DEVILS OR SAVIOURS

DEVILS OR SAVIOURS

A HISTORY OF DICTATORSHIP
SINCE 600 B.C.

by

GEORGE W. F. HALLGARTEN

Translated from the German

by

GAVIN GIBBONS

OSWALD WOLFF (PUBLISHERS) LIMITED
London
1960

MADE AND PRINTED IN GREAT BRITAIN BY
THE GARDEN CITY PRESS LIMITED
LETCHWORTH, HERTFORDSHIRE

CONTENTS

PART IV—DICTATORSHIP IN THE ERA OF WORKING-CLASS MOVEMENTS

PART V—DICTATORSHIP IN OUR TIME

Introduction

WHAT A DICTATOR IS

To people nowadays, the words "tyrant" and "dictator" have the same meaning. The expression "tyrant" comes to us from Greek, though it is of much older, probably Asiatic, origin, and the nearest equivalents in English of its original meaning are "lord" or "master". The word was used to designate the despotic ruler of a city state, the largest political unit known to the Greeks. He was supposed to have been elected democratically, though this was rarely the case. "Dictator", on the other hand, is a word which was coined by the Romans. It was first used as the title of a man who had to be of outstanding merit, to whom the Roman Senate had given unlimited political authority for a short period to deal with an imminent threat. Originally this period was never longer than six months. The sway of the Roman dictator extended over a much larger and more important area than those controlled by Greek tyrants. Indeed, the Roman dictatorships were tyrannies of the first magnitude, especially after the time of Julius Caesar, who was the first dictator for life.

The authority of a hereditary monarch, even when arbitrary and cruel, is based on traditional rights, but tyrants and dictators cannot rid themselves of the "evil smell of revolution", as a Prussian king once put it. Their breeding grounds are in the revolts and uprisings of human history, their bitter struggle to gain and maintain control forces them to extreme measures and gives all of them certain common traits already well known in antiquity. The famous description of the nature of tyranny contained in Aristotle's treatise *Politics* reads in many respects as if it had been written in the mid-twentieth century. In order to maintain his power, Aristotle tells us, the tyrant should cut off all those who are too high, he must put to death any natural leaders, he must not allow any common meals, clubs, education, and similar gatherings, he must be on his guard against anything

1

which is likely to inspire either courage or self-confidence among his subjects, he must prohibit literary assemblies or discussion groups, and he must take every step to prevent people from getting to know one another—as acquaintance leads to mutual confidence. A tyrant should also try to find out what his subjects are saying and thinking and should employ spies. The tyrant Hiero of Syracuse was in the habit of sending female detectives and eavesdroppers to any place where people were meeting. The fear caused by the knowledge that these informers might be present prevented people from speaking their minds, because, were they to do so, they would be found out more easily. According to Aristotle, a special art of the tyrant is to promote quarrels among the citizens, to set friend against friend, the people against the notables, and the rich against each other. He should take care to impoverish his subjects, thus preventing them from protecting themselves, as the people, having to give all their energy to working for a living, have none left to conspire against the tyrant. The construction of the Pyramids of Egypt, Aristotle states, is an example of this policy. Others are the offerings of the family of the tyrant Cypselus, the building of the temple of the Olympian Zeus by Pisistratus, tyrant of Athens, and his sons, and the great monuments put up by the tyrant Polycrates of Samos. All these projects were intended to give the people work and to keep them poor. Another practice of tyrants is to multiply taxes—Dionysus of Syracuse contrived within five years to force his subjects to bring all their property into his treasury. The tyrant also likes making war, so that his subjects may have something to do, and so that they can always look to him as a leader. While the power of a king is preserved by his friends, the tyrant must distrust those around him, as he knows that every one of them wants to overthrow him. Being near him, they have a better opportunity to do this than anyone else. Women and slaves—both regarded as of minor importance in classical times—are the tyrant's favourite tools, Aristotle tells us, and are given favoured treatment so as to control their husbands and masters. Tyrants always like bad men, because they love to be flattered, but no one with a spirit of independence in him will stoop to flattery. Good men love other people, or at least do not flatter them. Bad men are the best tools for bad work; "nail knocks out nail", says Aristotle, using a proverb coined in antiquity. This astounding passage ends by telling us that it is characteristic of a tyrant to dislike anyone who is independent or who has any special quality and to look on him as an enemy of his power—the tyrant always wants to shine alone in his glory.

It is no mere coincidence that the picture given in this analysis by Aristotle resembles closely all tyrannies up to the time of Joseph Stalin. When conditions are similar, it is only natural that we see similar results. The revolutionary conditions that breed tyrants and dictators give opportunities to people of a certain type of warped mind that would not exist in normal times. Such conditions allow these unbalanced men to develop a Government of diabolical maliciousness which has hardly any equal in history. But at the same time it must be admitted that some hereditary monarchs come very close to the tyrants in their cruelty. The European monarchs of the fifteenth and sixteenth centuries, for example, with their harsh brutality and shrewd cunning which paved the way to power for the European middle classes, compare with the worst dictators for their savagery and baseness. But while the display of tyrannical powers by hereditary monarchs depends on accidental circumstances, the use of abnormal powers by dictators is always essential. The stormy conditions in which dictators emerge force even the best-intentioned men to become tyrannical. Dictators must become hammers lest they become anvils. In some cases—in Stalin's life, for instance—it is the conditions surrounding the dictator that bring out the very worst in him.

Our presentation of the history of dictatorship—however sketchy—will show that the course of the revolutions that raised tyrants to power was not merely the result of coincidence. Neither were the way in which tyrants arose nor the methods they used when they seized control. As will be seen, specific circumstances favoured the rise of certain types of men, and hampered the ascent to power of men of different characteristics.

The types of men thrown up vary considerably, but there is always one common factor—where there have been no revolutions, there are no genuine tyrants, as distinguished from hereditary despots. This is why hardly any dictatorships are found outside the European and American spheres down to the twentieth century. This is especially true of the Orient, which is the field of hereditary despotism. Mass movements and revolutions, on the other hand, are usually characteristic of the Western world with its crowded cities and highly developed commerce. When eventually revolutions and dictatorships do occur in the Orient, they are the result of Western influence, of Western political ideas, and a reaction to Western expansion. This expansion ravaged and changed the Orient in our time much as the advance of Greek and Roman armies changed the old monarchies along the Euphrates and Nile twenty-five centuries ago.

The social unrest of the old world, whose revolutionary spirit lives on in Western civilization today, led to the rise of dictatorial régimes for the first time in human history. The cradle of tyranny is to be found in the cities of ancient Greece and the Greek colonies in Asia Minor and Sicily. Here were the stages on which were enacted the first successful mass uprisings in history. The seventh century B.C., in which this revolutionary development starts, sees also the first tyrannical figures appear like silhouettes through the fog of early Greek history.

Part I

THE DICTATORSHIPS OF ANTIQUITY

Chapter One

THE GREEK TYRANTS

The Collapse of the Aristocracy

IT is Aristotle who tells us about the form and course of the revolutions which brought the Greek and Sicilian tyrants to power. We read of small communities of noblemen who defended themselves with desperate courage against the landless crowds which vied with them for control. These struggles took place in the *polis*, or Greek city, which had grown up in large numbers, usually with a moderate population, in the mountain valleys of the Greek peninsula, on the Peloponnese, on the island world of the Aegean Sea, in Sicily, and in southern Italy, where the Greeks expanded in the great colonization period between 800 and 500 B.C.

Town and country were not sharply distinguished and often merged. The landless multitude, the *demos* of these cities, that hated the nobility, were a mixture of day labourers, debt-ridden small craftsmen, and landless younger sons of noblemen as well as peasants. The singular character of the Greek countryside, with its many mountain ranges making communications difficult, restricted the economy of the *polis* by limiting the area from which supplies could be drawn. This drove the younger landless men across the seas.

The great period of Greek colonization in the Mediterranean basin came to an end in the sixth century B.C., when it reached the Orientally despotic states of Carthage to the west and Persia to the east, and internal tension naturally increased. Demands for the remission of taxes and debts, for the admission of men who were not of noble birth to political control, for redistribution of the land, and for continuance of colonial expansion even at the expense of Greeks who had settled abroad, became increasingly strong. Aristotle describes the political scene in this tense atmosphere and the clash of the *demos* with the nobility—an embittered, stubborn struggle. Where such conflict of interests occurred, even the smallest incident, such as a quarrel about inheritance, about a girl, or a personal insult, could flare up into a political or complete social revolution. Disputes of this sort, more violent and of more frequent occurrence among the upper classes than among the poor, weakened the cohesion of the State and made the nobility especially vulnerable in their struggle with the *demos*. Aristotle frequently mentions instances where dissatisfied noblemen or high dignitaries deserted to the people and became their leaders. One of the biggest threats to the nobility was their use of mercenaries, as the general in command of these soldiers was almost bound to become a dictator. History, Aristotle points out, tended to show that almost all tyrants had begun as demagogues who roused the people against the nobility. In the earlier period—he is evidently referring to the sixth and seventh centuries B.C.—these demagogues had been generals as well, and had obtained political control in this way. In later years tyranny had suffered a setback, as demagogues were merely orators with no military training.

General Features of Tyranny

This remark of Aristotle is of basic importance. The Greek tyrants were frequently the military leaders of the lower classes against the harsh aristocratic rule in a struggle inflamed by over-population in the cities. However, in the fifth century B.C., as a result of the rule of the tyrants and the land reformers, the so-called *aesumnetes*, the class difference had been lessened and the people in the *polis* were no longer led by soldiers. The word "demagogue" as we use it today has not the same meaning as tyrant, but refers to an orator who deceived the crowds by means of rhetorical tricks. These orators performed on the Greek *agora*, where mass political meetings were always held. However, not all the tyrants were successful. Aristotle emphasizes that the attacks by the radical demagogues on the nobility during the earlier period had often led to the upper classes counter-attacking with great success—in Rhodes, Heracleon, Megara, and Cumae, for example, the tyrants had been expelled.

We are not, however, concerned with the ephemeral tyrants who were particularly frequent in ancient Sicily, where tyranny developed, as we shall later see, into something permanent, as it did centuries later in Latin America. The most important Greek tyrants were not merely the leaders of the dissatisfied peasantry, but were champions of the merchants whose trade had been fostered by Greek colonization in the Aegean and the West. The link between the poor from the city and countryside and the mercantile and banking interests was essential, if not indispensable, for the rise and success of all important tyrants in Greece and Asia Minor in classical times. The commercial and financial interests had not enough political strength, and the people were too poor to act on their own with great success.

In Sparta, an inland state of warriors which lacked a commercial class, the peasants were merely serfs, too weak to challenge the nobility. Even the Messenians, a warlike mountain tribe, were unable to resist conquest by the Spartans in the end. Consequently, tyranny in Sparta only emerged later, after the armies of the city had fought far from their homes in the so-called Peloponnesian War, and the city itself had had its social structure recast. Greek tyranny grew up first not in the inland towns but in the trade centres along the coast and in Asia Minor. It first appeared around 650 B.C. in the cities on the Isthmus, Corinth, Megara, Sicyon, and then spread to Ionia, the part of Asia Minor populated by the Greeks.

Just as the types of Greek city states varied greatly, so did the social composition of the groups that backed the tyrannies. Their history was also different. In the coastal towns of Greece and Asia Minor and on the Aegean islands, the tyrants naturally had much support from the merchants and financiers. Tyranny began there at the height of the colonization, which had greatly increased commerce and had resulted in large fortunes. In the Greek cities of Asia Minor the tyrants rose to power as a result of long struggles between the city masses and the nobility, or between cliques of noblemen.

These Greek tyrants and those of the Asiatic Lydians who conquered and exploited many Greek towns in Asia Minor possessed wealth which has become proverbial through the names of Gyges (about 600 B.C.), Croesus (564–560 B.C.), and Polycrates. Their end was varied but always unhappy. Croesus, King of Lydia, and more Greek than Asian, was overthrown by the Persians, although they allowed him to continue as a local tyrant (his burning at the stake is a myth), while the Greek Polycrates,

tyrant of Samos, one of the greatest merchants as well as rulers
of his time, was lured by a ruse into Persian territory and ended
on the cross (522 B.C.). Conspicuous by their wealth among
Greek tyrants are the Cypselidae, the rulers of the trade centre
of Corinth, the first of whom had been called Cypselus. The most
prominent member of the family, Periander, the leading figure of
the Greek world of 600 B.C., resembles Cosimo di Medici, the
greatest trader, capitalist, and patron of the arts of his age.

It is not true, however, that all Greek tyrants possessed great
fortunes. The British historian, P. N. Ure, one of the first to
stress the connection between the rise of commercial capitalism
and the Greek tyranny, who saw in his heroes the Vanderbilts
or Rockefellers of that age, has been carried too far by his joy
of discovery. Aristotle's remark at the start of his description of
tyranny, "the main aim of tyranny is wealth, for by wealth alone
can the tyrant maintain either his guard or his luxury", shows
that the accumulation of economic power was the result of the
tyranny rather than its cause. This does not mean that financiers
did not help the tyrant to power; they benefited from his success
and were prepared to lend him money, since they knew it would
pay. In the earliest days the tyrant was no capitalist, but a poor
man who proved useful to his financiers by leading the poor
people in town and country to help in the struggle against the
nobility. Conspicuous among these figures were disgruntled
members of the nobility desirous of revenge for their mis-
fortunes.

One of the earliest tyrants about whom we have precise information was Cypselus of Corinth, who in 657 B.C. ended the rule
of the wealthy Bacchiadae of Corinth. He was the son of a
princess from this old dynasty, who because of a physical defect
had married a member of the native non-Greek population.

Here, as elsewhere, Sicyon, for example, the lowest class sup-
ports the tyrant just as it frequently did in Sicily and still does
today in Latin America. As an "outcast" from the old nobility,
Cypselus held practically the same position between the lowest
class and the highest stratum as do the *mestizos* today in Latin
America, who are a cross between the ruling creole society and the
native Indians, and furnish most of the modern dictators of that
part of the world. The *mestizos* are inspired by a mixture of envy
and hatred of the wealthy upper class which is no less intense

than the feelings of their predecessors in ancient times, the Greek and Sicilian tyrants. We shall also find this jealousy of the wealthy nobility in the tyrants and dictators of the intervening centuries, in Renaissance Italy, in Cromwellian England, and in the Bonaparte family.

The tyranny in Sicyon resembled that of Cypselus not only in its support—a combination of the native population and the merchant classes—but in its psychological aspect. The ruling dynasty of the Orthagoridae, founded by a butcher, was delighted to be wooed by the hated nobility and was proud of its tremendous wealth and culture. Indeed, the daughter of Cleisthenes, one of the leading figures, was courted by noble-born swains from all over the then known world, her hand being won in the end by Megacles, a member of the Alcmeonidae family of Athens, in 575 B.C.

The impression that the ruling aristocracy would inevitably succumb resulted in a hereditary monarch sometimes taking the lead in the change to dictatorship, just as in Hitler's time, twenty-five centuries later, some Balkan monarchs turned dictator to retain their thrones. A man of this type was King Pheidon of Argos, a contemporary of Cypselus. He was reputed to have invented systems of coinage as well as weights and measures. If not true, this legend shows his connection with the rising new economic forces. In general, however, the tyrant rose from the people rather than descended from the ruling houses. He was either a fallen member of the old nobility or descendant of the lowest classes.

Tyranny in Athens

The best example of the rise to power of a fallen noble is the career of Pisistratus in Athens—almost the only powerful man of that age about whom we have detailed information. Starting in 561 B.C. tyranny in Athens comes later than in most other Greek tyrannies. While the tyrannies on the isthmus of Corinth, on the Aegean islands, and in Asia Minor opened the road to the commerce of the great colonization period and benefited from it, that in Athens was the result primarily of the pressure of a rapidly increasing population and the growing shortage of land for the peasantry. It did not appear, therefore, before the time when the

Athenians found the way to peaceful expansion blocked on the Greek mainland or Aegean islands.

Tyranny in Athens was preceded by a period of reforms with the object of relieving the land hunger of the peasantry by peaceful means. This reform is associated with the name of Solon. His family, the Medontidae, was a noble clan that immigrated to Attica, but did not possess sufficient land. This forced Solon to live on commerce and sponsor its cause in the political field.

Solon's much-praised achievements, his legislation safeguarding individual freedom, his cancellation of the debts of the small tenant farmers, his encouragement of commerce by attracting foreign merchants, and a monetary reform involving a mild inflation, did not go far enough, however, to satisfy the small peasant. These people could not continue without a new distribution of land and did not trust Solon's putting most of the political power into the hands of the rich. The problem of balancing the two main elements—the peasants and other small men with the wealthy traders—which always faced the Greek aristocracy, was not solved by tipping the balance too strongly in favour of the merchants. The tyranny of Pisistratus established the balance once more.

Pisistratus, like Solon, came from an old noble family, whose power was now based on commerce. He was prompted by a personal motive, just as Caesar later on, his financial state was precarious, supposedly because he tried to finance his first political rise to power with his own money. Like most tyrants Pisistratus first distinguished himself as a revolutionary general; he commanded the militia of poor peasantry from the mountains of Attica known as *diakrioi* in a war against Megara. When he had come back victorious to be deified by the masses, he used his resulting prestige to carry out a measure typical of a dictator— he started a rumour that an attempt upon his life had been made. To prove it, he drove through the city in a chariot spattered with blood, drawn by mules bleeding profusely, looking as if he were wounded. The infuriated people at once voted him a bodyguard. This was almost everywhere the first decisive step on the road to dictatorship. Supported by this bodyguard he occupied the Acropolis and became tyrant of Athens in 561 B.C.

His first attempt lasted less than a year, the radicalism of his followers alienated the wealthy merchants, who joined with the old nobility to expel him from the country. This alliance against Pisistratus did not last, as he succeeded in winning the support of the Alcmeonidae, one of the old merchant families, and strengthened this connection by marriage. About 559 B.C. he was brought back to Athens in a solemn procession, which was preceded by the goddess of the city, Athena, played by a pretty flower girl, in order to symbolize the change in sentiment.

As nearly always in the history of dictatorship, the relations between the tyrant and his financial backers deteriorated quickly, and after only a few years the breach between Pisistratus and the Alcmeonidae was so great that he had to flee a second time. It is not certain whether he actually left the country, but it is known that from then onwards he drew his support from the rich gold mines of Macedonia and Thrace. This made him independent of his former financial backers and permitted him to maintain an army of mercenaries. From about 550 B.C. he ruled the city for twenty-two years.

Like dictators all down the ages, Pisistratus was what we should call "left" nowadays. His sympathies were with the working men in the city and the small peasants, both of whom he assisted by reforming the courts of law, organizing rural credit, and easing the burden of taxation. He financed these measures, like most tyrants, by confiscating the estates of his opponents, and also by taxing the wealthy, which presumably explains his breach with the Alcmeonidae.

As the story of his *coup d'état* shows, he was skilled in the political tricks and manœuvres in which Machiavelli sees the essence of tyranny; after his unfortunate start he held the nobility to ransom by keeping its sons as hostages. Like most powerful men descended from the nobility, he had the ability for conciliation which distinguished him from the revengeful and treacherous figures who had risen from the city masses. This sort of tyrant is often found in ancient Sicily, and in their cunning and cold-bloodedness equalled Hitler or Stalin.

The problem of feeding the surplus population whose hunger for land had provoked the crisis was solved by Pisistratus in a truly tyrannical way. This was done partly by public building on a large scale, but also by political expansion and by obtaining a belated share in the general Greek colonial expansion. This increased trade improved the situation at home, and laid the economic foundation for what was to become the Athenian democracy, a community of property-owning citizens.

All this has a distinctly imperialist flavour, typical of many of these ancient and most later dictatorships; the Athenian tyranny follows in the footsteps of other early Greek tyrannies, especially those of Corinth and Megara. Like the tyrant Theagenes of Megara, who preceded him by about eighty years, Pisistratus championed the poor against the noblemen; he built an aqueduct, as well as fortifying the Acropolis and erecting the gigantic temples of Zeus and Dionysus. His public building and colonization gave work to the unemployed, but at the expense of the rich; this policy came to its logical conclusion in the establishment of an insurance system for veterans, just as Polycrates of Samos granted pensions to the families of the soldiers who fought his battles.

Art and Religion

Taken by and large, the Greek tyranny, like those of Caesar, the Renaissance dictators, Cromwell, the Bonapartes, and many others, has a decidedly liberal if not *bourgeois* character. This was combined with support for the peasant population, and the rural element settled in the city from which the tyrant's militia was drawn. Cleisthenes of Sicyon forbade the reciting of Homer as it was incompatible with the aims of his Government, and even the edition of Homer brought out by Onomacritus of Athens and three other scholars during the rule of Pisistratus shows proof of tampering with the text by the dictator's orders.

If the classes supporting the tyrant had no love for the world of heroes portrayed by Homer, they liked the vigorous peasant life described in Hesiod's works. Their favourite figure among the Olympian gods was Dionysus, the god of the Greek wine-growers, whose cult was deliberately fostered by Pisistratus and other tyrants. The rural Dionisin festivals were staged in Attica in December, when a choir of men dressed as peasants sang dithyrambic verses in honour of the god. These were interspersed with solos by popular poets; from the exchanges between the singer and the choir emerged the drama which was keenly supported by the tyrants. At the court of Periander worked the poet Arion, who perfected the dithyramb, at that of Pisistratus lived Thespis, the first dramatic poet.

By encouraging the popular cults, in contrast to the worship of the gods by the upper classes, the tyrant freed the masses from aristocratic control and won their support. But the great period of dramatic art came after the downfall of the tyrannies which benefited the development of democracy and even helped the aristocracy.

Seen as a whole, the rule of tyranny, in its treatment of religion and art, its encouragement of sporting events and national festivals, gave the small man a new pride and made him aware that he was a citizen of the *polis* which gave its name to the entire small state. Not unlike later liberal dictatorships, such as those of Caesar, Cromwell, and the Bonapartes, Greek tyranny in the sphere of culture destroyed aristocratic control and hastened a more democratic way of life.

End of the Tyranny in Greece

From the beginning of the fifth century B.C. tyranny began to lose power in the Greek mother country. There were two reasons : firstly, the merging of the social classes by the economic and social policy of the tyrants, and secondly, the development of the technique of warfare. Instead of fights between individual noblemen with or without small bands of armed retainers, a vast "phalanx" of heavily armed infantry, the so-called hoplites, was enlisted. Thus, politically, tyranny as the leading force of the rising commercial classes and the masses against the nobility was brought to an end; and militarily it was rendered unnecessary by the hoplites. Tyranny had played its part, and Greece had no more use for it. It was not easy to get rid of, for, like every other social trend, it had what the great German sociologist Max Weber used to call a vested interest in immortality, and the tyrants were loath to admit that the social wave that carried them to power had ebbed.

This desire to cling on to power was especially noticeable among sons of tyrants. Less qualified than their fathers, who had seized power as a result of much cunning, they were compelled to fight for their position at a time when tyranny had already begun to outlive its usefulness. This forced them to resort to even more extreme measures. Most sons of tyrants are famous for their cruelty, and few of them retained their power. After the death of the aged Pisistratus (527 B.C.) power descended to his

sons Hippias and Hipparchus, who, although morally above the
average, and singularly successful rulers, were unable to prevent
the end of tyranny. Hipparchus, the younger, managed cultural
affairs and public works and was quite efficient, but in 514 B.C.
fell a victim to the private revenge of two Athenian nobles,
Harmodius and Aristogeiton.

Incensed by what had happened and anxious for the future,
Hippias took extreme measures, and the murderers and many of
their friends were executed. Arbitrary taxes were levied, the
administration and judiciary were corrupted, the coinage was
tampered with, and inflation allowed to set in. The fall of this
tyranny was brought about by the Alcmeonidae family, who had
fled to Sparta, the enemy of Athens, and who persuaded her to
intervene on their behalf. Hippias fled to the Persian king and
later persuaded the Persians to make war on Athens—to their
undoing.

Similar events took place the same year—510 B.C.—in Sicyon
and Corinth, where noblemen, exiled by the tyrants, called in
Sparta to crush the tyranny. As these tyrannies had been the
result of revolutionary movements, they were followed by an
aristocratic reaction, which, like those which followed the dictatorships of Cromwell and Napoleon, did not last long. The
reason for this has always been the same; the cycle of history
could *not* be reversed, the economic and social changes which
had taken place remained, and it was hardly feasible to alter the
redistribution of property which had taken place during the
revolutionary period. The accumulation of commercial capital
remained unchanged, and the evolution towards democracy, even
if on a plutocratic and even imperialistic basis, continued.

Tyranny reached its end in Greece even before the start of the
fifth century B.C. Support for the fallen tyrants and candidates
for their successors were indeed found even during the golden age
of Athenian democracy, just as in our own day totalitarian parties
and people with a totalitarian outlook exist in the democratic
countries. But the menace of these would-be dictators was held
in check by the use of ostracism, a two-edged weapon, which
banished men grown too powerful.

The most important reason for the increasing Greek dislike of
tyranny was the support given by the King of Persia, the mortal
enemy of Greece, to these fallen tyrants and their would-be

successors. In his subjection of the Greek cities in Asia Minor, he used them to support his power. This helped to blacken the reputation of tyranny in Greece, which originally contained much that was good. If there had been anything to stress this unfavourable view it was the development of tyranny in Sicily, where it became permanent and where its demonic features were displayed to their fullest extent.

Chapter Two

THE TYRANTS OF SICILY

A Paradise for Power-hungry Men

SICILY was a colonial area in antiquity. The island was densely populated by emigrants from all parts of the Greek peninsula, who had settled there and in lower Italy in the golden age of Greek expansion, roughly between 750 and 550 B.C.

Greeks from Chalcidice and later on from Messenis founded Messina, Dorians and other tribes from the Peloponnesus populated lower Italy and the south Sicilian coast. They built cities like Tarentum or Acragas (Agrigenti, Girgenti), while the pride of the colonists from Corinth was the founding of powerful Syracuse.

The urge which drew these hordes of settlers away from the old country was not satisfied when they arrived in their new homes. The landlessness of the poor and of the younger sons of the farmers was one of the permanent features of ancient history. It caused the great colonization of the Greeks, and when all the land had been divided up, it led to furious internecine fights among the Greeks and fed the imperialism of Athens as much as of Sparta. The forces unleashed by these two features struck ancient Sicily like a Biblical plague, and finally shaped the history of Rome, who, by contrast, acquired too much land and by the consequent absorbing of foreign peoples helped to destroy antiquity.

In Sicily the fight for living space took on a particularly unpleasant form. The island lacked an outlet for its surplus population comparable with that formed by the Aegean islands for the mother country. As was to be expected in a colony, a considerable portion of the subjected population remained. Although useful for menial tasks, these people increased the number requiring to be fed. Worst of all, the western end of the island had been occupied for centuries by the African commercial power of

Carthage, representative of the Phoenician-Semitic race of peoples. Jointly with the Etruscans in Italy, they tried to stem Greek expansion. This led to an endless series of wars, external and internal, when one or other of the city states tried to establish political supremacy on the island. It also led to the rise of innumerable tyrants. Tyranny here became perennial.

Looked at from a political aspect, therefore, Sicily offers many parallels with Latin America, since the beginning of the nineteenth century. In ancient Sicily, just as in present-day South America, there were colonies, established by an upper class that had become emancipated from their mother countries; in both this upper class ruled a mixed collection of native tribes, and in both cases there was deep political disunion, continuous internecine class struggle and resulting from the lack of broad democratic classes, continuous tyranny and dictatorship. Ancient Sicily, like Latin America, centuries later, was one of the granaries of the mother countries, the landowners formed the nucleus of the population in many city states, and they were outnumbered by the merchants and craftsmen, while slaves worked on the estates of the landowners and in the vineyards and wheatfields.

As early as 600 B.C. we find a tyrant in opposition to the landowning classes in most of these cities. His unlimited power results from his being the leader of the multitude. The Sicilian tyrant came less often from the nobility than those in the mother country, perhaps because the nobility was less strongly represented than at home. Compared with those in the mother country and in Asia Minor, many of the Sicilian tyrants were plebeian, mean and base. Yet this made them especially capable of carrying out their historical task.

This is even evident among the very earliest tyrants, whose life-story is largely mythical. One of them, Panaitus of Leontini (*circa* 600 B.C.) portrayed as a leader of poor foot soldiers, overpowered the city nobles by a trick. As commander of the city, he ordered a general arms inspection. He separated the dismounted knights from their horses, surrounded them with the help of their grooms and his own men, and slew them.

Another of these early Sicilian tyrants, the ill-famed Phalaris (*circa* 570 B.C.), insisted on being granted a bodyguard for protecting the material collected for building the castle in his city, Acragas. He made use of this guard to subdue the citizens—a usual practice. The bodyguard was uniformed, and after the tyrant had been overthrown the wearing of this uniform (blue-grey shirts) was forbidden. To keep the city in terror, Phalaris roasted captured enemies over a low fire in a brazen bull, whose smoke-exuding nostrils allowed the groans of the victims to be heard. It is obvious that Phalaris—if Greek at all—had been influenced by the Carthaginian custom of offering their enemies to Moloch. The rôle played by non-Greeks in supporting Sicilian tyranny is important, just as the Indios in South America supported their local dictators. This came out clearly in the curiously interconnected histories of Gela and Syracuse.

Gelon and Hieron (491?–467 B.C.)

As happened so often, the aristocracy in Gela was overthrown by demagogues from its own ranks. These men became tyrants and relied on hired mercenaries, especially natives, for their support. However, the tyrants felt themselves threatened by all natives, whether in the army, in the cities, or in the country.

The first great Sicilian tyrant, Gelon, was famed for the cunning and brutality with which he ran the country he ruled. Having made himself master of Syracuse, the jewel of Sicily, he disappointed the masses who had opened the city gates to him by not allowing the expelled Syracusan nobility to return, but bringing in other nobles from the places he had conquered. The lower classes in those towns who had helped him as enthusiastically as those of Syracuse were sold into slavery as their reward.

Many subsequent instances of tyranny showed this "second act". Although military leader of the revolution, the tyrant was not usually to be found supporting the extreme left. Especially if a minor nobleman, he was anxious to check radicalism so as to maintain his power and impress his equals. The aversion of the aristocracy and the upper stratum in his own camp was lessened by his increasing conflict with his left-wing followers. Fearful of the dark spectre of social revolution, the aristocracy reluctantly gave the dictator a free hand and even at times helped him.

Like many other dictators, Gelon strengthened his power in this way. Yet the Syracusan lower classes, though grumbling about the favours he bestowed upon the upper classes, were grateful because he did not crush them completely, and they continued to support him. Gelon's prestige in Sicily became very great after he had defeated a huge Carthaginian army at the Himera river (480 B.C.) to help his brother-in-law Theron, tyrant of Acragas. Gelon's victory equals that of Salamis in the same year (according to mythology, on the same day) as one of the great decisions of history. In both East and West the Greeks had broken the threatening non-Greek forces which were surrounding them.

Gelon survived his triumph only by two years, and was succeeded by his brother Hieron (478–467 B.C.) Under Hieron the rise of Syracuse and the other Sicilian cities continued. His naval victory over the Etruscans near Cumae, a Campanian port which had asked for his help, repelled the last of the Powers which threatened the Greek world. The masses of captives from the Battle of the Himera fed the slave markets of Acragas and other towns for some time. The growth of the Mediterranean Powers after the Persian wars encouraged overseas trade. The march of progress on all sides gave the tyranny of Hieron a lustre and splendour which reminds one of the ages of Periander, Pericles, Augustus, and the Medici. Hieron gained fame himself by emerging as victor in contests in the Greek mother country, and was praised for this by Pindar and other poets whom he attracted to his court in Syracuse. Pindar was the greatest of Greek lyricists and glorified the ethics of the aristocracy. He was pleased that Hieron tried to make his rule a monarchy, and admired the way he founded a new city near the island's highest volcano, Aetna, presumably to avoid political trouble from the city masses. He proclaimed his son its king, and both were praised by Pindar. The name of Aeschylus is also connected with the new town. In the last years of his life he spent more time in Sicily than in Greece, and lived at Hieron's court. One of his dramas bears the title *The Woman of Aetna*. He stayed, as his self-composed epitaph shows, mostly in Gela, and he was killed there by a mountain eagle which attacked him when he was sitting in the sun.

The founding of Aetna is an example of the resettling of entire populations carried out with ruthless efficiency by Gelon and Hieron, who anticipated by many centuries similar measures of Hitler and Stalin. The increasing resistance to these measures was strengthened by the economic progress brought about by the tyrants, and Hieron had to lessen them as a result.

As Gelon's mercenaries had become citizens of Syracuse, he could no longer use them to support his rule, so he began to hire men and women from all ranks to watch over the people. These "detectives" of Hieron were one of the first examples of the secret police. The results were typical of more modern secret police forces. For example, enthusiasm was great for Polyzelus, Hieron's second brother. Gelon on his death-bed had entrusted his son to Polyzelus, who was also connected by marriage to Theron, tyrant of Acragas, co-victor at Himera. So Hieron dealt with Polyzelus as David had dealt with Uriah.

However, harsh measures such as these did not prevent the fall of the tyranny. Just as in Greece, tyranny had outlived its usefulness, due to the economic and cultural upsurge of the period. A year after the death of Hieron, his son Trasybolus was driven into exile. A few decades of freedom followed, marked by struggles between those who profited by the tyranny, namely the aristocracy and the mercenaries. Emerging victorious, the aristocracy took control of the city republics.

Dionysus I (405–367 B.C.)

The unusual political life of the island, together with the dependence of its landowners and traders on slaves, the pressure of an expanding population, and the constant threat from abroad made the development of democracy, or rather a mild aristocratic rule, very precarious, even in the best days of republican freedom. The peaceful period in Sicily ended when in the last decade of the fifth century, soon after the collapse of the Athenian attack on Syracuse, the Carthaginians began a large offensive against Sicily and subdued Acragas in 406 B.C.

Fierce attacks were made in the people's assembly against the aristocracy, who had carried on the war half-heartedly, probably from fear of conscription. The people's leader was an unknown soldier not twenty-five years old, named Dionysus, who had been at the defence of Acragas, and who had the rank equivalent to perhaps a corporal. Military duty in the service of an unsuccessful tyrant had stirred his ambition. He was fortunate in being well informed, as he served his generals as a clerk.

When the young uniformed demagogue was fined by the

chairman of the assembly for the intemperance of his speech—
he had complained that the front-line soldiers had been "stabbed
in the back"—he turned round and stared at the benches behind
him. Almost at once he was joined by Philistos, the wealthiest
man in Syracuse. He paid Dionysus' fine and urged him to continue, promising him that he would pay any further fine.

As a result of this "stab in the back" propaganda, financed by
"big business", Dionysus was soon granted a military command
by the people.[1] Dionysus marched with his soldiers to Gela, which
was being besieged by the Carthaginians. In an attempt to save
the situation by obtaining better leadership, he incited the citizens
against the patricians, whose leaders he arrested and executed for
treason. Although this move did not save the city, the property
of the legally murdered men enabled Dionysus to increase the
pay of his soldiers, and thus increased their loyalty to him.

When he had come back to Syracuse, Dionysus blamed the
other generals for the fall of Gela. The assembly, angry and
embittered, appointed him supreme commander—*strategos
autocrator*. He had come very close to tyranny, but still had to
take the final step. To do this in Syracuse would have been
dangerous because of the crowds. It was safer to do it at
Leontini, away from the city. To complete the action a "burning of the Reichstag" had to be engineered to cause a reason for
the final step. This was more easily staged in Leontini, away
from the city mob.

According to ancient custom, the assembly of the citizens was
always armed, so that an army on manœuvres could rapidly
transform itself into a parliament. If such an assembly were held
far from home, the older and more responsible citizens would not
take part in it, an additional reason for holding it at Leontini.
During the night Dionysus spread the word by means of his
slaves that their master had been assaulted by armed enemies.
The army assembled in haste, and the *strategos autocrator* was
at once voted a bodyguard, which marked the formal start of his
dictatorship (405 B.C.).

The tyrant hastened to placate a section of the aristocracy by
marrying the daughter of his deceased military commander, an
exiled aristocrat, and by marrying his sister to his wife's uncle.

[1] The reader will observe that this passage, particularly the phrases in
inverted commas, resembles Hitler's rise, told below, p. 228 et seq.

But the noble-born officers whom he blamed for the defeat at Gela were condemned as a result of his plea by the assembly and executed.

Although the political life of the city was outwardly unchanged, the vote of the assembly was "aye" from then on. This body was shunned by those hostile to the tyrant as his soldiers permitted no opposition. To help establish his rule, Dionysus surprisingly concluded a treaty with the arch-enemy Carthage. Its considerable concessions startled the world as much as the seemingly conciliatory foreign policy of Hitler immediately after he came to power. The reason in both cases was the same—to gain time for a later policy of revenge and expansion.

The contradiction between the tyrant's treatment of the aristocrats, whom he handed over to the mob to take their revenge, and his own apparently moderate policy towards the enemy led to a revolt of the aristocracy even before the conclusion of peace. The noble-born wife of Dionysus was captured, maltreated as a class traitress, raped, and driven to suicide.

However, the masses did not join the revolt, as Dionysus was considered the protector of the unpropertied multitude, especially of the freed slaves, the Sicilian native population, and the immigrants, from whose ranks he recruited his mercenaries and whom he made small farmers by distributing the estates of his aristocratic enemies. In order to strengthen his position further, he surrounded Syracuse with fortifications and protected tyranny from domestic as well as foreign foes by constructing an almost unconquerable fortress on the harbour island of Orthygia. The building of these mighty bulwarks needed 60,000 men, as well as 6,000 oxen drawing carts full of building material. Under the pretext that the use of slave labour dishonoured buildings serving to defend the land, the tyrant employed only free men—a thinly disguised form of state labour calling to mind the "voluntary" labour service of Hitler and Mussolini, and Stalin's methods of procuring workers.

The basis of this expansionist rule was naval shipbuilding and arms manufacture—both things with which Dionysus was familiar in every detail, and in which he took great pride. The invention of the catapult, the siege artillery of antiquity, is ascribed to him. He increased the size of the navy to three hundred units, many of them five-deckers. Both his navy and his army of 80,000 men were the biggest of their time.

These measures, like every rearmament, required great financial efforts. The wars, the building, and the splendid court, made the tyrant's rule unusually expensive. As well as confiscating the property of his enemies, Dionysus spoiled the temples, which were also used as banks, sold entire communities as slaves, a policy that hit even the Greeks, depreciated the currency, and, worst of all, levied confiscatory taxes. The tax revenues during his rule are said in five years to have equalled the total property of Syracuse, the largest city in the world at that time.

Despite these tremendous war preparations, Dionysus deceived the Carthaginians as to his true intentions no less efficiently than Hitler, centuries later, deceived the Western Powers and even Stalin. He even succeeded in obtaining aid from allies of Carthage in putting down a Syracusan revolt against his foreign mercenaries.

No one could expect gratitude from a man like Dionysus either in public or private life. In 397 B.C. he attacked Carthage, that hated Semitic rival of the Greeks in both the political and economic spheres. A blood-bath among the Carthaginian traders in Sicily was the signal for a world war—this, too, recalls the Hitler period.

The Syracusan offensive moved fast into the south-west corner of Sicily, but a year later the tide turned. A huge Carthaginian force landed and besieged Dionysus in his own capital. In the assembly of hard-pressed Syracuse, he was severely attacked by the nobility, and thus found himself in the position of the Syracusan generals he had himself attacked at the outset of his career. But the result was very different. In true dictator's style, Dionysus dissolved parliament with his cohorts. His luck helped him as much against his external as his internal enemies. The Carthaginian siege troops were weakened by a severe epidemic which destroyed their superiority in numbers. He was thus able to stage counter-attacks. On the flank of the mounted noblemen he placed unreliable sections of his mercenaries, and made sure that few of these latter returned.

The steadily decreasing support was countered by Dionysus as only a genius could. He secretly permitted the captured Carthaginian commander Himilko to escape, urged his mercenaries to surrender, and put them into his own service. In the history of tyrants and dictators almost everything is possible. So it is not surprising that after the glorious but not lasting peace with Carthage, 392 B.C., he took sides with the barbarians of Central Italy to fight the Greeks in the southern part of the peninsula. At their expense he carved out an empire the size of which had not been seen before in the history of the Western Mediterranean. It was clear that he planned to subdue the entire Italian peninsula.

The war was wearisome, a slow advance from mountain fortress to mountain fortress, from hill town to hill town, with Carthage in the rear which soon attacked him once more. The war was fought with all the Machiavellian technique of tyranny; the corrupting of local commanders who treacherously opened the gates of their towns to him, unexpected clemency towards prisoners who after thorough "brain-washing" were sent back to their cities as propagandists, brutal force where nothing else helped, and pitiless treatment of even the brothers of the tyrant if Dionysus sensed disobedience.

The resistance of some cities such as Rhegium, which delayed his schemes, could bring him to commit some fearful deeds. The city commander Phyton was killed in a manner too revolting to describe. Dionysus lacked all human feeling, he was a clear-thinking, acute, and shrewdly calculating man, crafty and cunning like Odysseus, a true Greek, but from the lower classes. He had no real sense of humour and he did not allow laughter. But he had some malicious irony, as when, for example, he confiscated a golden mantle from a statue of Zeus in the temple, declaring that this was good for the god's health, since the garment was too warm in summer and too cold in winter.

Dionysus was always eager for social recognition. In common with most dictators before the twentieth century A.D. he lacked the super-servility displayed to ingratiate himself with the upper classes he ultimately disappointed and disgusted. The choice of his wife showed his marked desire to impress the nobility, and so did his frantic urge to cap his gigantic military and political achievements by winning prizes as a dramatist and poet. He wanted his life to be, so to speak, an enormous symbol of *kaloka-gatheia*—the ideal of the beautiful and the good—which guided the proper Greek. In his private life, Dionysus, though he lived in official bigamy, was much more correct in his behaviour than noble-born tyrants because he was of middle-class background. He brought up his children in a most strict manner. His desire to be recognized as a poet lasted his whole life. He used the writing pad of Aeschylus and sent the poet Philoxenus to the stone quarries for ridiculing his verse. His dramas, *Adonis, Leda,* and *Almene,* are indeed reputed to have been of quite good quality, especially in their form. When he learned that another drama of his, entitled *Hector's Reward,* had been granted the long-hoped-for prize at the Lernian festivals of 367 B.C., he drank so much that he had a fatal stroke.

His son, Dionysus II, was typical of the tyrant's son held down by his father and kept out of politics. Twice he lost the supreme power in Syracuse to his uncle Dion and fled to Locroi, where he sought compensation along other lines. Together with his wife and daughter he corrupted the city. He maintained a harem which by means of force and by invoking a sort of *jus primae noctis* he replenished all the time. This infuriated the population to such an extent that after he had succeeded in escaping secretly to Sicily, the mob seized his wife and daughter and killed them with most cruel tortures.

Not lacking in political talent, Dionysus II seized power for yet a third time, but only in Syracuse itself; the other cities his father had ruled now had their own tyrants. All these tyrants were overthrown by an expedition from Corinth, the mother city of Syracuse, which was led by Timoleon and came at the request of the tyrant's foes in the various Sicilian towns. Timoleon's action in liberating Sicily from tyranny is paralleled by the exploits of Bolívar and San Martin in South America in more recent years. Dionysus II surrendered his power to Timoleon voluntarily and was sent to Corinth, where he led a stormy life. For some time he was a university professor, a vocation in which tyrannical traits are sometimes found.

> "Als Dionys von Syrakus
> aufhörte, ein Tyrann zu sein
> da ward er—ein Schulmeisterlein,"

says a German rhyme quoted by Goethe and Schiller.[1]

[1] The author was Schubart, a German eighteenth-century writer, who wrote it in an allusion to a despotic German autocrat who showed similar traits. In English it runs: "When Dionysus of Syracuse ceased to be a tyrant he became a little schoolmaster."

28 DEVILS OR SAVIOURS

The liberation of Sicily from tyranny was due to the fact that at the time of Timoleon's landing the tyrants were engaged in a war with Carthage and were in such sore straits that to some of them the "liberator" seemed more of a friend than a foe. Timoleon indeed succeeded in repelling the Carthaginians, but shortly after his death the pressure by the Carthaginians began again and led to the continuation of the system of military dictatorship, especially in the capital, Syracuse.

Agathocles (317–289 B.C.)

The new tyrant of Syracuse, Agathocles, ranked with Dionysus I as not only one of the greatest dictators of antiquity, but of all time. The problems faced by both dictators gave their rule similar characteristics. Both dictatorships fell after their deaths, but both fulfilled their purpose, that of checking Carthaginian expansion in Sicily by uniting the island temporarily against the bands of Punic mercenaries right up to the time when the expansion of Rome southwards relieved the Greeks of the task of fighting the African metropolis.

Agathocles was the son of an exile from the Calabrian city of Rhegium who worked as a potter in Syracuse, as did Agathocles himself at first. Right up to the latest periods of ancient Sicilian history, most exiles came as a rule from the higher ranks of society. This is probably the reason why Agathocles always tried to prove to the Syracusan nobles and citizens that his rank equalled that of the upper classes. He fought the local aristocracy to the bitter end, but did not display the inferiority complex which stood out so strongly in Dionysus, indeed he showed the traits of a Renaissance tyrant. He is usually pictured as a handsome and towering man, brutal and impressive, who, roaring with laughter, performs Herculean deeds, but who slaughters his enemies with the easiest conscience in the world. Sicilian historians describe him as a typical *condottiere*, that is, a recruiter and leader of mercenaries such as were hired by the Italian cities of the later Middle Ages.

In ancient Sicily the mercenary system had become permanent and was a plague, as it led to constant wars. Its leadership required brutality, fearlessness, and money. Money Agathocles obtained in a simple way; he married the widow of his commander, who had a vast fortune. Supported by these mercenaries,

Agathocles took part in the political life of his home town. Just like Dionysus, he sharply attacked the generals, who were of the noble class, accusing them of aiming at tyranny. Thus he led to their downfall and the downfall of the aristocracy.

Having used the help of the Carthaginians to overthrow the generals, he even obtained their active support in launching him in his career—just as had Dionysus before him. Several thousand Carthaginian mercenaries were put at his disposal as well as the garrisons of the other Sicilian cities which had been entrusted to him by the Sicilians themselves. The *coup d'état* staged by Agathocles to gain power is typical. Agathocles first packed the assembly with his supporters and surrounded the building with his soldiers. The fallen generals were arrested, led before the crowd, and harangued by him like a demagogue. They were then handed over to the executioner while his followers pillaged the houses of the nobles and slew all the noblemen they found. About 6,000 people are said to have perished the day Agathocles came to power.

Agathocles then returned to the assembly, took off his insignia of rank, and declared that he was resigning his leadership. This had the desired effect. The assembly, urged on by those who had became rich from despoiling the nobility, asked him "unanimously" to reconsider his decision, just as the supporters of Juan Perón, the Argentine president, requested him on their knees to remain in office when he threatened to resign in September 1955—which in the end only briefly postponed Perón's fall. Agathocles yielded to the demands of the assembly on condition that it grant him sole power, as he could not accept any responsibility if his colleagues broke the law. This made him supreme commander, as there was no equivalent supreme commander in the civilian sphere. He did not need a special bodyguard as did Dionysus, as the blood-bath at the outset of his rule had so reduced the numbers of his opponents that he appeared in the assembly without protection and his ribald jokes there were answered with loud laughs. The "unanimous" decisions of such bodies thoroughly purged of all opponents were naturally as little democratic as the "elections" under Mussolini, Hitler, Stalin, and all the other dictators of history. These acts are really plebiscites, an acknowledgment of the strong man and his qualities as a leader. All this made the

tyrant something like a feudal lord in the grand style. He expected "loyalty" from the masses just as a medieval king expected
it from his vassals; rebellion against him was considered breaking
this bond of trust and was therefore punished by him in person
and rarely by the ordinary courts.

Having become supreme master of the monster city of Syracuse
and all its resources, within a few years Agathocles conquered all
the Greek towns on the east coast of Sicily, and then, just like
Dionysus, attacked his erstwhile friends the Carthaginians, who
occupied Western Sicily. However, the Punic supremacy was
such that when Agathocles met them at the Himera, scene of
Gelon's great victory over them, he was decisively defeated, and
despite some brilliant defensive actions, especially in the defence
of Gela, was driven back into Syracuse.

The Carthaginians had learned from past experience; their
commander, Hamilcar, played the part of liberator from the yoke
of the local tyrants. This psychological warfare was so successful
that when the Carthaginians prepared to besiege Syracuse Agathocles had even less hope of success than had Dionysus when in
similar straits. The plan he thought out to meet the threat showed
tremendous energy and initiative with a creative combination of
fantasy and realism. Almost under the nose of the approaching
armies of Hamilcar, he embarked with his army on the Syracusan
fleet, broke through the Carthaginian blockade, and was the first
Greek in history to land at the head of his forces in Africa. He
burned his ships, not to improve the morale of his soldiers as
his propagandists declared, but to prevent their use by the enemy,
and then marched on the enemy capital.

Naturally it was not possible for him to conquer Carthage; the
vast metropolis surrounded by walls was too strong for him.
However, he spread terror throughout the city for weeks on end
as well as paralysing the Carthaginian army before Syracuse,
which enabled his countrymen there to break out and even to
capture Hamilcar, who was at once beheaded. Hamilcar's head,
dispatched to Africa, was shown to the Carthaginians in person
by Agathocles from the Greek siege walls. In the panic of those
weeks the Carthaginians sacrificed 500 of their children to
Moloch. But the tyrant did not win the war. His plan to besiege
Carthage and so match the siege of Syracuse resembled a game of

chess in which both players check each other's king and which finally ends in a draw.

His efforts to obtain reinforcements from the Greek mother-land, which had just conquered a large empire under Alexander the Great, did not succeed, and an internal conflict broke out which did his cause great harm. Revolts in his own camp and in Sicily, where the city of Acragas deserted his cause, forced him to return to Sicily twice. After his second departure, his army slew his sons, whom he had left behind as commanders, and as a band of mercenaries sold its services to the enemy. Agathocles slaughtered the families of the disloyal soldiers, and, full of spite and fury, proceeded against the Sicilian cities whose mutiny he blamed for the failure of his African campaign. The city of Segesta, which surrendered to him, was totally plundered and destroyed, and the populace slaughtered; he put the leaders of the mutineers into his catapults and shot them through the air or roasted them in ovens; the women met the fate of Saint Agatha. His feelings of revenge on his fellow citizens far exceeded his hatred of the enemy. To punish them he made peace with Carthage, and then, just like Gelon and Dionysus, he led the left-wing sections of the populace into a trap and ruthlessly slaughtered them. This brought him the support of many noblemen.

Different from other dictators, who were ruined by their dream of world conquest, it happened that the Carthaginians, the main foes of Dionysus and Agathocles, merely regarded Sicily as an area for colonization, and thus did not fight with the bitter determination that is found later among the opponents of Napo-leon and Hitler. The peace that Carthage granted Agathocles left him in control of roughly half of Sicily and thus enabled him to copy Dionysus by expanding in lower Italy. The Greek cities on the peninsula looked on him as a friend who protected them from the barbarians in the north rather than as a foe. His evident goal was the forming of a broad anti-Carthaginian coalition. For this purpose, too, he constructed a new fleet.

These plans, however, remained unfulfilled. He died, it seems, as a result of poison administered to him by a citizen of the city of Segesta who gained his confidence, in order to avenge the barbaric treatment he had given it. The murderer acted sup-posedly at the instigation of the tyrant's grandson Archagathus, who had just succeeded in doing away with a son of Agathocles by another mother, and who had tried to secure the succession. The dying tyrant, sensing this, gave Syracuse back her liberty in his last moments. But the freedom did not last. Military dictatorship in Sicily continued until, after the futile attempt of King Pyrrhus of Epirus to unify all Western Greece in one large empire, the Romans conquered the island.

Chapter Three

DICTATORSHIP IN ROMAN HISTORY

The Road to Revolution

DICTATORSHIP in ancient Rome[1] is closely related to the tyrannies of Sicily and Greece. But it assumed proportions which far exceeded the dictatorships of Dionysus and Agathocles in a very much later stage in Rome's history, some six to seven hundred years after the city's mythical foundation by Romulus and Remus. In Rome, just as in Greece, tyranny was the result of furious social struggle in which poor peasants and the city masses joined the capitalistic middle classes in fighting the landowning aristocracy. However, this struggle did not take place in very restricted areas as previously, and the contending parties—in the terms of that age—had universal significance.

Up to the second century B.C. Rome was neither a commercial centre nor was she restricted by space, and therefore had not the problem of overcrowding as had always been present in Greek cities. In her first centuries of existence, she lacked the middle class and capitalistic elements that could have supported any attacks on her nobility. Instead of internecine social struggles, Rome saw the aristocracy and the simple man in the city and country gradually drawing together, a union which lasted until long after there was any danger from foreign tribes and Rome had conquered the entire Italian peninsula. As a result of this expansion, the plebeians, or working class, were diverted from coveting the land and property at home, and the danger of dictatorship and social revolution was postponed. However, revolution could not be staved off for ever; it was the Roman conquest of all Italy that led to it, but on gigantic proportions as compared with what had gone on before in Greece.

---

[1] The word "dictatorship" is used here, as everywhere else in this book, in its modern sense. Used as a Roman official title, the word is, as explained in the Introduction, much older.

One of the most important results of Rome's many wars was the rise of a class of capitalists who made fortunes from disposing of booty and the selling of prisoners as slaves. They also invested gains thus made at high rates in the provinces. Instead of the individual financiers who supported the Greek tyrants, in Rome a large group of wealthy people existed who had a vested interest in conquest, slave-hunting, naval armaments, and the exploitation of provinces—in short, in imperialist expansion. Naturally they favoured the appointment of generals whose energy and aggressiveness promised success in this field. To check the aristocracy, who regarded these newcomers, known as the order of knights, as political rivals, these *nouveaux riches* allied themselves with the lowest classes, just as their opposite numbers had done in Greece and Sicily. These masses gained a size and importance in the years of Roman expansion which was unparalleled in the history of Greece and early Rome. Military service in the Roman Army and Rome's frequent campaigns on the peninsula had ruined the Italian peasant and had made him a victim of the Roman landowers and the wealthy, who robbed him of his debt-ridden property. Pressed by harsh creditors, and even more by the competition of the wheat shipped to Rome from the conquered provinces, the impoverished peasant moved into the city. There he swelled the ranks of the starving and penniless proletarians who were always ready to support any attack the knights launched against the existing political and social system.

The Roman nobility and its political instrument, the Roman Senate, faced this threat with no less concern that the Athenian or Syracusan aristocracy faced the events which led to the rise of Pisistratus, Dionysus, or Agathocles. To stop its immediate downfall, however, reforms on a still larger scale were required than the ones which Solon in a similar situation had brought about in Athens—though even he had not had very much success. The best thing to do would have been the release of public land in Italy, which had been seized by the Roman nobility during the occupation of the provinces, and to distribute it to the expelled and oppressed peasants. In addition, Roman citizenship should have been granted to the Italian communities which felt neglected. Rome indeed was not lacking in reformers from the nobility who were prepared to support such a programme, but like all men of this type they failed to overcome the egotism of their class. The Roman aristocracy died politically because it refused to be operated on by benevolent doctors. The Roman tribune (people's representative) Tiberius Sempronius Gracchus, who in 133 B.C. submitted a land distribution law to the assembly of the citizens of Rome, met with furious resistance in the Senate and was eventually murdered, and his energetic and clever brother, Caius Gracchus, who attempted the same reform ten years later, fared no better. The failure of the reforms left no choice other than to solve the social problem by imperialism, which did not please the aristocracy, since Rome's military expansion was likely to lead to the dictatorship of successful generals.

Marius and Sulla

One of the chief reasons for the misfortune that befell the Gracchi was the fact that the senatorial aristocracy at the time still held a firm grip on the army, which until the start of the first century B.C. consisted mainly of conscript citizens, landed peasants, and noble-born officers. Not long after the murder of Caius Gracchus, however, the picture changed. Rome's rise to world power necessitated the hiring of professional soldiers able to perform much more complicated and more technical military duty and imbued with a desire for plunder and higher rank rather than to return to their homes and property. Being the younger sons of peasants or country poor, these professional mercenaries could acquire land only through meritorious military service and the settling of veterans became one of the most burning problems in Roman history. This transformation of the army into a mercenary one naturally displeased the nobility as much as it was popular with the masses. The knights, too, saw in these new armies a much better weapon for continuous political and economic expansion than the old peasant army.

The father of the army reform, the general Gaius Marius, was consequently not a nobleman but a peasant's son from Corfinium, who had started as a successful business man before embarking on politics and finally a military career. The knights, being Rome's capitalist class, looked on him as one of their number from his former business life. The nobility hated him, but had no power to display their feelings, since his glory after his

victorious campaign against the African king Jugurtha, one of
the new-style colonial ventures, increased tremendously. The
chief merit for this victory and for the capture of the king by
treason was claimed, it is true, by a lieutenant of Marius named
Lucius Cornelius Sulla, a proud and phlegmatic representative of
the Roman nobility. The perpetual threat of an invasion of the
capital by the barbaric Cimbri and Teutons ended when Marius
won two glorious victories over them. This gave him the opportunity to have himself elected consul (one of the two state presidents) not less than six times—in direct violation of the Roman
constitution.

Fortunately for the Senate and the nobility, who watched this
development with uneasiness, Marius' party eventually disintegrated completely, which forced him to use his opponent to aid
him against his own left wing. The political weakening of Marius
aided his former lieutenant Sulla, who since the campaign against
Jugurtha had become jealous of Marius, and who gradually had
become the political trustee of the nobility and the Senate. Sulla's
success in the so-called Social War—a clumsy expression for a
war against Rome's Italian confederates which clamoured
for Roman citizenship—strengthened his position further. As a
result of these victories and his connection through marriage with
the veteran noble family of the Metelli, he was made Roman
consul in 88 B.C. Despite the support he received from the conservatives, he was, however, unprepared to exploit the opportunities open to a rather poor front-line officer like himself by
the growing Roman imperialism hated by the nobility. The urge
to rise, get rich, and live in appropriate luxury held this taciturn,
reserved man in its grip even though he kept it concealed behind
a mask of aristocratic correctness. Unable to hold in check the
fleeing chariot of Roman expansion, the Senate in those years
had to be contented if it somehow managed to keep the speeding
horses under control. It was therefore bound to welcome the
bitter opposition of old Marius to the plan of his former lieutenant to secure the richest of the overseas assignments, the command in the war against the wealthy King Mithridates of Pontus,
which meant that politically Sulla would remain in the aristocratic camp.

When he learned that a tribune of the people had persuaded
the assembly to transfer the command of the war against Mith-

ridates to Marius, Sulla became even more angry than when he
had had to see Marius march in triumph through Rome as the
victor over Jugurtha. He permitted his army, about to be shipped
to Asia Minor, to stone the messengers who had notified him of
his removal, marched at the head of his troops to the capital,
forced his way through the gates, mercilessly setting fire to the
suburbs, because the masses had backed Marius, even giving the
signal with a torch held in his hand, killed the people's tribune
who had deprived him of his command and leaving this trail of
vengeful destruction behind him, he embarked with his army for
Asia Minor to start his long-planned war against Mithridates
with the fullest vigour. That by his departure for Asia Minor
he abandoned the senatorial class to the revenge of Marius mattered less to him than his wish to avoid further delay in fighting
the Asian tyrant so as to take the expected booty.

The terrible outrages committed by Sulla's mercenaries in his
assault upon the capital marked the beginning of one of the most
blood-stained periods in Roman history. The senatorial and
people's parties fought each other with a ferocity not seen in the
internal struggles of early Rome. Marius had fled to Africa to
escape Sulla, and on his return to Rome he was given a tumultuous welcome. So embittered was he over the atrocities Sulla
had committed in the suburbs of Rome that he massacred the
Roman nobles, confiscated their estates, and exiled the survivors.
Marius died suddenly in the middle of his seventh consulate, and
his fellow consul, Lucius Cornelius Cinna, continued the anti-
aristocratic terrorism as a practically unrestricted dictator.

The plight of the Roman nobles was not alleviated until Sulla
had reached his objectives in the East, and had defeated King
Mithridates decisively, thus gaining the enormous booty he was
seeking. To the good fortune of Sulla and the senatorial party,
Mithridates proved his own worst enemy, for, instead of playing
the part of liberator from the Romans in the areas of Asia Minor
and Greece that he had conquered, he levied such crippling taxation that they deserted him in the decisive struggle. He was fortunate in being granted an armistice which demanded heavy
reparations but which spared him his life and his kingdom.

Thus Sulla had attained his objectives, and the subsequent
career of this first great dictator in Roman history was an attempt
to increase his gigantic empire reaching to Greece and Asia, to

make it secure, and to exploit it as much as possible. He took his revenge on everyone who hampered his activities or who had previously wronged him. Shortly after signing his treaty with Mithridates he returned with his army to Italy. In a few well-planned battles he broke the resistance of his democratic opponents, and in November 82 B.C. the civil war ended at the gates of Rome. These actions show him to have been a capable general as well as an efficient political leader.

The dictatorship which was formally conferred upon Sulla by the Senate has little more than the name in common with the earlier office of that name, as it was neither created to meet some outside danger nor was it given a time limit. Thus it resembled the form of dictatorship that we know today—it was a tyranny in the grand style. But it differed from dictatorships previously mentioned in one very essential factor : it was practically the first anti-revolutionary dictatorship in recorded history. Contrary to custom, its opponents were the city masses, the big business men or knights, and the mercenaries enrolled by the late Marius, whereas its supporters—and they were not too numerous—sat mainly in the aristocratic Senate. Just as Marius in his last days as seventh consul banished and killed the nobility, Sulla on his seizure of power resorted to large-scale proscription, which was aimed mainly at the capitalist class. He is estimated to have banished or murdered 2,600 knights. Whoever granted protection to banished persons shared their fate, and informers were well paid. Indeed the entire procedure was handled in such a summary manner that Sulla seems to have been trying to recover losses in financing the civil war.

Those prosecuted were denied legal protection; even professional criminals smuggled the names of men murdered by their hands into the proscription lists so as to escape punishment. Because dictatorships originating from the ruling classes usually lack the support of the masses, Sulla tried to enlarge the basis of his support artificially—an action typical of this kind of despotic rule. He increased the people's assembly by 10,000 freed slaves who had belonged to the murdered knights, choosing for this purpose mostly well-built young men who were tools in his hands. In honour of the aristocratic family to whom he belonged, he gave them the name of Cornelii. He also gave the veterans of his twenty-three legions land on which to settle at the cost of the

State. The Senate, which had lost many members as a result of the civil war, was strengthened by 300 knights, conservative in outlook, in order to split the remnant of the aristocratic opposition. The increase in the number of military courts, the limitation of the power of the tribunes of the people and of provincial governors, the extension of the senatorial authority over the civil courts, which had previously been under the control of the knights, and a general tightening of the criminal law were other measures which marked the progress of this dictatorship. But at the same time neither the Senate nor the aristocracy were satisfied.

Like all true dictators Sulla was as much a danger to his friends as to his foes. The illegal proscriptions and the outrages committed by the Sullanean gangs terrified many conservatives and even affected the dictator's own followers. The unusual pathological traits so typical of most dictators emerged with special vigour in Sulla, but in accordance with his own personality. Unlike most other impoverished noblemen who became tyrants, Sulla, being a professional Roman army officer, was not able to achieve his goal early nor did he achieve it as a revolutionary demagogue. As a typical officer, he had had to wait a long time for his opportunity. Both from the social and psychological aspect he was a case of retarded development; the final emergence of strange mental traits, the excessive appetite and sexuality of the ageing man resembled in its suddenness the breaking of the dam of a reservoir which had stored up water in many years of waiting.

Historians have always been mystified by Sulla's conduct in this final period, wondering why, for example, the dictator was always preceded by twenty-four lictors (guards) carrying fasces (bundles of rods), and why he, who was obviously aiming at kingship, suddenly renounced his office (79 B.C.). They attributed it to the resistance he found in his own ranks, a conflict that always exists between a dictator and the more radical of his followers. There are indeed proofs that the opposition among sections of the senatorial aristocracy was increasing, but it would hardly have led to his abdication had not his burning urge to make up for the frustrations of his youth driven him in his later years almost insane. His sudden resignation in 79 B.C., interpreted by his eulogists and by many historians as a proof of republican unselfishness, was thus inspired by the very same desire to make up for pleasures missed in the past which drove so many of the younger men into the arms of the masses and to tyranny. From the moment of his resignation to that of his death, not quite a year later, the ex-dictator spent his time on the huge estates he had taken from his adversaries, giving himself up to an uninterrupted series of festivities, drinking bouts and orgies of every description.

The Victory of Dictatorship: Gaius Julius Caesar

Despite their numerous secretly voiced complaints against him, the senatorial party saw in Sulla the saviour of their cause. In reality, Sulla's rule marked the beginning of the end of senatorial rule as a result of his political methods. The big colonial wars which financed Sulla's dictatorship remained essential, and the policy of robbery and expansion in turn increased the probability that the entire Roman State would fall a prey to some victorious general. The unending wars of spoliation led to a revival of the capitalist class which had been destroyed by Sulla, but the nucleus of this class was from then onwards formed by Sullanean *nouveaux riches* who had lined their nests with the belongings of the slain knights.

The recovery of capitalism and the increasing importance of the wars of spoliation, together with the mercenary armies, the import of slaves, and the city masses whose ranks were filled by the constant rise of slave economy in the country created once again the threat of a revolutionary Roman dictatorship. Natural candidates were the generals who under Sulla had accumulated huge fortunes and who both as military leaders and capitalists were interested in supporting a policy which was directly contrary to the ideas of Sulla and the Senate.

The prize in this race for dictatorship was won by the most successful of these military figures, Gnaeus Pompey, a young nobleman who both in his career and by marriage had been very close to Sulla and who had made a name for himself as a military commander by bringing seditious Spain back under the rule of the Roman Senate. Born in 106 B.C. and only about four years older than Gaius Julius Caesar, who was later to oust him from his position, he outshone his successor until both of them were well over forty. The final outcome of the historic duel between them was largely due to the dissimilar conditions in which they spent their early lives.

Pompey sprang from Sulla's entourage and reverted to the aristocratic fold. Despite his conflicts with them and his ambition, he was until his downfall a child of fortune from the higher ranks; vain, arrogant, spoiled, vigorous, but also sleepy and phlegmatic, he was to emerge at a late age as the winner in the clash with his dynamic rival.

Although he also belonged to the nobility, Caesar lacked everything which made Pompey's career easy and enjoyable : money, respect, political protection, and even robust health. Having come from a family which was not very well off, he was compromised in the eyes of Sulla and his supporters because his mother was a sister of Gaius Marius, and also because of his first marriage with the daughter of Cinna, the head of the terrorist leftist Government of the eighties which Sulla had destroyed. As a result Caesar was in such straits that he lost the rest of his fortune and only just escaped banishment and murder.

Destined to be an aristocratic leader of the masses, he could see that his career was blocked by the competition of the leading Sullanean generals, especially Pompey. All Caesar's biographers since Plutarch and Suetonius, in their understandable desire to give as complete a picture of his life as possible, have given too much emphasis to his early life. In actual fact, although he held some minor posts, Julius Caesar had, until after his fortieth year, as little importance in Roman history as had Adolf Hitler in Germany before 1920. After Sulla's death, which seemed to open the road to success to him, he returned from the East whence he had fled and tried to gain a reputation in Rome by indicting two mighty Sullaneans, but seeing that he lacked the necessary influence he returned to Rhodes to study at its university.

This early part of Caesar's career as well as his later years are illustrated by some anecdotes and gossip told by scandalmongers of the day. In later years Caesar's soldiers told ribald jokes about the relations said to exist between their general and the King of Bithynia; there was hardly any noble-born woman in Rome with whom he was not said to have slept. Many of these stories are probably enemy propaganda; as far as they are true, they show the way Caesar played the aristocrat. If these stories are open to doubt, the overall picture of the time is not. It suggests that

Caesar, like every other strong man, could never have risen to the top if his rise had not been preceded by vast social change. This change, inevitable since Sulla's rule, was going on at the very same time as Caesar was calmly pursuing his studies. It was as significant in his career as were the English and French revolutions in the lives of Cromwell and Napoleon, or the effect of the depression after the first world war upon the fate of Adolf Hitler.

The social change in Rome was caused by the constant wars of spoliation. The tremendous booty brought to Rome, especially the continuous influx of slaves from the Greek world, transformed the political and physical shape of the old capital in those years. Up till then it had possessed in its simplicity and severity something of the restrained nature of Sparta. The new capitalist class in Rome dominated the picture not only in the political field, by ousting the aristocracy, but also under the guidance of Greek immigrants and its Greek slaves transformed the entire life of the city. Greek fashions determined the mode of dress, Greek books the thought, Greek poetry the taste, and Greek architecture the building. The financing of the construction of the many modern buildings, temples, fountains, and public squares, as well as the entirely new style of life, caused vast expenditure; the need to cover these expenses, public as well as private, led in turn to the need for continuing the imperialist expansion which had originated the trend. The continuous move into the city of the poor from the country, who had been ruined by the rise of the slave economy, and the growth of urban handicraft, especially of the skilled type handled by freed slaves to the profit of their former owners, simultaneously increased the power of the lower classes, who hated the aristocracy. This made revolution more and more likely, and dictatorship became increasingly possible.

The young man who was pursuing his studies in Rhodes at that time was exactly suited to this period. A scion and not a servant of the Roman nobility, he was able to discuss its weaknesses with calm and aloofness and with a sense of judgment sharpened by Greek scepticism. He steeled his body by Greek gymnastics, although he could not quite overcome his epileptic disposition. As a capable but suppressed member of the Roman upper class he witnessed with unconcealed enjoyment the taming of that class by the Greeks it had subjected and the victory of Greek ethics over the harsh Roman way of life. Apart from this, the developments of those years created the conditions he needed for his rise to power, even though the outcome of the attempt was still hidden in the future.

The immediate fruits of this evolution could not be gathered by an unknown figure such as the young student in Rhodes, but were reserved for the powerful men of the time, especially Sulla's former generals like Lucius Licinius Lucullus, Marcus Licinius Crassus, and Gnaeus Pompey. The eighties and seventies of the first century B.C. were the years when these men flourished, especially Pompey, who knew how to use the deeds of others to add to his own glory. He put down an uprising in Spain after its leader had been slain by his own men; "terminated" the war against the famous slave revolt under Spartacus at the moment it had been almost won by Crassus; waged a war to clear the Mediterranean of pirates, forced King Mithridates, who had been decisively beaten by Lucullus, to surrender and flee his country, and ultimately conquered Jerusalem. The only hope a young man like Caesar without means or power had to compete with such mighty men was to know how to be useful to them.

The opportunity to do this arose quite naturally. As in the past, the senatorial aristocracy stubbornly resisted any attempt to concentrate power in the hands of an individual general. Men like Pompey were therefore forced to have the commanding positions they sought conferred upon them by the assembly. However, as a result of Sulla's reactionary laws, the Senate was even more strongly controlled by the senatorial aristocracy than before. If Pompey or Crassus wished to succeed, they had to remove the political restrictions applied by Sulla and make the assembly pliant by means of huge bribes. This was where Caesar, the nephew of Marius and the victim of Sulla, enjoyed the people's confidence and was able to render them real services. Caesar's connection with Crassus, Rome's wealthiest man, was the more important as he had contracted huge debts to finance his rise to power on his return from Rhodes about 74 to 73 B.C. Crassus was a typical representative of the kind of predatory capitalism established by Sulla. Using his advantage as an officer of Sulla, he acquired the best of the slaves shipped to Rome, and established regular slave schools to improve their quality and so increase their selling price; he also controlled the Roman fire brigade, which was instructed not to fight a fire until the wailing owners had sold their houses for a mere song to the great financiers who headed the fire brigade. It was in keeping with this that Crassus, Rome's greatest slave-owner, was entrusted with the command of the army which crushed the greatest slave revolt in history.

However, he was not able to seize a second important command; both he and Lucullus saw the rewards of their actions taken by Pompey, whom Crassus inwardly disliked. Since the time when Pompey had been given the command in the wars against the pirates and Mithridates, Crassus tried continuously to make up for the defeats he had thus suffered, and in Caesar he found the best ally. Since the beginning of the seventies the future dictator transacted business for Crassus on the Forum, the Roman market place which was also the centre of Roman political life, busily negotiating with people's representatives, party secretaries, and party bosses, and the never-ending stream of applicants for benefits.

However, Caesar could not hope for higher objectives than those for which Crassus was aiming as he was neither a military figure nor an influential politician. He would have to climb the prescribed ladder, which led from the office of quaestor (director of finance), to those of aedile (director of police), praetor (a high judicial magistrate), and consul (one of the two presidents of the republic), to give him a chance to be appointed governor of a province, a proconsul. To start at the age of thirty-six at the very bottom of this ladder was very disheartening for a man like Caesar, since in order to finance his rise he had been forced in all those years to promote the aims of men who were his inferiors intellectually, but who had more power than he. It was only natural that he should look for a short cut. After his year of service as quaestor, which he spent in Spain, he and Crassus gave their political backing to Lucius Sergius Catilina, an impoverished nobly born demagogue, whose candidacy for consul had been rejected at the behest of Marcus Tullius Cicero, which led the rejected candidate, half against his will and under the pressure of his election debts, to start an uprising. In Rome, which was full of the wildest rumours, it was said that Crassus planned to seize power as dictator, and Caesar as magister equitum (commander of the knights, that is, vice-dictator). Had Catilina conquered the senatorial party, Crassus and Caesar indeed would hardly have found it difficult to set him aside and seize control themselves; as it was, his defeat and death gave Caesar the opportunity to gain popular sympathy by making a speech against the execution of Catilina's followers, even though it was not successful.

The importance Caesar attached to winning over the multitudes is especially shown by the way he administered the office of aedile (director of police), to which he was appointed. The city crowds assembled in the circus could hardly believe their eyes when they saw what Caesar had produced for their pleasure; Greek chariot drivers; athletes from Thrace; dancers from Miletus; 112 lions; sixty enormous panthers; sixteen bears of the largest possible size; giraffes; elephants; tigers; and in addition to all this, 320 pairs of gladiators, who, guided by rules as in modern football championships, killed each other off amidst frantic applause from the spectators, until almost none of them survived. The Forum and the buildings housing the people's assembly were beautified by the new director of police, who was also in charge of public works; on the summit of the Capitol he erected a museum where he displayed his magnificent collection of art; the dilapidated main highway serving Rome, the famous Via Appia, was completely repaired by him. The money for this huge expenditure had, of course, to be procured by Crassus. This was paralleled in modern times by the wealthy Alfred Hugenberg, who, in order to foster his own political aims in Germany under the Weimar Republic, short-sightedly financed the Nazi Party which helped his rival Adolf Hitler to power. The debts contracted by Caesar amounted in the end to 1,300 talents (about £620,000); of this sum, 800 talents were paid in cash by Crassus, a considerable achievement even for a financier who gave his total wealth to be 7,000 talents (over £3,500,000).

The considerable propaganda staged by Caesar and the direction his career was taking show that even then he had decided to play a special part in history, which was to lead to his becoming consul and governor of a province. This was bound to lead to friction between him and the other candidates for unlimited political power. The millions spent by Crassus enabled Caesar to yield to his innermost urge, to act the part of the wealthy and snobbish modern nobleman in front of the Roman aristocracy, and to oppose the old Roman religion and ethics, which he despised, with the cultural ideas of the Greeks. He knew that the hatred felt for the aristocracy by the city masses would make him popular, and was not perturbed if the spiciest tales were told of his contempt for Roman traditions and his love affairs with the wives of many high-ranking men. During the climax of the Senate trial of the participants of the Catiline conspiracy, he arranged for a slave to hand him a document, affecting the deepest secrecy, and permitted the suspicious Cato Junior, an ultra-conservative, to intervene and read the paper to the entire meeting. It turned out to be a love letter from Caesar's favourite mistress, Servilia, a married woman of the best society and Cato's own sister, for whom Caesar is said to have sacrificed millions. She was, by the way, the mother of Marcus Junius Brutus, who with his companions was eventually to stab Caesar to death. Angrily the aristocracy saw how the upstart fought it with its own weapons; the tremendous sums put at his disposal enabled Caesar to play the benevolent, make large gifts, and even be courteous to his opponents, which the ruling classes found most obnoxious. In the letters of Cicero, who sympathized with the old aristocracy and adapted himself only temporarily and not completely to the dictatorship, we find Caesar's benevolence—his famous "*clementia*"—called a propaganda measure, not reflecting his true character. This view is as unsound as the view that Hitler's anti-Semitism was not rooted in his soul, but merely a political expediency, but it illustrates the importance of this characteristic in contributing to Caesar's final victory. Compared with the ethics of the old Roman warriors, his rule was humane and conciliatory, reflecting the spirit of the Greeks which animated the entire young rising Roman plutocracy, but in his hands this spirit was made an instrument of force.

Caesar realized well enough that the influence he exercised during these years was bound to disappear once the millions spent by Crassus had vanished without bringing the desired result. His fear of missing the right moment and of perishing prematurely by the slowness of his rise to consul darkened his best years. The constant necessity of doing political work for others, such as having to agitate for distribution of land, the lowering of the price of bread, tax relief for the masses, as well as the endless pressure by Crassus to obtain, through his services, a profit-bringing military command or a similar office—such as the chance to interfere with the affairs of Egypt—made him tired and weary. "Better the first here", he was heard to say when passing through a small town during his travels, "than second in Rome."

The decisive turn of his career came at the end of the sixties, when he had climbed high enough to reach for personal power, and when Pompey returned to Rome from his successes in Asia with his army and the enormous booty he had captured. The Senate once more feared dictatorship and military rule. In order to force the Senate into consenting to the settling of his veterans and the fulfilling of other promises made to them, Pompey readily accepted the proposal of Caesar and Crassus that they should pool interests by forming a political combination known as a triumvirate (rule of three men). It was the renewal of a somewhat loose agreement, which had first been entered into in 70 B.C. Its purpose was to secure control of all main political offices, especially those of governors of provinces (proconsul), by means of influencing the people's assembly and bribing electors and tribunes of the people. It was probable that this triumvirate would break up in a bitter quarrel between its participants. Caesar needed the triumvirate as he was preparing his candidacy for consulship. In order to get money for this step, Caesar had sought the office of pro-praetor (provincial head of the judiciary) in Spain. He used his stay there to gain some military experience and for accumulating money for election expenses by robbing natives and taking money from provincial Romans in need of his political protection. The year 59 B.C. finally brought him the long-desired rank of consul; he used the year of his consulate to obtain for Pompey the approval of the scheme to settle his veterans, and for himself, with the aid of a bribed tribune of the people, the office of governor of Cisalpine Gaul and Illyria. At the instigation of Pompey, who married his daughter Julia, and due to the death of a young governor who had been recently appointed, he was also made governor of Transalpine Gaul.

This was an appointment of the greatest historical significance. It was expected that when his consulate was over Caesar would get a rich province to despoil in order to strengthen his rule, but the chance that it was Gaul gave him a place, not only in the history of France and Europe but the entire modern world. The ostensible motive for his expanding the province he had been entrusted with to the Atlantic Ocean, the English Channel, and the Rhine was the threat of its being invaded by some frontier tribes, who, in turn, were being pressed by invading Teutons.

The energy which Caesar displayed in colonizing and subjecting this vast area was amazing. He was forty-four and had no military training worth mentioning. It all went to show that, like Sulla, he was a case of retarded development and that he was prepared to work hard to create for himself a base for his decisive bid for power. His task could only be accomplished owing to a disunited population—a factor which helped the *conquistadores* of later centuries like Hernando Cortez in Mexico or Pizarro in Peru. Apart from the division of Gaul into countless tribes, there were social cleavages; the noblemen, who were particularly strong among the Aedui, frequently sympathized with Rome. The conquest of the immense and trackless territory from which Caesar had first to expel the Teuton invaders was a very considerable feat, especially for a general without experience; it proved among other things that he had realism and great understanding of his men and especially for the problems of army supply. The vigilance with which he escaped all traps, so dangerous in colonial wars, the way in which he secured his supply lines under the most difficult conditions, and protected himself against surprise attacks gave him an especial place in the history of warfare.

The factors that decided Caesar's wars in his favour were his excellent organization, the good training of his soldiers, the discipline, the leadership, the arms, and the technical experience of his army. The fear of his army was increased by its system of taking hostages; by this means even areas through which it only passed were kept under control for many years. Yet despite this, the conquest of Gaul was still incomplete at the end of 57 B.C. The public proclamation of the annexation of the area by Rome, which was announced in the capital the following year and caused great enthusiasm, was probably a political trick. Its aim was to increase Caesar's prestige in the triumvirate and his popularity with the people, and also with the traders and financiers, whose agents followed the armies in order to buy slaves and ship them to Rome. The same motives explain Caesar's two expeditions to Britain, and on the right bank of the Rhine, but they also show his desire to explore by "armed reconnaissance" the best way of securing conquered Gaul; his first crossing of the Rhine was an answer to the appearance on the left bank of certain Teuton tribes whom he treacherously assaulted and annihilated.

The success of Caesar's propaganda in 56 B.C. was the more necessary since the anti-aristocratic party he had created in Rome terrorized the capital and created the danger of an aristocratic reaction. This party was led by the tribune Clodius, a *declassé* aristocrat and a former stool-pigeon. The Senate did everything it could to win over Pompey except giving him military power. Thus Caesar was once more able to repair the breach in the triumvirate and obtain by the usual pressure the endorsement of some new laws that extended his rule in Gaul for five years. These laws also gave Crassus, who for years had been dreaming of another predatory war in the East, the governorship of Syria, while Pompey received that of Spain. The breathing spell saved Caesar's work in Gaul, where the natives he had subdued rebelled against his rule with a determination that was extremely bad for his prestige. The revolts were encouraged by the fact that the Roman legions no longer appeared in one large close formation, but as garrisons scattered all over the country. One Roman detachment was lured into an ambush near Liège and annihilated; another, under the command of Cicero's brother Quintus, was relieved by Caesar at the last minute. The terrible Roman reprisals in their turn caused rebellion to break out in districts that had hitherto been quiet. What fed the flames of revolt most was the systematic spoliation of the province by the Romans. This embittered even the Gallic aristocracy, which until then had been Caesar's most reliable supporters. The revolt round Orleans, for example, led to the murder of Italian merchants who had their stores in that region, and also of a Roman supply officer.

The universal nature of these grievances gave the rebellion a national flavour, and brought it a leader from the most democratic circles. He was Vercingetorix, a young man from the Averni trible (in what is today the Auvergne), descended from an old royal family which claimed the right to rule the whole of Gaul. As the chief foe of the aristocracy, he had much in common with Caesar himself. The duel between the Roman general, over fifty years of age, and the prince half his age, who as an arch-enemy of Roman colonial imperialism aimed at leading the whole of Gaul, belongs to the great dramas of history. Both opponents in this struggle displayed great energy, stamina, and resourcefulness. The rebellion reached such proportions that Caesar, after a futile attempt to besiege his opponent near Clermont-Ferrand, was forced to evacuate the entire province. But because Vercingetorix was unable to keep his army of peasants away from their fields and homes any longer, he offered Caesar battle, and this saved the situation for the Romans. Caesar succeeded in encircling his adversary in the fortified town of Alesia, near Dijon, and after a siege that made history in the technique of warfare, during which there were some poorly organized efforts by the Gallic tribes to relieve their leader, Caesar compelled him to surrender by starvation. Pardoning of seditious natives was not the custom of the Romans; during the cleaning-up operations in the province, Caesar had captured tribal chiefs publicly flogged to death, and cut off the hands of entire tribes. Vercingetorix, whom Caesar held responsible for the whole rebellion and therefore for the delay of his political schemes, was kept prisoner for many years until Caesar celebrated his triumphs. He was then strangled.

The end of Caesar's campaigns in Gaul marked the beginning of his dictatorship. The triumvirate's system of influencing the assembly, bribery, corruption, blackmail, hunting for high commands, and spoliation of provinces had been going on far too long to permit one of its members to withdraw into private life in the provinces after his term was over. As a result the imminent expiration of Caesar's term of office signalled the approach of a crisis. After Crassus with all his army had been slain by the Parthians in 53 B.C., the relations between the two surviving members of the triumvirate deteriorated rapidly. The fear of an attack on the republic by Caesar led to a wave of aristocratic reaction which in 52 B.C. led to the death of Caesar's partisan, Clodius, leader of the city crowds. Pompey, carried away as a result of this feeling, protected the terrified Senate and gradually returned to the political policy of his earlier years, when he had defended the nobility. As a reward, the Senate entrusted him with an amount of political authority which it had denied Caesar. The Senate's request that Caesar should disband his army after the end of his time as Governor of Gaul led to an open breach between Caesar and Pompey in the first few days of 49 B.C. On

the night of January 10th-11th, 49 B.C., Caesar crossed the
Rubicon at the head of his legions. This river marked the boundary between the provinces he administered and the rest of Italy,
and as Governor he was forbidden to lead his forces outside the
province he governed. In this way, as he said, "the die was cast",
and he had formally become a rebel. Pompey, accompanied by
most senators and many other wealthy men, fled to Greece to
organize resistance with the help of the huge resources of the
Orient and of Spain, which he governed.

The vast scale of the social and political struggle was typical
of Caesar's dictatorship; it decided its form as well as its tragic
end. Had Caesar been tyrant of a small city-state such as
Dionysus or Agathocles he would have occupied the Forum with
his mercenaries, and would have formed a people's assembly,
would have court-martialled the leading aristocrats, killed their
followers, and, spurred on by the city mob, would have ransacked
their palaces. After a time a "plot" to assassinate the great man
would have been "discovered" and in the resultant riot the furious crowd would have granted him a bodyguard and unlimited
power. Supported by an army of secret police, he would have
forced the surviving nobles into his services and then would have
used them to fight the city masses and left-wing elements.

However, such a course was not open to Caesar, partly because
of Roman tradition and from political and technical objections.
In the Roman people's assembly sat Caesar's trusted followers, wooed, maintained, and paid by him for a long time; to
replace them wholly or in part by his army would hardly serve
his interests, especially when he needed every soldier he could get
for the coming struggle for world domination. In any case, the
Roman nobility had fled, which threatened to paralyse the functioning of the Senate and of the provincial administration which
had been in their hands. Instead of eliminating the aristocracy
Caesar was forced gracefully to accept the services of all noblemen who were not completely opposed to him, especially as he
needed them as a counter-balance against the people's assembly
and the city masses. Soon the world heard with surprise that the
dreaded man, instead of avenging himself on the nobility, freed
captured senators and supporters of Pompey, and even showered
them with gifts.

The political reorganization in Rome, speedily carried out by

Caesar in April 49 while passing through on his way to Spain, was restricted to a slight transformation of the political order without altering it completely, as well as making some key appointments. This policy did not really change; throughout the five years of his dictatorship, when the Civil War kept him mostly away from Rome, his rule was mostly extemporaneous. Prompted by the hope of reaching a more durable settlement later, he looked on the office of dictator as one which was renewed annually. At the same time he gradually reformed the Senate by filling it with his followers and a few men from the provinces until at last it had nine hundred members.

Plans of a more long-term nature were not made until shortly before his death. His method of rule for most of the time was in effect nothing but a continuation of the triumvirate, with one head instead of three. This policy enabled him to win the Civil War, but it also gave the moderate wing of the nobility an independence which would have been impossible under Dionysus or Agathocles, and thus induced the dictator to postpone the inevitable conflict with the friends of the Roman constitution, and the emphasizing of his autocratic position, to a time when it was too late for it—and this was to result in his untimely death.

Caesar conducted his war against Pompey on the principle of beating his enemies singly before they were able to join forces. He therefore did not molest Pompey himself at first, but marched against his supporters in Spain who were ultimately forced to surrender, despite an initial threat to his forces by Spanish natives who refused to supply them. Even during his campaign against Pompey himself he was brought into a very difficult position by Pompey's methods of attrition. He escaped from a position at Durazzo, where his forces were near starvation, to the east coast of Greece. The impatience of the senators who had fled with Pompey led to their chief's undoing. Their desire to return home led them to persuade their hesitant supreme commander to fight in the field, where Caesar was superior. By winning the resultant Battle of Pharsalus Caesar became master of the entire ancient world. (48 B.C.)

Pompey fled—with Caesar at his heels—through the Eastern Mediterranean and was assassinated while landing in Egypt. Caesar stayed in Alexandria, when the young princess Cleopatra, in order to win his support in her struggle with her brother

Ptolemy for the Egyptian succession, sneaked into his palace by night, and where he was besieged shortly afterwards by an army belonging to her enemies. Caesar's connection with Cleopatra is much more than a mere episode; it is a union of love and politics, comparable with, for instance, the relations between the Argentine dictator Rosas (overthrown in 1851) and his wife, or between Juan and Eva Perón, the Argentine dictator and his wife in the years after World War II. To the former student at Rhodes, a princess like Cleopatra, who had come from the Greek dynasty which had been placed on the Egyptian throne by Alexander the Great, was the incarnation of the Greek spirit which he knew and loved, and whose praise was sung by the Greek *nouveaux riches*, in whose circles Caesar moved without really belonging. Her refinement, and the tremendous luxury that surrounded her, appeared to him as the realization of the fondest dreams of this society of Roman snobs. His own circle would never have been able to compete with the splendour and extravagance of a queen who could count on the innumerable humans of an oriental monarchy, instead of captured slaves, to satisfy her whims.

Having become master of the world by his victories, Caesar felt he was the only man worthy of this woman. Caesar and the Queen of Egypt would be the marriage of Rome with the world of Alexander the Great, would be the symbol of the sovereignty of Hellenism and the downfall of that Roman aristocracy against which both Caesar and Cleopatra had to struggle. When he finally departed from Alexandria, where the queen was expecting a child by him, his decisions about the future was made; and in the story of his final disaster they play an important role.

The period of almost three years that followed Caesar's departure from Egypt were marked by three campaigns. First, that against Mithridates' son, which was short and victorious. It was from this war that he sent his famous dispatch *veni, vidi, vici* (I came, I saw, I conquered). Then came two strenuous campaigns against the Pompeians and other irreconcilable noblemen in Africa and Spain. Only after the midsummer of 46, when he celebrated four gigantic triumphs, did he find time for peaceful reform. After his last big victory over his enemies near the Spanish city of Munda, exactly one year before his death, he had no more need to fear action in battle, but danger of assassination grew. It was his peacetime reforms, and his urge to promote with his usual drive, the many measures he had had to postpone, that led to plots to murder him.

It was true that he was not as much of a social reformer as his aristocratic foes in Rome feared. The collapse of the last armed resistance to Caesar ruined all their hopes. The propaganda of the left-wing supporters in his party left him unmoved. In his social policy he favoured the rich; he dissolved the unions of craftsmen and lower middle class people which had been formed by Clodius, limited the public distribution of corn, the ancient form of unemployment relief, made criminal punishment more severe, and favoured social reforms only as far as it helped the army, the treasury or increased his prestige.

This policy did not indicate that he was interested in the welfare of the rich. His main concern was the upkeep of the state machinery and care for his veterans, for whose sake he put teeth into the legislation for veterans voted during his consulate, supervised its execution, and drafted a huge new settlement plan. The aristocrats and especially the very rich in Rome, although they had only felt lukewarm towards the Pompeians, saw with disgust how the dictator distributed the estates of the latter among his soldiers. From the booty taken in Africa, which came largely from this source, each soldier received 20,000 sesterces (roughly £180), the captains and colonels two and four times as much respectively; in addition to this, the dictator organized a huge banquet at public expense and a large distribution of corn. In order to increase his prestige and to lessen unemployment, Caesar, again at public expense, drew up a very large programme of public works, envisaging among other things, the rebuilding of Corinth and Carthage, and the draining of the Pontine marshes. To win the support of the provinces, Caesar advocated the inclusion of provincial representatives in the Senate, limitation of payments to the Roman tax farmers, and in general a modification of the system of robbery and spoliation Rome had applied to the provinces and which had been so profitable even to himself.

His policy angered the wealthy and powerful in Rome. Cicero tells us that he enforced it with the help of people who seemed most undesirable, bankrupts, fortune hunters, and professional criminals. These Caesar deemed especially fit to fight the nobility; among them was the double-faced Dolabella, Cicero's own son-in-law, who divorced his wife after having compromised her in public; the shrewd Balbus from Cadiz in Spain, Balbus' substitute, Oppius, and the corrupt and cunning private secretary, Faberius. One of the most scandalous figures among Caesar's followers was the dictator's official substitute, Mark Antony, who kept entire harems of male and female prostitutes, and who financed his immense waste by the confiscated estates of Pompey, which he obtained by public bidding, but for which he did not pay.

Some of the reports of the men sound like parlour gossip. In the end Caesar treated Mark Antony with reserve, and his selection of many of these men was certainly due to his need for clever non-aristocratic servants of his policy upon whose experience he could rely. It was just this increase in the prestige and weight of the dictatorship which, combined with its politics, led to resistance, especially in the ranks of the powerful and mighty in Rome, the richest members of the aristocracy which had unrestricted control of the Senate after the defeat of the Pompeians. Some of them, for instance, Gaius Trebonius, Marcus, and Decimus Brutus, Sulpicius Rufus, Asinius Pollio, and others, had, after Pharsalus, come over to Caesar in the hope that he would protect them and their interests against confiscation and limitation of the profits they made in the provinces. Great was their disappointment when they saw that their calculations had been wrong and that Caesar began to protect the provinces and communities, to clip the wings of the old predatory capitalism, to hand over the administration of the empire and provinces to his followers, and thus to eliminate their political and economic control for ever.

In the winter of 45-44 the signs increased that the dictator would reconstruct the empire with full force and that he would direct his energy against the very circles which believed they could control him until he reappeared in Rome at the end of the Civil War. In the eyes of his opponents the most immediate danger was his appointment of new officials who according to Roman rule were entitled at the end of their terms of one year to enter the Senate. These appointments made it obvious that after his return from his projected war against the Parthians, for which he had planned to set out on March 17th, 44 B.C., he would find a new, watered-down Senate, a pliant servant of his policy, and a willing helper in his plan to seize the royal crown, which was planned. His opponents had to steal a march on him, and to use the fact that the coolness of the Roman masses towards his dreams of kingship prevented him, to his disappointment, from staging his coronation before the Parthian campaign and to increase his personal safety accordingly. A king was independent of the people and did not have to renounce the use of a bodyguard as Caesar, in order not to arouse Republican suspicion, had done —to his own harm.

Caesar was not the first ancient dictator to aim at a royal crown. Hieron had had such plans and Agathocles had struck coins, showing himself as king. In their cases, however, it was more a matter of title, while Caesar's ambitions were evidently inspired by his connection with Cleopatra, who, to the disgust of the Roman aristocracy, visited him at that time in Rome, and disregarding his wife, Caesar invited her to stay in his house. She had brought along her little son from her connection with Caesar, who was named Caesarion. She also evidently had a share of the planning of the campaign against the Parthians which occupied Caesar in his last weeks. The death of Crassus would have been avenged and the great tradition of Alexander the Great followed. The campaign, if successful, would have extended the rule of Cleopatra and that of her intended husband, the Divus (divine) Julius, to whom sacrifices were offered in the temples, as far as the limits of the known world, and as a result of the tremendous booty involved would indeed have given the two reigning figures practically the rank of gods in the eyes of their contemporaries. There was already some talk of transferring the capital from Rome to Alexandria or Homer's Troy. These were gigantic plans, and as with everything that Caesar did, were a combination of fantasy and realism. The old Roman aristocracy and its spirit had been conquered; a grand style of despotism of Hellenism and humanitarian ideals was to triumph, supported by the city masses and the provinces now protected against robbery —and then Caesar was struck down by the fatal daggers.

The famous conspiracy was not a plot of his original enemies but was conceived spontaneously by members of his own party— though with the co-operation of some of his old foes. Two main conspirators, Trebonius and Galba, were leading Caesarian generals who opposed their lord and master's dreams of kingship for very much the same reasons as did the generals of Cromwell and Napoleon when they protested against these dictators' plans to become kings. Others, such as Marcus Junius Brutus, that very symbol of the conspiracy, and his namesake, Decimus Brutus, who persuaded the reluctant Caesar to appeal in the fatal session of the Senate on March 15th, were his close friends; the famous Servilia, mother of Marcus, and mother-in-law of the "lean and hungry" looking Cassius, was his favourite mistress. It was as if in later days commoners close to Cromwell had killed the great man when he dissolved the Rump Parliament or when he tried to take the crown, or as if members of the French legislative assembly had shot down General Bonaparte when on the second day of his famous *coup d'état* he appeared in that assembly to request extraordinary powers.

The difference between these cases and that of Caesar is of course that Cromwell and Napoleon were surrounded or shadowed by troops when risking a breach with their co-revolutionists in parliament, while Caesar who had just been voted dictator for life by his well-oiled election machine and whose dreams of kingship excited the public, was caught by the conspirators unprotected and was cut down in a public senate meeting before he had time to seek protection. Caesar was no social revolutionary, and it was practically certain that although he imposed sacrifices on the ruling classes he would finally have granted them protection, in the manner of Cromwell and Napoleon, in exchange for their giving up of claims to political freedom and parliamentary representation. But he perished as a result of the unusually long postponement and incompetent execution of his *coup d'état* and because he underestimated the risks connected with such a course of action.

The motives of Caesar's murderers, especially those of Marcus Junius Brutus, have been discussed repeatedly by historians and poets. That Brutus was strongly influenced by his bearing the name of an old foe of tyrants is certain; as seen from the sociological point of view, however, he and his friends were representatives of the rich Roman aristocracy which refused to see that the development of imperialism and spoliatory capitalism which had brought it such great riches was bound to lead to the rule of a strong man. History has indeed cast these men aside; not Brutus but Caesar signalled the direction of Rome's future history.

Part II

THE DICTATORSHIPS OF EARLY CAPITALISM

Chapter Four

THE TYRANTS OF THE RENAISSANCE

Change of Scene

NOT long after the death of Caesar the Roman Empire reached the zenith of its growth, but at the same time the nadir of its dynamic force. The spoliation of foreign peoples and the hunt for slaves which were the motives of the steady expansion of Rome came to a natural end as soon as the limit of the space available was reached. However, the over-sized state machinery, which had been built to run the gigantic empire, began to oppress Roman citizens as soon as the economic need for maintaining its dignitaries, its army of bureaucrats, and large mercenary forces vanished. The men in control were the Roman Caesars, and they had inherited their title from the greatest dictator in Roman history. The word Caesar still survives in the German word *Kaiser*. The Caesars gradually developed into mere instruments of state machinery and of the mercenaries, who in later years consisted almost exclusively of barbarians who together with the foreign barbarians that pushed into the empire across the frontiers brought the Roman domination of the world to an end.

The medieval and Germanic world that blossomed in the ruins of that Empire was ruled by feudalism and originally lacked large cities, mass movements, and dictatorships; it was only in its later stage when, like islands in the sea, larger towns emerged once more, especially in Italy after the twelfth century, that demogogues and dictators could arise once more. The period between the thirteenth and sixteenth century is one of the great times of tyranny. It was as if the ancient tyrants had come to life once more, surrounded by all the trappings of antiquity. Fedrigo of Urbino read Caesar's writings and loved them; Alfonso of Aragon—the father of Ferrante, one of the most ferocious despots

61

of that time—entered the city of Naples behind a laurel-bedecked Caesar who carried a globe; Sigismundo Malatesta of Rimini in turn—an even worse figure—erected a monument in the central square of his city commemorating Caesar's passage across the Rubicon river which flows through the town.

Looked at historically, however, that age fitted the Greek rather than the Roman world, as the defunct Roman empire had been replaced for centuries by a mass of small city states. As in ancient Greece and Sicily, these city states absorbed each other in endless conflicts. The commerce, chiefly with the Orient, developed rapidly from the eleventh century onwards, and had enabled these city states to rise and become powerful.

As centres of commerce and manufacture, these cities differed, it is true, very considerably from their ancient predecessors, which, although trade flourished with them too, were merely settlements of noble-born land robbers who subjected the native population. In the place of the city masses and the financiers who backed the tyrants of antiquity, the renaissance tyrants were supported by guilds of various kinds; in some of the guilds and merchants' unions are found, not infrequently, the remnants of the former nobility which in Italy was weaker than it had been in antiquity, and moved from the country to the city to adapt itself to its conditions.

The threat to these Italian towns, which forced them to display military power and thus tyranny was not the city nobility, but the foreign feudal world they had to face, the interference with their affairs by the rulers of Germany, the crowned Roman Emperors, who looked on this flourishing Italian world as an economic source of strength. The struggle with the Emperors into which Italy was forced, especially her clash with the Hohen-staufen (or Staufer) dynasty, determined and overshadowed the story of tyranny in Italy even after the memorable year 1250, when the Hohenstaufen rule collapsed at the death of the Emperor Frederick II. Renaissance Italy was never master of its own fate as were the Greek and Roman worlds; the last thousand years of Italian history were dominated by perpetual outside interference. A number of the Italian Renaissance tyrants, even though they rose from below, as in ancient times, became lieutenants of these foreign dynastic houses; foreign powers had

ended the political independence of the Peninsula at the conclusion of the Renaissance and subjected it to another three
hundred years of foreign rule.

Frederick II and Ezzelino da Romano

The Staufers' struggle for the control of Italy determined the
form of tyranny in Italy. The extent, vigour, and ferocity of this
struggle were partly due to the Staufers' gaining control through
inheritance of Sicily, a former domain of the Normans, and putting its resources to their use. While exploiting Sicily, Frederick
II, the most attractive and youthful, but also the most cruel ruler
of the Staufer dynasty, tested all those methods which he later
used in fighting against the Italian towns and vice versa, when
Roman emperor. His first victims were the Norman barons in
Sicily, whose leaders his father before him had publicly tortured
to death, forcing Frederick's Norman-born mother Constance,
who pitied the victims, to watch their agony. During this struggle
Frederick established a bureaucracy on very modern lines, a cruel
but efficient system of taxation based on Mohammedan methods,
a secret inquisition against enemies of the state, and worst of all,
a completely reliable and very cruel secret police controlled by
Saracens, which he afterwards used when fighting for supremacy
in Italy. Much of the technique he developed later became the
standard administration of modern great powers. What was
typical of the Staufer tyranny was the complete negation of the
rights of the individual. The state is the tyrant's god, all social
outsiders and potential mischief makers—such as gamblers, prostitutes, Mohammedans, and Jews—were dealt with severely, but
this did not mean that Frederick did not use these outcasts when
he required them for some special service. His lack of prejudice
in employing such outsiders was well known and stressed by him
with pride. His main aim, however, was to serve the state; he
cannot be called tolerant in the modern sense. In the last years of
his rule, when his struggle for supremacy in Italy and the Holy
Roman Empire had reached its climax he used the tricks of force
and violence typical of a man threatened by treason against his
arch-enemies, the Italian cities. The system of forcing hostages
from towns considered to be unreliable, a method Frederick had
used from the outset, was now extended so that individual cities
guarded the hostages of the others, thus connecting them all in

a kind of hostage network. Denunciations flourished, imperial officials were ordered to investigate every suspect, and to use torture if necessary. To give weight to this threat, the torture was administered by the Emperor's Saracen henchmen, who applied it with equal vigour to priests. If it were known that a bishop, for instance, had carried arms against the Staufers, or had broken the oath of loyalty he had sworn as a fief, he was dragged to the place of execution tied to the tails of horses. If the stallions did not act as expected, he was given special tortures and finally hanged, whereupon his body was cut down and dishonoured.

The tyrannical nature of the last years of Staufer rule won the heart of Ezzelino da Romano of Verona, who as a mere city tyrant, had formerly belonged to the opposite camp, but who had been betrayed by the union of the cities of Lombardy and had therefore sworn eternal vengeance upon them. Dante tells us in his Divine Comedy that he was covered all over with thick black hair. He used his connection with Frederick to secure one of the latter's illegitimate daughters as well as the means for the bloody persecution of his foes. The chroniclers portray him as a monstrous beast. The rule he established by obtaining control of the Alpine passes for himself and the Staufers was founded on all manner of crimes. When conquering the city of Friola he deprived all the inhabitants of their eyes, noses, and legs, and then exposed them to the weather; captured noblemen and their families were entombed by him alive by sealing their prison cells; his prisons were built in a way to make the prisoners suffocate; in one case he thus got rid of 11,000 captured soldiers from Padua within a few days.

Ghibellines and Guelfs

The dual rule of the Emperor Frederick and his son-in-law Ezzelino remained so strongly in the memory of that time that it later became identified with the concept of tyranny. A tyrant was in the eyes of most Italians a leading man of the "ghibelline" party (named after the city of Waiblingen, the home of the Staufers), composed mostly of small noblemen, or at least representatives of feudalism, while the anti-tyrannical and bourgeois section was symbolized in the eyes of contemporaries by the party of the Guelfs, or Welfs, named after the German opponents of the Staufers. This refers more to the descent and background of those figures than to their politics. Looked at politically and from the aspect of their social functions, the Italian tyrants were hardly less bourgeois revolutionaries than their ancient predecessors. Had the Hohenstaufen rule continued for another fifty or a hundred years, instead of suddenly coming to an end in 1250, many of the city tyrants known as "Ghibellines" would no doubt have opposed it, sword in hand. What connected the tyrants outwardly with the Staufers' cause was indeed the disappearance of the royal house. Now that the Staufers were dead, the tyrants had to take over some of their functions. The need to defend themselves against the growing power of the neighbouring cities and to stave off the rising pressure of the lower guilds and city masses, the desire to develop their trade with Germany, and the hope to check the popes, who had gained political strength through the collapse of the Staufers, caused the tyrants to view the Staufers in a magic light, and rendered them the Staufers' political heirs. In addition, the later Roman emperors, though they likewise on their travels from their native Germany appeared in Italy, gave up all thought of conquering her, which made it less risky to support the imperial ghibelline cause. From the point of view of political expediency, the Emperors' marches to Rome for coronation were very useful for the tyrants, as they were able to sell imperial dignities for hard cash and to make their position legitimate if not hereditary.

Basically, however, the tyrant remained the guardian of a revolutionary social order with very few exceptions, though he was by no means the mere leader of a city mob. Just as in ancient times, he was supported by the wealthy traders and bankers, who in the Renaissance were called the *mercadenza*. The *mercadenza* had the right in most cities to elect the leader of the multitude— he is here called the "people's captain" or "general captain"; the rest of the population had no part to play in these elections except to thunder shouts of applause. With the rising importance of commerce and manufacture, of guilds and mass movements, the title "captain" became increasingly popular, at the expense of the designation *podesta*, which originally referred to the city governors of the Hohenstaufen emperors. These newly risen rulers, even when they later received or bought imperial acknowledgment, had something illegitimate and not altogether respectable about them; many of them were born out of wedlock. The

Scaliger family of Verona consisted of "bastards", as the illegitimate sons were officially called. The Aragonians of Naples were descended from a bastard. The tyrant Cola di Rienzo in Rome claimed proudly to be an illegitimate son of the German emperor Henry VII. The legitimate birth of the tyrant Federigo of Urbino was in doubt. The Este and Malatesta families gave illegitimate and legitimate descendants equal rank. The sons of the popes enjoyed highest esteem.

Of course this "revolution in values" did not end hostility by those who felt damaged by it. The illegitimate sons never felt quite safe; like the figure of "Franz" in "The Robbers" by Schiller, or so many Shakespearean characters, most of whom reflect the spirit of the Renaissance, their rule was based on crime. In this atmosphere, nothing feeble could prosper; all half-hearted efforts failed; this age shows outstanding examples of almost superhuman figures who fought each other to the finish, despite tradition and law. Their emergence is due to the social revolution of the age, the rise of trade with the Orient, and to the cities, manufacture, and guilds; their final disappearance from the historical scene is due to the gradual ebbing of this revolutionary movement as in our own day.

Dwelling in inaccessible rocks or in dark citadels like that of Milan, the tyrant surrounded himself with foreign mercenaries, protected his sleeping quarters with a bodyguard carrying halberds, and had the food he ate tested by others so as to avoid poisoning. John A. Symonds described how the despot of that age shunned society and surrounded himself with artists, writers, astrologers, jesters, and exiles. The constant danger in which he lived envenomed his family life; his brother, son, or wife threatened to poison or stab him; his fear of his life was proverbial. Alfonso II of Naples saw the ghosts of his murdered victims in his sleep; Philippo Maria trembled during each thunderstorm and maintained several bodyguards, who watched each other. For the tyrant to die in bed was exceptional. In describing typical ends suffered by tyrants, Symonds tells us that Girolamo Riario of Forli was killed by his subjects in 1488, as had happened in 1387 to Francesco Vico dei Prefetti in the church of San Sisto in Viterbo. The entire tyrant family of the Vistarini was burned to death in 1402 by the rebel leader Fisigara in the market place of Lodi; Fisigara in turn died shortly thereafter of poison. His successor, Giovanni Vignate, was locked up by Philippo Maria Visconti in a wooden cage, in which he committed suicide. At the same time, Gabrino Fondulo, in his castle of Mastocormo, slaughtered seventy members of the Calvacabo family, to make himself tyrant of Cremona; he was executed in 1425 as a traitor. Among the most terrible events of the Renaissance is the story of the vengeance wreaked by the tyrant Corrado Trinci of Foligno on the clan of the Rasiglia who had killed two of his brothers. Having killed three hundred people by all possible kinds of torture, he loaded their maimed bodies on thirty-six mules which he drove in triumph through Foligno. His terrorism was finally terminated by Cardinal dei Vitelleschi, who had him and his five sons executed.

Under the Renaissance, the tyrants evolved from small to large. In the latter cases, crimes like the ones just described were less numerous as the number of candidates for power was proportionately smaller. At the same time, the numbers of *condottieri* (conductors) i.e. leaders of mercenary bands, who offered their dubious services to the cities, rose in numbers. As the cities grew richer, and so less prepared for war, they relied more and more on the services of these condottieri, who quite often became tyrants themselves. Later tyrannies over larger areas became more conservative, and were encouraged to do so by the example of the big European powers who at the end of the fifteenth century prospered under the rule of despotic kings. But even in this late period, entirely new tyrannies still emerged. The sons of the popes of that time used the political power of their fathers to create earldoms and principalities of their own. But, nevertheless, the golden age of the new and small tyrannies was in the thirteenth and fourteenth centuries.

Tyrannies of the Early Renaissance

As long as the Staufers were in power in Italy, tyranny took a radical form in the cities that opposed the royal house. The city of Milan was the centre of opposition to the Hohenstaufens until the second half of the thirteenth century. Here power was in the hands of the Della Torre, who, like so many of the tyrant clans in Italy, came from the Germanic nobility. Martino della Torre, who in 1247 was elected captain of the people of the city, fought the son-in-law of Emperor Frederick II, the ill-famed

Ezzelino. He gained great influence especially with the guilds and the lower classes. His funeral, in 1264, was an immense ceremony, though the Pope had banned him. His second successor, Napoleone della Torre, who began his reign in 1265, was the greatest tyrant of the early period; among other activities, he created a system of large canals which connected the city with the Adriatic, fostering its commerce; the citizens militia reached the very considerable size of 28,000 men under him. Its dimensions aroused the fears of the city nobility, which had a powerful backer in the shape of the Archbishop of Milan, of the Visconti family. Napoleone was finally captured by his enemy and died in an iron cage. The Archbishop gave the rank of captain to his great nephew Matteo Visconti, who, like all dictators, sought confirmation through "acclaim" by the people from time to time. In reality, this was only the upper guilds. Being a cautious person, he knew how to persuade the Roman Emperor to appoint him his Lieutenant (vicar) in Lombardy. This transformation of old dignities in a moderately revolutionary sense, have something in common with the time of Hitler and Mussolini, when various sovereigns and prime ministers turned themselves into Fascist dictators by copying the Führer and Duce. The connection of the Visconti with the Emperors made their dictatorship practically hereditary and made them natural chiefs of the ghibelline party, to the disappointment of the popes, who excommunicated many of them. Since the popes had been captured by the French and taken captive to Avignon in the first years of the fourteenth century, their edicts, it is true, could not do the Visconti much harm; tyrants even rose in areas directly subject to the pope. But the tyrants in these papal territories could not feel quite as secure as the Visconti and other ghibelline tyrants, the political heirs of the defunct Staufers and other supporters of the Holy Roman Empire.

The best-known representative of the type of tyrant developed on papal territory is Cola di Rienzo or Rienzi, the famous tribune of Rome known from Wagner's first big opera. Officially the son of an innkeeper and a washerwoman, Rienzi was in fact the illegitimate offspring of the Emperor Henry VII of a Luxembourg family. Unlike many of the hereditary tyrant clans, Rienzi did not belong to a family of nobles who had been known since antiquity. All his life Rienzi's attitude to the nobility was ambiguous; his lack of preparedness to destroy the Roman noble families he had overpowered led to his downfall. His attitude towards the nobility was similar to that of most tyrants both before and after his time, excepting the Communist, Fascist, and flatly counter-revolutionary figures. Instead of wooing the upper classes in a servile manner, as was originally done by the fascist leaders, most tyrants challenged them. The hatred of Rienzi for the noble born was increased by the execution of his brother, who was a victim of aristocratic intrigues, and led him to claim the proud title of "consul of the orphans, widows and poor", copying ancient ideas which were once more beginning to be revived. Later he called himself a "tribune of Rome" and, to the anger of the Roman nobles, offered the Pope unlimited power in Rome as the capital of the world. Thinking that the proud Roman lords needed their ardour dampened, the Pope permitted the arduous fighter Rienzi to continue for a while. Having come back from Avignon to Rome highly elated, Rienzi exploited his new position as papal notary in a most peculiar way. He signed his decrees with a silver pen, and summoned the Roman masses to inspect newly discovered Roman laws whose contents he described in large symbolic pictures which he explained in public to an enthusiastic crowd. He appeared on these occasions in a flowing toga with a white hat, trimmed with a band into which crowns were woven, and announced the renaissance of ancient Rome.

When the nobility invited him to banquets to make fun of him, he replied that he would have some of the great lords executed when he was in power. At Whitsuntide 1347 he invited the Roman people to assemble on the Capitol and appeared there surrounded by one hundred knights, in full armour displaying emblazoned banners, and forced the people to vote laws that gave him unlimited power. The nobles that were present were forced to swear an oath of loyalty as well.

Though grotesque in form, the rôle of Rienzi was the fore-runner of modern trends in dictatorships. He is one of the first of a long series of tyrants who aided the rise of the modern middle class. In their attempt to destroy the hated nobility, not only many renaissance tyrants, but many dictators in backward areas in our own times have paved the way for the development of a middle-class society and a money economy as well. It is significant that one of the books on Rienzi was written by a modern German middle-class land reformer, Adolf Damaschke, who saw in him a prototype. As a former notary, Rienzi was well aware of the inefficient enforcement of the law under the rule of the nobles, and took steps to depose corrupt judges. He had pending suits settled within a fortnight, punished those who made baseless accusations severely, and created special courts of peace to fortify the Christian family and counter the immorality of Rome. Charges that held up traffic such as tolls for the use of bridges and roads and excise taxes that burdened the city poor were abolished and were replaced by systematic tax-collection in the districts ruled by the big noblemen. The surplus was used for maintaining hospitals and for poor relief. Black marketing, especially in foodstuffs, were severely punished, and the food supply of the city was secured by establishing granaries. The ideas of Rienzi looked to the future—to end the disruption of Italy by aristocratic cliques he preached the ideal of Italian unity, and called a congress in Rome in 1347 in order to discuss it. His dream of an Italian republic was not to be fulfilled until exactly six hundred years later. The weakness and clemency of Rienzi towards the leaders of the nobility he had captured, which was the result of his inferiority complex as a plebeian, were in strong contrast with his self-imposed mission which needed super-human energy and harshness, and made his theatrical conduct and the ceremonial treatment that he insisted on being given look particularly ridiculous.

The increasing opposition of the wealthy trader class that had originally backed him, the hostility of the nobility, and especially the end of papal support made him panic and flee the city. After six years of exile he was reconciled to the Pope at Avignon, and returned to Rome with the support of a papal legate and mercenary troops. However, his attempt to re-create his former tyranny failed completely; while trying to escape in disguise, the former "tribune of the people" was recognized by his golden arm-bands, symbolizing his dignity as tyrant, which he had forgotten to take off. He was slain by the crowds and his body was suspended by the feet as was that of Mussolini in our own times.

Rienzi was not the only tyrant to find that it was more difficult to play tyrant on papal soil than on that of the defunct Staufers. His unfortunate experience was shared by the Bentivoglio dynasty in Bologna, which remained in power for over a century, but of whom several of the leading men were killed. Their entire rule was dominated by the hatred felt for them by the popes as usurpers of the property of the Holy See. The great Pope Julius II in 1506 finally drove them out. These Bolognese tyrants in their last years of power became typical *condottieri* who hired their mercenaries to any city in need, though in fear of revolts by their subjects, they were sometimes remiss in fulfilling their contracts. The city of Bologna, in its turn, did not like to see the tyrants use up its precious stores of arms, especially its cannon, which were then a new weapon, for their own purposes, or endangering the political interests by private agreements of that nature. The city of Venice, for instance, complained bitterly that the last great Bentivoglio in fulfilling his obligations to Ferrara, which was at war with Venice, had far exceeded the usual amount lent out. This sort of thing is typical of the age; the special methods and ethics of the *condottieri* and their bands helped to transform the nature of tyranny at the end of the Renaissance and to make it settled, economical, well-planned, somewhat less murderous, and rational.

While tyrants established on papal territory trembled with fear whenever a strong pope arose, the ghibelline tyrannies of the thirteenth and fourteenth centuries flourished. Chief among the tyrant families were still the Visconti of Milan, together with their successors, the Sforzas, the most important tyrant dynasty of the Renaissance. Reddish blond, tall, and stately men, especially in the first generation, clearly betraying their Germanic descent, the Visconti rarely answered the usual picture of a typical Renaissance superman. Pathological cruelty was combined in many of their cases with a type of cunning that betrays weakness. Bernabo Visconti, one of two brothers, who in the middle of the fourteenth century murdered a third brother and then jointly ruled their duchy of Milan, found as much delight in butchering people as did Ezzelino da Romano. It is true that he had a sinister kind of humour; he saw himself a kind of Robin Hood. But he was too much of a feudal magnate himself to act this part properly. He forced the people by means of heavy fines to take care of his five thousand over-sized hunting dogs, and blinded or killed everyone who, driven desperate by their damage to the harvest, harmed his freely roving wild boars. His favourite pastime was to have violators of his rules torn to pieces by his dogs; jointly with his brother, he invented the terror-inspiring *quaresima*, a forty-days-long torture, maliciously prolonged by insertion of breathing spells, during which the victims gradually lost their limbs and finally died of pain.

To the satisfaction of everyone Bernabo and his sons eventually fell into a trap they had dug themselves. Their conquerer was Bernabo's nephew Giangaleazzo Visconti, whom they had planned to kill by a clever plan. He used his reputation of cowardice, and dislike of physical exercise, belied by his stately physique, to convince his relatives that he was a religious maniac and thus quite harmless. He invited them on a pilgrimage, and suddenly arrested and imprisoned them with the aid of his German bodyguard. Bernabo died shortly afterwards as a result of poisoning. The greatest and most powerful of all Renaissance tyrants, Giangaleazzo had much in common psychologically with the despotic King Louis XI of France, portrayed in Alfred Neumann's excellent novel *The Devil*, who lived a century later than Giangaleazzo Visconti, and who is known as the Spider.

Both were figures from a background essentially non-aristocratic, both were calculating chess-players, and even bankers, as shown by some modern historians when they compare Giangaleazzo to a Wall Street magnate. In their hostility towards the feudalism of their time, despotic monarchs like Louis XI of France, Henry VII (Tudor) of England, and tyrannical despots like Giangaleazzo become allies of the rising bourgeois society and helped its prosperity and power.

The crafty manner in which the Milan tyrant created conflicts in the families of adjacent aristocratic dynasties and exploited them for his own benefit was exemplary. In disrupting the Gonzagas in Mantua, he proceeded exactly like Shakespeare's Iago, urged the head of that family of tyrants by deliberately false accusations to remove his wife, the daughter of Bernabo Visconti who hated him, Giangaleazzo, for having murdered her father. Then the tyrant made the murderer who, just like Othello, regretted his deed, responsible for this crime. To obtain control of Pisa, he induced the secretary of the local tyrant to murder his master and the latter's family, and to sell the city to him, and in much the same way he dealt with the Este family of Ferrara.

By such practices and by his model administration, based on that of the Emperor Frederick II, Giangaleazzo was able to extend his rule over a larger area than had been seen since the fall of the Roman Empire or was to be seen until the unification of Italy in the nineteenth century. He is rightly called the father of modern state economy and bureaucracy. In spite of the excessive splendour of his rule and the gigantic buildings connected with his name such as the cathedral at Milan and the magnificent Certosa of Pavia, his treasury was always filled—not the least because of his methods of tax collection which did not spare the clergy. The city of Pavia, where he had grown up and had lived at first, was close to his heart in every respect; he was a great benefactor of its university. In dealing with all non-Italian powers including the Roman Emperors who otherwise were so close to the Visconti, he emphasized his Italian nationalism. The city of Florence, which he regarded as his chief opponent, was accused by him of favouring the foreigners too much.

Though not a great general, Giangaleazzo was quite successful in directing the *condottieri,* who served him; among them was the Visconti's trusted Facino Cane who, faithful to them to the last, advised his wife Beatrice di Tenda, when he was dying, to marry the only surviving son of Giangaleazzo, who had died in the meantime. The son was the ugly, dark haired, and fat Philippo Maria. The marriage brought the Visconti heir, in addition to the hand of Beatrice, his senior by many years, the tremendous collection of treasures assembled by Facino; whereupon the grateful tyrant, since the ageing Beatrice had lost her charm, had her arrested for alleged unfaithfulness, and executed.

Although Philippo Maria was capable enough to enable him to reconquer almost the entire territory his father had ruled, and even to increase it by the addition of Genoa, the premature death of his father on September 3rd, 1402, must be regarded, like the death of Cromwell, and the assassination of Caesar, as one of the great turning points in the history of dictatorship. The disappearance of the greatest of the Italian tyrants made Italian unity impossible for another four and a half centuries. After the death of Philippo Maria, the last Visconti, in 1447, their *condottiere* Francesco Sforza rose to power. He was not interested in political adventures. By marrying an illegitimate daughter of the

last Visconti and after a victorious struggle against Venice, he
made himself tyrant of Milan, after three years of republican
rule, and political heir of his former masters (1450).

Tyrants of the Late Renaissance.

By the late Renaissance the larger political units were beginning to absorb the smaller tyrannies. The Aragonese had conquered Sicily, and by uniting her with Naples had founded a
large state which was ruled by Ferrante, one of the most ferocious
Renaissance despots. Other important figures on the Italian chess-
board were, in addition to Milan, the Papal States, and the two
Republics of Venice and Florence. Historians of Florence, starting with Villani (died 1348), Macchiavelli (died 1527), and
Guiccardini (died 1540), down to some historians of our own day
have attributed the political development of that city to its
indomitable love of freedom and have contrasted it with Venice,
which was ruled by a narrow and petty aristocracy or with the
despotism of Milan's tyrants. It was indeed the resistance of
Florence that prevented Giangaleazzo Visconti from making
himself master of the entire Peninsula. The difference between
Milan and Florence was, however, not mainly of a theoretical
nature. In Milan, distinct from Florence, the power of the
nobility was unrestricted. After its initial struggle with the
Staufers, the nobility strengthened political reaction, fought the
city crowds, supported the Visconti against the popes, collaborated with the Roman Emperors in the economic and political
fields, and ultimately held down Florence and Venice. Milan was
the most important centre of the munitions industry of the age,
and together with some score of sister cities under similar tyrannies—Bergamo, Brescia, Verona, and Mantua among them—
depended for its success on maintaining the connection with the
nobility, cities, and rulers of South Germany. The opposite was
the case in Florence. "The fact that Florence maintained its
republican constitution despite the general rise of tyranny", says
one of the experts of its history, Cecilia Mary Ady, "is mainly
the merit of its big merchant families, the so-called *popolo grasso,*
whose commercial interests embraced the globe." The centre of
these interests was the manufacture of cloth from wool imported
from England. Florence was connected with all parts of Western
Europe, especially France; it had a Western and republican

character, similar in some ways to the French republic of the nineteenth and twentieth centuries. What threatened this kind of liberty was not the rise of individual noblemen—they lacked strength and influence to stay in power for long periods—but the great financiers who lent foreign rulers the money they had made from the manufacture of cloth. This resulted in a number of connections with foreign dynasties which endangered the city's freedom, and in the accumulation of vast wealth by individual bankers. It also led to the fall of the republic after the fifteenth century when the importance of cloth manufacture dwindled owing to foreign competition. The family that profited most from this development was one of the most magnificent and most problematical dynasties of tyrants in the world, the Medici.

The rise of the Medici was helped because the city was ruled by wealthy Guelf cloth merchants, who had defeated the Ghibelline city nobility. They were ruthless entrepreneurs, hated by the lower guilds who had no share in the government, especially by the masses of poor home workers and day labourers. The alliance between the big capitalists and the city poor, so typical of the rise of tyranny, was therefore not directed against the nobility, but against the entrepreneurs who had taken its place and who were even more unpopular. Both were enemies of the Medici. The founder of Medici greatness, Cosimo di Medici, used his wealth for winning the have nots, and organized a regular political party. He acquired acclaim by his cautious and well-planned financial administration, and controlled elections by the simple device of allowing only the names of his followers to be put into the bags from which office holders were drawn by lot. Cosimo's grandson, the famous Lorenzo di Medici, went one step further. In 1480 he suspended the constitution and governed the city with the help of a "Council of Seventy" which he shamelessly appointed; the participation of the multitude remained restricted to the usual applause of the decrees so voted on the Piazza della Signora.

The name of the Medici will be connected for all time with painting, sculpture, and with philosophy and literature; it symbolizes a patronage of culture typical of most tyrants of bygone ages, especially of Renaissance rulers. As a nobleman or patrician become autocrat, the tyrant used all means at his disposal to excel in his display of pomp and splendour. Wherever the middle class was strong enough to force the nobility to move into the city, as was the case in Florence, these old clans aiming at tyranny competed with each other both in politics and in fostering the arts. That the tyrant led in the sphere of the arts cannot, however, explain the sudden rise of a large number of first-rate artists, nor can one credit him for employing them. The rise of a new society which allowed the individual to move more freely, with an upper stratum competing for the honour of employing great artists, is the cause of the emergence of a large number of Renaissance artists and scholars. Looked at with the eyes of those days, this hiring of talent by the tyrant was a challenge rather than something to give him credit for, especially as the culture thus developed suffered from the restrictions imposed on it by the tyrant's political interests. It is significant that the climax of the Florentine Renaissance would appear to have been during the time of Cosimo, when opposition to his rule had not been stilled, rather than that of his successors, when the ossification of the tyranny into rigid court life led to the Baroque style in art and the Counter-Reformation.

The reputation of the Medici as patrons of the arts and sciences diverts our attention from the way they obtained their power, especially under Lorenzo, when the economic picture darkened. We tend to overlook their economic imperialism, which in a way forecasts the nineteenth century, their confiscation of public funds, their depreciation of the currency, and the financing of foreign tyrants and despots. Measures such as the military campaign Lorenzo waged against the city of Volterra, which refused to let the Florentine cloth manufacturers exploit its alum mines for a trifling sum, or his confiscation of the municipal funds from which came the dowries of Florentine girls made Lorenzo very unpopular in Florence. The most important economic basis of Medici power was their state financing which they used to spread their system of political despotism. Cosimo had already had a brilliant success in this field. By supporting the *coup d'état* of Francesco Sforza in Milan in 1450 he not only ended the rivalry, which had lasted since the days of the Visconti, between Venice and Florence on the one side and Milan on the other, but he gained first-class customers in the Milanese. Francesco made the director of the local Medici bank in Milan his minister of finance. Cosimo's alliance with Sforza, enlarged by agreements with Louis XI of France, "the Spider", whom we have come across already, and temporary ones with Venice and the crafty Ferrante of Naples, began an era of political and economic co-operation between the Italian tyrannies as well as with the most autocratic of the European monarchies. The Medici looked on these monarchies as their ideal and did everything in their power to remain on friendly terms with them.

The only disturbing factor in this league of despots was the rising power of the Pope. Papal efforts to re-occupy Romagna, the hotly contested area of the "calf" of the Italian "high-boot" then covered with the castles of petty tyrants who rebelled against the sovereignty of the Holy See, were met by the flat refusal of Lorenzo to grant the Pope, Sixtus IV of the Rovere family, the means for this purpose. He wanted that district himself as a potential means of access to the Adriatic. Lorenzo underrated his enemy. Sixtus wished to settle his nephews of the Riario family in Romagna, and replied by taking the financing of the Holy See out of the hands of the Medicis, its old bankers. Worse still, the Pope transferred this most lucrative business to the old Florentine patrician family, the Pazzi, who were not only banking rivals, but who looked upon the Medici as upstarts. Although warned by the Medici, the Pazzi lent the Pope the money to carry out his plans in the Romagna. This increased the tension between the two families almost to a private war, and the director of the branch of the Pazzi bank at Rome decided to end the feud by murdering the heads of the Medici family. This led to the famous attempt against the lives of Lorenzo and his brother, Giuliano di Medici in Florence cathedral on Easter Sunday, 1478, from which Lorenzo escaped, wounded, and which resulted in the destruction of the Pazzi.

Attacks on tyrants in churches were not unusual in the Renaissance; the only times they appeared without a bodyguard were when they visited holy places. The murder of tyrants was so commendable, especially in the eyes of the aristocracy, that it compensated for the crime involved. It is significant that the Pope knew about the Pazzi conspiracy in advance; it was indeed the opening scene in the tremendous last act of Renaissance tyranny in which the papal state fought with the other tyrants and despots for its very existence, until all were drawn into the orbits of the new foreign powers that decided Italy's fate. The theatre of this struggle remained Romagna, or more precisely, the countless small tyrannies which along the road from the Adriatic north-west to Piacenza, known in antiquity as via Aemilia, followed each other like pearls on a string. Pesaro was ruled by the Sforza, Rimini by the Malatesta, Forli by the Ordelaffi, Faenza and Imola by the Manfredi, and Bologna, a much larger one, by the Bentivoglio. From the north-east the Venetians, from the north-west the Milanese, and from the west the Florentines penetrated into this area; along the Adriatic coast there was pressure from the kingdom of Naples and Sicily. The papal state in the south-west was therefore obliged to defend the Romagna from it rapacious neighbours and to prevent them from coming to the rescue of the terrified little tyrants. It was a game of big men with small men, and big men between themselves, and explains why tyranny not only affected the papacy but corrupted it completely.

If the papal state wanted to hold its own in the Italian world, it could not stay neutral in the feud between the Pazzi and the Medici in Florence. The defeat of the Pazzi incited Sixtus and his nephews, especially the crafty Girolamo Riario, to double their stakes in it. The struggle for the Romagna then reached its climax; the chagrin because of an unfavourable peace is said to have caused the death of Sixtus in August 1484. This led to the crushing defeat of his nephews and their failure to use his rule to establish personal tyranny on the territory of the papal state. Girolamo, even though he had tried to secure his position by marrying Caterina, the illegitimate daughter of Francesco Sforza, was slain by his troop leaders in 1488 in the city of Forli he had conquered, and his body was thrown out of a window by the infuriated inhabitants.

Girolamo's death was a warning to the most famous of these papal nephews (or sons as they were called by the end of the century), Cesare Borgia, son of Pope Alexander VI. Under Cesare, who, like Girolamo, began by conquering Romagna and subjecting its despots, Renaissance tyranny reached its technical climax, but at the same time approached its political end. The complete lack of sentiment in the political calculations of father and son was admired by the greatest political thinker of that age, the Florentine secretary of state, Nicolo Macchiavelli, who analysed their methods in his book *Ill Principe* (The Prince, i.e.

political ruler), one of the classics of political science. The crimes connected with the Borgias and many other tyrants of the time caused them to be condemned the more strongly by their contemporaries and later generations, as the tremendous financial needs of the Borgias and other papal families of those years increased the criticism of the Church which led to the Reformation. The hatred was so intense, that people were ready to believe the worst of them, though some of the best-known accusations launched against the Borgias are not too well documented.

It was once widely believed that Lucrezia Borgia committed incest with her father, Alexander VI and her brother. This tale goes back to her first husband, whom she divorced, and today the truth of it is doubted. Alexander's German master of ceremonies, Burchard, accused Cesare of murdering his brother, the Duke of Gandia, in order to become sole ruler in the papal state. All that can be proved is that the Duke left Cesare for a nightly ride to his mistress, and later his body, pierced by lances, was dragged out of the Tiber. Our interpretation of these events depends on the credibility of Burchard's personal comments. Throwing wealthy men, including cardinals, into prisons like the Castel St. Angelo to force them to pay ransom was a known practice of the age; it is uncertain how far poison was used to inherit from such men. Alexander's ultimate death and Cesare's grave illness at the same time, said to have been caused by their drinking accidentally a glass of wine prepared for poisoning a prince of the Church, are attributed by Burchard to natural causes, the marshy air and taking a cold drink after becoming over-heated in a ride.

That Alexander surrounded himself with women and courtesans, and Cesare's raping of women and men as well, such as the sixteen-year-old Astorre Manfredi, one of the local tyrants he had captured and later killed, have poisoned popular judgment of the Borgias. The pope and his son are more interesting for their political technique that had already captivated Macchiavelli than for their sordid private lives. Unlike Girolamo Riario, Cesare prepared his advance against the tyrants of the Romagna with the utmost care; he was supported by an Italian mercenary army under members of the Orsini family, and French auxiliary troops put at his disposal by Louis XI. However, his best allies were the local populations, who hated the despots for their oppression; as enemies of this feudal survival, even the proud, aristocratic

Borgias were more like champions of middle class society. Cesare occupied Umbria and Romagna, and established his own band of mercenaries with the aid of the French to rid himself of his helpers. The Orsini were suspicious, but were lured into a trap by Borgia. All this enchanted Macchiavelli, who was delighted when Cesare went on to betray the French by taking the side of the Spaniards against them, and planned to secure the rule of all Italy at his father's death. Borgia killed all the minor tyrants of the Romagna whom he had defeated as well as many members of their families; he checkmated the next pope in advance by winning the local Roman nobility to his cause by corruption, transformed the college of cardinals by poison and corruption, making it his tool; and he did everything with lightning speed. Only one thing, Macchiavelli adds, Cesare had failed to foresee, that at the death of the pope he would be too ill himself to put his plans into operation.

It is doubtful if Cesare, even if he had maintained control, would have been able to prevent the supremacy of the rising large monarchies of France and Spain. He and other tyrants of the late Renaissance, especially Lodovico il Moro (Louis the Moor) of Milan, had themselves called on their assistance in their struggles in Italy. After 1494, when the French under Charles VIII appeared in Italy for the first time, the evolution of the big European monarchies became inevitable. In 1499 the French captured Milan and imprisoned their ally, the Moor. After many years of continuous changing, Milan passed into the hands of the Spanish Habsburg monarchy, which eventually ruled all Lombardy.

The continuous advance of the Turks in the Mediterranean and the resultant opening of the maritime route from Western Europe to India, as well as the discovery of America moved the centre of European economic activity in a westerly and north-westerly direction after the end of the fifteenth century. While the Renaissance outwardly approached its climax, when Michel-angelo, Botticelli, Ghirlandaio, and Filippino Lippi worked in Florence, and Leonardo and Bramante in Milan, the political and social foundations of this world slowly withered away. In the second part of the fifteenth century many tyrannies had become civilized and assumed the style of courts, so well-pictured in Baldassare Castiglione's *Il Cortegiano*, the famous description of the life around the dukes of Urbino of the Montefeltro dynasy. The evolution to hereditary monarchy which took place had become typical of the few surviving Italian tyrannies in the sixteenth and seventeenth centuries. The political forms became more rigid, the stagnation of the economy lead to a gradual stopping of the revolutionary pressure and the dying away of mass movements. The surviving tyrannies, protected, comforted, acknowledged, and given privileges by the big European powers which dominated Italy during these centuries became symbols of conservatism; in the sphere of the arts, this change is reflected by the styles we know as Baroque and Rococo.

Chapter Five

DICTATORSHIP IN THE ENGLISH
REVOLUTION: OLIVER CROMWELL

Reformation and Dictatorship

ON the whole tyranny remained confined to Italy in the sixteenth century. In the rest of Europe the middle classes were
neither sufficiently vigorous nor developed to destroy feudalism
and to promote the rise of dictators. The main rewards of the rise
of the pre-industrial middle class were reaped by the absolute
monarchs, originally big feudal lords, who with the help of these
new social forces had risen above the level of their peers. This
trend was continued by the Reformation, which brought most
European monarchs a great increase of power, even where they
remained Catholics. In the Protestant countries, especially in
England, where Henry VIII reformed the church, the power of
monarchy grew as a result of confiscating church property. In
the second half of the sixteenth century a gradual reaction set in.
The growing importance and development of overseas commerce
led first in the Netherlands, and later in England and France,
to the rise of a new commercial and partly bourgeois society
which opposed and limited the absolute monarchy, and finally
overthrew it. In the Netherlands, essentially a maritime nation,
this development produced a revolution, but no dictatorship.
Dictators are as a rule supported by land forces. Conditions in
England and France, whose civil wars were fought by land
armies, were therefore more favourable for the growth of dictatorship. The English Revolution of the seventeenth century
caused the rise of the first great dictatorship in modern history;
the "Protectorate" of Oliver Cromwell.

The Social Aspect

The life of England at the beginning of the seventeenth century was still based primarily on agriculture, as was that of all
the major powers at the time. Roughly three-quarters of its

population of about five million lived in the country. London at that time had about 530,000 inhabitants, Bristol, the next largest city, 48,000. Even in those early years English economy showed features that distinguished it sharply from the development on the Continent. Its backbone was sheep breeding, and the resultant production of wool and cloth, and was often connected with rural production and shipping. Many a big sheep breeder worked in close connection with the City of London, and textile production received a strong impulse by the constant rise in prices during the first six decades of the seventeenth century.

The same rise in prices that encouraged the rise of a commercial middle class society hampered the activity of the crown which lived on fixed revenues, which decreased all the time. This forced the monarchs to add to their incomes by every possible means—taxes of questionable legality, and the granting of monopolies. This led to endless disagreements between them and the English Parliament which claimed the right to vote taxes, but which did not yet represent the total population, but only its upper layers, the landowners and commercial classes. The difficulties of the monarchy were accentuated by the fact that the English crown had passed to the Scottish house of Stuart at the beginning of the century. The new king's faith was Roman Catholic, much hated in England. The Stuarts—James I and, after 1625, his son Charles I—based their power, apart from the support they received from a large section of the nobility, on the Church of England, heir to the prestige and the large estates of the Catholic clergy, and on trade monopolies which stifled the rising independent producer and merchant. It was little wonder that their opponents, especially in the city of London, became ardent followers of Calvinism which opposed the Church of England and which found support in the merchants and financiers and among the enemies of the Stuarts in Scotland.

The development of the struggle against the kings from Scotland drove many an English noble who would otherwise have supported the crown into the camp of their opponents. This makes the English Revolution even more difficult for a foreigner to understand. It is not even possible to decide whether the great struggle was caused by a rise or decline in a revolutionary society. It seems certain, however, that the Calvinist middle class and the high nobility which often made common cause with it did better than before. Opinion is still more divided as to the lower classes. The small freeholders presumably had their share in profiteering from the rise of prices from 1603 to 1660, although it is not certain how numerous they were, since the estimates of the enclosure of arable land by the sheep-breeding landowners differ. The agricultural tenants, the rural workers, and the city populace certainly suffered from the rise in prices, which partly explains why their revolutionary fury was aimed even more against the upper strata of the revolutionary society than against the monarchy as such. As in many other revolutions, this led to a most complicated game of intrigue, in which disappointed parties frequently made common cause with political enemies against people they disliked in their own camp.

The Dark Horse

The struggle between the monarchy and Parliament, which had already led to constant clashes under James I increased in intensity after the succession of Charles I in 1625. In the Petition of Rights, 1628, Parliament among other demands, once more underlined its right to vote taxes; in March 1629 Charles arrested its leading figure, Sir John Eliot, who had zealously defended the privileges of Parliament. He was sent to the Tower, where he died. Parliament itself—it was Charles' third—was dissolved and was not reassembled for eleven years. Among the members of this third Parliament of Charles I was a large stocky M.P. who represented Huntingdon. He attracted no special attention and only once before the Parliament was dissolved did he make a speech. It was short and vehement. He complained that his old schoolmaster, a certain Dr. Beard, an ardent Calvinist, had been forced by the bishop of his diocese to preach a sermon sympathizing with the Roman Catholics.

The surname of that M.P. was already well known; it was Cromwell, and came from Thomas Cromwell, brother-in-law of his ancestor Morgan Williams, whose son Richard changed the name from Williams to Cromwell in honour of his famous uncle. The memory of the name Williams remained just as the Schicklgruber tradition in the family of Hitler. Even in his marriage contract, the seventeenth-century dictator is called "Oliver Cromwell alias Williams". Some students of Cromwell's early life have attributed his later career, and especially his hatred of royalist nobility, to his descent from this Welsh family, whose blood, it is true, was diluted by Norman and Saxon ancestry. A strong influence on Cromwell was the memory of his namesake, Thomas Cromwell, who is known in English history as *malleus monachorum*, the hammer of the monks—the statesman under whom the dissolution and spoliation of the monasteries was carried on. They did not foresee that another Cromwell would avenge the monks and be known as *malleus monarchorum*, the destroyer of the monarchy.

It is tempting to retell the little that is known of Cromwell's youth in Huntingdon, and to state that he was indeed chosen by Fate to bring down the régime of the Stuarts and to cause the death of King Charles I himself. Cromwell is said to have beaten the future king in some childish game when they were both young. However, this is to reverse the course of history. It is more useful to examine the circumstances of a man in his position. This shows us that a man of his kind had little hope of achieving much. Just as with the lives of Napoleon and Hitler, the early life of Cromwell was studied only comparatively later, when it was realized that he was going to hold high office in the land. To their contemporaries, all these men, and indeed as most dictators in their early years, were not only nonentities, but people who did not harmonize with their surroundings.

The scanty information that we have about Cromwell's youth has been summarized by the meticulous German historian Leopold von Ranke in the following words: "Having become independent at too early a stage through the death of his father, he went through a period in which he indulged in the amusements of an exultant and spendthrift youth, eager for pleasure." As it happened, his birth in 1599 coincided with the rise of harsh ascetic Calvinism, especially in the English middle class, to which, in 1620, Oliver became linked by marriage and was already related by family connections. Under these circumstances, Oliver was soon seized by a grave feeling of personal guilt which he shared with many contemporaries, and which, as was usual at that time, caused him to seek religious salvation, though in a strangely personal way that distinguished his career from others. The physician at his birthplace, Dr. Simcott, later stated that Cromwell had called for him very often in those years, as he suffered from hallucinations (fantasies), which were centred

especially round the cross in his town. Even when Cromwell attended his first parliamentary meetings the London physician, Sir
Thomas Mayerne, made an entry in his notebook that he had
treated Cromwell whom he had found very depressed (*valde
melancholicus*). "Had the main business of Parliament", said von
Ranke, describing the Cromwell of 1640, just before the Civil
War, "consisted of making routine speeches"—Cromwell had
been a member since the early years of Charles I's reign without
being noticed—"he would hardly have played a great role even
then. His untidy appearance, the dark red colour of his face and
peasant clothes made him look almost eccentric. With his harsh
voice he uttered statements that violated the existing political
constitution, and which once led to a motion to make him kneel
at the bar of the House, asking pardon."

Von Ranke emphasized that only the "swing towards
radicalism" gave a man like that the chance to seize power. As
with all dictators, this was the important point. In order to
become what in later years was called the Lord Protector, Cromwell needed specific social conditions, that is, a situation which
allowed him not only to break through the social barriers but
also to permit him to use his many—negative—qualities as levers
of his policy, and to transfer the struggle into a sphere in which
he was unequalled. The stocky small landowner from Huntingdon, more a farmer than a gentleman, a victim of carnal temptations, but unable to carouse as would a lord in Elizabethan days,
and even half ruined by trying to do so, began in his disappointment and even embitterment to remember both his physical
prowess and the ties that connected him to other men of his
station in life. These were the freeholders, not from Norman
stock, but somewhat above the bulk of the population to which
they belonged. The time was not far off in which the combination of this stratum with the "outsider" of the Parliament, the
M.P. for Huntingdon, gained significance for England and even
for the world.

Political Earthquake

The decisive turn of events came not long after the ill-famed
eleven years in which King Charles I ruled without Parliament,
and which ended in 1640. The King was in sore need of money
and called another Parliament despite what had just occurred.

The reason for the King's financial difficulties was that he was having trouble with the Scots, who especially hated his religious policy, and who saw in the Calvinist English middle class, particularly in the City of London, their natural allies. City and Parliament used the King's plight to deal him a series of heavy blows; in 1641 they forced him to execute his chief adviser and minister, the Earl of Strafford, whom they held responsible for violating the Constitution by governing without Parliament; they obliged him to consent to summon Parliament at regular intervals, and suspended his authority to dissolve the Parliament then in session. They also abolished the Star Chamber and several other institutions which had been the bulwarks of absolute monarchy, and brought the rule of the bishops to an end.

The general excitement reached its climax when, in October 1641, a tremendously bitter uprising in Ireland began. The Catholic population, suppressed for centuries, feared that the thoroughly Protestant Parliament would treat the Irish even more harshly than the monarchy had done. Parliament's refusal to grant the King the money to crush that revolt unless he submitted to Parliamentary rule, induced the King to attempt a *coup d'état* against the Commons, as the leader of the two Houses of Parliament. The failure of this *coup*, in the first days of 1642, led to the open breach. In July, Parliament set up a committee of public safety, as happened later under revolutionary France. The Earl of Essex was entrusted with the leadership of a special parliamentary army; the revolution, then called the "Great Rebellion", thus led to civil war.

In its first eighteen months, the war went badly for Parliament. This led to a situation in which a man like Cromwell was needed. If it had not been for the weakness of the Parliamentary party, called Roundheads from the way they cropped their hair, the Protector would not have come to power. The Parliamentary party had the larger means, its troops were commanded by nobles not inexperienced in military matters, but the men it had hired, especially its cavalry, could not stand up to the royal army of "Cavaliers", with its large numbers of gentry, well trained in riding and fencing, which gave the King's party its name. It was Cromwell's special merit that he recognized the weakness of his own party and that he succeeded, notwithstanding his own subordinate military position, in organizing the remnants of the free

English peasantry, freeholders and yeomen, in such a way as to form the nucleus of a completely reliable army, whose spirit, discipline, and fighting power were unparalleled at that time. The youthful, brilliant and dashing, but careless, Prince Rupert, the leader of the Cavaliers, recognized the qualities of Cromwell's new soldiers when he named them the Ironsides.

The religious fanaticism for which Cromwell and his Ironsides are famous was partly due to most of them being peasants and their opponents being the gentry whom they looked on as oppressors. They thus displayed radical views that terrified the merchants, master craftsmen, and wealthy people of the towns such as the City of London, and the M.P.s whom these troops were serving. Thus a situation was created which is typical of most dictatorships; an army of peasants, or peasants that had moved into the cities, fought for the wealthy in the cities against the nobility, achieved victory, and finally terrorized its own allies. The later developments of the English revolution strongly resemble events we have already studied. After the Parliamentary Army gained its first big victory at Marston Moor in 1644, owing to Cromwell's decisive intervention, the rising leader and his troops saw with increasing anger how their generals, who as big lords rather sympathized with their opponents, did nothing to exploit the victory, thus tipping the scales once more in favour of the defeated King. Under these circumstances, Cromwell could only follow the road of Dionysus and Agathocles; in November 1644 he appeared in the House of Commons and accused his immediate commander, the Earl of Manchester, of military inactivity and of giving support to the enemy in the civil war. Manchester on the other hand charged Cromwell in the House of Lords with hostility to the aristocracy and encouraging political radicalism.

The Earl's fear of radicalism was already shared by members of both Houses. It was well known that the army sympathized with the views of the Independents, one of the many sects of the working classes of that time. Parliament and the City of London, on the other hand, clung to their rigid Calvinism which replaced the rule of the bishops by that of priests (presbyters) and thus was known as Presbyterianism. So Cromwell was in a less favourable position than his predecessors in ancient Syracuse who had known how to persuade the citizens' assembly to arrest and execute the incriminated supreme commanders. He therefore said unctuously that, being a Christian, he had the best intentions, and instead of insisting on the punishment of the generals, in the first part of 1645 he succeeded in making Parliament vote the so-called Self Denying Ordinance which excluded members of both houses from holding military or civilian office during the civil war. The ordinance automatically deprived the Earls of Essex and Manchester of their commands, while Cromwell was deemed so indispensable a leader that the law was suspended so that he could retain his command. As a result, he succeeded in reforming the entire army on the lines of his Ironsides, and the reconstructed army was called the New Model. He defeated the King at Naseby in June 1645. As with his earlier successes, his victory was partly due to the fact that the originally victorious royal army under Rupert had carelessly begun to take booty.

The blow was so decisive, that in the spring of 1646 King Charles fled from the English witches' cauldron to his enemies in Scotland. In February 1647 they handed him over to the English parliament in return for £400,000 back pay.

The King Checkmated

This move created a most interesting political situation with especial significance in the history of dictatorship. The imprisonment of the King of England coincided with the clash of interests between the victorious army and its wealthy political supporters. This was typical of the "second act" of most old-style dictatorships and led to a triangular struggle between the Crown, army, and Parliament. The ruses and intrigues in this struggle would have pleased Macchiavelli. The tactical positions of the champions in this contest changed almost daily, but the social interest involved and the aims of the rising dictator remained very much the same.

While the relations between Parliament and army deteriorated constantly, Oliver and Charles I had something in common. At the bottom of his heart Cromwell held the money bags of Parliament in little higher esteem than did the King. During the period that he had ruled without Parliament, Charles had done much for the working classes and his policy by no means justified the damning verdict of the partisans of Parliament at the time and the subsequent Whig historians. A very intelligent and sharp witted, though completely faithless monarch, stately and over-bearing, Charles I was as ready as Cromwell to use social questions as weapons against his foes.

Cromwell understood the English peasants who had fought a losing battle against the large sheep-breeding landowners. This had become evident before the Civil War, when he protected the moorland farmers, fishermen, and reed-cutters of his country against the Duke of Bedford, who planned to use his riches to drain the moors. Though closely related to the City by family ties, Cromwell was quite ready to threaten it with rebellion, in a way reminiscent of tyrants of ancient days, if it failed to submit to him. The demands of the left in the army and among the masses for equality, universal suffrage, and the continuous clamouring of the army for the payment of arrears were met most cleverly by Cromwell making the City of London and Parliament accept him as mediator between centre and left and by strengthening his own political position. To the dismay of the left-wingers, Parliament voted him a salary of £2,500. His power grew steadily, he saw in the divine light which in the opinion of all Protestant sects inspires all true Christians, a confirmation of his personal political mission. To the French ambassador, who enquired about his future plans, he gave the famous answer, "No one rises so high than he who knows not whither he is going". In his role of "protector" of society, as he was later called officially, he would have liked to have had the support of the crown. Both he and his adversaries, the Presbyterian-minded Parliament, outdid each other in political offers to the captured King, in order to win him over; Cromwell even went so far as to promise him the reinstatement of the hated bishops—in the name of religious freedom. However, Charles I was playing his own game and only listened to these suggestions in order to gain time for his own plans to mature. When he finally escaped from his jailers at the end of 1647, and fled to the Isle of Wight, Cromwell had to break off negotiations. He had much trouble from his own soldiers, who suspected his secret dealings with the King.

In the course of events, the flight of the King is paralleled by the escape of Louis XVI in the French Revolution. Radicalism grew in the excitement up and down the country, and gave the Revolution the upper hand. The Presbyterian Scots invaded

England in the hope of persuading the English Parliament and the English Presbyterians to come to the rescue of the King. Their defeat by Cromwell at Preston brought to an end the King's hopes of outside help. The King was allowed to move about almost without restriction, and the news that he had almost reached an understanding with Parliament led the army to take him prisoner once more and to "Pride's Purge". This was the expulsion or arrest of the majority of the members of Parliament by a group of soldiers under Colonel Pride, and the members that remained, known as the Rump, decided to break off negotiations with the King and to indict him, as the army desired. The order for Pride's "purge", which was to give its name to similar actions right down to the days of Soviet Russia, was not signed by Cromwell himself, but by General Thomas Fairfax; but Cromwell endorsed the *coup*, when he appeared in Parliament next day.

Cromwell had despised Parliament for a long time, although he himself was a member. He realized that the majority of its members had enriched themselves by seizing the property of the gentry slain in the war, and he shared his soldiers' fear that Parliament planned to discharge them as quickly as possible, so as to get rid of the fear of oppression, of additional expense, and of the need to pay the arrears to the soldiers. He obviously planned to enlist the King's aid to end Parliamentary control, satisfying the army, and finally, as so many other dictators, playing the part of saviours of society by checking the radicalism of the Left, which was causing him anxiety as a landowner. The King's friendliness towards Parliament, however, and the excitement this had caused in the army, forced him to side with the soldiers, to exploit the *coup d'état* they had started without him, and to carry through his programme without and even in opposition to the King. Even then he tried to save the life of the ruler, but learned to his dismay that the latter, presumably in the hope of rescue, was refusing any concession.

The outcome was inevitable. In the first days of January 1649, the Rump voted the necessary acts which gave Cromwell supreme power in everything but name, and it then indicted the King for having violated constitutional principles by his armed attack upon Parliamentary institutions; in the third week of the month Charles appeared before the judges who had been selected by the Rump to try him—there were about eighty of them—whom he declared, with sound legal argument, incompetent to function. He laughed loudly at the paragraph of the indictment accusing him of tyrannical rule, noticing the irony of the situation. It was clear from the outset that the prosecution demanded his head— to allow another tyrant to take his place. On January 30th King Charles I ascended the scaffold. When his body lay in its coffin in Whitehall, waiting to be transferred to the vault in Oxford, it was approached, it is said, by a disguised figure, who, regarding it with emotion, is understood to have uttered the words "cruel necessity". The apparition vanished without letting its face be seen, but the guard in charge claimed to have recognized its voice and step—they were those of Oliver Cromwell.

Dictatorship of Toleration

Having become almost completely a dictator by mutilating Parliament and executing the King, Cromwell at once performed the political manœuvre so characteristic of tyrants of his social background : he began the open struggle with the left wing of his followers, who had carried him to power. It was the end of a conflict which had begun in the last years of Charles I. While Cromwell and his officers were often ridiculed in the political pamphlets of the day as "gentlemen-independents", i.e. as noble-men who had joined this radical sect for opportunity alone, the nucleus of this sect, which controlled the army, came from the craftsmen, merchants, and copyholders, and aimed at a far more extensive reform of society than Cromwell had envisaged. The army had elected a regular soldiers' council to which each regiment sent two representatives and whose deliberations make very interesting reading. As members of sects and opponents of both the then defunct Church of England and the Presby-terianism which prevailed in Parliament and the cities, the soldiers and most of the officers wanted toleration of all existing sects. From these sects such as the Familists, Antinomists, Ranters, Quakers, Anabaptists, and numerous others, many of whose members were forced to emigrate after the Restoration, there emerged the nucleus of modern America, and the spirit of religious toleration which characterizes it.

Even Cromwell, himself a sectarian, followed these principles, though only as far as they were compatible with his rule and did not undermine the society which he felt he represented. Already in 1647, during the months before Charles' flight to the Isle of Wight, he had had to contend with the Levellers, the radically democratic wing of his army led by Colonel Lilburne and Colonel Rainsborough, which at that time demanded general and equal suffrage. Rainsborough, originally a craftsman, told Cromwell to his face that he knew of no divine law which said that a lord could send twenty, a gentleman only two, and the army no members to Parliament.

Coloned Rainsborough was murdered in the time of Charles I by the reactionaries who hated him, but his political work was continued by Lilburne, the most colourful man of the age, who had once been pilloried by the King, and had spent many years in prison under appalling conditions. A firm and intrepid leader, and of a sharp, logical, and persuasive mind, Lilburne opposed the English strong man and the Rump after the execution of Charles I. His aim was, instead of military rule, the establishment of a truly democratic republic. The programme of reform he developed in his numerous pamphlets reads like a wonderful list of all the institutions on which modern democracy is based; he demanded among other things, a cabinet responsible to Parliament, limitation of the length of Parliament, free elections, protection of the accused, trial by jury, the prohibition of a second arrest of a person on the same charge, complete religious freedom, the right of conscientious objection, and restrictions upon the monopolies, which had the same sort of position as the trusts today. The fact that many small merchants from the ranks of the Parliamentary party rose to become monopolists, formerly the prerogative of good royalists, partly explains the resistance which the Rump and Cromwell put up against the demands of "honest John", as Lilburne was called by the people. What made Lilburne especially hated by the reactionaries was his attack on the army. Furthermore there were even more extreme radicals than him, and he was blamed for their doctrines as well. These were the "true Levellers" whose ideas were similar to those of Socialists today. In 1649 a group of these men appeared at Cobham in Surrey, settled as squatters on the estates of some noblemen and started tilling the ground.

As a landowner, Cromwell felt attacked by this move, which gave him an excellent chance to show himself as the saviour of

society, both to the old ruling class and even more so to the
nouveaux riches who had helped themselves to the estates of
royalists slain in the fighting, and to the high-ranking officers
who ostentatiously displayed their wealth. It was in these years
that his son-in-law Fleetwood received the country seat of Wood-
stock, General Lambert—it was no coincidence that he was the
leader of the Conservative wing of the army—the estate of
Wimbledon, General Okey that of Ampthill, and so on. With
these mighty interests behind him, Cromwell could spurn mincing
words. "I tell you," he shouted at the members of the Council of
State he had formed, banging the table, "there is no way to
handle these men"—pointing towards Lilburne, whom he had
had arrested—"than to smash them, else they will smash you."
Lilburne and his friends were sent to the Tower, and two months
later Cromwell dispersed an allegedly Leveller-inspired mutiny
among his troops who refused to march against Ireland, which
for the second time in the English Revolution had risen against
English rule. The outcome of this action, in which Cromwell
showed his usual courage, was clear from the outset; the rising
English social imperialism absorbed the resistance of the masses
against him; his enemies stood on the whole more on the extreme
Right than on the Left.

What he did in Ireland will never be forgotten; "Cromwell's
curse on you" has remained to this day the worst thing an
Irishman can say to a man. The cause of the Irish hatred was
not only the appalling slaughter of the populations of Drogheda
and Wexford, but even more his well-planned robbery and suppression, which was the climax of the English oppression of
Ireland which had begun with the Reformation. The bigoted,
intolerant, and uneducated Protestant leader of the English army,
who had already invested heavily in the loans issued for the
reconquest of Ireland, believed he was chosen by the Lord to
destroy a nation whose papal religion had been struck off the
list of creeds he promised to tolerate and which appeared willing
to offer the son of the beheaded Stuart, later King Charles II, a
springboard for the reconquest of England. As well as this, Cromwell had to defray the debts of the first reconquest of Ireland, the
pay of his troops, and the demands of war speculators and army
suppliers from the proceeds of his Irish campaign. In order to
obtain the three and a half million acres necessary for this pur-

pose, he robbed about two-thirds of the Irish population of their soil and partitioned their land among the creditors of the purchasers of their titles. This new class of owner further broadened the ranks of his revolutionary aristocracy. The Scots had also rebelled against the revolutionary English government and were defeated by Cromwell at Dunbar (on September 3rd, 1650), and at Worcester (a year later to the day). In contrast to the Irish, Cromwell treated them with moderation as they were Protestants. Cromwell's dictatorship became increasingly an all-Protestant affair, though not necessarily one of all Protestants. The Presbyterians and the members of the defunct Church of England looked on Cromwell's military rule with the gravest concern. The soldiers tended to dominate Cromwell, rather than the other way round. The history of this dictatorship was a triangular struggle between the army, Cromwell, and the remnants of parliamentary society. In this struggle the army interest turned the scale.

Right at the very start of his career, just after the execution of the King, Cromwell found that neither the Council of State, which took over the functions of the monarch, nor the Rump could be used quite so easily to fulfil his purposes and those of the army. The Rump, just like its predecessor, promoted mainly the interests of the cities and capitalists; for instance in October 1651 it voted the Navigation Act, which gave England a monopoly in trading with her colonies, and thus caused a naval war with the Netherlands which ran counter to Cromwell's all-Protestant foreign policy, and which he therefore tried to bring to a conclusion as quickly as he could. There were many other troubles. The Parliamentary committees were slow, the Rump neither hurried to endorse the draft of a Constitution desired by the army, nor did it set a term for new elections.

The constant resistance caused Cromwell in the end to dissolve Parliament by force. The scene—it was on April 20th, 1653—has often been pictured. Cromwell at first took part in the debate, became angry, called the Rump to task for its sins with mounting anger, and then ordered his soldiers in, who escorted members from the hall, while he himself hurried excitedly around the chamber. When the leader of the opposition, Sir Harry Vane, started to leave, Cromwell stepped in front of him, shouting in anger: "Sir Harry Vane, Sir Harry Vane, may the Lord deliver me from Sir Harry Vane." It was, as with most *coups d'état* of middle class dictatorship, aimed at his own political followers from the revolutionary period. The army, realizing that the country longed for peace and quiet, especially the wealthy, and that there would be nothing more than protests, was no longer willing to submit to any control, even by persons sharing its opinions. Before very long, Cromwell replaced the Rump by Barebone's Parliament, sometimes called the Little Parliament, which, as with similar institutions under Hitler and Stalin, consisted only of men of his liking or picked by him. The members of Barebone's Parliament were mostly Sectarians, comprising Quintomonarchists, Baptists, and Quakers. For the history of the rise of modern democracy and middle class society, the debates of that assembly, like those of the Levellers, are of very great interest. However, Cromwell could not work with it since it refused to create a state church which even he, despite his policy of religious toleration, felt he could dispense with as little as the Stuarts had done. In any case, the influence of Barebone's Parliament did not affect much the government of England, which was carried on almost entirely by the landowners and the wealthy traders, the backbone of the administration.

The Protector and his End

The leading army officers, who formed the nucleus of the revolutionary aristocracy and who greatly exceeded the old nobility in their arrogance and snobbery had mistrusted Barebone's Parliament as a mouthpiece of small people, craftsmen, traders, and God-inspired shopkeepers. The dissolution of this second Cromwellian Parliament and the necessity for providing proper administration and collection of revenue gave them the upper hand. The new constitution, drafted by General Lambert and known as the Instrument of Government brought Cromwell, under the title of "Lord Protector", the position of king in everything but name. It further created a Parliament in which the gentry that backed the Stuarts was prominent, a change quite in keeping with the army's aversion to the upper middle class, the social claims of its commanders, and especially with the fact that nobody else enjoyed adequate administrative authority. Sectarian and lower class circles regarded the Protector as hardly better than a traitor, ridiculed his pious expressions, and saw in his eternal evoking of Providence and the divine blessing of his rule a caricature of a genuinely sectarian creed and deliberate hypocrisy. This was probably somewhat exaggerated; the Protector hardly ever forgot the bonds that connected him with the common man and regarded his political role rather as a necessary sacrifice, in order to retain as much as possible of the idealism of the Independents. He could hardly forget the fact that for a man in his position his real enemies were on the Right, despite his recent actions against the Left.

The passive resistance of the gentry which controlled the self-government strongly influenced the fate of his dictatorship and prevented him from undertaking far-reaching reforms. His greatest administrative achievement was the appointment of professional public servants by his capable "secretary of state" John Thurloe, who was also in charge of the secret police, which were already well-developed under this dictatorship. Together with the great John Milton as Foreign Secretary, and the naval hero Robert Blake in charge of the navy, Thurloe headed a cabinet of high calibre. But to break the might of the gentry was more than even the best cabinet could do. Faced with parliamentary resistance to the Constitution proposed by the army, the Protector was forced to dissolve even this Parliament. As a result he ruled alone for a time, a more absolute dictator than even the Stuarts. He levied taxes arbitrarily and despatched military governors, the so-called major generals, into the individual counties. The increasing financial plight could not, however, be met by these methods. He lacked the necessary machinery for collecting taxes; without Parliamentary approval his rule could not be financed, and at the time of his death in 1658 he continued to make experiments in parliamentary government.

The sabotage of his dictatorship from the right and left was also marked by attempts against his life. All were foiled by Thurloe's well-trained secret agents before they were carried out. The best known of them, undertaken by Sindercombe, caused Parliament to offer the "Lord Protector" by the "Humble Petition and Advice", the kingly crown. The City of London, which backed this move, feared the anarchy that his death was likely to cause, in case the question of his successor remained unsolved. But even his handling of this problem showed clearly how strongly he depended on his generals; for fear of their jealousy he finally turned the petition down, though its acceptance seems to have appeared to him as the best guarantee for securing the survival of what could be called the Cromwellian system.

One of the important features of the Cromwellian system was its foreign politics. Cromwell was a keen champion of the Protestantism in both internal and international politics. His aim in foreign affairs was to develop relations with the Swedes and the Dutch, his main enemy being Catholic Spain, against whom he staged daring raids, to settle Protestant colonists, and to fill his empty treasury. He succeeded in capturing the Spanish silver ships; a big colonial expedition, however, which had been rather carelessly prepared, failed completely. This led him to seek the alliance of the French, old enemies of the Spaniards, to make up for what he had lost.

Though in the end he dressed in purple at public ceremonies, carried a sceptre, and surrounded himself with pomp and splendour, he could not make Europe forget his origin. The diplomats at his court and the nobility told stories about his typically middle class daughters, said to claim all the honours of princesses, and waited with sardonic smiles for the pleasure of seeing their mother, a plain and simple woman, playing the gracious queen; the envy of the generals' wives who refused to recognize this rise in rank was regarded as the main reason for the Protector's failure to become king.

Cromwell's was a dictatorship which stood and fell with its founder. The monarchist reaction which had started even in his lifetime, triumphed shortly after his death. His incapable son Richard was speedily removed from the government; within only two years of his death, the Stuarts returned to the throne. It is when history turns the complete circle, which it does so frequently in dictatorship, that the impression is created that the march of time has stopped.

As in all these cases, however, the picture had decisively changed. The revolutionary society that had risen under Cromwell and waxed rich, began from that time to collaborate in shaping the fate of England. The new Stuarts lacked the power of the old ones; when they tried to return to absolute rule, they were removed once more. The ideas, however, which developed in the time of the Lord Protector, though hardly as a result of his actions, have gained decisive importance in modern history.

Part III

DICTATORSHIPS DURING THE RISE OF INDUSTRIAL CAPITALISM

Chapter Six

DICTATORSHIPS OF THE FRENCH REVOLUTION

Prelude

S EEN from the point of view of world history, the great English
Revolution of the seventeenth century which led to the dictatorship of Oliver Cromwell was merely a stage in the rise of
the middle class, and of democracy and progressive thought in the
lands bordering the Atlantic. The next important step on this
road, the revolt of the Thirteen Colonies against the English
mother country, resembled the Revolution of the Netherlands by
not leading to dictatorship. The farmers and traders of the United
States, ardent enemies of standing armies, had no use for figures
such as Cesare Borgia or Oliver Cromwell; after having shaken
off English rule, they returned to their fields and shops.

This was far from being the case in the next big development,
the French Revolution of 1789 and the troubles that followed it.
A strong army was necessary for the new forces that had been
unleashed, and this led inevitably to dictatorship. In contrast
with the revolutionary society in the Anglo-Saxon countries,
island countries with regard to their political structure, a continental power such as France could not for a moment dispense
with protecting itself by armed force; especially during a revolution, where the traditional struggle between the continental
powers was accentuated by the contrast of the social systems
involved and the political theories behind them.

Despite superficial similarities, the French Revolution differs
from that of England. It was caused, as in England, by the
financial plight of the absolute monarchy, who, in their grave
embarrassment, acknowledged doubtful old privileges, granting
the French Estates-General, consisting of the nobility, clergy, and
middle class, the voting of tax laws. Another resemblance was that
the middle class, represented in Parliament in England by the

Presbyterians and in France by the Girondists (from the place in France where this group was the strongest), yielded eventually to a radical lower class, the equivalent of the Independents in England being the Jacobins. In both cases it was this lower stratum that was responsible for beheading the king for having betrayed it and aimed for its annihilation. Both revolutions culminated in the dictatorship of a general of the revolutionary army, who protected the middle classes against the lower strata, and after whose end reaction set in.

But this is where the similarity ends. While the England of the seventeenth century already possessed a comparatively modern society, due to its sheep-breeding and manufacture of cloth, which had transformed the peasant into a free labourer, France lagged far behind her neighbour. The serfdom of her peasants, the complete lack of a modern central administration, the restrictions imposed on trade, commerce, and traffic by a medieval system of feudal dues and levies, the feudal ownership of land which hampered agriculture and industry, the enormous estates of the church which magnified these evils, and finally, the repercussions of all this on the revenue forced the French to carry out a far more drastic reorganization of their society than did England. This made the French Revolution more thorough, bitter, and bloody than its English counterpart, in which the class struggle was of little importance and did not lead to the mutual slaughter of lower middle class and middle class or of capitalists and reactionaries.

The proportions of the social problems in France, the fury of the inner struggles of the French Revolution and the constant danger from outside explain why no dictatorship was set up which corresponded to Cromwell's tyranny to save society. The constant danger of foreign intervention threatened peasants and middle class with political reaction in the persons of the landlords who had fled and who might be forced back on France by the bayonets of the armies of the European monarchs. As long as this danger lasted, no one in France dared promise the society created by the Revolution sufficient protection. Nor could the safeguarding of society against the lower classes be successful as long as the country, constantly threatened by reaction, was shaken by some sort of revolutionary fever. The few French generals who at this early stage attempted to master the revolutionary flood and pose as saviours of society were either forced to flee to the enemy, as did the famous General Lafayette in 1792, or General Dumouriez the following spring, or were executed as was General Custine in August 1793.

The Dictatorship of the Lower Middle Class: Robespierre and the Committee of Public Safety

In the French Revolution, dictatorship did not begin in the familiar way, but in a quite different fashion, as the forcible rule of a lower middle class, not much interested in capitalism and never fully understood or supported by the peasantry. This form of dictatorship does not lack predecessors in history, but they are rare. Under the Medici in Florence there arose the monk Girolamo Savonarola, a determined foe of the tyrants in control, who was supported by craftsmen and apprentices. During the Reformation struggles, the city of Münster, Westphalia, saw the rise of the Anabaptists, whose Radicalism made them something like Bolshevists in the eyes of their contemporaries. The Anabaptists looked for their support to the upper ranks of society in this struggle; their leaders, Jan Mathys, and later Jan van Leyden (correctly, Bockelsohn) knew how to exploit the competition between the Catholic Bishop and the Lutheran patricians for the control of the city.

This fact was significant. Since the lower classes everywhere lacked training in arms, they were unable to seize control unless the upper classes were weakened by internal struggles or by enemy invasion. Even in these instances, the lower classes were usually reluctant to set up an open dictatorship. What finally forced them to act was generally the sudden worsening of their position owing to the civil war unleashed by the upper classes or the national war and the invasion of the enemy.

Thus it came about that in the first years of the French Revolution the lower middle class and workers were the most active but not in command, the system known as the Reign of Terror is only an outcome of the phase of the Revolution that followed the giving of the constitution, the meeting of the states-general, the "oath of the tennis-court", the storming of the Bastille, the rise of the peasants, the flight of the nobility, the voting of the Constitution in 1790, and the "legislative" period that started in 1791.

Playing a most important part in these later years was the Girondist party, formed by deputies from the Gironde district around Bordeaux. The commercial interests of these wealthy financiers, traders, and liberal intellectuals played a great part in the history of the French Revolution. The lower middle class, organised in the Jacobin club in Paris accused the Girondists of being over-anxious to protect not only their rule, but their newly seized estates from interference by European monarchs and for these purposes to try and provoke a war to the detriment of the small man. That the conduct of this war, combined with the inadequate system of tax-collecting, led to a devaluation of the currency embittered the lower middle class and workers even more. Jacobin circles stated angrily that this devaluation which was so pernicious for the working classes even brought great profits to the Girondists since it increased the value of their property and encouraged speculation. In any case the Jacobins were not certain that the Girondists war would lead to the defeat of the foreign monarch, and of exiled royalists who were trying to bring down the revolution. The best speaker among the Jacobins, Maximilien Robespierre, lived in constant fear that the start of the war might induce one of the nobly-born officers, who had joined the Revolution for purely opportunistic reasons, to stage a *coup d'état* and betray it.

An unimportant barrister from Arras in northern France, Robespierre, distinguished himself from other extreme radicals such as Karl Marx or Lenin by his originally moderate conduct. When the newly crowned French King Louis XVI, and his queen Marie Antoinette (later hated for being Austrian) returned in 1775 from Rheims, where they had been crowned, and were fêted in the College Louis le Grand, the seventeen-year-old orphan Robespierre, the best pupil of the year, had given the official Latin welcoming speech. Even in the first years of the Revolution, Robespierre hardly went farther than to demand that the royal power be restricted by constitutional guarantees. But it is wrong to suppose he was a moderate liberal. The veneer of moderation upon his character was as thin as was the top layer of French society—half a million nobles and one million "bourgeois"—in comparison with the estimated 25 million working population, nine-tenths of which lived in the country.

Robespierre was a psychopathic case. Shortly after the death of his mother, his father, apparently mentally unstable, had disappeared, leaving two sons and a daughter in great distress. This had made Maximilien astute, pitiless, determined, straight, narrow and hard as steel, as if he were trying to replace his vanished father as head of the family. He was not yet a revolutionary politician. Modern psychiatrists have attributed his self-admiration to his need to give himself and his relatives—by his exemplary conduct—a new father, so-to-speak, a model of the correct observance of middle-class ethics.

A man of this type, it is true, had to be supported by the peculiar forces of his time. Men like him are not infrequent, but do not usually arouse very much attention. In a quieter period, Robespierre might have died a respected barrister, or even a magistrate. In the years when France under German occupation veered towards Fascism, he would have ended in a concentration camp. He was swept to power by the Leftish trend of the Revolution during his best years. He was not responsible for this, but it enabled him to play a great part in history, and to develop certain traits of character more than he might have done under normal conditions.

The decisive turn of events was brought about by the Girondist conduct of the war, which led to some French defeats at the beginning, and made the Jacobins think that the Gironde, the King, and the foreign monarchs had conspired against them. The bitter mood of the Paris masses worked up to fever pitch when the unfortunate manifesto of the Duke of Brunswick, commander of the approaching Prussian troops, became known in the first days of August 1792. This, in modern terms, amounted to quite unjustified meddling with the internal affairs of France. It threatened Paris with annihilation and its citizens with firing squads if they hurt the King and Queen, virtually held prisoners in the castle of the Tuileries in the centre of Paris. The logical result was the storming of the Tuileries by the infuriated crowds to end the treasonable connection between the court and foreign potentates as well as the setting up of a revolutionary municipal government, known as the Commune and the transformation of the central parliament into the so-called National Convention. Elected democratically, but by an astonishingly low proportion of voters, the Convention reflected the mood of those turbulent weeks between the storming of the

Tuileries and the black day of September 2nd, 1792, when the capital was shaken by the news that the King of Prussia had taken Verdun, only 180 miles distant. This caused the infuriated crowds, who thought they were being betrayed, to slaughter more than one thousand prisoners said to have been reactionaries.

On this wave Robespierre was swept into power. His prestige in the Jacobin club and among the small shopkeepers, craftsmen, and municipal employees of the capital increased steadily, although, or more strictly, because, the government was still run by the Girondists, without royal sanction, the King having been deposed. In the face of the shouting crowds in the galleries, which directed the Assembly and threatened its members in the name of the Paris Commune, the Girondists and other adversaries of Robespierre could not make themselves heard, though they held the majority. The crowd clamoured for the death of the King, "Louis Capet" as he was called after his dethronement, using his family name. Robespierre, unlike the middle-class Cromwell who wanted to save the monarchy, had no reason to like the King or his Queen, Marie Antoinette, centre of a web of intrigue. The royal couple appeared to him as the main support of his enemies, the Girondists. On top of all this, the suspicion of treacherous links between the King and foreign potentates grew steadily, and has been confirmed by later historical research. Accused of treason against his country and its Constitution, the King was brought before the Convention, condemned, and on January 21st, 1793, guillotined.

The execution of Louis XVI was a severe defeat for the Girondists, as the party of property and order, and it was not the only one. Shortly afterwards a big alliance of all European powers, including England, was formed against the Revolution; two days later the Royalist peasants of the Vendée rose against the government; on March 18th, General Dumouriez, successful up till then, was beaten at Neerwinden; in the beginning of April, General Custine was forced to evacuate the conquered city of Mainz; and the same day, news was received that Dumouriez, after a futile attempt to play the society-saving dictator, had gone over to the enemy. Once more, as in the preceding summer, the Parisian mobs feared that their internal enemies had combined with foreign potentates to strangle the Revolution and that only one man and one party could save them, namely Robespierre, who because of his political reliability and correctness in money matters was called "L'Incorruptible" and his political party, the Jacobins.

Robespierre did his utmost to encourage the Paris mobs in this view. He was not an orator on the grand scale, but masterly in expressing clear thoughts, sharp as a knife in public debate and hard as steel in his logic, he helped by intervening almost daily in the Convention and Jacobin club to forge the weapon for replacing the rule of the Gironde; the so-called Committee of Public Safety, the executive instrument of France in one of her darkest hours. Until July, the leader in the Committee of Public Safety was Georges Danton, a powerful rival of Robespierre in the leadership of the masses. His replacement by Robespierre cast a shadow over the future.

The Girondists handled their foes during those months as if struck by blindness. They did not realize that the military defeats and the distress of the populace caused by the depreciation in the value of the currency called for the utmost caution. Instead they chose this moment to proceed against Jean-Paul Marat, the popular political writer and newspaper editor, a leading representative of Jacobin thought, though not a party member. His acrimonious attacks on reactionaries, black marketeers, and economic saboteurs as well as his vulgar style made him the god of the Parisian slums. Marat was acquitted by the Paris court before which he had been forced to appear by the Convention, still controlled by the Girondists, and this led to huge demonstrations in his favour. The second mistake made by the Girondists was to arrest in reprisal Jacques Hébert, the leader of the homeworkers, small craftsmen, and the city poor. He stood even more to the left than Robespierre, and to the common man he had become the symbol of the struggle against loan sharks, profiteers in the illicit trade in foodstuffs, and other speculators. Then, on top of all this, the Gironde finally proceeded against the revolutionary municipal council of Paris, the Commune. No wonder Robespierre's demands that the Convention be purged found universal approval. One cannot help recalling "Pride's Purge" of Cromwellian days. On June 2nd the Convention suffered a political blood-letting administered by the Commune and its tool, the National Guard. The leading Girondists fled or were

arrested, and the Committee of Public Saftey governed henceforth almost uncontrolled.

These events brought the country close to anarchy, though
most of the former provinces, anxious to secure the revolutionary
achievements against the foreign invader, supported the leftward
trend with enthusiasm. But not only the peasants of the Vendée,
but also, to mention a few cases, the cities of the Midi dependent
on trade with England, such as Marseilles and Toulon, or Lyons,
which lived on its silk trade, declined to have anything to do
with the Republic, not to mention the commercial centre of
Bordeaux, the capital of the Gironde. Infuriated by the bloody
terror in Paris, these cities listened to the few Girondists who had
escaped arrest and execution and opposed the Jacobin agents
whom Paris despatched to enforce the rule of the Convention.
That it had to protect the food supply of Paris and other cities
by sending armed detachments to requisition rural products,
which the peasants refused to sell because of the depreciation
of the currency, steadily increased the number of the foes of
the Convention. The meagre success of this way of procuring
food, on the other hand, embittered a section of the workers,
who, incoherent at the time, saw with dismay that the Convention froze wages but was quite unable to stop the rise of prices.

These conditions explain the fearful bitterness of the struggle
taking place at that time both inside and outside France. They
also explain why a man like Robespierre was able to seize power.
Would-be dictators of a different nature, a man like Hitler, for
example, would not have been suitable. From the technical
aspect, Robespierre remained merely *primus inter pares*, chairman of the Committee of Public Saftey, a group of twelve equal
men, and even this modest rank was merely given him by un-
written law. Only in the course of his thirteen months of power
did his position become a dictatorship proper, one of the shortest
but also most interesting in history. The nucleus of the Committee of Public Safety (*Comité du Salut Publique*) the executive
power of the Convention, was formed by three men, none of
whom entered it until July 1793. In addition to Robespierre
there was firstly Couthon, a lawyer the same age as Robespierre.
Physically handicapped, he was the most fanatic of the twelve.
His wheel-chair—he was immobilized by gout—is still shown
in Paris museums. Finally there was the energetic, youthful

Léon de Saint-Just, tall and handsome, secretive, a true arch-angel of the Revolution, who as commissioner of the Convention helped with great success to forge the armies of the new France into instruments of victory. The most outstanding figure among the other members was the great military planner Lazare Carnot "the organizer of victory". Some of the others stayed in the background on purpose, among them Barrère, whose multiple capacities from diplomacy to organizing the theatres were used by later governments; on the left of the committee were the actor Billaud-Varenne and the dramatist Collot d'Herbois.

The "purge" of the Convention on June 2nd, 1793, removed the last obstacle in the way of the Committee of Public Safety and Robespierre to exercising unlimited power. Still, they faced a tremendously difficult task. To destroy the spectre of counter-revolution they used the weapon of terrorism which blackens this period of French history. The uprising in the Vendée of the royalist peasants, abounding in outrage, was suppressed by them in an even more gruesome way; since the guillotine did not work fast enough, about two thousand men caught with weapons in their hands were simply shot; and when this method likewise proved too slow, the commissioner of the Convention, Jean-Baptiste Carrier, organized the infamous *noyades*, slowly sinking barges which drowned their human cargo. Other victims were merely tied together and thrown into the water. Because of the mass of these floating bodies the mouth of the Loire was so badly polluted that an epidemic broke out in Nantes which caused the death of thousands of its inhabitants.

The officers who lived in Nantes and the wealthy citizens were escorted to Paris to face the revolutionary tribunal, the court of dictatorship, inseparably connected with the Reign of Terror. The services of agents such as Carrier were a liability to that system, as he misused his power to stage a long series of orgies. Robespierre recalled him when he heard about them, but dared do nothing further, despite his position. Just as with Lenin, Robespierre did not wish to see anyone blunt the republican terror he deemed necessary for his rule. This terror, as in Lenin's time, reached its climax after plots against it, the best known being the assassination of Jean-Paul Marat by Charlotte Corday, who was influenced by Girondist propaganda. One of the victims of the terrorist reaction was the city of Lyons, which the

Convention wished to erase from the map. But in reality only forty houses were pulled down, and the fanatic Couthon, who was in charge, dared guillotine only two thousand people, whereas five thousand people had perished in Nantes. In Bordeaux, the arm of terror was stayed by the action of the high bourgeoisie. With the help of the pretty daughter of the banker Cabarrus they seduced and bought Tallien, the commissioner of the Convention. Robespierre's effort to destroy the corrupt couple had a boomerang effect. Toulon was one of the worst hit towns, and the military genius of the young captain Bonaparte led to its recapture by the Jacobins, who slew eight hundred counter-revolutionaries. The English men-of-war which were evacuating the remainder were in the end forced to fire on them as their panic was endangering the sailing of the ships.

Paris and France in those years outwardly offered a picture of the wildest party strife and anarchy. Soon, however, a unifying trend appeared in this confusion, the organization of national defence against invading foreign armies and *émigrés*. This produced a strong reaction in favour of the revolution, made possible by a war-socialism which tried to protect the small man against misery and which was supported by the terror. At this stage the Revolution was diametrically opposed to anarchy. The greatest mistake that a defender of the Revolution could make was to advocate unlimited freedom. Previously liberal and bourgeois ideals had triumphed and even been supported by Robespierre, and it was only the Reign of Terror which fully showed his powerful traits of character. "During a revolution," he said then, "the government must be based on virtue and terror. Virtue without terror spells defeat; terror without virtue lacks power. Terror is nothing but swift, severe and flexible justice." The Revolutionary Tribunal which owed its existence to the storming of the Tuileries allowed the defendant to plead his cause, but usually without attorney or the chance of cross-examination. It provided a trial by jury in which the judge fixed the sentence. It was not as inconsiderate as is usually assumed; in 1793–1794 it condemned seven hundred and fifty persons and freed five hundred; its victims were not always priests and noblemen, but more often employees, innkeepers, shopkeepers and even workmen, often charged with violating the law of maximum prices, or with disregarding the wage laws which were fixed in such a way that the whole régime might be called middle class socialism.

The Committee of Public Safety knew well how its war economy was endangered by such violations; at that time the concept of economic sabotage was born. Rumours about the gold, which the arch-enemy of the revolution, the British Cabinet of the younger Pitt, distributed in the country, never stopped. While fourteen French revolutionary armies magically produced by Carnot stopped the foreign armies and even invaded their countries, Robespierre and the Convention feared a stab in the back. With his middle-class background, Robespierre had only accepted the idea of price-control with hesitation and the first laws on it were still very incomplete. When finally in the spring of 1794, an explicit regulation on price-control came out, drafted by a special committee, though an interesting achievement, it was too late politically. Inflation had stirred up the peasants, the main supporters of the revolution, against the capital for having taken their products by force and had driven the day labourers and small employees to despair and revolt. Their spokesman was the unstable Jacques Hébert, whose temporary arrest had incited the masses of the "Commune" to bring about the fall of the Girondists. The rising Leftist opposition was marked by a revival of the attacks on churches and priests.

Robespierre was concerned lest his toleration of this might alienate the small shopkeepers, the revolutionary peasants and landowners, and some of the new "departments"—the administrative districts created in 1790—so he was ruthless; Hébert and his followers were guillotined and the power of the Paris Commune that supported them was lessened. Robespierre thought he had to display his opposition to atheism. As he could not placate the Catholic church, he organized the famous "Festival of the Supreme Being" in June 1794, in which he himself, in tricorn and blue tails, and more made up than usual, appeared before a tremendous crowd, burning the symbols of anarchy and atheism and offering a bouquet of flowers on the altar of the new goddess, who was represented by a female figure. It was a rebuff to pure reason, a sign of his arrogance, and aiming at thought control.

Politically the Festival was a sign of weakness, especially since Robespierre had damaged his party after the Hébert coup and even more so by the trial and execution of his old school friend

Georges Danton. Ugly, a wastrel, and with suspicious sources of income, Danton was the most powerful of the radical revolutionaries. He had risen by organizing the national resistance in the bloody weeks of September 1792, and had pushed the movement leftwards. Then he had suddenly declared his intention of protecting the wealthy, similar to many a middle class dictator. Robespierre, not without reason, suspected that English gold was behind this change of heart; as a royalist agent, Baron de Batz advanced large sums of money from foreign financiers to many influential members of the Convention. For fear of punishment they withdrew their support from the government.

This affair, known as the Indian Company affair, which entailed the sale of bogus shares, shows how much economic sabotage can damage a community built on state socialism. Robespierre's purge of these doubtful supporters weakened its structure so much that it could not stand a second experiment. The end came when the shady Tallien and the even more corrupt Barras supported the others to destroy the three leading men just before an incredibly severe new law would have given Robespierre power for a second purge.

Robespierre sensed the coming of the coup. On July 26th, 1794, the day before it was planned, he made a speech in the Convention which has been called his political testament, in which he defended the first purge and the increasing severity. He promised the same fate in a scarcely veiled threat to other members whom he named. Next day, when about to continue, he was shouted down by the opposition, indicted by the Assembly, and arrested, together with Saint-Just, Couthon, and Augustin Robespierre his brother. The guards allowed their prisoners to escape to the town hall, seat of the Commune. But it was no longer the old Commune; Robespierre's coup against the Hébertists had alienated the masses, and while the future of the fallen leader was being discussed, Barras and some armed guards entered and fired at Robespierre to prevent his escape, and shot away half his chin. Next day he was driven through the streets of jubilant Paris and guillotined with his companions.

Transition to the Dictatorship of Bonaparte

The fall of Robespierre was welcomed with joy by his foes, especially by the workers and the old and new ruling classes, but

it ended neither the Jacobin party nor the system of dictatorship. The government went to the men who had brought him
down, men of doubtful reputation like Barras and Tallien, or
the sly director of State Police, Joseph Fouché, who had callously
killed thousands, and having become rich, rose to be Duke of
Otranto under Napoleon. The new society surrounding them,
called "Thermidorean" from the name of the month in the revolutionary calendar in which Robespierre was overthrown, was eager
to safeguard the property it had acquired during the revolution.

Robespierre's downfall freed this class from the threat of
confiscation of its property and from price-control, and also gave
an opportunity for lucrative dealings with public officials. *Enrich-
issez-vous* (make money) was the slogan of this new upper class.
Paris soon became elegant again. In the centre of this new society
were the beautiful women of doubtful reputation who had joined
the corrupt members of the Convention; Madame Tallien, the
heroine of the 27th of July, which her husband helped stage to
release her from prison and save her life—she was known as
Notre Dame de Thermidor; Madame Beauharnais, mistress of
several of these men, especially Barras, a depraved but capable
nobleman who had joined the revolution; and finally Madame
Récamier, intimate friend of both of them, and like the others
made famous by the works of the revolutionary painter David.

These *nouveaux riches* stood, however, on shaky ground. The
city masses were angry about the abolition of consumer protection; this split in the revolutionary camp increased the chance of
a monarchist reaction which threatened the property of the
nouveaux riches. It was true that the Republican armies, due
to the continuation by Carnot of the *levée en masse* begun under
Robespierre, gained victory after victory, forcing Prussia to
conclude the Peace of Basle, which secretly promised France the
left bank of the Rhine, and destroyed a detachment of English-
men and French *émigrés* that had landed on the French coast.
But this did not remove the danger of a restoration of the
monarchy and nobility. The agents of the brother of Louis XVI,
who lived in London, exploited this split especially in Paris,
where the royalist wing of the middle class, conspicuous in the
first years of the revolution, began to reappear. Due to the
abandonment of the state socialism established under Robespierre, to the increasing speculation, to luxury production, and

the rising value of real property caused by monetary inflation and political changes, the political pendulum during those months veered to the right. After Robespierre's fall, part of the nobility had returned to Paris; its sons, thirsting for revenge, joined the young snobs of the *nouveaux riches* in turning on the Jacobins.

The Convention, which was still regarded as the legal parliament was just drafting a new constitution, and under these circumstances dared not fix a date for its own dissolution; its members and the *nouveaux riches* who owned estates of noblemen or Girondists would have faced arrest and vengeance. Driven into a corner, the assembly tried to master the situation by voting laws extending the terms of most deputies, a risky game considering the mood of Paris. The monarchists, furious to see the chance of revenge disappear, stirred up the old rich bourgeoisie and the National Guard, which had moved constantly towards the right. On the news that the nation still sympathized with the Jacobins, and had endorsed the new constitution, known as the Directory, as well as the controversial extension of terms of the deputies, the monarchist leaders prepared for an open rebellion.

The Convention faced a dangerous situation as it had only 5,000 men to fight the National Guard, estimated at about 15,000. It could not expect to be defended by Paris mobs which it had abandoned to inflation and the fury of reactionary terrorists. Consisting of *nouveaux riches*, profiteers, parliamentarians and officials, the ruling party possessed neither local political support nor the power to break the wave. At this critical moment, Barras, a typical unscrupulous profiteer, remembered one of his personal friends, an employee in the topographical department, and in spite of his youth (he was only twenty-six), a revolutionary general. It was the former Captain Bonaparte, to whom the revolution owed the reconquest of Toulon, and whose rise had been meteoric. He was dismissed from the army because he had refused to be transferred from the artillery to the infantry. At that moment he was in a very bad mood and two months previously, in August 1795, he had considered suicide.

"General Vendémiaire"

The request by Barras to help the Convention by taking command of the defence against the threatened revolt gave Bonaparte the chance to reach the top of his career. His task was typical of a middle class dictator, to protect a wealthy class against monarchist reaction and the lower classes. More than four years elapsed before the ambitious general's first *coup*— known by the name of the month on the revolutionary calendar in which it took place, 13 Vendémiaire (October 5th, 1795)— and the start of his dictatorship, but the background remained the same. As a minor nobleman, he was specially fitted to become dictator at that time, whereas men like Robespierre and Lenin would have failed.

The tremendous gifts of Napoleon, his universal achievements, his adaptability, his drive, his immense capacity for work, his penetrating intellect, and his limitless energy, which enabled him to play one of the greatest rôles in history, have produced the most literature on any one human being except Abraham Lincoln and Shakespeare. They have also led to much discussion of his youth and the reasons for his rise, though little attention has been given to comparing him with other, less colourful, dictators. Bonaparte's history differs from those of the dictators in quality and proportions only. As with most of these men, Bonaparte was looked upon as eccentric as a youth. His development started when, as the gifted son of an impoverished Corsican noble family he entered the war academy at Brienne, to be trained with other cadets of aristocratic family. His family, although poor, was one of the leading in Corsica, and the young Napoleone Buonaparte (his name was not spelled the French way until later) entered a society which differed in language, manners, dress and moral conduct, and which looked down on him as foreign and uncivilized, from a country only just conquered by the French crown. Nothing infuriated Napoleon more than to be despised on account of his background; a noble-born cadet, who made such derogatory remarks was assaulted by Napoleon with such vehemence that the latter was detained for some time, while his offender was not punished as he came from a high-ranking family. All this determined Bonaparte's character, expression, and general appearance.

The boy Napoleon had the look of an enraged hawk, which did not disappear until he had become First Consul in 1800. In his earlier years he resembled his mother Letitia, who had been wild and passionate in her youth, while later, as statesman

and emperor, there was more resemblance to his father's features,
strengthened by the imperious expression of Caesar. The change
is symbolic; he had won the game he was playing, and he and
his family were then recognized as equals by the ruling houses
all over Europe. This led him to play for higher stakes—world
domination; his mental tension continued, but in aristocratic surroundings he was genial and affable in the tradition of his
paternal ancestors, Florentine noblemen who later served Genoa,
and who intrigued with the leisurely calm of experts.

While Napoleon was at the academy at Brienne, he longed for
a new Corsican war of liberation against the French nobility
among whom he worked. His hero was Pasquale Paoli, the
Corsican leader under whom the islanders had risen unsuccess-
fully in 1769, the year of Napoleon's birth, against the French
who had bought the island from Genoa. At first Napoleon
thought that the French Revolution would be the chance for
Corsican liberation, but as the leftward tendency grew and with
it the chance for ambitious young soldiers like him, his enthusiasm for Corsican freedom diminished. Promoted to captain by
the new rulers after the storming of the Tuileries, he turned on
Paoli, who was fighting the French, and eventually fought him
openly, forcing his family to flee to the mainland. This rift
between Bonaparte and Corsica gave France her Emperor, just
as Hitler's hatred of Austria gave the Third Reich its Führer.
In both these cases, however, just as with Stalin's alienation from
his native Georgia, other elements were involved, too.

Bonaparte, who knew his Plutarch well, had already dreamed
of deeds like Caesar and Alexander when at the military
academy. He was a Spartan, a born nobleman warrior. For the
luxury and lack of any sense of duty shown by the noble-born
cadets around him he had only hatred and contempt, but he
respected their class to which he was proud to belong. He was
never a democrat. His later career betrays his wish to lift himself
and his family to the rank these high-born snobs held by birth,
to make members of his family, as well as those who had helped
him, princes and kings, and to bring admirers from the aristocracy into his service. He was promoted first by the French left,
and made general after distinguishing himself in the struggle for
Toulon, but became involved in Robespierre's downfall and
nearly lost his life; it was not until the offer by Barras, that his

fate suddenly turned. The seed was now fertilized and France moved towards the greatest dictatorship the world had ever seen —and was to see until the days of Hitler and Stalin. Asked by Barras if he were prepared to take up the unenviable task of protecting the Convention by force against vastly superior numbers, he asked for half an hour to consider. With his typical gift for making quick decisions and his indifference to human life, he accepted, and during the night ordered the cavalry of his brother-in-law Murat to place four hundred cannon round the Tuileries where the Convention met, and in particular, at the corners of the Rue Saint Honoré near the Place de la Concorde. The firing from these guns reduced the attacking mobs to bloody heaps of human flesh, and saved the Convention, the government and the new Directory—a moderately republican form of administration named after the directors who formed the cabinet. It gave the man who had broken the political opposition his first nickname—General Vendémiaire.

Rise and Coup d'Etat

At his request, Barras and his fellow directors gave the command of the armies in Southern France to their saviour, who intended to use them to invade Italy. This decision was also prompted by the desire to remove as far from the capital as possible a potentially dangerous young general. His plan was to disengage the Rhine frontier, where war was being waged against monarchist Europe, by a march into Italy. Austria, one of the arch enemies of France, would be threatened by such a move. No one foresaw that this very decision paved the way to power and glory for the coming dictator. Bonaparte was able to put the miserably equipped soldiers with whom he had been entrusted to much better use than the other leaders whose men were better cared for. In his first proclamation, the young general stirred up the wild lusts of his men to seize the "fertile plains" of Italy, thus inspiring them with a devotion to duty and keenness which were not matched even among the revolutionary armies, although these armies surpassed the mercenary forces of the monarchs in mobility, speed and manœuvrability, as they were democratically enrolled. Revolutionary armies could be moved from country to country and be ordered to requisition their food, while the mercenary armies had to drag along their entire forage,

since if allowed to requisition or fight in modern dispersed forma-
tions, they were practically certain to desert. Revolutionary
armies were led by much younger officers than those of the
monarchs, where the officer's career depended on length of service and influence. Bonaparte's army had as well as these advantages, the unique drive resulting largely from hunger and need
and forceful leadership.

These advantages were temporary, as were later those of
Hitler. Dictators of that kind believe their successes to come from
their own qualities and are never able to understand why fortune
finally deserts them as soon as their enemies imitate their army
organization and military technique. The combination of unique
conditions with their relentless drive lifts them to the top with
such speed that they have no time to analyse their progress until
they have fallen, by which time it is too late. Bonaparte's campaign of 1796–97 in Italy is the dawn of his power, it is an epic
of personal courage, military leadership and art, which made his
name famous throughout the world. The figure of the slender,
youthful general, tricolour in hand, at the head of the troops
storming the bridge at Arcola in the face of the Austrian guns
became the symbol of the power of the revolution, of the expansion of its aims by the setting up of a sister republic on the soil
of Italy freed from the Habsburg yoke. In reality this "Cisalpine
Republic", so named by the classically minded Napoleon, whose
leadership he put into the hands of the Italian upper middle
class, was merely a puppet state, of the type familiar in dictatorships of the twentieth century, and France annexed some portions
outright, and forced others, such as the papal states, to pay
tribute.

Bonaparte knew quite well what the "liberation" of Italy really
meant. "Do you think that the idea of freedom could make these
spoiled, superstitious, avaricious, and fickle fellows commit great
deeds?" he wrote to the Directory in Paris, speaking of the Italian
population, ". . . in my army there is hardly a true Italian,
merely 1,500 ne'er-do-wells, picked up in the streets, who loot
and are not worth their pay." He believed in making examples
to maintain authority, killing the entire populations of Lugo
and Binasco, for example, including the children, and then
burning the cities down. In Pavia and other places he simply
shot the city authorities without trial and allowed his soldiers

twenty-four hours to loot the town. These actions were all in answer to Italian resistance to his "liberation".

Unlike the decadent fascist dictator of the twentieth century, Napoleon did not use cruelty for its own sake, but had reasons of state for it which knew no limits. The tremendous mountain of skeletons which accumulated, and the pitiless war policy carried out under his rule disturbed him not at all, the yardstick for all his actions was political expediency and the interests of the Bonaparte family. His law-making activities in Italy led to the formation of a governing class similar to that of France, but this benefit was offset by the theft of money and looting of art treasures from Italy, the latter being exhibited in galleries all over France. The originally impecunious general returned a rich man from Italy. His Italian campaign and the resultant Treaty of Campo Formio (October 1797) proved less successful politically than they did financially. Even though he had decided during the campaign that he would not share his power much longer with "those Parisian advocates" as he called the Directory, he had a long way to go before he could stage a *coup d'état*. All France greeted him on return, army, middle class, peasants, and even the workers in the suburbs, as the man who had forced monarchist Europe to sue for peace and who had thus given the French Revolution its rightful place in the international field; no one would have understood why this new freedom should be taken away. In order to exclude certain competitors, Bonaparte had given the Directory some compromising material disclosing the monarchist intrigues of certain generals and government-members he disliked, which had led to a *coup d'état* on 18 Fructidor (fruit month—September). So he was even less able to turn Barras and his colleagues, whom he had just saved for a second time, out of power by a sudden stroke.

While confident of final power, he was satisfied with military command for the time; he was backed by the Directory in his conquest of Egypt, a project which combined his dreams with practical reality. The dream to conquer the Orient, which had plagued dictators from Alexander and Caesar onwards, was coupled with the commercial ties of France with Egypt and Bonaparte's desire to threaten British rule in India. Barras and his colleagues were only too pleased to remove the over-successful general for a time from French soil in this expeditious way. The naval expedition to Egypt was planned by Napoleon with his usual drive and talent for organization to the smallest detail, and he brought an army of 30,000 men and a staff of scholars, technicians, and engineers to his goal without incident, as he had concealed his intentions by a ruse which misled Nelson and his fleet. His conquest of the area was aided by its being ruled by the so-called Mamelukes, a military nobility put in control by the Turkish sultan which suppressed the native Arabs and poor *fellahin,* a circumstance which Bonaparte used most cleverly in his proclamations to the natives and his army.

His expedition was very important for the scientific exploration of Egypt, otherwise it was a failure. Dictators such as Bonaparte, whose whole characters are dominated by certain hatred complexes formed in their early youth, easily become unscrupulous gamblers who spurn the most elementary caution whenever they are able to satisfy these basic impulses. Traits of this kind become manifest at an early age, even if—to the misfortune of their contemporaries—the rising dictators still succeed in mastering the situation. In all these cases—such as Hitler and his "Brauhaus" *putsch*—the appearance of such gambling habits in an early stage of their development bodes ill for the future.

Napoleon had staked all when he smuggled his three hundred ships through the Mediterranean, which was dominated by Britain, but with an opponent of the calibre of Nelson their safe return was an impossibility. The expected happened when Nelson attacked Bonaparte's fleet and almost wiped it out. This sealed the fate of the expedition. The English naval superiority not only encouraged the resistance of the Turks, the legitimate masters of Egypt, whose garrisons Napoleon tried to drive out from all the eastern Mediterranean, but it cut off the French army from its mother country. Bonaparte himself, like a stubborn schoolboy, did what he could to speed its doom. His strategically useless attacks on the Turkish coastal fortresses led to the slaughter of entire city populations, as in the worst days of the Crusades, and the shooting of thousands of Turkish prisoners whom Napoleon was unable to feed. The picture of his retreat from Syria to Egypt, at the head of weary, limping stragglers, anticipated his withdrawal from Russia in 1812.

The ethics of Napoleon's behaviour when upon the news of the bad military situation at home he secretly deserted the expedition without proper orders and, after deceiving the patrolling British ships reached the French coast has often been strongly criticized. Any ordinary military man who had done the same would have been court-martialled. But Bonaparte had ceased long ago to be an ordinary military man. The entire population of France became jubilant on hearing of his landing. His ride from the coast to Paris resembled the triumph of a Roman emperor. The entire event is most significant in the history of dictatorship as it illustrated the rôle played in the careers of these men by social change. Even a leader of Bonaparte's stature was entirely dependent on the circumstances.

Two years previously, in October 1797, after a victorious campaign, he had been received in Paris with enthusiasm, but had been unable to seize power as the current ran against dictatorship. Yet, despite his being a beaten troop leader who had deserted his men, for which an ordinary soldier would have been court-martialled, his seizure of control was everywhere expected. This was because of the changed situation in Europe, not because of any change in the hero's character. While he had been in Egypt a new war had started in Europe in which France had lost almost all Bonaparte's Italian conquests. All were now threatened with Bourbon vengeance; certain industries, such as the Lyons silk manufacturers, stood to lose their raw materials, and the lower classes, which had been stirred up since Robespierre's downfall by the rise in prices, were once more agitated. In short, it was a situation in which everyone wanted strong leadership, for which they were prepared to sacrifice some of the meagre republican liberties offered to them by the Directory.

Yet the actual staging of the *coup d'état* was not at all easy. Bonaparte had no devoted army in France under him, and he had not only to get rid of the Directors, who were led by Barras and practically formed the Cabinet, but of the Council of Elders, the upper chamber, and the Council of the Five Hundred, the commons as it were. For fear of the city masses it seemed wiser to stage the *coup* outside the capital if possible. The same reason had led Dionysus to pick a small garrison far from Syracuse. In the weeks preceding the *coup*, Bonaparte negotiated with a number of highly placed people who offered him their services. Among them was the Abbé Siéyès, a member of the Directory, who, in those months, just like an employer, had interviewed several would-be dictators among the French generals before deciding on Bonaparte. If Siéyès, a former priest, represented first and foremost the upper bourgeoisie in whose name he had once drafted the first constitution of revolutionary France, a second prominent person negotiating with Napoleon at the same time was the Duke of Talleyrand, a genuine member of the old nobility. Napoleon's old mixture of love and hatred for the nobility, which he could never conceal completely, made him dependent on Talleyrand in a strange fashion, like the son on a father. He was certainly a strange kind of father. Crippled in childhood through the neglect of his nurse, Talleyrand with his club foot and his insuperable cynicism had something of Mephistopheles in Goethe's *Faust*. Having fallen out with his class at an early stage he had worked for the separation of the Church and the State, although himself a prince of the Church, and as a result of the dictatorship that was about to be set up he veered to the right once more, only to betray his lord and master to the Bourbons, whom he continued to serve as Foreign Minister even after the Corsican's downfall. To keep the influential three-man group that sponsored the *coup d'état* in style, it even comprised a genuine Jacobin : the Chief of Police, Joseph Fouché, a dry bureaucrat of mass murder—like Heinrich Himmler of later years.

From his association with these men, and the advice they gave, Napoleon had little trouble in staging the first part of the envisaged *putsch*. Early on the morning of 18 Brumaire, 1799 (November 9th, by a strange chance the date was to be important in the life of the Weimar Republic and Hitler), a member of the Council of Elders, helping the conspirators, moved during the session of that body that owing to an imaginary plot it would be advisable for the safety of the two parliamentary bodies to move them from the capital to the castle of St. Cloud, and entrust General Bonaparte with the command of the Paris troops to protect the assembly and to execute the suggested measures. Remembering the mobs which had threatened Parliament during the revolution, the Council of Elders voted the motion. At the same time the Directory dissolved peacefully; two had gone over to Napoleon, anyhow, and Barras was easily persuaded by

Talleyrand that resignation was the best step he could take to protect his own future.

Things ran less smoothly next day when the two assemblies met at St. Cloud. Embittered by the concentration of troops, both assemblies were unwilling to entrust power to Napoleon, whose poor speech did little to help—he had had little experience in rhetoric. Still worse was his experience when he entered the Council of the Five Hundred, half of which consisted of Jacobins. Amid cries of "Down with the robber", "Down with the dictator" the deputies surged upon him, beating and striking him. Someone even tried to strangle him, and he was half unconscious when dragged out of the hall. At the suggestion of his brother Lucien, President of the Council in the Council of the Five Hundred, he incited his soldiers by the account of his experiences, which he called "an infamous plot". The ignorant soldiers rapidly emptied the hall of the Five Hundred. Later in the evening, some of the members, brought back by the soldiers on Napoleon's orders, "voted" him the powers he required. Simultaneously the Council of Elders, convened again by candlelight, did the same thing. The most famous *coup d'état* in history had succeeded.

Tragedy of Europe

To most French people, as with the Germans in 1933, the dispersal of the Directory was a joke—even historians have treated the spectacle of the red-robed deputies jumping from the windows and running in fear of the bayonets of the soldiers in a light-hearted manner. In fact, just as with the burning of the Reichstag in 1933, this was one of the greatest tragedies in world history. The possibility of peaceful democratic development had been nipped in the bud. Still more pernicious were the repercussions of these events on the rest of Europe, which as a result of its effort to conquer Napoleon was hampered in its natural development, and the political reaction which set in after his downfall had an unhealthy influence upon the future of the Continent.

That the man who ruled France through this dictatorship was a genius made the situation worse rather than better, as Napoleon's extraordinary capacities enabled him to carry out his fatal activity on a surprisingly vast scale that astonished both his friends and his foes. His contemporaries did not see the negative side at first. The French bourgeoisie, reshaped after the revolution, welcomed his domestic reforms and his international policy. The peasants and town workers saw in his activities the victory of the revolution. Many of the institutions created when France was outwardly ruled by three consuls—but in reality only by Bonaparte, the First Consul—have survived to the present day, especially those set up in the first years of his sway. Among them are the centralized administration, the powerful rôle of the prefects, who represent the will of the Government, and the *départements*, the new administrative districts. Bonaparte's ruthless suppression of robber bands, his subjection of the peasants in the Vendée by stick-and-carrot methods, and his successful struggle against the administrative corruption that had sprung up under the Directory, earned him the thanks of the wealthy middle class. Much of his creations, however, had been planned by the revolution on more independent, liberal and humane lines.

Although Bonaparte had originally been close to the Jacobins and was hailed by France as a protector against European monarchs and the return of the Bourbons, he wished to end these connections when in power. His harsh treatment of criminals contrasted strongly with the humane principles of ᵗʰᵉ revolution. His financial policy of indirect taxation fell on the shoulders of the masses, although it must be admitted that this was set off by his conquests when entire nations were made to pay tribute to France. Strikes were punished by the law. By forcing workmen to carry so-called labour books, he almost delivered them into the hands of their employers. His famous Code Napoleon, which is still the basis of French law, although admired by the legal profession for being clear and precise, was a retrograde step after revolutionary law, especially regarding women, illegitimate children, prisoners or any physically or legally handicapped people. The newspapers were almost completely suppressed and the police organized with great efficiency to forestall any uprising. Education was adapted for military needs as France was transformed into a gigantic barracks in which all men were brought up for war. Even religion was put in the dictator's service. After signing a concordat with the Pope, the French clergy were in duty bound to announce Napoleon's mission as a saviour. "God", said the official catechism after Napoleon had crowned himself emperor, "has created the Emperor Napoleon as a symbol of His might and as His image on earth. . . . He who resists the Emperor Napoleon, resists Divine Providence, and his soul deserves eternal condemnation and hell."

The basis of his system was perennial European war. Already in 1800 Bonaparte was again at war with the Habsburg monarchy; by his victory at Marengo he began his revision of the map of Europe to which he owes his place in history, and which belongs to European and even world history. We are concerned in this book only with the individual characteristics of his rule and its place in the development of dictatorship. Napoleon's rule shows with singular clarity what disaster the rise of figures such as he cause to the world. The gambler and adventurer in him already displayed during his invasion of Egypt emerged even more strongly. Just as with Hitler in our own day, Napoleon at first could hardly have had more than vague plans as to what he was going to do with the old Continent, and notions of the "European" Napoleon, just as with Hitler, are mostly later inventions by historians affected by the dictator's propaganda, giving an exaggerated picture of things which resulted chiefly from historical coincidence. His "European" mission was simply the outcome of his defeat of the House of Habsburg, which was also the bearer of the crown of Holy Roman Emperor. This medieval survival collapsed like a house of cards, and the numerous small German princelings competed with each other for favours, mainly territorial. The honour and dignity of the princelings were quite forgotten, and one of them even went so far as to post himself behind the Emperor's chair as he played cards and to kiss his hand repeatedly without the Emperor seeming to notice anything!

As a result of all this, as well as of his defeat of Austria at Austerlitz in 1805, of Prussia at Jena the following year, and the subsequent Treaty of Tilsit, the map of Europe was completely changed. The Emperor ruled over the vastly increased French territory, which included Belgium, West Germany, Piedmont and Genoa. He was master of Switzerland, King of Italy, and Protector of the Confederation of the Rhine, which was joined by most South German princes, and Saxony; his brother Louis ruled Holland, his older brother Joseph Naples, his younger

brother Jerome Westphalia; French troops occupied all Han-
seatic towns. A French army under Marshal Davout controlled
Poland; large parts of the Adriatic and even the Aegean Sea
had fallen into French hands. Napoleon was free to act as he
pleased; the incompetent Joseph was shortly afterwards made
King of Spain and the throne of Naples thus vacated he gave to
Murat, his brother-in-law. The occupied countries had to bear
the cost of all this; France did not pay a cent. The "kingdom"
of Italy, though theoretically independent, paid thirty-six million
gold francs per year as "subsidies"; the Prussians, whom
Napoleon treated with deliberate maliciousness, were forced to
contribute a billion. The flourishing condition of the French
treasury enabled Napoleon to shower his marshals and other
dignitaries with donations. Marshal Lannes received a million
gold francs, Ney a yearly pension of 300,000; his chief of staff,
Bertheir, an initial payment of over 400,000 gold francs and an
annual pension of 500,000.

The bitterness of the rapidly developing European nations was
increased by Napoleon's deliberately making them his vassals in
the economic field also. He attempted to kill two birds with one
stone in his economic policy. By the so-called Continental System,
the closing of all Europe to imports from Great Britain, he tried
to hit the rising English industrial power in its most vulnerable
spot. Combined with this were far-reaching measures in favour of
French industry, to ensure French economic supremacy in
Europe at the expense of the subject or dependent European
states, which were unable to import cheap industrial goods or
sell their agrarian products. These regulations adversely affected
even Continental manufacturers, the only people to benefit from
the Continental System. On top of all this, the Emperor was
forced to guard and supervise all Continental countries, a task
which encouraged him in his war policy and increased his
ambition to conquer the world.

The worst result of these actions was the increase of international hatred due to the wanton disregard of the interests of all
who were not French, including even those who had befriended
France during the revolution. Seeing the entire Continent becoming a slave of French imperialism, the liberals in her neighbouring
countries became her most outspoken foes. The anti-French
speeches made in Berlin University by Professor Fichte from

French-occupied Jena, formerly one of the most ardent admirers of revolutionary France, were equivalent to the loss of an entire campaign for Napoleon, though he failed to see it. Joseph Görres was another former admirer of French liberal thought who as a result of his great disappointment became an intolerant adversary of France. What was worse, many of these foreign thinkers rejected the good with the bad and became foes of the republican ideas they themselves had once cherished and up to a point still invoked.

The French dictatorship committed many tactical mistakes, such as the shooting of the Duke d'Enghien, the bookseller Palm, Major von Schill, Andreas Hofer, and its embittered struggle against the patriotic anti-French movement in Spain where whole city populations were slaughtered. These made many people, especially German patriots, regard Napoleon as the incarnation of the devil, the Antichrist forecast in the Book of Revelation, sentiments which lacked sense or moderation. They led to the rise in Europe of the new idea of irrevocable hostility between the nations, compared with former development a very retrograde step, which, strangely enough, was to become the more bitter as economic development and railways lessened the distance between the nations involved.

> "Fill the Rhine with their dead bodies
> Make it o'er this dam of fear
> Flow westwards from its present valley
> Thus to form the 'Rhine Frontier'."

> *"Füllt den Rhein mit ihren Leichen.*
> *Lasst, gestauft von ihrem Bein,*
> *Rücklings um die Pfalz ihn weichen*
> *Und ihn so die Grenze sein"*

thundered Heinrich von Kleist, giving the cue to generations of young Germans.[1] Napoleon, faced with this unforeseen resistance, carried on with redoubled vigour. The link between the old monarchist Europe and these new middle-class enemies made him even more stern and inflexible and stimulated his fatal urge to play *va banque*. His campaign against Russia in 1812 showed

[1] These verses are contained in Kleist's *Hermannsschlacht,* which celebrates the victory of the Teutons over the Romans, but which was really aimed at the French.

that France was not strong enough for the rôle that Napoleon wanted her to play. The collapse of the Napoleonic armies on the wintry steppes of Eastern Europe and the War of Liberation that followed re-established the natural proportions of Europe. But even Napoleon's downfall, two years later, could not undo the events that took place while he was master of Europe. France had lost one million soldiers, a huge number in those days. The rest of Europe lost four or five times that figure.

The pernicious result of Napoleon's rule was the strengthening of reaction among the European Powers to such an extent that even the British, the chief victors over Napoleon, turned against it. The German middle class, which by a *levée en masse* had helped the monarchs win the war, felt betrayed and deprived of the political fruits of their victory. This does not mean that it had now become revolutionary or democratic. Instead, the Wars of Liberation against Napoleon of 1813–15 produced that bitter anti-Western and even anti-democratic mood of the outwardly liberal Prusso-German middle class and intelligentsia which was to have such fatal results for the future of Germany and Europe and which also seized other countries formerly occupied by Napoleon. This feeling of hatred and aversion to the West and its humanitarian ideal has determined the subsequent development of Europe to a large extent and has made the conflicts in the Old World breaches which until recently were almost impossible to heal. This rule of the dictator Napoleon was the start of the chain of German troubles and European struggles which finally led to Hitler's Reich in which the neo-Prussian and anti-Western traits were so conspicuous, even though the Führer was personally more anti-Russian than anti-French.

Chapter Seven

THE NEPHEW AS UNCLE: LOUIS NAPOLEON

Armed liberty

NOT unlike England after Cromwell, France was ruled by its exiled monarchy after the fall of Napoleon, the Bourbons being forced on the French by the bayonets of the conquering foreign armies. In both cases the restored monarchy did not last long, as it overrated its power. In 1830 the Bourbon king Charles X was replaced by Louis Philippe, from another branch of the royal house, the Orléans, under whom the upper middle class took the place of the nobility. In 1848 this bourgeois monarchy in its turn was overthrown, a victim of the middle class and the Paris workers, and gave way to the Second Republic, but in the same year a nephew of Napoleon I, Louis Napoleon, was elected President of this short-lived republic, and in 1851 he seized power as dictator. Just one year later he proclaimed himself Emperor Napoleon III. After he had been captured by the Germans at Sedan in 1870, the Government of France was called the Third Republic, which survived until 1940, when France was overrun by Hitler's German troops.

This constant change in the form of government is less surprising if one examines the reasons and comparison is made with parallels in history. The resistance of monarchist Europe to the revolution forced the democratic elements to rely on the Army as their defender to an extent unkown in other countries. While this lasted, most crises led to dictatorship. Only in the 1880s had democracy become so firmly implanted that the Army emerged second best from its struggle with the Republic, as shown in the so-called Boulanger crisis and the famous Dreyfus affair, in both of which the Republic finally triumphed over the Army.

This situation is exactly paralleled in ancient Sicily, in the Renaissance, and, more recently, in Latin America, where the republics were constantly at war or in the throes of an internal revolution. There is a great difference between Anglo-Saxon democracies, where the Navy was predominant, and those where the Army prevails. France in the nineteenth century was an example of the latter. The tremendous importance of Napoleon I to France won the respect of the people for members of his family and made the path to dictatorship easy for them. This was the trump card of the great emperor's nephew, Louis Napoleon.

In Louis Napoleon's early youth the Bonaparte family, to which he was so proud to belong, were under a cloud. In 1815, Napoleon I escaped from his exile in Elba and returned to France for a hundred days. After his final defeat at Waterloo he was banished to St. Helena, where he died in 1821. But it was just this proscription of Napoleon by the reactionary monarchies that paved the way for the rise of his nephew. In the clever propaganda put out by Napoleon and those round him the exiled emperor proclaimed himself the martyr of the revolution, ignoring his suppression of the French Republic, the left, and non-French nations and his sacrificing them to his own personal ambitions. He was presented as the young Bonaparte, "Général Vendémiaire", the conqueror of Egypt and the "liberator of Italy". The European middle classes, oppressed by the monarchist reaction, began to look on the cause of the great man, slowly dying in exile, as their own.

Useful Martyrdom

Louis Napoleon grew up under the strong influence of his mother, Hortense, *née* Beauharnais, daughter of Napoleon's first wife Josephine and wife of his brother Louis, King of Holland. From childhood he was brought up to believe that he would follow the great man. His family was proscribed in most of Europe, and he spent his youth in the family castle of Arenenberg on Lake Constance, and in Augsburg, and he therefore spoke French with a heavy German accent. Although technically a "prince", being the son of a once-ruling member of the family, he knew only too well that the nobility despised him. He was brought up by Hortense to believe that the Bonapartes were destined to be the saviours of humanity. By exploiting this idea properly, the road to power for Louis Napoleon would be easy.

It was just what he wanted to hear. The deaths of the young son of Napoleon I and his own brother made it easier still. More than that, as quite apart from the circumstances adversely affecting his family, his own personal case was aggravated by his knowing that his legitimate birth was strongly questioned. Until recently it was generally believed that Louis Napoleon was not the son of his supposed father, who had separated from his mother, but of the Dutch admiral Verheul; an impression confirmed by the lazy, slowly calculating nature of the subsequent emperor, with his yellowish face, his goatee, his shuffling gait, and his predilection for heavy Havanas which showed much more the traits of a sugar planter of the Dutch East Indies with creole features than those of a Napoleon. One modern scholar has doubted whether the admiral really was the father of Louis Napoleon, but what is certain is that Louis Napoleon was aware of the doubts of his legitimacy, which must have strongly increased his desire to seize power and rule—to show the world he was a true Napoleon.

An imitator of a dictator like Hitler later on, Louis Napoleon belongs to the ranks of the dictator-mimics. Curiously enough, his one trump card, his name, was for decades a liability to him. Until 1848 the classes most susceptible to the St. Helena propaganda, especially the French peasants, had no say in politics. The class in power, the upper middle class, deemed that a Bonaparte dictatorship was not only unnecessary, but even dangerous. It looked as if the hopes of the scheming Prince would be frustrated and his succession as emperor remain just a dream, like the attempt of Napoleon I to lead a free France against the monarchs on his return from Elba, or the freedom struggles of those days such as took place in Spain or Poland which ended with complete victory for the reaction. Indeed he and his brother became involved in a freedom movement in Italy in 1830, as a result of which his brother died from fever and he himself escaped only by the great risk of his mother, who staged a daring *coup*. These were melancholy years in which the defunct Napoleonic empire looked almost unreal and in which Hortense, in the best romantic and early-Victorian style, rendered for her son in the castle of Arenenberg her talented poems and songs, among them the *"Partant pour la Syrie"*, which later on under the new Napoleon played the rôle of the Badenweiler March under Hitler.

With the stubbornness of a monomaniac Louis Napoleon strove for his only goal, power. Concealing the "obstinacy behind gentleness" he was unwilling to accept the postponement of his wishes. There was already an established Bonapartist group in France under the leadership of an adventurer named Fialin, who called himself the Comte de Persigny. In October 1836 the Prince, partly with Persigny's help, but even more as a result of the assistance of an energetic and pretty vaudeville singer, a Mrs. Gordon, who knew how to captivate the chief of a French infantry regiment in Strasbourg, Colonel Vaudrey, staged his first *coup*. In full uniform he led the Vaudrey regiment through the streets of the town. The *coup* collapsed within an hour as the other troops of the garrison remained loyal. The Orléans Government deported Louis Napoleon to the United States. But even then the propagandist power of Bonapartism became visible; the Prince's helpers, when put on trial, defended themselves with such vigour that the court did not dare to punish them.

An even more absurd plot took place in 1840, when Louis Napoleon, then living in London, with fifty-six followers, half of them servants put into French uniform, landed near Boulogne. The participants had no idea of the object behind this apparent pleasure trip of one of the leaders of London high life. It was not revealed to them until they had all been made quite drunk. This plot failed even more hopelessly than the other. The Prince approached the garrison in his great uncle's uniform, circled by a well-trained eagle. But his harangue to the soldiers had no effect on them, and with his followers he was literally driven into the sea, where they were picked up and arrested while swimming back to the boat. In the subsequent trial theatrical scenes were staged as did Hitler in his trial after the "Brauhaus" *putsch*. It was of little avail to Louis Napoleon. While the Bonapartist phrases were spreading from the courtroom all over the country, Louis Philippe, head of the House of Orléans, to raise his own prestige brought the remains of Napoleon I back from St. Helena to the Paris crypt at the Invalides—but meanwhile Louis Napoleon had been imprisoned for life at the fortress of Ham, near Péronne. It is not enough to imprison would-be dictators, unless they are handled according to Renaissance methods and shown a short cut to Heaven. Louis Napoleon used his time in the fortress for learning and recreation. Just as Hitler wrote *Mein Kampf* when in Landsberg fortress, Louis completed various political writings in Ham; indeed, he later referred to his six years' imprisonment there as terms spent at the "University of Ham". The Prince was perfectly aware that the world had made great progress since the death of Napoleon I and was quite willing to calculate and act accordingly.

The collapse of the First Empire had terminated the supremacy of France on the Continent, and the new Napoleon was unwilling to change this situation radically. Having grown up in an age when the idea of nationalism, kindled by the French Revolution, had seized all European nations, he, as the potential champion of the progressive forces of those years, was obliged to take the lead in this movement instead of fighting it. It was a tricky decision. His support of the unification of countries like Germany and Italy meant territorial changes in favour of France as his price, and this gave him considerable trouble after he became Emperor. At Ham, too, Louis Napoleon learned much about labour problems, which he wanted to handle according to modern concepts. As a dictator, Napoleon III stands in the half light between the liberal revolution of the end of the eighteenth century and early nineteenth century and the totalitarian dictatorships of the twentieth century. Modern sociologists, inspired by the experiences of our century, see him as a pace-maker of either Fascism or Socialism, according to their viewpoints—but both without reason. The younger Bonaparte was too much a son of the French Revolution, too humane, too liberal, and not sufficiently totalitarian to be considered as a precursor of Fascism. On the other hand, he was far too closely tied up with the money economy of his time to be rated a Socialist. Not unlike our own century, the rise of the industrial working class forced every serious politician to give some thought to the problem of Socialism and to offer the public a programme for the solution of the social question, without this entitling us automatically to call Louis Napoleon a Socialist.

An adventurer and crafty schemer, Napoleon III borrowed many a political idea from contemporary thinkers and used them in his pamphlet *On the Extinction of Poverty*, in which, however, his Bonapartism shows only too clearly. He realized, as did his uncle, that the middle classes had to be scared by Bonaparte's mystical connection with the city masses. He also saw that as well as the smaller banker and businessman who tried to limit the State power by parliamentary institutions, a new group of bankers arose who were prepared to centralize the savings of the masses in monster banks and use these huge funds to cover the country with a network of railways. Later on, being a cunning political schemer, he used these men as allies against the liberal entrepreneurs, but was not able to claim historical or ethical merit for it. His support for these measures did indeed benefit the workers to some extent, but Louis Napoleon never helped them directly; he did nothing for the trade unions, and cannot be called a forerunner of either trade unionism or Communism.

The would-be dictator concentrated first and foremost on his bid for power, and was naturally concerned that he was not allowed to "graduate" from the "University of Ham". Eventually he escaped by a *coup*, by disguising himself as a workman, many of whom were engaged on the rebuilding and enlarging of the fortress. He was helped by his old doctor, who showed the inspecting officer the face of a wax doll that had been put in the Prince's bed as a dummy.

Having returned to London, Louis Napoleon renewed his connections with English society and with the *demi-monde*. Although he had not been entirely devoid of female company at Ham, he displayed his desire of making up for the lost years when he regained his freedom. One of his most intimate friends, the most renowned *cocotte* of the big city, was a Miss Howard, who had financed his *coup* at Boulogne, and who stood by to help him with further support. In all this, Louis Napoleon was more a Beauharnais than a Bonaparte, a genuine offshoot from the sub-tropical and decadent atmosphere from which his grandmother Josephine Beauharnais and his mother Hortense had sprung, both of whom were known for their extra-marital adventures. He had practically nothing of the martial spirit of the Corsican and Italian Bonapartes, which had at first been embodied in the mother of the great Napoleon. His unmilitary mood, unbecoming to a dictator and not to be confused with true humanitarian ideas, was later to deprive him of his throne.

The "Eighteenth Brumaire" of Louis Napoleon

That a political opportunist, which is all that Louis Napoleon ever was, succeeded in becoming master of his country astonished most contemporaries, especially as he spoke the language with a strong foreign accent, as had his uncle. When, later, he congratulated Bismarck on his impeccable French the latter is said to have replied that he wished he could return the compliment. The explanation lies in two facts alone : the name Napoleon, which had a magical effect at the time, and the good fortune of the middle-class revolution of 1848, which was European in its extent. The volcanic eruption that helped Louis Napoleon to power was the second or third of the social movements of that type that spread over Europe and which were followed in our own century by a series of proletarian tremors, even though the features varied according to where the uprising took place.

In France, as in Germany and other countries, the royal power was shaken by the radical middle classes, who, in turn, feared the rising industrial proletariat. In July, bloody struggles took place between the middle and working classes all over France, in which the former, supported by the Army, emerged victorious. This radically changed the political scene at once. When banks and stock exchanges trembled, a Bonaparte was in his proper place. Overnight the chances of success of the adventurer from London who had accepted a seat in the French National Assembly mounted sky-high. Shrewd financiers who foresaw the result—not only the always-helpful Miss Howard, now the mistress of the rising man, but also more serious figures such as the banker Achille Fould gave money; on December 10th Louis Napoleon was elected President with over five million votes; the next candidate, General Cavaignac, who had put down the workers' revolt, obtained four million less.

The election shows how senseless it is to call Louis Napoleon a Socialist. The millions of votes he received came rather from peasants and lower middle class who believed his election propaganda that he was the "saviour from Socialism". The election was a plebiscite type in which the voters, regardless of the party they supported, voted for a well-known military name from fear of revolution or social crisis. The election of Field-Marshal von

Hindenburg as German President in 1925 and General Eisenhower as United States President in 1952 and 1956 shows the same trait. Elections of this kind easily lead to the verge of dictatorship in countries where democracy is not yet well established. In the case of Louis Napoleon an election of this sort was the only way in which he could reach his goal, since he lacked military talent and influence.

That Louis Napoleon would not give up his position as President of the Republic even after the end of his term was practically certain, as he was a Bonaparte; all his actions as head of a republican State aimed exclusively at the preparation of his *coup d'état*. From the outset he surrounded himself with Bonapartist pomp, appeared whenever possible in uniform and on horseback, removed those high-ranking officers not known for being completely devoted to the Bonaparte tradition from the Army and, to increase his prestige as guardian of the established order, dispatched French troops to Italy against Garibaldi, to re-establish the papal authority which had been shaken in the first months of 1848. This blow to the cause of Italian unity which he had proclaimed all his life shows the true nature of Napoleon III. He was an opportunist who betrayed the revolution wherever possible while posing as its symbol.

Internal support for this ambiguous policy was easy, as in her fear of a working-class uprising an ultra-reactionary Parliament (*Corps Législatif*) had been elected by France. The three years which elapsed between Louis Napoleon's election and his *coup d'état* almost exactly on its anniversary form a model example of how to become a dictator. The opponents fought with each other's weapons, like Hamlet and Laertes, the dictator unctuously advocating progress, while the parliament wished to set up a monarchy to defend its own working. Luckily for the dictator, the masses of the peasants and lower middle classes who backed him had since the French Revolution been almost deprived of participation in parliamentary life, which made the parliamentary cause gain its main support from the wealthy middle class. This situation changed only after the downfall of Napoleon III, which deprived Bonapartism of its foundation.

Under these circumstances the dictator candidate had no difficulty in endearing himself to the masses by means of well-publicized journeys round the country; all he had to do was to surround himself with the right men in order to convince the wealthy upper middle class that it would be better to deal with him, the dreaded dictator and friend of the people and supposed Socialist, than with a Parliament which had indeed been elected by the upper middle class but which had lost all credit politically.

The figures he selected for the decisive act were just the right characters to back an adventurer such as himself to the hilt. There was Louis Napoleon's half-brother de Morny, an illegitimate son of his mother Hortense from a connection with Talleyrand's illegitimate son, the Count de Flahault, a cold and calculating financier and absolutely unscrupulous careerist; there was General Saint-Arnaud, who, having been dismissed from the Army for his gambling debts and sent, to reform his character, to the struggle against the Riff-Kabyles, committed hideous crimes there but became Louis Napoleon's Minister for War; there was the Prefect of Paris, Maupas, and the military commander of the city, Magnan, who were won over by immense bribes, and there was, finally, the "white eunuch", the overseer of Louis Napoleon's harem, Mocquart, who served the President also as private secretary.

The outward reason for the *coup d'état* was the refusal of the French Chamber to extend his office beyond its normal term; the date of the *coup* (December 2nd) was chosen, in the style of the older Napoleon, as it was the anniversary of Austerlitz and the coronation of Napoleon I. According to a well-informed source, bribes flowed freely before the *coup*, and at first everything went well. Maupas arrested all the leading members of the Chamber, while Fialin-Persigny occupied their main meeting hall with troops. On the morning of December 2nd the population of Paris read monster white posters declaring the Assembly dissolved, re-establishing universal suffrage it had abolished, and making the people arbiter between the President and Parliament by means of a plebiscite. But then the unexpected happened. General Magnan withdrew his troops from the city, probably because de Morny felt that his half-brother was being too liberal and had to be forced to pose as a protector of law and order. If so, de Morny was most successful, as after the withdrawal of the troops the Paris masses became rebellious. Public gatherings took place and barricades were erected. This is what the wirepullers wanted. Shots rang out and the military returned to enforce law and order. The *coup d'état*, which had been planned to be bloodless, cost at least 380 lives.

"Saint-Simon on Horseback"

Once in power, Louis Napoleon had to follow in the footsteps of all dictators in his policy towards the middle classes, however distasteful it might have been to him. His experiences with soldiers had been unfortunate, his intervention in Italy had been foiled by armed force, and so had his two earlier *coups*. His imprisonment led to a longing for freedom, which made the first, or liberal, stage of his dictatorship last longer than usual, and a strong liberal trait remained one of the chief characteristics of this dictatorship. In course of time, however, the dictator, although badly prepared, had also to play his rôle in the second act in which liberalism becomes the opposite.

The prominence of the first act was due to a large extent to the discovery of gold-mines in California, which started a boom throughout the world which in France removed at first all traces of the difficulties of 1848. The Emperor Napoleon III, who adopted this title on December 2nd, 1852, was able to promote his favourite economic schemes, especially the building of railways. This was made possible by the support of the new big deposit banks, especially the *Crédit Mobilier*, which, under the brothers Jacob and Isaac Péreire, fought the private banks led by the Rothschilds to tap the French savings and put them into the service of the nation's industrial development.

The *Crédit Mobilier* supported the construction of most of the important railway lines. In 1851 the mileage of the system was only 2,196 miles; in the heyday of the new Empire, from 1852 to 1857, this was increased by 6,408 miles, and by 1867 France had 14,890 miles of track. While this made the Emperor popular with the small man, the chief investor in the new banks, and increased his confidence in him, it earned for Napoleon the enmity of the private banks. The admirers of the Empire saw him as "Saint-Simon on horseback", as he and his ministers, as well as the new-type bankers and industrialists, seemed to be influenced by the ideas of the Count of Saint-Simon.

However, this did not mean that Napoleon III was a Socialist; it showed, rather, that he followed Saint-Simon's ideas of monopoly capitalism. The big banks formed in those years have determined French history to the present day. The economic boom enabled Napoleon III, like all dictators, to carry out immense building programmes and encourage culture, if the latter were still possible in that age of crinoline and gas-lamps and the mass production by machinery of small ornaments. Many of the great writers of the time—Mérimée, Gautier, Augier, Flaubert, Sainte-Beuve, George Sand, Taine and Rénan—were associated with the Imperial family, and Haussmann, prefect of the Seine *départe-ment*, drove gigantic boulevards through Paris and made it the city with which we are familiar today. The monster world fairs, especially the second in 1867, made Paris the centre of the world.

The "Débâcle"

All the time, however, social forces were working silently and steadily which were to bring the dictator down, in the reverse way from his uncle. While Napoleon I overreached himself and challenged all nations, "Napoleon the Small", as he was contemptuously called by Victor Hugo, tried to adapt himself to current political thought and to the wishes of the nations around him, and perished because he displayed insufficient military power. Napoleon III, a political speculator, lacked the ruthless energy and creative imagination of his uncle, qualities which especially in those years of the unification of Germany and Italy would have been very necessary in the leader of France. A dictator protecting a middle-class society could hardly afford to be friendly or even indifferent to movements of this nature. The ruling classes in his country expected him to guard not only their economic but also their political interests; the conservative wing of French society, especially the Catholics, saw in the unification of Germany and Italy a dangerous threat and made the Emperor responsible for it.

The star of Napoleon III rose as long as these developments over the borders of France were invisible or temporarily suspended. The Second Empire reached its climax in the Crimean War, where allied with Great Britain, it fought Russian tsarist tyranny. After 1856 the sun of the new Napoleon began to sink as his policies suffered defeat after defeat. This was not recognized at once by people at the time, who thought that Napoleon's support of Lombardy against Austria in 1859 was the climax of his empire, but the loss of Savoy, the original home of the new

Italian royal house, to France as the price of her support, and the ending of the Pope's temporal power in Italy angered Catholics all over the world, not least those in France.

The opposition to Napoleon III had reached his own family. Their mouthpiece was the Empress Eugénie Montijo, outstandingly beautiful and ambitious, but uneducated, extremely superficial, and therefore politically dangerous. Catholic policy was to resist the development of the new nations, and to carry it out would have needed tremendous personal energy and material resources, both of which Napoleon lacked. Yet he was never able to free himself from Catholic influence. He thus ended as a dictator who failed in the "second act". Under the constant prodding of the Empress he yielded to the Catholic and Conservative policy all the time without being able to execute it properly. Catholic and other right-wing pressure made him desert the cause of Italian unity and to support the Habsburg monarchy as the leading Catholic Power in Europe. For the same reason he embarked on various colonial adventures, partly to avenge murdered Catholic missionaries and partly for capitalist speculation. For the same reason he protected the Pope, as he had done when President, when the Italians tried to drive him from Rome. These measures alienated the liberals, without wholly pleasing the Catholics.

Among Napoleon's worst blunders was the expedition to Mexico to force the Mexicans to accept the Habsburg Archduke Maximilian as Emperor, an expedition for which he lacked power and funds. His desertion of Maximilian, who was finally shot by Mexican patriots, lost him prestige in Catholic eyes. And when Protestant Prussia attacked Austria about the same time, in 1866, and defeated her at Königgrätz, thereby gaining the political supremacy in Germany, the contempt for Napoleon's policy among the Catholics reached a new height. The battle of Sadowa (named after another place in the vicinity which was easier to pronounce) was looked on as a blow against France, and henceforth they longed to "avenge Sadowa". Napoleon III, feeble and sickly, was unable to meet their demands. To stem the onslaught from the right, he tried to win over the French liberals and to persuade Bismarck to grant him some territorial compensation as a price for his support of German unification under Prussia. His much-discussed, confused and contradictory political combinations in those final years in which he tried to secure part of the Rhineland, Luxembourg or Belgium are much more the result of his weakness and political embarrassment than of a malicious mentality, eager to conquer foreign territory.

It ended when the Catholic group, led by his wife, forced him against his will to start the war of 1870 against Bismarck's Prussia, for which he was quite unprepared both in the military and strategic field. France was completely defeated in the first months and Napoleon III was captured by the Prussians at Sedan on September 1st, 1870. This led to his downfall, which internal opposition had been too weak to achieve on its own. It was the complete collapse of the dictatorial system, the "Débâcle", from which Bonapartism has never recovered.

Chapter Eight

DICTATORSHIPS IN THE SPHERE OF SPAIN AND PORTUGAL

The Common Denominator

WHILE dictatorship gradually disappeared in France and had no opportunity at all in Eastern and Central Europe before the power of the monarchs who ruled there was thoroughly shaken, the Hispanic world on both sides of the Atlantic became a stronghold of this type of rule—and for several good reasons. Poverty, illiteracy, lack of political education and the overwhelming power of the landowners and clergy prevented until quite recently the growth of an efficient democracy in the Hispanic world on both sides of the Atlantic. The only stable element were the armies, whose political preponderance dated from the first decade of the nineteenth century, when Napoleon invaded Spain, causing the Spanish colonies in America to revolt against the mother country and at the same time aroused the Spaniards at home to fight the invader with arms. In the New World across the Atlantic the leaders of the revolutionary armies replaced the former Spanish governors. This put the political control of these countries into the hands of the military and led to the constant change of presidents with dictatorial powers, known in the Latin American world as *personalismo*. Instead of carrying through a full-dress social revolution, the leaders simply staged a military *putsch*, a so-called *pronunciamiento,* outlawing their political predecessors and proving their point with bayonets. This was as true of Spain's former colonies across the Atlantic as it was in the evolution of the mother country, which until the first third of the nineteenth century was governed by the old Bourbon dynasty, re-established after Napoleon's downfall in 1814.

The Bourbons were not quite so secure on the throne after their return as they had been before. The experience of the preceding decades, and the continuation of bourgeois and revolutionary propaganda during the reaction after 1815, enabled the Spanish generals to make themselves indispensable to the monarchs. Being allies of the middle classes, which developed slowly in Spain, most of these military figures are in the category of bourgeois dictators; almost all were inspired by Bonapartism and saw Napoleon I as their god. In the nineteenth and early twentieth centuries most of these individuals, like the bourgeoisie of that age, were liberal and anti-clerical. The desire to increase the revenues of the Army drove many of them into the camp of bourgeois freemasonry and led them to attack the privileges of the Church and the nobles. It is true that there were some exceptions, even in the nineteenth century. In the Fascist era some of these dictators, like the middle classes of that period, were more or less outspokenly in favour of the policy of Hitler and Mussolini. The general conflict between the Western world and the sphere of the Soviet Union and Communism after World War II made the anti-revolutionary and anti-liberal type of dictator preponderant.

Almost everywhere in the Spanish and Portuguese world dictatorship became an established institution, since the Army from whose ranks the dictators emerged was for many decades the only stable element in the life of those States. Until quite recently the political form of military dictatorship was the common denominator connecting the mother countries with their former colonies. Only in the last few years when much of Latin America overthrew their dictatorships did this situation change, making the New World once more look more progressive than the old one.

Spanish Dictators before Hitler

The history of Spain from the downfall of Napoleon to the 1830s is the story of the struggle between the returned Bourbons and the power-hungry generals, who vied with each other in suppressing and controlling the Spanish people. Under Ferdinand VII (1814–33), an almost Fascist figure in purple, and a sadist, the foes of the Government were tortured in the fortress of Monjuich. One of the victims of this system, a leader of the popular movement against Napoleon who under the Bourbons supported the liberal cause, was exposed every Sunday in an iron cage to the insults of the peasants visiting the local fair. They harried him with sticks and spat on him. At last the tortured giant, while on the way to the place of execution, broke his chains like Samson, and seizing his own sword with which his torturers had ridiculed him perished along with them. Ferdinand was the most counter-revolutionary among all Spanish kings since Philip II, but even he, towards the end of his reign, could not govern successfully without the help of military dictators of the bourgeois and liberal brands. The resistance of the nobility to his plan of having his daughter Isabella recognized as heir to the throne led to a general reshuffle in the political world. To Ferdinand's great disappointment the nobility, and especially the Church, supported the candidacy to the throne of his brother Don Carlos, in whom they saw a devoted instrument.

In view of the armed resistance of Don Carlos to the new order in Spain, the rule of the young Queen, represented by her mother during her minority, would doubtless have failed had she not been backed by the leader of the "liberal" military clique, Baldomero Espartero. The section of the populace that benefited most from the appearance on the scene of the military dictators—the "liberal" Espartero and his more "moderate" rival Leopold O'Donnell, Duke of Tetuan, a Spaniard of Irish descent, was of course the Army, especially the officer corps. In 1872 experts stated disgustedly that the Spanish Army which at that time numbered roughly 300,000 men, with a reserve of 100,000, had enough officers to command an army of two million men! Espartero's "liberal" dictatorship saved Isabella from the Carlistas or Carlists—the followers of Don Carlos—whose main support came from the Basque region in the north, and thus gravely damaged the cause of the Church. But the clerical party, defeated in this minor theatre of war, transferred the struggle to Madrid and staged a counter-revolution under the leadership of General Ramón de Narváez which brought about Espartero's downfall.

Narváez, an aristocrat of the old school, who was quick to gain young Isabella's confidence, is the first great counter-revolutionary dictator in Spanish history. He removed the national militia, which was supported by the city population, and replaced it by a civil guard mainly recruited from the country. He suppressed the newspapers, created a system of spies and stool-pigeons, brought the parliament, known as the Cortes, under exclusive conservative control, changed the Constitution to serve his purposes, and during his lengthy rule, which was interspersed by liberal interludes under Espartero and O'Donnell, drove the liberals underground. The inhabitants of Madrid became accustomed to the sight of captured opponents of the dictator, chained with common criminals, being driven through the streets of the capital to do forced service in the nearby labour camps. When the dictator was on his deathbed he was warned to forgive all his enemies. He is said to have answered that this was unnecessary as he had killed all of them. As with many other dictators, Narvaez was helped by the industrialization of his country and by the beginning of railway construction, which stopped the resistance of the population. He died in April 1868 during his last dictatorship, and his death deprived Isabella, who had become fat and ugly through over-indulgence in love—and chocolate—of her indispensable political adviser and protector. The fear lest the power of the dead might fall into the hands of the lover of the Queen, an Italian, caused the generals to expel the dynasty later in the year. But as the Crown represented the political unity of Spain while a republic endangered it, most generals continued to stand in the monarchist camp.

After a short reign by an Italian-born king and a short, tragic period of republican rule, in which the central republic had to fight armed resistance by individual provinces, political authority automatically slipped back into the hands of the generals, who finally called the son of the banished Isabella, Alfonso XII, to the throne. Under this king and under his son Alfonso XIII Spain went through a period of more advanced industrialization and participated in the general European prosperity of that time, which for Spain, as a non-belligerent country, continued through the period of the first world war. During those years the Army stood rather more in the background. As the country was a monarchy, Spain was not in need of military dictators if the Crown had other ways of ruling. But with the postwar problems, which were shared by most other nations, political control once more reverted automatically to the Army, which always had the upper hand when the situation called for the use of force.

Social conditions had undergone a decisive change since the days when Espartero had defended the Crown against the Carlistas and the nobility. The years of "liberal" dictatorship had passed. The new dictator, General Miguel Primo de Rivera, who came to power in Spain a year after the rise of Mussolini, resembled not so much Espartero, but rather his conservative opponent, Narvaez. The *putsch* and the rise of Primo de Rivera were doubtless inspired by those of Mussolini, though Primo de Rivera could not match his idol. Unlike the leader of Fascism, Primo de Rivera remained a conservative military dictator of the old brand. The old powers—nobility, Church and Army— applauded his policy and backed him up as long as he served their interests. However, he lacked the most essential prerequisite of all modern large-scale dictatorships, the support of the masses. Embittered at Primo de Rivera's kid-glove treatment of the Church and the advance of the clericals in the Administration, the bourgeoisie, which had originally welcomed his rule, soon withdrew its support. The Army, dissatisfied with his pacifist policy in Morocco, did likewise. Had his rule not coincided with a general boom which allowed him to carry out many public works and so widen the basis of his support, he would have probably fallen from power much sooner.

The end came inevitably when the boom gave way to the big depression of 1929 and subsequent years, itself a favourable condition for the rise of dictators. However, in the Spain of Primo de Rivera the social basis was lacking which might have allowed a Hitler to exploit the depression politically. In view of the disastrous collapse of the Spanish currency, a result of the economic depression and the withdrawal of American credits, the dictator lost the support of the Army and in January 1930 had to ask the King to accept his resignation. His downfall led to the collapse of the monarchy not long afterwards. By backing the dictator the monarchy had tried to save its throne in vain, and thus suffered the same fate as did the Italian royal family fifteen years later.

Chapter Nine

LATIN AMERICAN DICTATORS IN THE NINETEENTH AND EARLY TWENTIETH CENTURIES

The "Liberators"

WITH the chief exception of Francisco Franco, Spanish dictators usually governed in the name of the monarchy. On the other hand, the dictators in Latin America came to power in territories which had shaken off the rule of the Spanish or Portuguese crowns. The history of Latin American dictatorships starts towards the end of the first decade of the nineteenth century with the revolt of the overseas colonies against the States of the Iberian Peninsula, which at that time had been overrun by Napoleon's troops. After the downfall of Napoleon it was expected that the colonies would return to their old political connection with the mother countries, but this did not materialize; the re-established powers in Spain and Portugal were not sufficiently far-sighted to grant them the political concessions they required.

The bloody and decisive struggles in which Latin America broke loose from the Old World did not at first produce the rise of a revolutionary stratum, nor lead to the rise of mighty dictators which represented it. Instead of the modern bourgeoisie which in this backward sphere developed only sporadically and slowly, Latin America possessed the so-called creole class, consisting of descendants of European immigrants, a stratum which was looked on as inferior by the populations of the mother countries. Basically aristocratic and owning property, proud of its traditional culture, creole society resented this moral discrimination with special bitterness—but in keeping with its aristocratic tradition also disliked its own revolutionary rôle. It realized its vulnerability and knew that the Spaniards, deeply offended at the revolution, would stir up the lowest classes—both coloured Indios and half-castes (*mestizos*)—to do it deadly injury.

This explains the lack of final success of the so-called *liberta-dores* (liberators), men such as the Venezuelan national hero Simon Bolívar, the Argentinian San Martin or the Mexican leader General Iturbide, all of them representatives of the creole stratum who directed the great struggle against Spain and who therefore seemed chosen for the rôle of dictators. The necessity of winning the war spoiled the political chances of all these "liberators". The unchaining of the coloured native population by the Spaniards, the hideous maliciousness with which the last Spanish viceroys caused the gauchos of the pampas or the *Llaneros* in the plains of the Orinoco to attack the frightened creole class, forced Bolívar to turn the tables and to fight the Spaniards with that very same weapon. The co-operation of the natives and of an International Brigade—mostly English veterans who had lost their livelihood as a result of the end of the Napoleonic wars—brought Latin America the desired independence. But Pandora's box had been opened; the social forces that had been unleashed could not be suppressed once more.

To the great disappointment of the creole upper class, which blamed the "liberators" for this development, it was henceforth threatened by the forces from below. Unpopular with the coloured masses they called in of necessity but only temporarily, the "liberators" found that even their own class regarded them with considerable mistrust—not unjustifiably. Some of them, including the "forerunner of Latin American freedom", Francisco de Miranda (1754–1816), Bolívar himself and San Martin had spent a great part of their lives in revolutionary Europe. Iturbide and even Bolívar had some coloured blood, and San Martin, though of Spanish parentage, had peculiar personal experiences which made him a revolutionary. Iturbide, like Bolívar and several other "liberators", aimed openly at absolute dictatorship, but with the sole exception of Dr. Francia in Paraguay, none won the support of the Indios—the only way to success.

Iturbide showed a marked desire to win over the creole upper class and thus to make it forget his ancestry. Thus he first played a counter-revolutionary rôle and crushed a first attempt to liberate Mexico, under the priest Hidalgo, who was supported by *mestizos* and Indios. The long-overdue separation of Mexico from Spain had to wait until an accidental revolutionary turn in the policy of the mother country enabled him to bring it about in the name of the conservatives, the Church, the creoles, and even the Spaniards living in the country.

Bolívar, being a big landowner, was less of a reactionary than Iturbide, the former small officer eager to mingle with the mighty, who finally under the name of Augustin I had himself proclaimed Emperor of Mexico. A demon consumed by passions, Bolívar collapsed morally after the sudden death of his very young wife. He spent several inherited fortunes in Paris. But even he was unwilling to sacrifice the class interests of the creoles, though this policy ruined the success of his work. Lack of support by the Indios was one of the reasons for his failure as dictator.

The most unselfish figure among these "liberators" was General San Martin, Argentina's George Washington, Bolívar's equal as a strategist and statesman and his superior as a man. Unlike Bolívar and Iturbide, somewhat social misfits from their slight admixture of coloured blood—despite their assimilation to the creole class—San Martin always remained the genuine gentleman. He was born in America but was the son of a Spaniard who had served Spain in Europe most of his life. The climax of his career was the dramatic moment when after his famous crossing of the Southern Andes, the liberation of Chile, and the expulsion of the Spaniards from Peru, he met Bolívar, who had performed similar exploits in the North. He placed the welfare of South America above his personal desires, and after several days of negotiations he yielded to his rival, who was consumed with ambition and who wished to reserve the expulsion of the remaining Spanish armies to himself. Instead of settling the question in Latin American fashion with the help of arms, he transferred the rule over the city of Lima, which he had conquered, to Bolívar and spent the rest of his life in retirement in Europe. His parting message to the Peruvian Parliament contains the unforgettable words: "The presence of a successful army leader, however unselfish he might be, is a danger to newly established republics."

The Caudillos

San Martin's statement gives the clue to the understanding of the entire history of Latin America. Had San Martin's example been followed, this evolution would have been very different. But after the expulsion of the Spaniards Latin America lacked genuine aristocrats, especially in the control of the armies which

had brought about the independence of the former colonies.
Most Army leaders, starting with Bolívar's generals, were
mestizos, descendants of intermarriages between the creoles and
coloured Indians, which made them ideal military dictators. In
contrast to the "liberators" such as Bolívar who took great care
to conceal any admixture of coloured blood in their veins by a
strong pro-creole attitude, the hybrid descent of most *mestizos*
was too conspicuous to be hidden. Mistrusting the creoles the
mestizos desired, however, to be their social equals or superiors.
The *mestizos* stratum was a hotbed of that mixture of envy and
hatred of the nobility which inspires many a bourgeois dictator.

This sentiment, which in the case of Cromwell or Napoleon
appeared in splendid isolation, became the dominant feeling of
an entire social class in Latin America, which provided sufficient
numbers of men infected by the germ *"Bacillus dictatorialis"* for
the institution of dictatorship than was the rule here. Looking
down arrogantly on the pure-blooded Indios or negroes, the
mestizos at the same time needed them for carrying out their
politics; the *mestizo* stratum formed the upper class of the
coloured population without whose support it would have been
unable to check the creole nobility. In the coloured population
the *mestizos* possessed the mass basis which the creole "liberators"
lacked. This explains why most great creole politicians had little
success.

About one year after his coronation as Emperor, Iturbide was
expelled by representatives of the lower classes and was slain
when trying to return by force; Bolívar, in turn, at the end of his
life, had to witness his most important political creation, Greater
Colombia, lose Ecuador and Venezuela and break into three
pieces roughly corresponding to the old Spanish administrative
districts in this area. The egotism of the dominated territories
became evident; the aversion of the creoles in the various districts
to submit to central dictatorship, even creole-controlled, was
cleverly used by Bolívar's *mestizo* generals, Flores in Ecuador
and Paéz in Venezuela, to fight him and ascend to power. Outwardly these generals defended the ruling classes of their districts;
in reality, however, they were mainly interested in their own rule,
which they could only maintain with the help of the natives.

Just as in Spain, the main seat of power in all Latin American
States was the Army, to whose wishes the Church and nobility

had to submit, though often with great repugnance. The Army leaders rising to power, the so-called *caudillos,* were steadily threatened by the jealousy of the other generals. The greater the lack of firm social foundations, as for instance in Central America and Bolivia with their terribly poor and ignorant native and Indio population, the more bitter and numerous were the individual generals' struggles for control; the half-century after Bolívar's disappearance was a time of complete political anarchy for many Latin American States. On the whole, this customary race for power known as *personalismo* offers few features of general interest. The combatants in this struggle had usually no historical significance unless they succeeded in terminating the universal anarchy, and for this purpose to enlist the support of the more stable forces of their age. From the basis of their support the bourgeois-type dictators can be distinguished from the champions of the anti-revolutionary creole society, which, living on big estates, enhanced the rôle of feudal overlords.

The picture was most colourful. The only thing the Latin American States had in common was their aversion to the political aspirations of the former mother countries, Spain and Portugal; the social structure of each dictatorship varied very much. Before the revolt of the colonies the policy of the mother countries, like that of most European States, had been determined by the rise of the bourgeoisie and the French Revolution, and was thus liberal, but it became reactionary after Napoleon's downfall. Consequently American politicians of every creed found some convenient argument for challenging the trend in the mother countries and for justifying their dictatorship morally.

In the old Jesuit State of Paraguay, for example, whose spiritual directors had been forcibly removed during the liberal era in Spain, the mother country was attacked for just this reason. Paraguay's "liberator", Dr. Gaspar Rodriguez de Francia, regarded himself as the avenger of the Jesuits, to whom he owed his education. Setting himself at the head of the coloured natives whom the Jesuits had lovingly patronized and trained but at the same time kept in ignorance and slavery, he struck with bitterness against the Spaniards in his country, and, though a creole himself, kept the rest of his class under the strictest control, not infrequently calling in the executioner. As the man who had lifted the Spanish yoke but who at the same time was the leader of the natives, he combined the functions of a "liberator" in the Bolívar style with those of a typical *caudillo* —almost the sole example of this kind. A Caesar and a high priest as well, he was rather like Stalin in clerical garb. He surrounded his country with a kind of purple curtain which nobody was permitted to lift without his permission, and kept it in almost demoniacal dependence. When he died in 1840, after a rule of twenty-six years, nobody dared to believe he was dead; suspicious lest he might have disguised himself, the natives of Paraguay greeted each other with the words: *"Viva el dífunto!"* (Long live the deceased one!)

If Francia was a creole—though significantly enough like Bolívar and Iturbide not of entirely pure blood—his successors, the two Lopez, father and son, were genuine and very typical *mestizos*. The younger Lopez, Francisco Solano, an ugly, small lad, saw in himself a second Napoleon I and copied this idol of many Latin American dictators in a way not achieved by any of his colleagues. This is true even of the way he treated the Catholic Church, which, as Dr. Francia had done, he forced to educate the ignorant natives in a spirit of absolute obedience to him as the Lord's anointed servant. The nucleus of the population of fanatics was the Army, which Lopez junior served as Minister for War during the dictatorship of his father. He recruited it and trained it for his future needs. This recalls the career of Frederick the Great, but other features of the rule of this most pernicious of all Latin American dictators are similar not only to the rule of Napoleon but also to that of Hitler. As with both these dictators, Lopez shared a certain underestimation of his enemies and an overestimation of the initial advantages he had secured by his well-planned armament policy and by his invasion of weakly protected territories of enemy countries. In foolhardy blindness he not only attacked the gigantic State of Brazil and the Republic of Uruguay which blocked his way to the sea, but at the same time Argentina, which tried to stop his march through Uruguay. His ignorant Guarani Indians, whom he had convinced that their foes killed all prisoners, were told by him that the war would end in three months—which in the style of Hitler he seems to have believed himself.

In reality the tremendous struggle lasted five years, during which the population of Paraguay, which had numbered over a

million people, sank to 220,000. Like Hitler, Lopez was firmly
resolved not to stem the mischief he had conjured up, but rather
to drag his entire nation into the abyss. The poor Indios and
their women and children, believing that the enemy left them no
choice, fought to their last drop of blood. It was a "total
mobilization", just as in the German Third Reich later on. The
women carried the supplies for the army, and when collapsing
under the burden were left on the road to die. Like Hitler, Lopez
was plagued by fear of treason, the more so the longer the war
lasted. He arrested his own brothers and shot them. His mother,
who implored him to save their lives, was publicly flogged. The
only person who exercised some power over the practically
insane dictator was his pretty Irish mistress, Ella Lynch, whom
he had met in France and who equalled him in intelligence and
cruelty. She cut a splendid figure on horseback and helped him
fight his battles. As in the cases of Napoleon and Hitler, the
Lord in the long run supported the stronger forces. Driven into
a corner, the tyrant finally had to flee into the roadless territory
of the Gran Chaco. Just as with Hitler, he was convinced that
his end spelled the doom of his nation. It has indeed still not
fully recovered from the terrible blow it received at that time;
impoverished and with its population reduced, it is still limping
along behind its neighbours. Lopez, it seems, died like Hitler by
committing suicide at the moment when the enemy surrounded
him (April 1st, 1870). According to other reports he was captured
and killed.

That the example of this madman was not followed was not
due, of course, to any lack of such figures, as Latin America,
with its countless *mestizos*, is probably richer in men of this type
than any other part of the world. Probably the true reason was
that before the advent of the modern totalitarian State there
was hardly an instance in history where the population of an
entire country had been trained for totalitarian use as it had
been in Paraguay under the Jesuits, Dr. Francia and the elder
Lopez. In the rest of Latin America the Indios were much too
disobedient as a rule to give their lives blindly to a *mestizo* and
to fight his wars of conquest, though naturally countless efforts
were made to use them in this way, especially in Bolivia. One
of these exploits is connected with the name of General Santa
Cruz, a descendant of the Incas, who in the way of Lopez junior

tried to gain access to the sea for Bolivia, and as a result came into conflict with her neighbours, Peru and Chile. Attacked in the rear by Argentina's dictator Rosas, Santa Cruz had to abandon this endeavour and, threatened by a revolution, was forced to flee from the country.

The evolution of Bolivia is one of the best examples in history of a surplus of dictator candidates who lacked a suitable mass basis. To look for support of a dictatorship among the emaciated Indios from the former Spanish silver mines was like building on quicksand. From 1825 to 1898, Bolivia had no less than sixty revolutions; six of her presidents were murdered, and a great many others driven into exile. Among those exiled was the grotesque Melgarejo (1864–70), one of the best examples of an insanely vain *mestizo* dictator, who, in addition, was illegitimate. As so often among people of his type, his longing for recognition was shown in the erotic sphere. He was filled with great pride because he had succeeded in making Juanita Sanchez, a girl from the upper classes, his mistress. To intimidate the women of the upper classes, who looked down on Juanita with contempt, he terrorized their husbands, and thus forced the culprits to kneel before the girl begging her pardon. Utterly faithless and without any scruples—he personally slew his predecessor, who had magnanimously spared his own life—Melgarejo, in typical *mestizo* style, soon attacked the very coloured stratum from which he had partly descended, and deprived the poor Indios of their land. His end came when the clan of la Sanchez, which had provided him with his mistress and in return had been granted tremendous financial privileges, began to oppose him, rather in the way of the murderers of Caesar, who likewise had been very closely connected to their victim. During an attempt to enter their mansion by force he was shot down by his own son-in-law.

It was typical of most of these leaders that they turned against the coloured stratum from whence they had come. It corresponded to the "second act" of the bourgeois dictatorship, but with a distinction. The Latin American dictators did not usually come to power as the helpers of a middle class which they later betrayed, but their political somersaults, in view of the weakness of the middle class, benefited the landowners and also very often the Church as well. Some of these *caudillos* were excellent in changing sides; the champion in this field was the "Napoleon of Mexico", the shrewd Santa Anna. A most unsavoury creature, a traitor and a liar, he was conspicuous for an urge for recognition, unusual in its intensity even in that classical breeding-ground of egocentrics. This urge made him lose all sense of proportion and led to a stupendous self-glorification. His very tenacity made him a typical representative of that period of transition, in which the anarchy of the liberator age gave way gradually to the more stable years of capitalist penetration. He shared this fate with his more important opponent, Benito Juárez, a man of far higher ethics and his ultimate successor, and also with contemporaries such as Ramón Castilla of Peru, Rosas of Argentina, and also with Rafael Nuñez of Colombia, who flourished some decades later.

In contrast to Juárez, the pure Indio, Santa Anna was a typical *mestizo* who by his theatrical ventures was just the man to captivate the poor Indios and make them his instruments. He started as a rebel against the reactionary Iturbide in 1823 and in 1830 occupied the capital Vera Cruz in fighting for the liberal cause against the conservative president Bustamente. But when the liberal régime he had supported started to carry through truly liberal reforms such as the abolition of the Church tithe and of political control by the clergy, a reform of the universities, a reduction of the army, and especially the secularization of a fraction of the Church property, the crafty leader of the Indios saw a welcome chance to offer his services to the infuriated landowners, and especially the Church. He destroyed the Government he had himself brought to power, and, turning military dictator, became the hero of the conservatives. His reactionary rule caused the defection of Texas, which joined the United States. The effort of the "Napoleon of Mexico" to stem this move by force led to the ill-famed slaughter of American partisans in Fort Alamo in San Antonio. Shortly afterwards Santa Anna was decisively defeated by the American general Sam Houston in 1836. This brought about the collapse of the dictator. The history of Mexico until 1853 is full of his attempts to regain power; no less than six times he became president and almost dictator, but lost control once more because of his ostentatiousness and lack of moderation. A medium-sized, black-haired man with penetrating dark eyes as well as a melancholy look, Santa

Anna saw himself to be the martyr which in a sense he was; a victim of his lust for power which urged so many *mestizos* to pose as powerful men. After his conquest of the capital his carriage was drawn by four white horses; he rode in golden coaches which were burned when he fell from power; in 1838 he lost a leg in defending the country against an attempted French invasion and staged a solemn cortège for this limb and had it entombed in a beautiful monument.

Though a protector of landed property and the Church, a man of the type of Santa Anna, who led the poor Indios, must be distinguished from the conservative and reactionary dictators whom he closely resembled. Counter-revolutionary dictators often emerge in Latin America from the hinterland, which is usually at loggerheads with the liberal *porteños*, i.e. those in the coastal towns, or they seek their support on the high plateaux, the old centres of Spanish might, from where Army and Church watched the coloured natives among the mountains. This is true, for instance, of Colombia and Ecuador, which supported Bolívar's counter-revolutionary troop leaders, Paéz and Flores. Ecuador later produced one of the greatest conservative dictators of Latin American history: Gabriel García Moreno.

The verdict on García Moreno (1860–75) differs even today, depending on the political views of the person giving it. Catholic and especially Jesuit historians see in him the most important statesman of Latin American history; liberal historians a bigoted monster. The truth lies between these extremes, as he was indeed both. He was attorney for the Jesuit order and tried to prevent their expulsion from Ecuador; in this he enacted a similar rôle to that of Dr. Francia of Paraguay, the avenger of the Jesuits. His solemn conduct and religious zeal made the tall, lean man with the piercing black eyes look like a hypocrite to the liberals; they refused to believe in the alleged conversion the former free-thinker had claimed to have undergone in his youth, and they mercilessly ridiculed his zealot's vituperation of Paris and of French morals which repeated sojourns in Europe made increasingly insufferable to him.

The far too vigorous way in which the dictator protected the rights of the Church by proceeding in a manner which embarrassed even the Pope, looked like hypocrisy to the liberals; the exile Press drew caricatures of the humble manner in which the mighty ruler, lifting his hat, bowed to each priest he met, begging the Father not to answer this greeting. But in fairness to García it must be stated that an anti-clerical attitude often benefited the big liberal speculators and the Army, both of which profited from the wasting of Church property, and that the average liberal leaders did nothing for the native population, which conservative figures such as García firmly protected. For this very reason progressive and socially minded Catholic writers such as the American Richard Pattee put a laurel wreath on the head of this dictator. After fifteen years of office he at length became a victim of his liberal opponents, whom he had handled most cruelly and whose partisans cut him down on the steps of the cathedral at Quito.

If García, as champion of a "Republic of the Heart of Jesus", was practically a priest, the most widely known of the counter-revolutionary dictator type, the Argentine Don Manuel de Rosas (1835–52), was a general, as were most Latin American dictators. But Rosas was not one of those liberal and anti-clerical figures so frequent among the ranking military of those days. Coming from a family of big landowners, Rosas, of impressive appearance and a typical nobleman, grew up among the *gauchos* of the Argentine pampas, where the estates of his clan were located. This gave him the dash of independence and arbitrariness a nobleman needs for playing dictator. A good deal of his success, however, was due to his mother and especially his wife Encarnación Rosas, both of whom were looked at askance by the haughty society of Buenos Aires because of their connection with the *gaucho* leader. They avenged themselves with the cunning and spite of the offended female. The collaboration between men and women in the exercise of this dictatorship anticipated the era of Juan and Eva Perón in the 1940s and early 1950s, almost exactly one hundred years after Rosas.

To find out about the activities of her opponents, the wealthy and commercial circles in the capital, Encarnación Rosas kept check on them through their laundresses and chambermaids. The city poor and especially the employment-seekers were admitted to her boudoir and were used by her to spy on their employers, just as Eva Perón did a century later. Encarnación Rosas handled Press and censorship, and particularly the licensing of marriages. She thus became a power in the capital, as was her husband among the *gauchos* in the country; both, like the Peróns, possessed a sharp instrument in the secret police, the dreaded Mazorca.

The struggle against his liberal opponents, whom he called atheists, made Rosas look towards the Church, which was on cordial terms with his friends, the landowners, and was supported in the provinces. His effort to make the Church, like so many an early Latin American dictator, his obedient instrument exceeded, however, the limits of what was compatible with Catholic doctrine; his image stood upon the altars with incense burning before it, and was carried along in religious processions; he issued his own index of prohibited books and established a special clergy of his own choosing to which he issued orders. His favourite colour, red, was painted on all corners and walls, like the black of Fascism later on. His enemies disappeared in the torture-chambers of the Mazorca; the more important ones, governors of the different provinces, were likewise jailed, in spite of Rosas's posing as the sworn foe of the centralist principles maintained by the liberal Unitarios, and were court-martialled and shot, or murdered. The dictator's final downfall was accelerated, just as was Juan Perón's, by the death of his influential wife, for whom the people, in a general state of mass hysteria, staged, as they did a century later for Eva, a monster funeral. The factor that obstinately undermined his rule, and which Rosas was never able to overcome, was the bitter hostility shown to it by all major foreign Powers. Due to the permanent blockade of Argentina by the French fleet, the port revenues declined; the régime's effort to replace them by increasing taxes made Rosas unpopular. The alliance of a provincial governor threatened by Rosas with the inhabitants of Entrerios province, whose commerce suffered from the blockade, finally led to a general uprising which was also supported by foreign countries. In 1852 the dictator, just as Juan Perón 103 years later, under cover of darkness went on board a foreign man of war anchored in the port and became an exile, ending the most important dictatorship in Argentine history.

Caudillos and Capitalism

The dictatorship of Rosas was transitional and showed how capitalism cemented the power of the *caudillo*. But industrial development here did not come from within, as elsewhere, and as a result no middle class arose. Instead Latin America fell under the rule of foreign adventurers, speculators, bankers, exporters and traders, and became a target for foreign imperialism. Consequently, the social effects of modern economic development in other countries did not become manifest here, capitalism strengthened the might of the individual *caudillos,* but until recently it failed to stimulate the rise of a democratic middle class.

A good example of the way in which the individual dictator was supported by the rise of modern capitalism is the dictatorship of Antonio Guzmán Blanco of Venezuela (1873–88). Guzmán Blanco was the son of a corrupt politician who had been ousted by the conservative *caudillo* Paéz, the best known of Bolívar's generals, and thus had gone over from the conservative into the liberal camp. This interlude determined the further career of father and son even after Paéz's temporary disappearance from the scene. The final outbreak of a grave civil war between the Venezuelan central authority, once more headed by Paéz, and the individual provinces of the country, which fought under the liberal flag, caused Guzmán junior to switch from a diplomatic and political to a military career and to excel as a general in the service of the liberals.

The peace he finally brought about in the civil war made him seem a traitor to fanatic liberals. Guzmán's main aims had certainly little connection with the promotion of the liberal cause. He knew that the party of his foe Paéz had negotiated a loan with the London bank of Baring Brothers, and he saw in his intervention in this affair an opportunity for personal enrichment, and thus for the stabilization of his further career. Made Vice-President by the leader of the liberal federalists, to reward him for his military exploits, he succeeded in being entrusted with the final negotiations on the London loan. His right-hand man in this work was the private secretary of the vanquished Paéz who, when his master began to lose more and more control, told Guzmán about the chances for enrichment presented by the loan deal in return for a promised share of the profits.

The loan led Guzmán Blanco to take over the custody of certain customs agencies under the pretext of having to supervise the prompt payment of interest to Baring Brothers. There was never any accounting of these revenues, which from November 1864 to June 1865 alone amounted to one and a half million dollars. A financier who paid in advance on these revenues and in doing so had cheated the dictator was beaten up in prison by Guzmán's agents until he gave in and handed back what he had stolen to the original thieves. Thenceforward everything moved like magic. Guzmán, the darling of the European stock exchanges, made his country contract heavy debts and profiteered greatly from the commissions he kept for himself according to the amount of the loans. At a later date he stopped payment on the loans and thus betrayed the bondholders.

The influx of foreign capital, however, enabled him, like so many Latin American dictators, to change the face of his country. Guzmán Blanco presented Venezuela with her first railways, he constructed highways and bridges, built mines, assisted agriculture, and tried to transform his capital, Caracas, into a "Little Paris". When his breach with the conservative dictatorship of Paéz involved him in severe conflict with the Church, he replaced the clerical system of education by founding two thousand lay schools. His fight against the Church, though partly due to the bishops' refusal to help raise him to Heaven, in the real sense of the word, led to the attempt to create a National Church which, significantly enough, was based on priests from the ranks of the *mestizos* and Indios. Other measures of this type were his licensing of civil marriages, an improvement in the legal position of the Jews, the secularization of Church property, the dissolution of monasteries and other places of Catholic instruction. His was a policy based on force. Guzmán had no inhibition against confiscating the property of his enemies and in suppressing newspapers, especially if they offended his vanity, which exceeded that of all other dictators of his age—which was saying a lot. That the people knocked down his monuments and statues during the final rising against his rule, when he resided mostly in Paris, almost broke his heart. He died in exile in 1899, eleven years after his downfall.

There was much resemblance between Guzmán Blanco's rule and that of Porfírio Diáz in Mexico; perhaps the most significant and one of the longest dictatorships in Latin American history, it lasted thirty-five years (1876–1911). It was the typical history of a *mestizo* leader, a hard, cold, egocentric, bitter, vain, but very capable military man, with great political gifts, who knew how to make foreign capital serve his political ends and open up the country. Diáz's youth—he was born in 1830—coincided with an age when the creoles all over Latin America were fighting a losing battle with the *mestizos* and coloured people for control. Diáz brought relief to the creoles, but only under the condition that they let him govern unrestrictedly. He achieved much, but his rule was expensive for his country. When he came to power in 1876 Mexico had a total length of 430 miles of railway; at the time of his downfall in 1911 it was 15,336 miles. During the same period Mexico developed a very considerable textile industry from practically nothing; in 1911 there were 146 textile factories employing 33,000 workers. This progress was, however, paid for in misery by the masses. While in his younger days a fighter against foreign tyranny and one of the troop leaders who defeated the Emperor Maximilian of Mexico, later on he became an even worse tyrant, supported by the rule of machines which made the life of the abysmally poor Indios still more miserable than they had made that of the working man in early-Victorian England.

As with Stalin later on, young Diáz had been chosen for the priesthood. To the despair of his clerical tutors he turned his back on the seminary and fought with the liberals against the aims of the Church. Under the presidency of Benito Juárez, the great man of Mexican history and conqueror both of Napoleon III and the latter's *protégé*, the unfortunate Emperor Maximilian, the young general moved steadily into the foreground, though both as a *mestizo* and a military man he resented the rule of a full-blooded Indio, a determined representative of civilian control. An attempt by Porfírio—Diáz was often called by his Christian name—to rise against Juárez failed completely, however; it was only the premature death of the President which enabled him to continue his career of a general playing politics. At the time of the death of Juárez he had fled in priest's garb to an isolated part of the country. The decisive moment came for him under the successor to Juárez, whom he succeeded in removing from the presidency; his rise to power was connected with submissiveness to United States capital, which looked for concessions, and apparently with an understanding with the Church to which he secretly promised cancellation of some reforms it especially resented.

His association with these two powers shaped his entire dictatorship. The "second act" of bourgeois dictatorship was very conspicuous with him; his deliberate policy of reconciling the reactionary forces explains the length of his rule. The influx of foreign capital allowed him to stabilize his tyranny by systematic corruption; recalcitrant generals or high officials received railway, mining, fishing, gambling-casino or other concessions, or were silenced by the handing out of monopolies or large estates. Unconcerned about the final results Porfírio staged a real "sellout" of his country, which made him extremely popular abroad and among the thin stratum of Mexican *mestizos* and landowners, but which caused the poor coloured *peóns* (small farmers) to curse him.

After his downfall in 1911 it turned out that over one billion dollars of the Mexican national wealth, which was then estimated at a total of 2,400,000,000,000 dollars, was in the hands of United States capitalists, while British capitalists held roughly 300,000,000 dollars; taking into account the holdings of some other nations the share of the Mexicans in their own capital was not even one-third of the total. The worst feature was that Porfírio ousted the poor Indios from their common lands, the *ejides*, without any scruples, and in addition deprived them of all land to which they could not show title, which was usual in the case of the illiterate natives. That illiteracy did not vanish was to a great extent due to Porfírio's educational policy, which remained restricted to the execution of the laws abolishing clerical schools promulgated by his predecessor, without replacing them by lay schools. The situation of the poor *peóns,* who were literally put out on the street, was pictured as truly frightening by contemporary observers; these conditions caused the country to develop later into a social-minded republic. Apart from the Church and the landowners, the only class that had profited from this dictatorship was that of the *mestizos,* whom Porfírio deliberately favoured as public servants; they were joined by the "new creoles", the Mexicans of white but non-Spanish descent.

Even Porfírio himself, although he had a heart of stone and the characteristics of an Aztec god, often displayed the traits of an unbalanced *mestizo*. When he received complaints about the results of his actions, he often began to weep profusely, but of course without showing symptoms of repentance in his policy. In general, as it tried to balance social strata with varying coloured skins, Latin America offers an ideal field for sociological research, as long as the mentality of these different groups is not attributed to their "racial" qualities. The individual's connection with one of these strata decided whether he was entitled to certain social or economic privileges, which determined his attitude as a social being.

The figure of Porfírio Diáz, who was finally driven out of the country by his enemies in 1911 and died in exile in Paris in 1914, has made history among twentieth-century Latin American dictatorships. All these dictators, big and small, vied with each other in opening their countries' raw materials to foreign Powers; depending on the production of the nations involved one could speak of oil, rubber, guano, nitrate, sugar or tobacco dictators. A character like Juan Vicente Gómez of Venezuela (1908–35), the dreaded "tyrant of the Andes", connected himself with the Rockefeller oil interests; our contemporaries Anastasio (Tacho) Somoza of Nicaragua (assassinated in 1956), Rafael Leonidas Trujillo of the Dominican Republic and many others made tremendous fortunes like this. All these men based their power on *mestizos* and neo-creoles rather than on the creoles proper, who rarely sought the support of the creoles, who even now look down on them as people not to be trusted.

Part IV

DICTATORSHIP IN THE ERA OF THE WORKING-CLASS MOVEMENTS

Chapter Ten

TOWARDS THE TOTALITARIAN STATE

W ITH the increasing importance of industrial production the social conditions determining the growth and type of dictatorship changed considerably. The rule of the Bonapartes, especially that of Napoleon III, and the prominent Latin American dictatorships of the last hundred years were strongly influenced by the advance of modern machine production, and this is true to a far larger extent of the dictatorships of Communism and Fascism.

Curiously enough this type of dictatorship—usually referred to as "totalitarian"—did not emerge in the Atlantic and Western world, which was the cradle of modern capitalism and industry. They rose instead in countries that were late arrivals in this development and which deflected it according to their social structure. To the surprise of most contemporary sociologists, especially the Marxist ones, the industrial workers whom they expected to be the champions of the revolutionary movement proved on the whole to be the most reliable supporters of the existing form of society and to be outspoken foes of dictatorship in any form, both Fascist and Communist.

While Marx had assumed that the more capitalism developed the more the misery of the workers would increase, which would automatically culminate in a proletarian revolution, in actual fact the workers in the Anglo-Saxon countries, the cradle of modern capitalism, and in many other countries co-operated on an increasing scale with the ruling industrial society. It was evident that the working classes preferred to form trade unions and stage strikes wherever possible, thus winning higher wages and relief from misery, than to wait impassively until the capitalists by creating gigantic modern enterprises involving a disproportionate increase in the output of the means of production started a revolution against themselves. The revolutionary proletarian

movements—anarchist syndicalism and, later on, Communism
—flourished the more strongly the more backward and un-
developed was the capitalism of a given country. The most
important Communist dictatorship rose in a country where
according to Marxist doctrine those movements possessed the
smallest chances of success—while the Communists failed in the
United States, in England and in Germany, to mention only some
of the most important areas which according to Marxist theory
appeared ripe for them.

The United States, England and Western Germany are nowadays the main bulwarks of the democratic and reformist labour
movement. It is true that the old democracies were the only
nations in which the rise of this movement led to no bloodshed
—or very little. In Germany and Italy, where no bourgeois
revolution had taken place to smash the social remnants of
feudalism and absolutism and clear the way for the ascent of the
new classes, the new political order did not gain stability until
after a tremendous and desperate struggle put up by the reactionary strata under the leadership of totalitarian dictators, and
after a second world war in which these powers were overthrown.

This movement led to the strongest possible criticism of the
existing society. The rise of Communism and Fascism was
inaugurated by a revolt in the field of ethics and a rebellion
against traditional political and social doctrines, including the
prevailing religious ideas and principles, which have hardly an
equal in history. Almost all previous dictatorships had maintained the existing ethical and religious traditions, and had interpreted any deviations from the norm as being improvements on
an ethical heritage whose value they recognized. The deliberate
policy of the dictators of the age of the proletarian mass movements to break with these principles created a completely new
situation. They obviously recognized instinctively that the social
aims of their movements were incompatible with the traditional
claims of the Christian Churches to guide ethics and social
behaviour and that their policy called for the application of
means which flatly contradicted Christian ethics. Large-scale
attacks against the Church and its priests had already taken place
in the French Revolution. During the period of Robespierre the
city masses, especially in Paris, had followed the lead of Jacques
Hébert in staging furious onslaughts on the priests for their

support of the ruling classes, which by speculation and black-market deals made food prices soar. However, this movement did not last. Had not Robespierre, who followed the old school in such matters, ended that agitation by force, it would doubtless have subsided automatically after the end of the French monetary inflation and the common misery, since not even Hébert himself had planned to lift atheism to the rank of a new religion.

In the course of the nineteenth century, however, the situation changed rapidly. The victory of the Industrial Revolution, first in England and later on the European continent, and the misery of the international industrial proletariat in that early period of modern capitalism in which the machine ruined the craftsman and the entrepreneur was not confronted with organized Labour, created the impression that the plight of the lowest classes called for a dictatorship from below. The appearance of these new elements invited a new kind of opposition to the ruling classes, and a hostility to Christian methods and ethics that was more than tactical. Social changes of such impact always stimulate new thoughts reflecting the new social interest.

The rise of these new social tendencies encouraged a man like Karl Marx to change from being a Berlin coffee-house littérateur, who gave a radical slant to the ideas of his teacher Hegel, to becoming a critic of society as a whole, and for this purpose to join Ludwig Feuerbach in systematically attacking the Christian religion. At this stage, however, Marx stopped. Despite his theoretical criticism of the Christian religion he never planned to turn his back on Christian ethics and to base his policy on lies, betrayal, deception and deliberate misleading of friends and foes.

While this might be due more to lack of opportunity than to personal merit—Marx would have been the last to yield to moral scruples—it is an historical fact that the freeing of Communist ethics from the last remnants of moral inhibitions was not the work of Marx, but that of men who, unlike him, were engaged in an actual struggle for political control. They were members of the Russian intelligentsia of those years, which means people who by fighting the Tsars tried to give their country the basic constitutional guarantees then enjoyed by the middle classes in most other European countries. Given the political backwardness of Tsarist Russia, this policy involved terrorism, and thus opened the door to violating all rules of political behaviour customary

in civilized areas. One of the leading Russian terrorists of that
age, the pitiless and gloomy Sergej Nechaiev, a fanatic in action
and in suffering pain, and a pupil of the anarchist Michael
Bakunin, followed the principle that everything was permissible
that served a political purpose : falsification of documents, lies,
assassination, betrayal, theft of State secrets, and similar deeds.
The political organization of these men, known as the Will of the
People, murdered the Tsar Alexander II and was about to kill
his son, Alexander III, when it was caught by the police, which
led to the hanging of the planner of the second attempt. The
name of the terrorist executed should be noticed. It was Alexander Ulianov, the brother of Vladimir Ulianov Lenin. Lenin's
ascent to power later on showed what he had learned from Marx
and Nechaiev.

The breach with the Christian religion and its ethics was not
limited exclusively to the radical left wingers of that age, especially European and Russian intelligentsia. The attack of these
elements upon the Churches and the existing order was supported
as well by men on the extreme right wing of the ruling classes,
though of course for exactly the opposite reasons. The rise of
industrial capitalism and its social results not only embittered the
proletarian classes, but also the monarchist circles and aristocratic
landowners, and they even shocked individual members of the
middle classes, making them wish to join the nobility in fighting
social revolution and to erect a dam against the danger from
below. Mistrusting their own class, these men, among them
Nietzsche, signalled the coming disaster by their warnings like
birds fleeing from a hurricane. That Nietzsche, living in Switzerland and unrecognized in his native Germany, gave many of his
thoughts a pro-Western and anti-German shape, must not conceal that his philosophy was basically anti-human, anti-democratic, anti-social, anti-proletarian and super-aristocratic, that is,
basically anti-Western, and that he was very eager to free those
struggling against the city multitudes from scruples and moral
chains likely to hamper them in defeating and suppressing the
masses—especially from the commandments of the Christian
religion. Though Nietzsche, that sworn enemy of the masses,
would probably have wrung his hands in despair if faced with
National Socialism, he cannot escape the verdict that his attack
upon Christianity as a whole—both its dogma and its ethics—

helped pave the way not only for d'Annunzio, but also for
Mussolini, Hitler and especially—Himmler.

Released from any regard for traditional Christian behaviour,
the Communist as well as the Fascist dictators tried every method
to make the masses follow their lead and to render them subservient. In Stalin's Russia just as in Hitler's Germany the day-
dream of General Erich Ludendorff, German commander in the
first world war, described in his book *Total War* materialized :
the unrestricted mobilization of the entire nation in the service of
a leader for whom every period of peace was a continuation of
war with other means. This reversal of Clausewitz's old dictum[1]
was basically offensive both to democracy and Europe's old
ruling society, including even that of Prussia, which clung to its
military tradition and often provoked the impression that the
"totalitarian" dictatorships of the twentieth century represented
something fundamentally new, and without precedent in the
history of dictatorship.

This impression was increased by the political rôle the dictators
of our age used to play : they were no longer revolutionary
troop leaders, as had been so many dictators in the past, but
party heads; their prestige was not based on victories in the field,
but rather on successes in beer-halls and political riots in which
they threw their foes bleeding down the stairs; their original arm
was more the Press and radio than the machine-gun; their
followers consisted, according to the circumstances, of the small
middle classes, the farmers, or the masses of proletarians in the
modern monster cities.

In reality, however, the dictators of the past did not differ
from those of the present to such an extent that would justify
drawing a sharp distinguishing line between them or regarding
the totalitarian dictators as something altogether novel and
unheard of. The distinctions that exist are more of form than
content. The totalitarian dictators merely used a new technique
and new methods for tackling tasks known as well to the earlier
dictators, but not always solved by them. Lenin's Communist
dictatorship, as mass rule set up by a preceding revolution in
socially higher spheres, had forerunners in the dictatorships of
Robespierre and the Paris Commune of 1871, which will be

---

[1] In his classic book *On War*, the Prussian general (died 1832) had coined
the slogan : War is the continuation of politics by other means.

mentioned in the next section. Fascism and its younger but bigger brother, National Socialism, were a modern form of the counter-revolutionary dictatorship, based on broad masses. The notion of party leaders, connected with totalitarian dictators, is misleading. Their so-called parties were not genuine in the sense of parliamentary democracy. They were rather bodies consisting of personal followers of the "Führers", which was true not only of the Fascists but even of Lenin, who by the overwhelming weight of his personality deprived his colleagues of influence. Wherever the totalitarian parties took part in parliamentary routine work they served primarily the personal aims of their leaders as well as doing sabotage; Hitler, in order to emphasize the character of his party as that of a body of personal followers, withdrew the hundred-odd deputies of the Nazi Party who had been elected in 1930 from practical parliamentary work.

The new factors in the totalitarian dictatorships were the use of modernized art and techniques to win the masses, the lack of any scruples in carrying out their aims and in the mass terrorism and scientifically planned *coup d'état*, in which Lenin especially excelled. Their rule was based on certain social classes which hitherto had played a minor rôle. The harshness and maliciousness of the totalitarian leaders expressed sentiments in those classes which had been long subdued, and they succeeded in exploiting old ideas such as pan-Germanism and pan-Slavism, which were either popular with those groups or which by the victories of the dictators received a new meaning. This evolution, however, was the result of a sudden historical development which started during the first world war and which will be analysed below, and not—as some students assume—the result of a special totalitarian spirit which they say was entirely new in history. Incredible as were the forms dictatorship assumed in the totalitarian age, they represented nothing but "new wine in old bottles"—as a comparison of their technique with Aristotle's analysis of tyranny will show.

Chapter Eleven

THE RISE OF COMMUNIST
DICTATORSHIPS

General Background

WHEN Marx and Engels drafted their famous programme of
action in 1847 which was originally only planned to develop
the political philosophy of a small workers' organization called
the Communist League, they felt greatly elated that their pamphlet for this reason bore the title *The Communist Manifesto*,
thus avoiding the term "Socialist". The Germany of that time
was still so far behind the big Western democracies politically
that German Labour could hardly hope to reach its goal without
a thorough revolution of the European state system, and needed
more than merely Socialist reform.

Except in Western and Northern Europe, the Jews shared the
workers' fate of being practically second-rate citizens. Neither in
Central Europe nor in Russia had the Jews received the equal
political rights they enjoyed in the areas affected by the French
Revolution and also in England. In Germany and Russia, only
the collapse of the old political order and the victory of Labour
at the end of World War I finally brought them the desired
equality.

This explains why many Jewish intellectuals were Labour
leaders in Central and Eastern Europe in contrast with the
Western nations, where the Jews rose alongside the middle classes.
Their opinions differed strongly, of course, according to personal,
geographic, social and international peculiarities. A brilliant
speaker and would-be nobleman such as Ferdinand Lassalle, for
example, distinguished himself strongly from that eruptive
volcano, Karl Marx, who through the clouds of tobacco that surrounded him made pitch and sulphur drop on the ruling classes.
In addition, most German and Jewish Socialists of the later
period, satisfied by the achievements of the Weimar Republic,

in turn showed little understanding for their comrades from
the East, who embraced the ideals of Bolshevism. Whether Marx
himself would have endorsed the Bolshevist dictatorship which
was established more than thirty years after his death and which
up to this day claims his political heritage is not quite certain. It
is undeniable, however, that he and Lenin, the founder of the
Bolshevist-Communist dictatorship, shared many personal and
philosophic traits. The boundless hatred with which Marx all
his life attacked monarchist and reactionary Prussia, whose
citizen he had been, anticipated the bitterness with which Lenin
fought against the Tsars.

Differing from the Silesian-born Lassalle, who came from a
province whose non-Catholic elements had welcomed Prussia as
a liberator, Marx grew up in the Rhineland, which during the
French Revolution and the Napoleonic period had enjoyed civic
equality and which did not welcome the Prussian domination. In
the 1840s, the formative period of the young Marx, Prussia met
universal resistance in the Rhineland, backed by industry,
Catholics and workers. An inexorable critic of the ruling classes,
Marx realized that most of his fellow citizens aimed merely at
forcing the Prussian Crown to grant them better conditions. Since
it seemed certain, however, that any understanding with Prussia
would be at the expense of men such as himself, who in old
Prussia had no chance to rise, he hated the social elements that
surrounded him in the Rhineland still more bitterly than even the
Hohenzollern dynasty, and decided to overthrow them by taking
the lead of the proletariat.

His fear of any reconciliation with the upper classes is a trait
he shared with Lenin; both hated all shades of liberalism—
whether in the bourgeois or the Labour camp—still more
emphatically than the reactionaries. This spirit also permeated
all Marx's theoretical works. They expressed his urge to prove
the imminent annihilation of the powers he hated; their tremendous scope displayed the vehemence of his desire. His natural
inclination to interpret the evolution in this sense was accentuated
by the circumstance that he wrote in the early period of machine
capitalism in which it seemed as if the proletariat was heading
for ever-increasing misery. This does not mean that he did not
make discoveries of the greatest scientific importance. Without
his methodical digging into the secrets of modern society, and

without his reversal of the contemporary philosophy of history which regarded man's social existence as the result of spiritual forces, modern sociology would not exist. But in formulating the immanent laws of this evolution, which he analysed in the thick volumes of his work *Das Kapital*, he was bound under these conditions to fail; the real development of capitalism moved largely in the opposite direction from what he had assumed; the more strongly the system rose, the weaker became the tendency towards a proletarian revolution.[1] It is true that Marx, in spite of this firm belief in the final collapse of the capitalist class, differed from his most famous pupil, Lenin, inasmuch as he did not possess a clear picture of the envisaged "dictatorship of the proletariat". Even though individual events, particularly in the so-called Paris Commune of 1871, looked to him like forecasts of the new social order of which he dreamed, he and Engels did not yet think their age was advanced enough to produce the general upheaval; in addition, his life in his London exile prevented him from being as familiar with the actual technique of revolution as were the contemporary terrorists in Russia, who lived in an atmosphere of murderous attempts against individuals and society.

The overestimation by Marx—and later Lenin—of the Paris Commune as a proletarian uprising was due to the rôle the Paris workers played during its decisive battles and also to the fact that the most important political party of the Commune, the "radical Republicans", was surrounded by Socialist factions, comprising members of Marx's First International. In reality, the uprising of the Commune—a word which referred to the city community— was prompted less by the attitude of the Paris labourers than by that of the shopkeepers, craftsmen, employees and other *petit bourgeois* elements who during the German siege of Paris in 1870–71 and the resultant holding up of business life had accumulated debts, and who, with the conclusion of peace in sight, were exposed without any public protection to the pressure of their creditors. The refusal of the Paris population to dissolve the National Guard it had formed and to hand over its arms to

[1] The well-known neo-Marxist view that the impoverishment of the proletariat forecast by Marx was temporarily postponed by imperialist expansion is true with strict limitations only, and does not explain the development in a series of capitalist countries; in some instances, such as the evolution of the U.S.A., it at least fails to cover the complete picture.

the public authorities, who showed no consideration for its plight, led to a mass attack of the "defenders of property and order" upon these poor tormented people which finally culminated in the atrocious slaughter during the first week of May 1871, which took the lives of about 20,000 "Communards".

In spite of his belief that a proletarian revolution had to start in the capitalist West, Marx in his last years was very much impressed by the consolidation of Western capitalism and the growing number of acts of terrorism in Russia. Both slightly modified his views and made him admit that a peasant revolution in Russia might be in the offing, to form the prelude to the proletarian uprising in the West.

Rise of Lenin

For Lenin, the most successful follower of Marx, the hope of this revolution in the East was the goal of his entire career. In this respect Lenin followed in the footsteps of the Russian intelligentsia of his time. The fate of the Russian intelligentsia was determined by the rôle of the middle class, which in Russia, still more than in Germany, was a late-comer and a misfit. Weak since its inception and lacking the kind of support the commercial and industrial development of Western Europe gave the Western bourgeoisie, the wealthy upper middle class was in doubt whether to be more afraid of Tsarism, which refused it all the rights which the middle classes of other countries possessed, or of the revolutionary agitators who began to stir up the peasants and workers against the existing order. The growing misery of the Russian peasant, a result of the "liberation of the peasants" by Tsar Alexander II, was reversed by aristocratic pressure, and gave the crisis of Russian society its special edge. This being so, the Russian intellectuals had no choice but to carry out their struggle against the Tsars at their own risk and in opposition to the middle class, to which they belonged socially. In this respect their situation resembled that of the radical wing of the Jewish intelligentsia in Germany, which aimed at an absolute political equality with the upper classes, and among which men like Marx were conspicuous. In Russia, however, the industrial proletariat was at that time, the end of the nineteenth century, still so insignificant and feeble that the Russian intellectuals could not yet marshal its forces in the service of their political aims. The Socialist opinions of the leading Russian revolutionary thinkers of those years, such as Alexander Herzen, reflected chiefly the sentiments of an intelligentsia infuriated by the cowardice of the bourgeoisie, and did not yet originate in deep revolutionary planning. The Will of the People, the terrorist organization that was the political instrument of the anarchist Michael Bakunin and his pupil Nechaiev imprisoned by the Tsars, thought that Socialism would not yet work in an area as backward as Russia, and for the time being the revolutionaries should concentrate on bringing about a division of the big landed estates and on winning the general political rights which the Western countries had established many years earlier. In 1879, however, a small group of intellectuals under the leadership of George Plechanov left this organization and emigrated to Western Europe, since it rejected terrorist methods. While in Europe, this group became familiar with the ideas of Marx, which fully corresponded to its plan of bringing about the revolution in a natural non-terrorist way. In consequence it founded a small unit for spreading Marxism in its country in 1883.

The young Vladimir Ulianov, later known by his pen-name of Lenin, was born on April 22nd, 1870, in Simbirsk on the Volga. He was the son of a fairly well-to-do school inspector, and was deeply impressed by the tragedy of the hanging of his brother Alexander. This made Vladimir an easy target for anarchist and terrorist influence. Being a member of the younger generation, however, he lived in an age when many a young revolutionary wanted more than terrorist liberalism disguised as anarchism in which his brother had been involved. It was just at this time that group Marxism began to spread through Russia, due to the work of Plechanov. As early as 1889 the young Ulianov, just nineteen years old, founded a small Marxist group at Samara. At the time he was studying law and was under suspicion for his political activities. He had little success in his professional career and for most of his life existed on his mother's money. In the beginning of the 1890s he transferred his activities to St. Petersburg (now Leningrad) and before long led the local Marxist movement. A journey abroad brought him into personal contact with Plechanov himself, who spent most of his time at Geneva, and at the end of the same year that he went to Switzerland Lenin was arrested working on the first Marxist newspaper in St. Petersburg.

Unlike Plechanov and his circle, somewhat forbidding and professorial, whose emigration had originally been an escape from internal Russian problems which they did not consider ripe for Socialist intervention, Ulianov-Lenin envisaged the preparation of revolution from the outset. A medium-sized, tenacious and stubborn man, who was occasionally on the verge of a nervous breakdown, Lenin had a reddish, pointed beard, protruding cheeks, squinting eyes and a somewhat insulting smile which indicated possible Kirghiz or Kalmuk descent. He impressed everyone who knew him as a person of the highest mental capacity, gifted with a will of steel, who did not reject terrorism as such, but planned to limit its use according to his political needs. Lenin's ethical concepts were shaped by the terrorist utilitarianism of the super-Machiavellist Nechaiev. Lenin deemed everything possible that helped him attain his goal. The difference between him and the Bakunin form of terrorism was mainly that he tried to give the revolutionary and terrorist action a broad, carefully considered class basis, and to strike only after he could reasonably expect a mass upheaval. The scrupulousness of his policy and his rigorous rejection of any compromise with the ruling classes, including liberals of all shades, distinguished him, on the other hand, from the Plechanovists—later called Mensheviks—who aimed at a real and not mere working-class democracy. His inflexible refusal to compromise in any way with the upper class, including the ruling stratum of the working class, had in Lenin's case, as in that of Marx, a pathological slant, obviously reflecting the terrible experience of his youth when his brother had been hanged.

It was Lenin's great good fortune to live in an age when a man with this mentality could hope to succeed. If the events of 1914 to 1917 had not worked in his favour he would have remained the stubborn eccentric and insufferable dogmatic he appeared to most of his contemporaries. Before the first world war, his career was a series of political moves which were ethically questionable and dishonest acts which lost him many valuable friends. The career of Stalin shows a similar phase. Lenin's nervous energy was taxed by these constant quarrels with those near him and he had to seek relief by escaping to Nature; during his lengthy and not disagreeable exile which followed his arrest in 1895 he became a hunter and wandered in the endless tundras of that vast region as well as an expert skater; when during the party struggles at the beginning of the twentieth century he faced a nervous breakdown he was only saved by several months of hiking, in company with his wife Krupskaya, in the mountains of Switzerland. Lenin's exile in Siberia in the last years of the nineteenth century came at a time when the industrial proletariat, which in the time of Marx and Engels was very wretched, had already risen from the bottom, thus putting the Labour movement under the influence of the trade union revisionist. In the more advanced industrial nations such as England, and especially Germany, where the Socialist Eduard Bernstein became the spokesman of the movement, this evolution led to almost a collaboration between the working class and the very powerful industrial imperialism of those years; in Russia, in turn, the ideas of the time were reflected by Economism, the theory of rightist Socialists who tried to limit the workers' movement to the economic field and improve its position within the framework of the existing economic order.

Lenin was a sworn enemy of this trend, as it deprived him of the spoils of his struggle, the destruction of Tsarism. He opposed it the more strongly as a man of his calibre had more difficulty than other people to maintain his position against opposition. As Hitler saw when imprisoned in Landsberg, Lenin watched with disgust political competitors trying to replace him as head of the movement while he was absent in Siberia. This continued even after he returned to the scene in 1900. For a professional revolutionary such as he was, his release from Siberia was merely an exchange of exile inside his country for exile abroad. From his Siberian period he was known by the most popular of his pen-names, Lenin, derived from the Siberian river Lena. Despite the esteem shown to him because of his qualities of leadership and mastery of logic, Lenin had to fight right up to the 1917 revolution against political competitors who attempted to oust him and his organizations, especially the newspapers which he directed and which were smuggled into Russia from his place of exile.

The struggle had no political boundaries; but it was particularly bitter among the Russian émigrés, where the paper Iskra

(The Spark) which Lenin had founded and edited finally slipped from his grasp. The struggle for actual control of the Russian Social Democratic Party was closely allied to it. During the party rally of 1903 which began in Brussels and was transferred to London, Lenin received an insignificant and accidental majority which in no way reflected the real views of the Russian workers. From then onwards, these "majority members" (Bolsheviks) and "minority workers" (Mensheviks), originally led by Martov (Zederbaum) faced each other as deadly enemies; from this split the history of Lenin's Bolshevik Party begins. This party was later called the Communist Party. The foes who scolded Lenin bitterly for aiming at dictatorship over his paper, and even at dictatorship over Labour instead of dictatorship of Labour, were met merely with his haughty and somewhat scornful smile. A true pupil of the revolutionaries of the nineteenth century, he could not understand how anyone could think of a revolution without training a group of professional intellectual revolutionaries; in this respect as well as in being free of all traditional ethical inhibitions, he was much more a pupil of Russian terrorists than of Marx.

Even though Lenin was a magnificent leader, a highly qualified organizer of the lowest strata of the huge Tsarist empire, and a passionate spokesman for the many Russian-controlled nationalities, in order to be successful he had to await the virtual collapse of the existing form of society, which could only be brought about by a war. Without the defeats of Russia in the Russo-Japanese War (1904–05) and in the first world war, the establishment of the Communist dictatorship in 1917 would have been as unthinkable as, for instance, the rule of Robespierre and his Jacobins without the mortal threat to Girondist-controlled France by the European monarchs of his time. It is this complete dependence on the start of a crisis in the upper strata or on the loss of a war, or on both, that distinguishes the dictatorships of the lowest classes from the bourgeois type and the counter-revolutionary dictatorships.

Cromwell and Napoleon, generals of a victorious revolutionary movement, could go about quite openly and could make arrangements to remould their movements according to their aims in full publicity without fear of being disturbed. Robespierre and especially Lenin, working in the cellar of society, were frequently forced to hide themselves and watch for straws in the wind to show when the time was ripe for their undertakings. Such precautions had been particularly necessary for Lenin, as he was not protected by parliamentary immunity as had been Robespierre. Lenin was a master of concealing his game, and even after the start of the revolutionary movement in Russia following the Japanese victories in 1904–05 rarely appeared in Russia in person, and then only under the strictest security precautions. The comparison between him and Robespierre comes from those years, and was made by Plechanov and Leon Trotsky, an eager reader of Lenin's *Iskra*, and one of the agents of its vast network, who had come to see Lenin in exile. In spite of his high self-esteem, his tendency to contradict people, and his rather Menshevist political philosophy, Trotsky was destined to join the master in playing a leading rôle in the Bolshevist revolution.

The development of the revolutionary movement in Russia in 1905–06 proved clearly, however, that even high-class revolutionary leaders cannot accomplish their tasks unless supported by external circumstances. While the defeat in the Far East had strongly damaged the prestige of Tsarism, it had failed to shake Russian society to the same extent as the first world war did later. Leaving aside the chronically bad situation of the Russian peasants, the Russian economic situation could not yet be called critical. Most troops remained faithful to the Government. The first bloody clash between the Russian proletarians and the Tsar was the work of a loyal Labour leader and Tsarist stool-pigeon, the priest Gapon, who had been misled by conflicting backstage influences about the Government's true intentions. The much more serious revolts in the autumn of that year, in which a Soviet, or workers' parliament, appeared for the first time in St. Petersburg in order to direct a general strike, failed because of lack of organization and discipline due to the passive attitude of the peasants, and, finally, because the revolutionary propaganda within the ranks of the Tsarist Army was still insufficient. In those months Lenin always tried to check the other leftist parties, especially the Mensheviks, who sought a political compromise, as well as the Social Revolutionaries, a new party which continued in part Bakunin's terrorist group the Will of the People, and vied with the Socialists in trying to capture the support of the peasants. But Lenin's relentless attitude did not as yet match the situation, indeed his furious attacks on the moderate Socialists, including even Plechanov, whom until then he had succeeded in keeping in line, were rather a boon to the Tsarist Government, and were used by it for holding in check the moderate Socialist as well as the bourgeois parties which tried to lead Tsarism along parliamentary lines. The Tsarist secret police was under orders not to disturb Lenin's meetings at that time.

Was this a mere coincidence? We know that to Lenin everything which served to promote his aims seemed permissible. In order to beat the despised Mensheviks, he, for instance, distributed pamphlets deliberately distorting the truth, defending this action with the argument that the end justified the means. When after the failure of the first revolution his party ran short of money, he organized well-known raids upon bank trucks in which he was helped by young Joseph Stalin. Such a man, when he found it expedient, could indeed at times co-operate with the police. It is certain that the leading party positions were for many years in the hands of a certain Roman Malinovsky, whom Lenin clearly knew was in the service of the Tsar's secret police. As far as Stalin is concerned, a photograph exists of an authentic document which shows that he was for a certain time at least in the service of the secret police, possibly for the purpose of shortening one of his numerous prison terms by handing over to the authorities the names of some of his many competitors vying for political control in his native Georgia.

The fanaticism with which Lenin fought any idea of a compromise with the Mensheviks or bourgeois parties also permeates his political and scientific writings. Of limited interest as to their theoretical value, they show shrewd realism in the evaluation of everything which might be politically useful to their author. A man such as he had little in common with other Labour leaders of that age. During the congress of the Second International at Stuttgart in 1907 or Copenhagen in 1910 he was hardly visible, except during the sessions of the Russian section, in which he stood alone in his opinions. For the development of the Western workers' movements and their compromises with capitalism and imperialism he had the utmost contempt. His despair about the other Socialist parties' attitude on the outbreak of World War I inspired, among others, his study *Imperialism—the Last Stage of Capitalism*—in which he hinted, misinterpreting the facts, that the rapid growth of Western monopoly capitalism and of the Western "Labour aristocracies" would culminate in a general proletarian revolution. When the revolution finally came, it succeeded only in countries in which monopoly capitalism was far behind and very backward; otherwise he could never have become a dictator.

The October Revolution

Lenin's thesis that World War I had to be transformed into an international civil war to establish the dictatorship of the proletariat was not even endorsed by members of his own Bolshevik Party before the Russian Revolution of 1917. They were professional revolutionaries, many of whom had become soldiers of the cause because of the persecution of the Jewish intelligentsia in Tsarist Russia, and while they agreed with Lenin's desire to put an end to the ruling classes, most of them refused to join him in threatening the Jewish middle class to which so many of them belonged. In this respect there was only a small difference between the Mensheviks proper and the intellectuals in Lenin's camp who in their eagerness to speed up revolution had chosen the way of force. Of the later leading Bolsheviks, only Zinoviev agreed entirely with Lenin, and was therefore often called Sancho Panza in party circles.

Even when Lenin, angry at the support given by the Socialist parties to their governments during World War I, called a conference of leftist Socialists close to him in the village of Zimmerwald in Switzerland for the purpose of replacing the Second International with a third one from the belligerent countries, he had hardly any success even within his own camp. The majority of the Zimmerwald conference flatly rejected his proposition to transform the first world war into an international civil war, and in this way the plan of founding a new workers' International on this political basis failed as well. Were world history guided by the formation of democratic majorities, Lenin, who usually met with resistance from his own followers, would hardly have achieved much.

However, as in the case of so many dictators, the outward conditions suddenly changed in a way which enabled a man of this type to succeed. Viewed in the light of the time, his sudden meteoric rise appeared to have been due to his superior intellect,

which for years had made meticulous plans for taking over the
Government. There was some truth in this view. The fact that
the Russian working classes saw in him the man to lead them out
of their misery was indeed due to his patient clandestine work in
the preceding decades, to his establishing a network of agents,
and especially to the underground papers he issued in which he,
with never-failing patience, acumen, and clarity of thought,
hammered away at the crumbling edifice of Tsarist Russia. In
this respect a man of his kind, who by both his appearance and
conduct seemed to have come from the Turkish and Tartar
elements which under Genghis Khan and his successors ruled
over the Russian steppes, was no doubt far superior to the
other members of his movement. But without the final outbreak
of the long-hoped-for political and social crisis in Russia—for
which he was hardly responsible—he would have remained the
dreaded queer character, insufferable alike to his foes and most
of his friends.

Fortunately for him, the Russian Revolution of March 1917,
which finally led to his rise, proved to be much more serious than
the first one. Unleashed by the anger of the middle classes and
elements of the nobility about the indecision, corruption and
incapacity of the Tsarist régime to fight the first world war, it
at once revealed the strong dissatisfaction of the broad masses
which had been stirred up by price rises, hunger and the general
plight of the Russian economy which had been cut off from the
West. The so-called Provisional Government, which after the
abdication of the Tsar in March 1917 came to power in Russia,
was a political instrument of the Russian bourgeoisie which
resembled the cabinets formed in revolutionary France by the
Gironde, and it tried, just like them, to wage an energetic war
against its country's enemy, Germany. During the outbreak of the
revolution, Lenin was living in Switzerland; he was assigned by
Fate the rôle of Robespierre, the enemy of the bourgeoisie and
leader of the lower classes, whose example he was known to
adore. Just as Robespierre, Lenin fought against his nation's
participation in the war, which in his eyes served only the interests of the bourgeoisie, and not those of the workmen and
peasants. The difference between revolutionary France and revolutionary Russia was that while France had been surrounded by
one single belt of enemies, the opponents of revolutionary Russia

were divided into two camps, Germany and Austria, with which
she fought openly, and the Triple Entente, led by Britain and
France, Russia's former allies in that war, who threatened her
with reprisals in case she concluded peace with the common
enemy.

Lenin was a sworn foe of any kind of reconciliation with the
ruling classes of his country, and even while in Switzerland
vehemently denounced any thought of joining the Western allies
in continuing the struggle against Imperial Germany. Instead,
he accepted an offer of the Imperial German Government to
take him and his friends in a sealed railway carriage through
Germany to Sweden and thus to Russia. Upon his arrival there,
he contemptuously rejected all efforts of the new Russian rulers
to use him for their own political purposes. His intransigent attitude alienated many followers of his own camp, Bolsheviks as
well as Mensheviks. Not a few Bolsheviks of Jewish and bourgeois descent, seeing their fondest dreams fulfilled by the downfall of the hated Tsar, displayed some desire to continue the war
against Imperial Germany together with the Western democracies. Their ranks were joined originally by Joseph Stalin, who
had just returned from one of his numerous periods of exile in
Siberia, and who, before Lenin arrived, believed that this policy
would offer a man like him a short cut to a leading political rôle.
Lenin realized, however, with great satisfaction, that his own
attitude, if it did not please the intellectuals and their sympathizers, was wholeheartedly accepted by the anonymous masses of
the labourers and peasants and of the soldiers, who were tired of
the war. It was a moment when the psychological experience and
conduct of the leader and the masses suddenly coincided. This
happens in all true dictatorships, when the leader appears as the
chosen spokesman of the masses. The sympathy of the Petrograd[1]
masses for Lenin's policy went so far that they upset his plans by
premature mass actions, thus giving the Provisional Government
the pretext for proceeding against the leading Bolsheviks, which
forced Lenin to flee to Finland.

In this difficult situation for himself and his party, Lenin
received invaluable help through the political activity of Leon

---

[1] The name of St. Petersburg, being German, was changed to Petrograd in
1914 on the outbreak of war with Germany. The city was later named
Leningrad in honour of the Communist leader.

Trotsky. Ugly and much needing the attentions of a barber, slightly taller than most other Bolshevik leaders and of great bodily strength, Trotsky, like most other Bolshevik leaders, concealed his real name (Bronstein) behind a revolutionary cover. He was almost the only one among these men besides Lenin who was aiming not only at a leading but a principal rôle. A Menshevik or conservative Bolshevik rather than a radical, and a typical member of the Jewish intelligentsia, he was illegally arrested and detained in Great Britain while returning from exile and saw with dismay the most important positions controlled by the Mensheviks and their friends being given to his rivals. In midsummer 1917 he openly joined the Bolsheviks and soon became indispensable to Lenin. His value to the party was mainly his influence on the local Petrograd Soviet, an assembly of the capital's lowest classes, which Trotsky had already directed during the first Russian Revolution and which in 1917 was originally mainly under the control of the Mensheviks and their allies, the Social Revolutionaries. The existence of these Soviets had the same fundamental importance for Lenin and his Bolsheviks as the Commune had for the Jacobins and Robespierre. It was a revolutionary municipality which they used at a battering-ram for staging their *putsch* from below.

In transforming the Petrograd Soviet into an instrument of Bolshevism and a weapon against the Provisional Government as well as in preparing the entire revolt, Lenin and Trotsky were helped by three special conditions. Firstly, the war-weariness of the masses; secondly, the incredible mistakes of the Provisional Government, especially in internal politics, where it was controlled by anti-Socialist industrialists and other middle-class politicians; and, thirdly, because the Tsarist reaction, to prevent the Provisional Government, under its moderate Socialist leader Alexander Kerensky from veering to the left, staged a military *coup* led by General Kornilov, a counter-revolutionary. This last event was decisive. Counter-revolutionary dictatorships, except when terminating a dying revolution, almost always fail. This promotes a radical revolution from below.

In the history of Lenin the *putsch* undertaken by Kornilov, who was forced to surrender within a few days, played exactly the same rôle as the unsuccessful plot of General Dumouriez against the radical revolution in Paris in the career of Robespierre.

The collapse of the *coup* deprived Lenin's chief opponent, Kerensky, of his main instrument of power, on which he was forced to rely even when struggling with its leader, and he was thus exposed without sufficient military cover to the pressure of the Bolshevik masses. Worse still, the danger of counter-revolution caused the Petrograd as well as the Moscow Soviet, formerly controlled by Lenin's opponents, suddenly to join the Bolshevik camp: the ascent of Leon Trotsky to be president of the Petrograd Soviet and the way in which he used that office decided things in favour of Lenin. The news of the advance of the Germans, then still the enemy of the country, in the direction of Riga and even further, caused Lenin to fear he was lost if he did not stage his *coup d'état* with the same energy with which Robespierre had destroyed the Gironde, and thus counteracting the threatened co-operation of Dumouriez with the advancing Austrian and Prussian armies. The customary resistance in his party was silenced by the usual verbal clashes with his party members, although even his faithful Zinoviev joined his critics on this occasion. Supported by the Soviet military guards commanded by Trotsky, by armed workers' units, revolutionary parts of the Petrograd garrison, and the navy at Kronstadt, the Bolshevik leaders assumed power without bloodshed or special trouble on November 6th, 1917. Kerensky fled, and the other members of the Government surrendered. From its place in the old Russian calendar (October 24th), the event is known in history as the October Revolution.

The Kaiser's Pyrrhic Peace

The ascent to power by the Bolsheviks gave the signal for one of the most thorough revolutions of human society known in history. The new Government's directions about the seizure of the banks, the industrial enterprises, and the landed property merely legalized a situation which in the first years looked very much like anarchy and which led to the total destruction of the existing order. Members of the former ruling classes who did not emigrate and proved themselves acceptable to the new rulers tried to secure for themselves a position in the officer corps of the rapidly growing bureaucracy, which in most cases was only possible after the lapse of a few years; immediately after the revolution, and especially during the civil war which followed it, the system of terrorism against all beneficiaries of the former régime prevailed without restriction. Lenin himself, although he was not concerned with the details of this enormous change, had neither the time nor the intention to stop his followers, but considered their actions essential to his system and its attack against the former ruling classes and their foreign friends. His time was more than fully occupied with the task of preventing the badly damaged Russian State, surrounded by enemies, from drowning in the mire of his movement.

His most important problem was how to make peace with Germany and her allies, so as to protect the new order in the former Tsarist empire against outside intervention. The way he tackled this task was most unusual. In radio broadcasts, directed "to everybody", Lenin and Trotsky invited the whole world to stop the war. Though Germany showed no intention of making concessions, the Soviet Government worked ardently to undermine the fighting spirit and military morale of its own armies. Lenin's propaganda among his own soldiers was practically a military betrayal; he left it to the Germans to determine the price they expected for granting the Russians peace unilaterally. The peace conditions of the Imperial German Government, presented to the Soviet peace delegation under Trotsky and Joffe in January 1918 at Brest-Litovsk, were of such a kind as to amaze even the most ardent pacifists among the Bolsheviks. The customary discussions within the party became more bitter than ever.

Led by Trotsky, men like Bukharin, Uritzky, Joffe, Krestinsky and Lomov fought against the German conditions to the very last moment, when Germany, through her spokesman, General Max Hoffmann, presented the Soviet Cabinet with an ultimatum, which Lenin proposed to meet with merely a passive attitude. Members of the Jewish intelligentsia who were practically in the bourgeois camp were evidently satisfied by what the Revolution had achieved up to that time and were ready to join the Western democracies in fighting German militarism, as its representatives in Brest-Litovsk showed marked indications of anti-Semitism. But as usual, this wave broke when it hit the rock-like will of the leader, who had but one goal : to prevent the planned course of his proletarian revolution from being deflected by military adventures. Lenin knew that, viewed from this angle, he had merely to see that the centres of the Russian Revolution, Petrograd and Moscow, did not fall into German hands. That the Germans, despite the imminent peace in the East, had to continue fighting in the West was a sufficient guarantee for him that the peace conditions imposed on the Soviets at Brest-Litovsk were hardly worth the paper on which they were written. What mattered to him was to obtain a breathing spell for Russia and thus to free his hands for the proposed mental undermining of the whole German nation. By signing this treaty he achieved both goals. The peace treaty he finally concluded with the Germans at Brest-Litovsk in March 1918, while outwardly bringing the Germany of William II tremendous gains, was in fact for the Kaiser a Pyrrhic peace, whose results helped to destroy his rule. The final outcome became visible after only a few weeks, when the armies of occupation which the Germans were forced to leave in the East for securing their new conquests were absent from the West when they started their big offensive. Still worse for them was that the peace treaty permitted Lenin during the very months when the Central Powers began to collapse to spread his ideas and agents all over Central Eurpoe, where they helped to bury German imperal rule

The Dictatorship of the Proletariat

For Lenin the collapse of the Central Powers simplified the political situation very much and caused him to play the part of Robespierre to an increasing extent. In place of two different groups of enemies, the Soviets faced one single political camp, and at least in the West had their hands free. As the Soviets' struggle for self-preservation was directed against the Entente Powers from thenceforward, it assumed in the eyes of Lenin's followers an increasingly defensive shape, and helped him to strike at his internal foes who secretly sympathized with the Entente nations. The feeling that they no longer fought for imperialist interests but for the defence of their revolutionary achievements made the lower classes, although they had refused to continue the world war, bear the terrible burden imposed on them by the civil war which immediately followed the Lenin revolution.

Just as with Robespierre, the civil war gave Lenin's Government the decisive prestige among the broad masses needed for carrying through its task and for fighting the upper classes. Given the complete stoppage of industrial production and the resultant depreciation of the currency, Lenin was obliged to ensure the supplying of the most important Russian cities by forcibly requisitioning food and by spoiling the country. Though he tried hard to support these confiscatory expeditions by stirring up the poor peasant against the wealthy, the peasantry as a whole was not favourably inclined towards the Bolsheviks. During the elections for the Constitutional Assembly which Lenin considered a farce but which, since he had endorsed them, he could not stop, the Bolsheviks were completely eclipsed by the Social Revolutionaries as representatives of the peasantry. The start of the civil war and the encirclement of the country by a series of counter-revolutionary generals who threatened to deprive the peasants of their lands brought a temporary political turn towards the Bolshevist side; and when, after the end of the civil war, the peasants started to react against the eternal confiscations and to revolt against the régime, it had become too late. Meanwhile Lenin had gained a decisive advantage in timing and had used it for building up his system of revolutionary terrorism which was to form one of the strongest foundations of Communist rule.

The father of the revolutionary terror was Felix Dzershinski, a lean, thin-lipped Pole with a goatee, who came from a wealthy family, but had embraced the Socialist cause and had spent a great part of his life in prisons and in Siberia. A cold, dutiful bureaucrat of death, Dzershinski had much in common with the attorney-general of the French Revolution, Fouquier-Tinville, with Napoleon's cold but fanatic minister of police Joseph Fouché, a former commissioner of the Convention famous for his staging of massacres, and with the director of Hitler's Gestapo, the dreaded Heinrich Himmler. The nuclear units of the "Extraordinary Commission" (Cheka), as the revolutionary State police was originally called, consisted of non-Russians or half-Russians, especially a detachment of sharpshooters from Latvia, of Chinese, Polish or Ukrainian Jews, and even a few Germans and French. Their ranks were increased by class deserters from the former ruling strata in Russia, who like all renegades served their new masters with especial zeal.

Established in the spacious premises of the former Russian Insurance Agency on Lubianka Street in Moscow, given to it after the Government had been transferred there from Petrograd, the Cheka and its successors, the O.G.P.U., N.K.V.D. and M.V.D., formed a special political body with their own clubs and administrative offices, newspapers and special code of honour. Before long the name "Lubianka Street" gained a special meaning, comparable to Prinz Albrecht Strasse in Berlin, where Himmler's secret police was located. The routine killing of prisoners used to take place in the basement of that building in Lubianka Street by revolver shots in the head from behind, usually on Tuesdays. In addition to these official acts there was the mass terrorism which reached a certain climax after the assassination in August 1918 of the dreaded local chief of police in Petrograd, Uritzky, and the shots fired some weeks later by Dora Kaplan, of the Social Revolutionary Party, at Lenin himself. These tremendous waves of political and often personal revenge enabled sadists and perverts who like to join such movements to satisfy their personal desires. This explains some of the many reports of the burning, crucifying and boiling or burying alive of political prisoners, or the sinking of entire ship loads of captives in unseaworthy vessels—acts that recall certain features of Jacobin terrorism.

The institution of the Cheka and the general terrorism allowed Lenin to make his will felt unrestrictedly and to direct the Government in a way which practically amounted to dictatorship. What was called the Soviet Constitution—the product of the crossing of the Communist aims with the workers' soviets— did not restrict the dictatorship in any way. The all-Russian Soviet hardly ever met and had no chance to interfere in any sphere with the decisions made by Lenin and the other ministers —people's commissars, as they were then called—of the Union.

But the increasing power of the Cheka had considerable disadvantages for the régime. Although they were still kept under some control during Lenin's lifetime by his mere prestige, they very soon displayed a marked tendency to become autonomous and influencing the Administration decisively once he disappeared from the scene. Their only serious but not equally powerful rival in the imminent struggle for power was the Red Army. In February 1918, when it was founded, the Red Army was planned to be an *élite* troop consisting of hired soldiers from the old Tsarist Army and of young workers, but already in

August 1918 the position of the Soviet Union in the civil war had become so dangerous that, instead, a mass army based on conscription was formed and put under the command of the former Tsarist officers, under the supervision of Soviet commissars, of course.

The participation of the broad masses in the civil war put its stamp on the Soviet dictatorship for the future, made its sharp centralism popular, and gave the population the strong determination to defend the achievements of the revolution, a conviction which did not even vanish after the "beleaguered fortress" of Lenin's first years had become the mightiest State on the European continent, whose policy determined the actions of all other nations.

None of this was foreseeable in 1918. Lack of foodstuffs, starvation, the stoppage of production, anarchy, lawlessness, and the attacks, backed by the European Western Powers, of anti-Bolshevik generals from the north, the east and the south made the situation of the Soviet Union wellnigh desperate. Then Lenin's work was saved overnight by the collapse of the Central Powers. The downfall of Germany and her allies in the autumn of that year freed Lenin in the west and south-west from a neighbour who, in spite of the peace signed at Brest-Litovsk, had remained a foe, to all intents and purposes, and it also demoralized the military units of the Western Powers which helped his enemies in the civil war. With Germany and her allies beaten, these units saw no reason why they should still fight on to keep Russia in the anti-German camp and demanded to be sent home. Left without Western assistance, the Russian counter-revolutionary generals lacked the strength to carry on. In addition to this, the peasants mistrusted them, since they feared that the restoration of Tsarism might deprive them of their land. In the beginning of 1920 the danger was over for Lenin, and the Red Army even felt strong enough to start an offensive against Poland, which, however, was a failure.

From the end of 1920 the balance of power in Europe was re-established and remained so for a decade and a half, until the rise of Hitler endangered it once more. This development, measured by the yardstick of Lenin's aims, was most disappointing for the Soviet dictatorship. All his life Lenin had firmly believed in the outbreak of an international revolution which would at the same time give the Russian revolution the much-needed international protection. The left wing of the participants in the Zimmerwald conference was merely awaiting his signal to give the ruling classes a mortal blow in the various belligerent countries. But apart from the Soviet Union itself, there were hardly any countries whose social structure favoured such a trend. Central Europe and particularly Germany, in which Lenin had great hopes, proved immune to a large-scale proletarian revolution, in spite of the loss of the first world war. The mighty development of heavy industry in Germany did not stimulate a rebellion, as Lenin had expected, but rather the evolution of trade unionism, which was strictly opposed to it, thus matching Germany's conservative political outlook, which was determined by the existence of a strong lower middle class and land-owning peasantry. Wherever the French Revolution had brought about a liberation of the peasants from the bonds of feudalism—and that was the case in all Western and Central Europe—the peasantry, unlike that of Russia, stood in the conservative camp. The temporary aversion of many German peasants to the existing order, especially in South Germany, disappeared with the termination of the system of price controls and food requisitioning introduced during the war. Under these conditions the hopes for a general Communist revolution in Germany were futile, and the same was true for most other countries. The Communist efforts to exploit the German revolution of November 1918, by staging a kind of German "October Revolution" the following year in the style of Lenin, were foiled without very much trouble. A Communist revolution of a more serious kind which developed at the same time in Hungary also failed owing to the opposition of the victorious Allied Powers, especially the kingdom of Rumania, which had no intention of tolerating the emergence of Communism in its defeated neighbour. After the Rumanians had put down the revolution with armed force they supported the establishment of a counter-revolutionary dictatorship under Admiral Horthy.

After the end of 1919 the great moment for staging a Communist world revolution and building international proletarian dictatorships of the Moscow brand was gone. From the point of view of the new Russian Soviet State it might have been better to renounce this political programme based on imagination rather than a realistic appraisal of the international situation, which was bound to create enemies for Lenin's State even among Powers that would have been willing to co-operate with it. But the idea of world revolution had long since become a standard item in the Communist political inventory. In March 1919 there was created in Moscow the Third International, whose aim was to unleash the world dictatorship of the proletariat but under the circumstances often produced the opposite effect: a terrible confusion in the Labour camp, including even the local Communist parties, consternation among Russia's political friends, and a series of victories of international political reaction. The great rift which existed between the foreign policy of the Soviet Union, chief director of the Third International, and the genuine interests of the Communists and other leftists in the different countries involved, was by its very nature too deep to be bridged over. This made the history of the Third International, abbreviated to "Comintern", very problematic.

Just as in his international policy, in the end Lenin had to yield to realities to a certain extent, and thus lead his country in the opposite direction from the one he had wanted. The socialization of his country's economy that he had planned was dependent on the existence of well-functioning individual enterprises. The existing industrial plants, however, had been so badly damaged during the war, by the lack of experts and raw materials, the impossibility of complete repair, and especially through being directed by untrained men from Labour circles, that they not only made no profit but also impeded the customary exchange of industrial goods for agricultural products. This forced the Soviets to proceed to a systematic spoliation of the rural districts by military units ordered to requisition food, and thus automatically created the danger of a counter-revolution. Immediately after the termination of the civil war the despair of the peasantry about this situation led to the terrible uprising of the garrison of the fortress of Kronstadt, which was a result of this discontent, and which forced Lenin to wage a military counter-move that endangered his entire programme. Lenin succeeded in mastering the crisis. He was stronger than Robespierre, who possessed no firm class basis and whose corrupt agents, co-operating with the black marketeers, put an end to his rule when it was threatened by similar dangers. But Lenin's effort to go to the roots of the evil and to bring temporary relief to the suffering peasants drove him away from the goal he had set himself. The temporary relaxing of the Socialist economy, the New Economic Policy, (N.E.P.) was practically equivalent to an abandonment of his basic idea, at least temporarily. Lenin was stricken by illness in 1922, and at the time of his death in 1924 handed over to his successor Stalin a political establishment surrounded by capitalist nations, and which, to a large extent, had re-erected capitalism even within its own territory, and not a Socialist country surrounded by a group of similar nations. In contrast to the "dying State" of which the Marxist doctrine had spoken, this structure carried perhaps the strongest State the contemporary world possessed, and instead of symbolizing the dictatorship of the proletariat, the State machinery became an ideal instrument of a primarily personal tyranny.

Chapter Twelve

TOTAL COUNTER-REVOLUTION: FASCIST AND NATIONAL-SOCIALIST DICTATORSHIPS

The New Elite

FEW dictatorships have proclaimed their revolutionary nature more emphatically than have Fascism and National Socialism. In reality, however, these systems were essentially modernized issues of counter-revolution, that is, dictatorships of anti-revolutionary leaders, who, different from most other representatives of this type, sought the support of the broad masses and who, to the chagrin of the older counter-revolutionary strata, made those masses the principal beneficiaries of their political struggles. This definition explains the limitations in time and space to which this type of dictatorship is subject. In contrast to the revolutionary movements previously pictured here, counter-revolution down to modern times lacked the broad popular mass basis. Hard pressed by burghers and peasants, the upper social strata, nobility and monarchy, lacked sufficient protection against the common man in the fury of a revolution. This isolation mattered little as long as the nobleman sat in his castle and fought in armour on horseback as he did in the Middle Ages. But with the approach of modern times, with their mass armies, firearms, big cities and large-scale revolts, his situation became precarious. The only way which remained open to him was to divide his foes politically and geographically, not always easy to do.

In the West, the cradle of modern democracy, the chances for forming counter-revolutionary mass movements were small. In Germany and Italy they were better, though they emerged rather late. Due to the tardy development of industry and the age-long political division of these areas, with their wealth of dwarfish principalities and states, both countries possessed a social structure which in itself favoured a development of this kind. Under the influence of the depression of the 1870s and 1880s—the worst of its type before that of the late 1920s and 1930s—both Germany and, incidentally, Austria-Hungary indeed produced some sporadic reactionary and lower-middle-class movements, with an anti-Semitic programme. But the rule of the monarchies in those countries which resented any competition in the leading reactionary strata prevented the anti-Semitic leaders of those days— the Court preacher Stöcker in Berlin or von Schönerer and Mayor Lueger of Vienna in Austria—from anticipating Hitler and Mussolini and their rôles, and the participation of all the big European Powers in the imperialist race soon absorbed whatever unemployment there was, depriving those movements of their followers. Italy at that time lived on her tourist trade and migratory labour that sought work in foreign countries, and during those years she did not even see the beginnings of such a movement. All these phenomena postponed the chance of the growth of reactionary mass movements, but not permanently. Their hour came after the first world war, through the ending of imperialist expansion and the growing plight of those countries, which caused grave social disturbances.

The evolution after the first world war was of decisive importance for the formation of non-Communist European dictatorships. Without the tremendous shock of those years—the German revolution of 1918, its aftermath, and the proletarian movements in Italy which culminated in the occupation of the industrial plants by the workers in September 1920—neither Fascism nor National Socialism would have come to life. This does not mean that there was even a nucleus of truth in the well-known contention of Mussolini and Hitler to have saved their countries from Communism. These oft-repeated allegations lacked any real foundation, both as far as the immediate after-war period and the depression of 1929 are concerned. In 1920, when the Italian workers seized the plants, Mussolini's still diminutive Fascist group had hardly taken any political action, and Hitler during the decisive months of 1918 and 1919 was nothing but an unknown little corporal who was used for reporting on local political groups by the Munich sections of the German Army, which had been dissolved. It was not their alleged achievements in fighting Communism that gave the political organizations of both men their later weight, but the inherent social dynamics of those movements, which gained momentum in a period that favoured mass actions.

Instead of the old social *élites* of the past which had become too small, thin and fragile to stem the tide of this century, there emerged a new anti-revolutionary but much broader society under the direction of those leaders. It might be termed an ersatz *élite*, detesting the lower classes, but at the same time competing politically with the earlier *élites* and viewed by them with the utmost suspicion. In the framework of this ersatz *élite* the lower middle class played an outstanding rôle, at least in the chief formative period. The German and Italian lower middle classes stood at the end of a long tradition which made them ripe for their rôle. They were different from those in Great Britain, where a lower middle class in the Continental sense hardly existed, as well as France, where it boasted of its revolutionary tradition, and finally from Russia, where its nucleus had been suffocated by Bolshevism. "The small middle class", Karl Marx had already written seventy years before Hitler, in his classical sketches of the German revolution of 1848 published in the *New York Tribune*, "is especially numerous in Germany, due to the meagre development of the classes of the big capitalists and industrialists in that country. In the big cities it forms almost the majority of the population, in the small ones it prevails absolutely. . . . Its intermediary position between the class of the major capitalists, merchants and industrialists, the bourgeoisie proper, and the proletarian class determines the character of this stream; it aims at the position of the former, but the smallest mishap throws the individuals of this class down into the ranks of the latter. In monarchic and feudal countries the small middle class needs the patronage of the court and the aristocracy for its existence; the loss of this patronage can ruin most of it. In the small towns the welfare of the smaller middle class is very often dependent on a garrison, a district government, a district court. To take away these institutions would mean ruin to the small merchants, the tailors, the shoemakers, the carpenters. Consequently, they constantly waver between their hope of entering the ranks of the ruling class and the fear of being pressed down into those of the proletariat and even of the paupers, between the hope of promoting their interests by gaining a share in directing public affairs, and concern at provoking by their ill-considered opposition the ire of a government which determines their existence, since it is able to deprive them of their best customers. Small are the means they own, and the insecurity of their property increases in inverse proportion to its size. In its political opinions this class is most fickle. Humble and hypocritical under a strong feudal and monarchic government, it turns towards liberalism when the bourgeoisie is rising : it is seized by violent democratic paroxysms as soon as the bourgeoisie has assumed control, but is a victim of the most pitiful timidity if the class below it, the proletariat, dares to make an independent move."

Since the days when Marx wrote this, the situation of the small middle classes both in Germany and Italy had changed decisively. The political unification of both countries and the growing administrative centralization, especially in Germany during the Weimar period, deprived those classes of the patronage of the many courts and established local authorities; with the rise of modern capitalism, of the textile and shoe industries, and the departmental stores on the other hand, pushed the craftsman and small shopkeeper into a corner; the growing might of the workers in turn threatened their former social privileges and made them the more bitter, the more rapidly they declined economically. For some time these feelings were mitigated because members of these declining classes found employment as "white collar workers" in the offices of the new industrial monster firms. But the crisis of the postwar period and especially the slump of 1929 stopped this and led to the simultaneous collapse of the old and new lower middle classes, particularly in Germany. The impact of this sudden disaster made the lower middle classes only too eager to listen to the propaganda of the political figures who at that time started to cater for them and woo them. The Christian Churches—the only serious competitors of Hitler and Mussolini in trying to gain the sympathy of these classes—found it difficult to keep them in their control unless the dictator, such as Mussolini in Italy, made them some concessions, as he needed the Churches for political reasons.

The ersatz *élite* was even broader than the lower middle classes proper in Germany as in Italy. After 1918 it started to aim for the position of the old ruling classes and ultimately tried to re-place them completely. In both countries the Fascist movement in its beginnings was composed of people from the ranks of the young non-commissioned officers of the first world war who were unfit to become civilians, and by stray intellectuals and students. In Italy as early as 1922 this group was joined by unemployed from the rural districts who had been deprived of their livelihood by the anti-immigration laws brought into force at that time in the United States and other countries. In Germany after 1929 the unemployed eventually became an essential element in the Fascist movement: to them must be added the medium and small peasants, who had been ruined by the depression; all these people with their families gained such importance in the end that when Hitler came to power they almost obscured the original lower-middle-class nucleus of his party.

Origins of the Fascist and Nazi Weltanschauung

Since the time of the French Revolution the European aristocratic society, which had still been so lively and optimistic in the eighteenth century, had been sunk in a deep pessimism, particularly in countries like Germany, which, unlike France, were still anticipating the coming of their revolution. This pessimism was the more deeply rooted in Germany since it corresponded to traits in the German character which connected the Germany of that period with the world of ancient Germanic demons and gods: the interest in the unknown and unknowable, the mental relationship of the fighting hero with the hereafter and the world of eternal night, the spirit which Thomas Mann characterized as "sympathy with death" in one of his early political writings and which he found expressed in the symbols of the cross and the tomb. The presentiment of imminent disaster, the conviction that they were doomed to succumb, without any hope of avoiding it, to the new society of money power, democratic freedom, equality and fraternity—ideals to which only lip-service was paid—inspired the nobility with melancholic pride.

Not everyone in this political camp, however, was prepared to renounce all future existence and accept being buried alive. Instead of taking opium, as did Thomas de Quincey, or collapsing with a bottle of absinthe in his hands, like Baudelaire, some partisans of the aristocratic cause deemed it more worthy to perish in open fight, arms in hand. Friedrich Nietzsche, the super-conservative scion of six generations of Protestant ministers on both sides, had absorbed aristocratic ideals to such an extent that he found the capitulation of the so-called decadence before the imminent storm flatly shameful. Others, as for instance Richard Wagner, in whom plebeian traits, human baseness and tremendous artistic gifts were combined in the strangest fashion, dreamed of the services of a saviour they could render to the old world that was decaying.

Wagner was about one hundred years ahead of his time politically. His career and much of his philosophy anticipated the development of the German lower-middle-class society that in his time was still connected with the upper strata, but which later, after the first world war, played an autonomous rôle and became an ersatz *élite*. Richard Wagner was the scion, it seems, of an illicit connection between an energetic and talented actor, Ludwig Geyer, and the illegitimate daughter of a Weimar prince who had married the Dresden director of police, Wagner. He suffered from the feeling that his mother did not love him and of being unwelcome to her. All his life he longed for the love and understanding of a woman, half mother, half beloved, and of princely station. In *The Flying Dutchman* he expected his salvation from a woman of that type; in *Tannhäuser* he even tried to enforce his salvation through a person of that kind and, if refused, threatens to become a kind of rebel; in the *Lohengrin* drama the hero changes from an object into a subject of Grace whose messianic mission, however, is foiled by a sinister intrigue of the aristocracy, which plots against him. All these ideas are taken from mythology, but Wagner transformed them into symbols of his own weird fate, of his hatred of the Paris of the 1840s, which had refused to open its doors to the little German conductor, then unknown, of his misery and his futile efforts to get rid of his eternal debts, of his longing for the royal German courts which he hoped would help him to erect the theatre of the future he planned and thoroughly to reform the entire opera, and of his desperate struggle against monarchs and bureaucrats who kept their pockets closed to him.

In his feeling of superiority to those above and below him, Wagner anticipated many of the features characteristic of Germany after 1933 in his life and creations. During the worst troubles of the revolution of 1848 he breathlessly appeared on a public platform, warned his audience of the dangers of Communism and—an unwanted saviour—suggested that the King of

Saxony, whom he served as conductor of the orchestra, should be made hereditary president of the Saxon Republic. His conduct during that year—in the pre-Hitler period erroneously considered democratic by most observers—had in reality much in common with the attitude of both Mussolini and Hitler, the later leaders of the ersatz *élite*, who, like Wagner himself, tried to force their services of saviour upon upper classes unwilling to accept them.

By his innumerable political writings and letters we are very well informed about his development. The *Tetralogy*—a series of four musical dramas—*The Ring of the Nibelung*, which revolves around the figure of Siegfried, is basically a symbol of Wagner's ill-fated efforts to make the reluctant German upper classes serve him and his vast schemes of artistic "reform", and thus to bring about their "salvation". The leitmotives of the frustrated seeker after salvation bemoaning his fate (The *Dutchman* and *Tannhäuser*) and the disappointed heroic bringer of Grace (*Lohengrin* and *Siegfried*) are interconnected in Wagner's own thought and even in reality with his memorable relations with the Bavarian king, Ludwig II, who saved the maestro from terrible misery, finally to become his victim both mentally and politically. Wagner, who at first saw his "Parsifal", that is his saviour, in the young king, before long realized the latter's own mental isolation and thus changed from the rôle of bemoaning Tristan of the third act or of Amfortas crying for help to that of a believer in his own *Parsifal* mission, the "pure-hearted fool" of his last great creation who is aware of the faults of the ruling Christian society and thus is able to cure them through "regeneration"—the infusion of new blood.

Beneath the Christian veneer under which this work was concealed, contemporaries failed to see the main meaning of this stage consecration drama, as it was called. In reality the drama is totally un-Christian and even anti-Christian, since it shows that Christ's blood, contained in the Holy Grail, has lost its magic power that "saves" the aristocratic stratum, unless it be regenerated by a new saviour who is thus apparently stronger than Christ Himself. Viewed in the light of Wagner's development, the *Parsifal* drama which aroused Hitler's enthusiasm must be regarded as the symbol of the rise of an ersatz *élite* which believes in its magic superiority over the old Christian society. In the Wagnerian thought it had a sacred character. As the drama that consecrated the Bayreuth stage, it was to be performed only there, in the temple Wagner had erected for it, and by those chosen for presenting it, who were in part connected with very personal experiences with the mission of the "saviour" of the German nation and culture. Among them especially was his mistress and later wife Cosima, the very gifted daughter of the great pianist Franz Liszt from his connection with the Countess d'Agoult, and wife of his friend and admirer, the conductor Hans von Bülow. Cosima was tall, basically ugly, a stranger in Germany, of illegitimate birth, but eager to compensate for these defects by serving Wagner and helping to create the new German cultural *élite*, even at the risk of her good reputation.

The anti-democratic and anti-Semitic traits of political Wagnerism, which under Cosima's influence became the more conspicuous as time went on, were accentuated after Wagner's death by the activities of Houston Stewart Chamberlain, an Englishman educated in France and a severe neurasthenic—he finally became totally paralysed. In his psychopathological hatred of his own country he became the apostle of super-pan-Germanism and put his talent as a writer into Cosima's service; his work *The Foundations of the Nineteenth Century* transformed Wagner's political doctrines into proper racial ideology. It is true that at the close of the 1890s, when this work was published, monarchy in Germany was still on solid ground, and this restricted the activity of the pan-Germanist ersatz *élite*, that applauded Chamberlain's ideas with glee. As distinguished from the Nazis later on, the pan-Germanists of the imperial era consisted chiefly of geographers, engineers, intellectuals, bureaucrats and other middle-class colonialists, who found Imperial Germany too moderate and lacking energy.

The main epoch of political Wagnerism came after the end of the first world war, and especially after 1929, through the rise of Fascism and particularly of National Socialism; it of course in itself did not prevent the older forms of the ersatz *élite* and its ideas from living on. Along with National Socialism and the older, more bourgeois pan-Germanism, there still blossomed the school of Nietzsche, more proud, hard, anti-pacifist and hostile to the masses than the old nobility, but for this very same reason also opposed to political Wagnerism, as being too mass-minded and plebeian. Curiously enough, it was not a political Wagnerian but mental scion of Nietzsche, the Italian poet and author Gabriele d'Annunzio, who helped the birth of Fascism.

The Beginning of Fascism in Italy: Gabriele d'Annunzio

Although contemptuous of the masses, like Nietzsche, d'Annunzio possessed more of the qualities for leading an ersatz *élite* than most of his contemporaries, which for a time almost forced him to play the mass leader. A tiny, almost girlish creature of somewhat dubious noble descent, he tried all his life to excel as a Hercules, super-aristocrat, snob, dandy and military hero, and to present his exploits in literary form. Whether he, still a schoolboy, appeared in the most fashionable restaurants, ordering for instance lemon ice cream with caviare; whether still at a tender age, he started scandalous relations with the most eagerly wooed daughters and married women of the high aristocracy who finally rushed upon him in swarms; whether dressed by Europe's best tailors, whom he always forgot to pay, he exposed his super-polished shoes, his derby and his bald head with the little pointed beard in parliamentary sessions, to cause incidents there; whether living in the Villa Capponcina near Florence with the great actress Eleonora Duse, he employed eighteen servants and filled his mansion to the brim with objects of exotic luxury; or whether, sick of this peaceful super-debauchery, excelled in the war as an officer, speed-boat commander, aviator, and chief propagandist, his life always followed the same line : to create sensations by performing unheard-of tricks in all fields of human life, to arouse in this way the admiration of the crowd and the women—especially those of noble birth—to present his experiences in literary form, and thus to make partial payments to the most stubborn of his creditors.

Before the first world war he had to flee to France because of his debts, and there he maintained his usual style by living with a Roman marchesa, a famous equestrian, on a handsome estate on the Côte d'Argent. This made him the principal figure in the efforts of France and the other foes of Germany and Austria-Hungary to lure Italy into the Allied camp after the outbreak of war and make her fight her former political friends. The mass agitation for driving Italy into the war, known as Interventionism, which was sponsored by the Allies and their political partisans and seized all Italy, appealed to the liberal and democratic traditions and sentiments of the Italian bourgeoisie. But at the same time it caused the rise of a middle-class militarism which in the future could also be used for anti-liberal and anti-progressive aims, depending on the circumstances. The interventionist propaganda thus gained great importance in the history of the movement that later became Fascism. Two radical interventionist leaders, d'Annunzio and Benito Mussolini, a renegade from the Socialist camp who had joined the interventionist cause, transformed the social remnants of Interventionism into the social nucleus of the Fascist movement. In this way, just as they had done when bringing about Italy's entry into the war, they forced the reluctant monarchy and its cabinets as well as the aristocracy and the conservative wing of the middle classes to accept their will or their rule. The students, intellectuals, the newspapers fed by French money, and the bourgeois and lower middle class mass organizations which agitated for Italy's entry into the war in 1915, furnished the foundations of the movement which, after the signature of the Versailles Treaty, developed under the leadership of d'Annunzio and Mussolini into an ersatz *élite* hostile to the working class, and was reorganized and absorbed the old ruling class.

D'Annunzio at first outranked his rival in competing for the leadership of this class, due to two advantages which were later to become hindrances : his enormous popularity among the intellectuals and that he was no Socialist. From the sociological angle his activity is the exact counterpart of the propaganda of the pan-Germanists in the North, who likewise based their might on a bourgeois ersatz *élite*. Before 1918 Europe was more imperialist than Socialist. It was only after the first world war that agitation among the working class became the main task of a leader of this kind, and this decided the final victory of Mussolini. D'Annunzio was too much a littérateur and aesthetic to wage a full-fledged fight for power with his rival.

The climax of the political activity of d'Annunzio was reached in 1919, when the victorious Allies denied Italy the right of keeping the city of Fiume she had occupied. This inspired the Italians with the same bitterness as the Versailles treaty the Germans. Encouraged by the officers of an Italian detachment which shared the command of the city with the English and French troops, pending the decision whether it was to be given to Italy or Yugoslavia, the poet and politician marched at the head of three hundred men upon Fiume[1] and amidst the jubilation of the populace established a political dictatorship there, while the foreign troops looked on without interest. The youth of the Italian middle class, and the demobilized officers who resented going back into civilian life, the high school and university students, and small employees and technical assistants whose plants suffered from the strikes of the workers, saw in the fate of Fiume their own cause. *Giovanezza* (youth) became the battle-cry of Fascist Italy, which was born on the main square of Fiume in front of the city hall. From the balcony of this building overlooking the little square the ageing poet, whose bald head resembled that of Caesar more and more, harangued the masses night after night to fight the ideals of the Western world. D'Annunzio's knowledge of antiquity, his keen sense of the dramatic, of music and rhythm, set the pace for the Fascist movement, its pulsating and flexible technique, its reviving of the ancient battle-cry *"Eia eia allala"*, its theatrical way of obeying the leader and its carefully practised collective yells, and also the way in which it treated its foes, particularly the manner of exposing them to ridicule.

The mass of his followers—a mixture of demobilized soldiers, *arditi* (hotspurs), legionnaires, *bersaglieri*, grenadiers, and even armed Amazons, littérateurs and artists—had, it is true, only a faint resemblance to ancient Greek or Roman heroes. The blockade of the harbour of Fiume by the Allies, who resented d'Annunzio's *coup*, led to a tremendous rise in prices, a black market, organized smuggling, prostitution of both sexes and to a systematic spoliation of the city by the followers of d'Annunzio and a chain of crimes which introduced the era of European Fascism in a fitting manner. A snobbish super-aristocrat rather than a mass leader, d'Annunzio possessed neither the political nor the economic knowledge the situation required. Being mainly a comedian and a poet, he was much less interested in political success than in a dramatic ending of the tragi-comedy he had staged, which was not slow in coming. His refusal to evacuate the city forced the Italian Government, after signing an international

---

[1] Since the cession of Fiume to Yugoslavia after the second world war, it has been known as Rijeka, its Croatian name. Both Fiume and Rijeka mean the same thing—river

agreement on the future of Fiume, to expel him by gunfire from Italian warships, which killed fifteen of his followers and from which he only narrowly escaped himself. A melodramatic funeral ceremony followed, during which d'Annunzio, weeping profusely, kissed the coffin of each of the victims. The dead were buried soon after in the park of his estate near Salo on Lake Garda, the property of a daughter of Richard Wagner confiscated during the war, where he sought refuge from the hardships of his political career and "consumed" pretty women on the assembly line. . . . Near the tomb, guarded by a sentry, stood the deck of the torpedo boat *Puglia*, which he had commanded for some time and from whose deck gun a shot was fired every day at noon at his orders.

The Rise of Mussolini

The collapse of d'Annunzio's Fiume adventure brought the leadership of the rising Fascist movement automatically into the hands of his rival Mussolini, twenty years younger than he was. Mussolini had helped him with his Fiume venture in a rather dubious way; he was accused in public of using part of the funds collected for Fiume for the publicity of his own group, the *fasci di combattimento*, then still small and founded in the spring of 1919. As well as this, d'Annunzio's supporters bitterly accused Mussolini of having concluded a secret agreement with the Cabinet of the Italian Prime Minister Giolitti, in which he abandoned d'Annunzio's cause in return for political and presumably financial support. If true, this would be the first of the frequent cases where middle class and conservative elements were attracted to the Fascists, as their supposed saviours, to regret it later most deeply.

Mussolini was the right man for the part he was to play. A scion of Romagna, that once Byzantine area at the calf of the Italian boot where Girolamo Riario, Cesare Borgia, and many smaller Renaissance tyrants had ruled—he grew up in a time when Socialism in Italy and also in other Latin countries still showed revolutionary and anarchist traits. The weaker the development of heavy industry and trade unionism, the more emphatic is the trend towards self-help. Benito's father, a smith in the hamlet of Predappio and an ardent Socialist, had at an early stage of his life been imprisoned several years for having been associated with Michael Bakunin, the father of Anarchism, and even the young Benito, unbending, pugnacious and unmanageable but also insidious and terribly vindictive, was something of an anarchist. As a fight to a finish against the ruling society, Anarchism usually flourished best in backward countries with an absolutist régime, where the modern proletariat was still underdeveloped, such as in the areas which later succumbed to Communism. In the case of the Mussolinis, father and son, in spite of their emphatic Socialism they were both *petit bourgeois* rather than proletarians, which made Benito especially suitable to lead an ersatz *élite*; one of his biographers, Monelli, has entitled his work about him "the *petit bourgeois* Mussolini."

Having become *Il Duce,* Mussolini often emphasized the great impression made on him at the Salesian convent where he was brought up, as the boys ate their meals in three different groups, according to their means. "Such an experience", Mussolini used to add, "makes you a Socialist." It was an error. Treatment of that kind hardly makes a Socialist, but rather a Fascist, a man who acts less from love of the working class than from envy of the upper class, and tries to raise himself to their level. Few social movements have emphasized their revolutionary character more strongly than have the Fascists and National Socialists, and revolutionary conditions and enormous energy were needed to make the ruling classes yield to the ersatz *élite*. Yet the Fascist goal was not the starting but the control of the much-discussed proletarian revolution, that is, not a rebellion proper, but the replacement of the ruling society by a new antirevolutionary stratum which by its excesses far outdid the original one.

This endeavour to play the master constitutes the very nature of Fascism, its leaders and faults. The leaders of Fascism rose because their individual development preceded and anticipated that of the ersatz *élite* in time and intensity; their entire life was a series of efforts either to blackmail or to serve the upper classes slavishly—nobility, middle classes and bureaucracy—depending on the circumstances, and to prove their power to the workers. Mussolini followed the footsteps of his father and was a Marxist Socialist until his thirty-second year; in his case the inborn traits of his nature remained outwardly concealed, but in the light of later development they appeared rather early.

The violent, uncanny, fanatic young man with the big coal-black eyes who wielded a knife became a teacher in primary schools and was dreaded for his tyranny. Before long he fled to Switzerland to escape military service like many of his country-men. While there, not unlike Richard Wagner in Paris and Hitler in Vienna, he experienced a sudden decline from a *petit bourgeois* existence to the very bottom of society and with few interruptions spent almost two years as a vagrant, beggar or wandering propagandist. During this time he received the first few of his fifteen prison sentences, which were for vagrancy and political misdemeanours. The period was formative for his sub-sequent career. The descriptions we have of it are largely based on his own stories and bring to mind certain passages in Hitler's *Mein Kampf*. Among them is the story of his vain efforts to earn his daily bread by working as a mason; like Hitler he was chased away with disdain since his fellow workers found him too spoiled and his dress too gentlemanly. From thenceforward he was com-pletely dominated by his feeling of shame for his decline and his desire to force the ruling classes to pay more respect to him and his deeds, no matter what the price. His experiences during those years also caused his subsequent fanatic hatred of the British : the sight of the overdressed British travellers who love to visit Switzerland and Italy proved to him, the former school teacher, that he had declined almost to the ranks of the begging *lazzaroni*, a discovery which almost crushed him.

Between 1904, the end of his unhappiest period, and the start of his career as an independent political leader ten years elapsed, which he spent in furious agitation for the Socialist Party, for which he fought like an incensed bull confronted by the prover-bial red rag. At the time of the Italian occupation of Tripoli in 1911 he became the centre of public attention by organizing war-resistance and acts of sabotage all over the country, and once more was sent to jail. The decisive turn in his life came at the end of 1914, when the Italian party proclaimed complete neutrality in the war, while he himself, editor-in-chief of its most important newspaper *Avanti*, and apparently a furious anti-militarist, sud-denly turned round to become a warmonger. It later turned out that this obvious class treason, which resulted in his immediate expulsion from his party, was inspired by the secret activity of French agents, who offered him money to found a paper of his own—the *Popolo d'Italia*—to support the cause of the Western Allies. But it would be an exaggeration to ascribe his big change of front exclusively to the effects of French money. As he was already the chief editor of the mightiest Socialist paper, Mussolini lacked neither means nor political influence. The decisive factor was that he, the violent bull with the *petit bourgeois* background, had all the time regarded violence as one of the instruments for exhibiting his power in the eyes of his country, especially its ruling classes, and thus to amalgamate with them. That the Western Powers for whose cause he fought stood for the preservation of democracy, while Germany and Austria-Hungary, the targets of his warmongering, represented the cause of the monarchies, could increase his illusion of continuing to defend Socialism even though he had broken with the Socialist Party.

After the war, when the ruling classes had no more use for his services, he indeed played the unswerving Socialist once more. The Fascist programme of 1919 exceeded even the Communist platform in its political radicalism. This attitude, however, had mainly the result of raising Mussolini's political price. The hour for his movement came after the failure of the proletarian occupation of the factories in 1920, when the Italian postwar crisis led to the formation of an Italian ersatz *élite*. The mass protests and lamentations of the demobilized officers, veterans, lower middle classes and unemployed, especially in the rural areas, who were all sinking into misery, suddenly gave the voice of Mussolini the force of a loud-speaker, after he had been alone in his views for many years.

Even then he still tried to postpone the final decision in the struggle between Socialism and Fascism. In July 1921 he concluded a written agreement with the Socialists to prevent further bloodshed and prepare for mutual toleration. Evidently he, the former Socialist, began to mistrust his own political friends. But he could not rid himself of the pressure of the social forces he had joined when expelled from the Socialist Party. The less since his *squadri d'azione*, the shock troops of the Fascist movement, had destroyed not less than 120 centres, raided 234 Socialist Party meeting places, killed 202 workers and wounded over 1,000 in the five months preceding the political armistice, and were eager to continue in this way. Prior to their famous "March on Rome" in 1922, the Fascists altogether burned down 500 workers' meeting places and dissolved 900 Socialist political meetings by force, mostly under the protection granted by the State authorities to the "well-disposed" Fascist Party.

In other words the movement had become so strong that even its leader could no longer stop it. Under the prompting and cursing of his lieutenants such as Grandi, Farinacci, Tamburini, Bastianini, Arpinati, Misuri and Caradonna, who used to rule their districts like feudal lords, the weakest traits in the character of *Il Duce* and the Fascist movement emerged—the desire to please and the eagerness for public applause. This is very conspicuous in Mussolini's photographs of the 1920s and 1930s, which display his satisfaction that he, the former penniless schoolboy, had succeeded in conquering his much-desired seat at the opulent table of human pleasures as a result of his violent political measures.

This "Socialism" was misnamed "Fascist political philosophy", as it served the personal aims of its chief propagandist above everything else. He never tired of presenting himself to his fellow men as a universal genius and sportsman, who sacrificed all his former ideals to this urge. The main *motif* of his nature was not strength, but human weakness, which explains the miserable end of this idol of many contemporaries when it finally fell from its stand. The over-emphasized brutality of this *petit bourgeois* playing Caesar, with the protruding chin and self-satisfied expression, did not indicate real vigour, but a fanatic determination to remain at the top of his movement even if it meant abandoning every ideal he once worshipped.

That Mussolini would have to empty the cup of self-humiliation to the last drop was due, among other things, to the general economic depression of 1921, which provoked great unrest in Northern Italy. This caused the big landowners and leaders of heavy industry to urge the leader of Fascism with threats and promises to proceed against the lower classes. To accentuate their demands, the big landowners openly supported Mussolini's most dreaded competitor with his party, the bold demagogue Dino Grandi, who terrorized the Po valley at the head of bands of unemployed and who helped the landowners to hold in check their starving rural workers, driven desperate by the monetary inflation. Mussolini, cornered, was forced to drive out the Devil with Beelzebub. At the Party Congress in Rome at the end of

1921, he checkmated Grandi by deliberately outbidding the latter's anti-Socialist policy, and thus simultaneously gained the support of the industrialists, whose cause he had begun to sponsor since 1920; among his financial backers were Commendatore de Benedetti and Ugo de Cocogni of the Turin Industrial League (*Lega Industriale de Torino*); the directors Benni and Gino Olivetti of the general industrial federation (*Confederazione Generale dell'Industria*); Director Mazzini of the machine and accessories producers' association (*Associazione fra Industriali Meccanici ed Affini*), and many others.

After the decisive swing against the leftists, Mussolini's Blackshirts made rapid progress, especially in small rural places, where they appeared in motor trucks in the middle of the night, and with the help of the local landowners, dragged the leader of the rural labourers out of his bed, stripped and tortured him, and finally abandoned him chained to a tree along the highway, unless they preferred to kill him outright. Mussolini's revolutionary past and his connection with the futurists and other modern artists gave his struggle a certain ironical and humorous colour, which lent it deceptive humanitarian traits. The Fascist election propaganda originally resembled an expressionist carnival, and the mass infusions of castor oil with which the enemies of Fascism were temporarily put out of action concealed the bloody terrorism of the stylishly bearded sadists such as Italo Balbo and Dino Grandi, whose hair style and mode of dress set the fashion in the Fascist movement, to the chagrin of the Duce, who was almost bald. The struggle was not only directed against the Socialists, but even more against the Popolari, the Catholic reformist party, which under the leadership of the far-sighted and energetic Don Luigi Sturzo opposed the drift towards dictatorship, just as the German Centre Party opposed Hitler in 1933. The Catholic reformist party was finally outsmarted and cast aside by a direct understanding between the Vatican and the dictator, who temporarily played the rôle of protector of Christianity. In doing so Mussolini—as had d'Annunzio—played the heir of ancient Rome. His increasing intimacy with the Roman Church, which he tried to make a servant of his world-wide aims by concluding a concordat with the Pope in 1929, and the organizational structure of his shock troops (*squadri*), which meticulously copied the Roman legions, were for him symbols of his position of Roman emperor.

From the beginning of 1921 the weakness of the State authorities to the Fascists led to outright revolts, for instance in Ferrara, where Italo Balbo did a thorough piece of work, in Trento, Fiume and all Tuscany. The Fascists were not victors everywhere. In Parma the workers resisted them in a bloody battle, and during an attack on Sarzana Mussolini's men lost twenty dead, whom they promptly celebrated as martyrs. In proportion to their opponents, the Fascists were much weaker than the National Socialists to their opponents even until they seized power and afterwards; in the spring of 1921, when Italy's last pre-Fascist elections took place, 141 Marxist deputies (including 20 Communists), 107 Popolari and only 35 Fascists entered Parliament. The lack of unity on the left, the country's weariness of labour troubles and especially the benevolent attitude of both the Vatican and industry finally brought Mussolini to power.

Mussolini's attacks on freemasonry won him the heart of the clergy; his destruction of all workers' associations—whether Socialist, leftist-Socialist, republican, Catholic, anarchist, syndicalist, or co-operatives, made no difference—brought him the support of the producers. Neither in Italy nor later in Germany were the industrialists completely Fascist-minded, but with Don Sturzo they could be called philo-Fascist, as they used the revolutionary lower-middle-class movement for their own aims, and, not always successfully, tried to make the Fascist State serve their purposes. The leading Italian trusts were hampered in their production by the postwar depression and the backwardness of Italy's industrial establishments, and they saw a chance to secure large public orders or other economic advantages in the rise of Mussolini. For instance the Banca Commerciale Italiana, which was insolvent as a result of financing the debt-ridden Ansaldo combine, supported Mussolini in the expectation that he would buy its Ansaldo shares at a favourable price, which he promptly did after the "March on Rome". The industrial pressure to make Mussolini Prime Minister was accentuated by intervention on behalf of the Army, which, just as in Germany in 1933, harboured a pro-Fascist group. In this group were several officers who were accused of being partly responsible for the ignominious Italian defeat at Caporetto during the first world war and who tried to protect themselves from possible demotion. One of the pro-Fascists in the Army, General Vaccari, planned to replace the King of Italy, Victor Emmanuel III, called *Il Re Bambino* from his small stature, by his cousin, the ambitious Duke of Aosta, if necessary. Even in the King's immediate surroundings Fascism had supporters; a few days before the March on Rome, at the end of October 1922, the most glamorous figure among the Fascists, the war hero De Vecchi, and the commander of the Fascist shock troops, had a talk with the Queen Mother, Margherita, who enthusiastically welcomed the "good cause".

The psychological attack upon the ruling authorities by promises, grants of protection, flattery, threats and blackmail were indispensable prerequisites of the Fascist way of seizing control. The Fascist rise was not due to genuine revolution, but to the supposed "saving" of society by a rising ersatz *élite* which under pretext of its good intentions attempted to oust the old, genuinely conservative stratum and acting supposedly in its interest, took over the struggle against the proletariat. The final victory of Fascism in Italy was basically merely the triumph of the most energetic over the other counter-revolutionary groups, which it is true professed other political ideas, but which were too strongly connected with Fascism socially to use force to spoil its victory. This form of seizing power made it necessary to avoid premature provocation of the sympathizing groups—nobility, middle class, and clerical petit bourgeois—by the troops of the Fascist movement and in many cases forced the Fascist leader to temper or disavow fanatic hotheads. The March on Rome, already planned by d'Annunzio and carried out by the four great men of Fascism —Bianchi, De Vecchi, Balbo and De Bono—in contact with the pro-Fascist Army and circles, was therefore terminated by Mussolini as soon as it had served its aim : to procure for *Il Duce* the appointment as Prime Minister of the intimidated King, Victor Emmanuel, and it culminated in a final parade which—like Hitler's *Tag von Potsdam*—was to blur the impression of political blackmail which preceded it, and to offer instead a radiant picture of perfect national unity.

Fascism in Control

The new man had not participated in the march of his shock troops on Rome and according to Balbo had even disapproved of it until the last minute. He reached the scene after the decision had been brought about, travelling by sleeping-car from his safe quarters in Milan, and began his rule without any fixed programme. What was later called "Fascist philosophy" was the subsequent product of flattering propagandists like the tiresome Paolo Orano, overrated parlour philosophers like the vain Giovanni Gentile, who called Fascism the highest form of liberalism, overpaid professional babblers like the oily Luigi Villari, or "synchronized" former foes of the régime such as the absurd Giovanni Prezzolini, whom Mussolini, along with an entire Italian cultural institute, put at the disposal of Columbia University in New York to make his cause popular.

Leader of a minority party in the Italian Chamber, rejected by the Press and the tremendous majority of the population, Mussolini could only maintain his rule by resorting to ever-increasing violence. His special hatred was aimed at the brilliant young leader of the Socialists in the Chamber, Giacomo Matteotti, a fearless scion of the upper bourgeoisie who mercilessly disclosed the economic background of the new régime. Among the affairs he exposed were the Ansaldo transaction of the Banca Commerciale; the public purchase of 18,000 shares of the mineral oil refinery at Fiume; the State's underwriting of bank credits given to the Federation of Italian Industry; and the granting of a monopoly for selling petroleum to the American Sinclair Oil Company, which brought millions to some of the dignitaries of the new régime. Systematic corruption was typical of the Fascist form of dictatorship. In Fascist Italy as in Nazi Germany an entire new class of dignitaries and party functionaries rose which grew rich at the expense of the victims of Fascism. Ciano father and son—both addressed as counts, though only the father, as recipient of a high military decoration, was entitled to it— became the wealthiest men in Italy; among other representatives of this type were the long-nosed Achille Starace, secretary-general of the party from 1931 to 1938; his predecessor in this position, the violent and disgusting Roberto Farinacci, a former railway worker nicknamed the "Ras" (feudal vice-king, Abyssinian style) of Ferrara, to whom the Fascists gave the title of "Doctor of Law" and who used to collect princely gifts for influencing the law courts; and, finally, the minister for the supervision of currency, Rafael Riccardi, who made his millions by granting import licences.

Just as with most dictators, Mussolini displayed little desire to prevent his followers from indulging in murdering, torturing and stealing—without good reason. The enumeration of an endless series of such crimes by Signor Matteotti in the Italian Chamber of Deputies simply made him furious; he indicated his wish that this foe of his would vanish from the scene in the Press and in written hints sent to some of his followers. In 1924 this wish was suddenly fulfilled, and when it turned out that a Fascist gang headed by the Italo-American gangster Dumini had kidnapped the deputy in a car, murdered him in beastly fashion, and cut his body to pieces, the master of Fascism washed his hands of it in the manner of most dictators. He might have had as little advance knowledge of the intended murder as Hitler seems to have had of the Reichstag burning, but as leaders of their movements both men were morally responsible for such deeds, especially as they benefited enormously from them.

It looked at first as if Mussolini would be swept from the scene by public indignation over the assassination of a deputy, who was inviolable in law. The Matteotti affair produced not only a social crisis, but also a very grave psychological crisis for a man who came from the Socialist camp and who had never ceased to believe in the possibility of a final reconciliation with his old comrades, though the type of Socialism he professed was primarily intended to serve his own career. Being confronted with the dilemma of choosing between letting the murderers escape and so to accept responsibility for their dead, or infuriating his own party by proceeding against some of his men, he sank into black despair, which for a time led to his complete isolation and to great indignation in his own camp; that the ship of Fascism did not capsize in the storm was mainly due to the inactivity of the leftist opposition, which proved incapable of exploiting their excellent tactical situation. This delivered the pilot into the hands of his most radical followers, until the ship finally crashed on the rocks of international politics.

From the angle of day-to-day politics, the turn after the assassination of Matteotti, for which he assumed public responsibility, in the end proved favourable to him for the time being; the awful crime is correctly regarded as the starting-point of his unrestricted dictatorial rule. He personally ordered the maltreatment and even the assassination of prominent foes of Fascism; among his victims was the deputy Amendola, who was assaulted by Fascist *squadristi* (shock troopers) and died later in exile from this maltreatment. This was on the direct orders of *Il Duce*, as the master of Fascism used to be called, and De Bono, his obedient right-hand man. Other victims were Professor Pierro Goberti of Turin, who shared Amendola's fate; the deputy Misuri, "roughed up" by the supreme chief of the *squadri*, Italo Balbo; the deputy Forni, whose torture was supervised by the first chief of Mussolini's secret police, O.V.R.A., Cesare Rossi; the Fascist deputy Ravalzolo, who had fallen into disgrace; and a large number of others. Rossi, whom Mussolini made the scapegoat of the Matteotti affair and whom he dismissed, finally fled to France and put down what he knew in two memoranda. He was lured to Switzerland by Fascist agents, with the help of a pretty woman, and after being dragged by force across the Italo-Swiss frontier he disappeared in an Italian prison. Another famous scandal of those days was the case of Ricciotti Garibaldi, a son of the great freedom fighter of Italy, Giuseppe Garibaldi, who was put on trial for having served Mussolini as an agent provocateur among the political exiles in France for a more than handsome remuneration. Towards the end of the 1920s the O.V.R.A. became something like an official institution, especially after a series of attempts against the life of the dictator had been staged, all of which failed, but which, in the manner of all tyrants, he used most cleverly to serve his aims.

The outward picture of that period, the initial stability of the Italian lira, the increasing imports, the apparent pacification of the country, the start of public works including the draining of marshes, the erection of hospitals, orphanages and homes for foundlings, the cessation of strikes and the decrease of unemployment—mostly natural results of the economic recovery after the first world war—gave the Italian public, and foreign countries as well, an exaggerated notion of the achievements of that dictatorship which still lives in the works of some of Mussolini's biographers, who speak of a golden age of Fascism. Frightened by the emergence of a big Communist State among the world Powers, not only the Fascists of all nations but even wide circles of the democratic West, especially its upper classes, looked with satisfaction upon the much-discussed conqueror of Communism, the man who forced the trains in Italy to pay scrupulous attention to their time-tables, the Caesar-headed leader of the movement, who, with his correct stiff collar, dark jacket, striped trousers, and mania for wearing cream-coloured gaiters, appeared as the true symbol of a permissible revolution, one that could be approved of by decent people.

What was not known was that the great man, yielding to his upstart urge, extended his mass conquests to the female world, and each afternoon had a *tête-à-tête* with one of the countless women who used to flock to his audiences. These were mostly full-bosomed matrons of the bourgeois and—less frequently—of the aristocratic Roman society who socially outranked his low-born and modest wife Rachele, and whom he used to receive in his gigantic but sparsely furnished studio in the *Mappa Mondo* hall of the Palazzo Venezia, which had nothing but carpets for the accommodation of visitors of the more informal kind. The Italian public, which in late years ascribed his increasing physical and mental fatigue to his connection with the gracious Clara (Claretta) Petacci, which became known then, had the correct idea, though it erred as to the immediate cause; neither *Il Duce's* relations with Claretta nor the other comparatively extensive connection in his life—that with Margherita Sarfatti—ever occupied him to the same extent as his habitual relations with the mass of women who remained anonymous. Sarfatti, the later biographer of her lover, joined Emil Ludwig, who by publishing his *Conversations with Mussolini*, rendered the democratic cause for which he stood a distinctive disservice in preserving that thoroughly fallacious notion of the "good" Duce of the 1920s in the memory of mankind. This wrong picture was emphasized by the tremendous popularity Mussolini enjoyed in the ranks of the Italian lower middle class, and especially of the youth, by the success of his *Dopo Lavoro* scheme, which like Hitler's *Kraft durch Freude* organization took care of the workers' and employees' spare time, and by the activity of his gigantic youth organizations such as the Opera Nazionale Ballila, which roused the enthusiasm of the new generation.

However, in reality in those years in which the international boom of the mid-1920s helped Fascism to gain some popularity the very worst traits of this system appeared. It began with the

chaining of the free Press which had started in 1924, the year
Matteotti was assassinated. In the first months of 1925 the complete destruction of freedom of speech and assembly followed.
Combined with it was the ruin of Parliament, which in the first
two years of the Fascist régime had still been functioning, and
the suppression of the freedom of teaching as well as of the
regular Civil Service. The de-commissioning of Parliament in
turn and the rise of the Fascist Party deprived the King of his
most essential prerogative, to appoint a Prime Minister responsible to the parliamentary majority, and thus transferred the
supreme authority automatically into the hands of the Fascist
Grand Council directed by Mussolini. The judiciary was permeated by Fascists, and a special Fascist tribunal was established.
The free exercise and choice of professions and the free right to
move about vanished likewise. The eight-hour day and the right
to strike were suppressed.

A gigantic international publicity campaign celebrated Mussolini as the saviour from Bolshevism. In reality any Communist
danger in Italy had disappeared long before he came to power.
If anything fostered Bolshevism, it was the disastrous inequality
in the division of property and land in Italy, which Mussolini,
however, just as Hitler in Germany, left essentially unchanged,
and the Fascist wage system, which worsened the situation of the
very poor industrial worker and still more that of the rural
worker. The "pump-priming" of the economy by public works
and later by armaments burdened the nation with heavy debts,
undermined its currency, and favoured price rises and black
markets, while the prohibition of strikes and the activity of the
Fascist Labour organizations kept the worker and his wages
chained to the bottom. Theoretically both capital and labour
were subject to the rule of an "impartial" third party, the Fascist
State, whose agents controlled the Chambers of Labour in which
the entire production was organized. But in view of the constant
rise in prices, the system worked against the labouring man in
practice and led to a sinking of real wages. The suppression of
the right to strike abolished the only efficient weapon the workers
had to fight exploitation. The Fascist Chambers of Labour,
though it would be erroneous to call all of them one-sided and
pro-capitalist, were too cumbersome and lacked legal authority to
prevent this development, since they were bound to fix wages in

8—DOS

such a way that most existing enterprises, even when they had become unprofitable, could continue to exist. The efforts of *Il Duce's* first Minister of Finance, De Stefani, to stop the inflationist development and to balance the budget failed, due to his being replaced by the very rich trust magnate Count Volpi di Misurata, under whose auspices the big combines such as Snia Viscosa (synthetic fabrics), Montecatini (chemical products) and Fiat (cars and heavy industry) controlled the State almost unrestrictedly, and received tremendous credits from the United States. The result of the excessive industrial expansion was the start of an industrial crisis which preceded the world depression of 1929 by not less than three years, but which was politically useful for *Il Duce,* since the general need for State intervention tightened the ties between the people of the Fascist system.

Mussolini's international policy during those years was cautious, on the whole, though it was marred by an unforeseen and cowardly naval attack against the undefended Greek island of Corfu, which was prompted by his personal lust for vengeance for what he regarded as a slur. His caution was due to the needs of that period in which the influx of the American billions and the political and military situation of Europe, still then unprotected by an armed Germany against what appeared to some as the Russian threat, seemed to call for a strong collaboration between Italy and the Western world. Under these circumstances *Il Duce* was forced to shelve his anti-British complex temporarily; it was only after Hitler's rise had prompted him to accelerate the execution of his imperial plans, which the British opposed, that his anti-British complex gained unrestricted control over him. This led him to embark on a thoroughly unrealistic and typically dictatorial policy which finally caused his downfall.

The Dictatorship of National Socialism: The "Poor White Trash"

While Roman-Italian Fascism in its whole style reflected the tradition of an empire which had ruled the world 1,500 years earlier, National Socialism by the name of the State it created— the Third Reich—and by its nature continued the territorial claims of a political structure which had been in existence until the beginning of the nineteenth century and whose spirit had not yet perished. The much-criticized words of the German national anthem, composed by a liberal German in the first half of the nineteenth century, "Von der Maas bis an die Memel, von der Etsch bis an den Belt",[1] prove that the tradition of the First German Reich, better known as the Holy Roman Empire, which had ruled over vast parts of Europe, had not even disappeared in the first and best period of German nationalism, which was still humane and liberal. Wholly in the twentieth century, when nationalism in Germany had assumed reactionary and imperialist traits, this tradition gained momentum, especially after the signing of the Versailles Treaty, which cut down the size of Germany in a way which had not been seen since the time of Napoleon.

The Germans abroad and the German victims of the Versailles Treaty, who included the many Germans driven out of the newly founded nations in the east—the Baltic States, Poland, Czecho-slovakia, Yugoslavia and others—played a considerable part in the founding of the National Socialist movement. While the nucleus of the new party was formed, especially after the start of the international depression, by the German postwar ersatz *élite*, the lower middle classes and the white-collar workers, its leaders often consisted of expelled intellectuals and of other victims of the postwar development in the lost areas across the German boundaries and in the former German colonies across the seas.

Even Adolf Hitler himself belonged in a certain sense to this category. He was in the Imperial German Reich (the Second Reich, which lasted from 1871) at the start of his career, a root-less German from a boundary district who refused to return to his native land. The German element in the Habsburg ruled the Austro-Hungarian Dual Monarchy in which he had grown up, and had been separated by the war of 1866 from the nucleus of the German population. In Hitler's earliest years it even lost its preponderant position in the Habsburg lands where it had been the ruling stratum. The rise of the non-German nationalities in the old Dual Monarchy, though merely a natural result of the general development which was causing the formation of new nations all over the world, hit the Germans in those territories with especial force, since they were numerically inferior.

The upper strata of the German-Austrians—nobility, clergy,

---

[1] "From the Meuse to the Memel, from the Adige to the Belt."

officials—and the business world, where the Jews played a leading rôle, were too firmly connected with the fate of the Dual
Monarchy and the ruling imperial house to fight the Habsburg
monarchs openly when they started to solicit the political co-
operation of the non-German nationalities and to respect the
latter's political interests and wishes in the 1870s. But in a section
of the middle and lower middle classes, as far as they were not
completely controlled by the Church, pan-German, anti-Slav
and anti-Jewish ideas, gained ground, and even the strongly
clerical wing of these elements which rejected the pan-Germanist
ideas displayed a strong anti-Semitism, especially in the years of
economic depression. Among the pan-German-minded Austrians
before the turn of the century, Georg von Schönerer made head-
way with his propaganda, which in many respects anticipated
National Socialism. Among the clerically inclined Viennese lower
middle classes worked another great demagogue, the anti-Jewish
Mayor of Vienna, Karl Lueger, an eminent man in his way,
whose art of leading and treating the masses was later copied
by Hitler. The Führer himself, born in 1889, grew up at a time
when von Shönerer's great period had passed, but Lueger was
then reaching his zenith.

Young Adolf Hitler was more the son of his mother, whose
facial traits he inherited, than his somewhat rough father, who
was proud to have advanced to the position of a medium customs
official. He showed none of the characteristics of the small
peasants of the Waldviertel, near Linz, from whom he was descended on both sides, but both physically and mentally had
something in common with the versatile and flexible Slav race.
It seems certain that he had a drop of Slav blood in his veins—
though four generations earlier, through the family of his
mother. The suggestion of his Minister of Justice, Hans Frank,
that he was partly Jewish is not yet proved. A former Munich
attorney who had been Hitler's personal legal adviser and who
was later hanged by the Allies for having committed fearful war
crimes, especially in Poland, Hans Frank wrote memoirs in the
months preceding his execution in which he contended that
Adolf's grandfather Aloys Hitler, illegitimate son of the maid
Schicklgruber, and acknowledged *ex post facto* by the latter's
subsequent husband, Georg Hiedler (the spelling varies), several

decades after the conclusion of the marriage,[1] had in reality been the son of a Jew from Graz, who paid support for him. Coming from so well informed a source, this testimony is interesting, though it is uncertain whether Aloys's alleged father, one Frankenberger, was a Jew. Instead of laying undue stress on this kind of hypothesis, one should rather emphasize the special conditions under which Hitler's character developed as well as the unique situation which finally allowed him to rise. Both would suffice to explain the Hitler case.

As a rule dictators are rarely shaped by descent—the parents of Robespierre, Napoleon I, Lenin, Mussolini, Hitler, Stalin were no more than average persons—but are formed by social tensions causing a sensitive character to turn neurotic and thus make him a candidate for dictatorship. Revolutionary periods such as the years after 1918 usually stimulate a mass emergence of dictator candidates; most of them usually disappear after a short time. That Adolf Hitler won the race was especially due to his personal experiences making him one of the last and most active followers of von Schönerer, and at the time of his political rise a man of that type was in demand.

The decisive moment in Hitler's career was his failure as a would-be student of painting in Vienna, which led to his social decline from the rather sheltered *petit bourgeois* existence his parents had secured for him. Certain of his success as an artist, young Hitler—he was about nineteen when he finally settled in Vienna—had put all his money on this one bet, which failed, and had even neglected his general education to such an extent that any other way to the top remained blocked to him. The grave psychosis which developed in him during the four years

[1] According to the thorough investigation undertaken by the eminent Austrian expert on Hitler, Dr. Franz Jetzinger, in the files of the Austrian civil and Church authorities, the belated acknowledgment by Georg Hiedler that Aloys was his son would appear to have been a fake, performed many years after Georg's death by relatives and friends of the family, apparently to remove a stain from the shield of Aloys, the Government official.

The Hans Frank version of Adolf Hitler's descent in turn calls to mind a story related during World War II by the British psychologist Harold Baynes, according to which Hitler in the years of his misery in Vienna tried to raise money from a Jewish ancestor, but was thrown out of the door. If proved, Hitler's alleged Jewish descent could of course not be considered the "cause" of his actions, but at best as an element that increased the bitterness and the anti-Semitism which developed in him in the days of his social decline.

he spent among the dregs of the Viennese population in flop-houses and poor-houses was increased by starvation and physical weakness, a remnant of lung infection,[1] and also by the suppression of his sex life, which he evidently intended to ignore until he had regained some social respectability. We are now informed through a report of a friend of his youth, August Kubizek, that for years he worshipped a girl from the middle classes in a platonic fashion whom he, apparently under the conviction that he had nothing he could offer her as yet, did not even dare to talk to, but whom he merely used to stare at silently, placing himself at a street corner which he knew she had to pass.

The more strongly developed was his desire to achieve speedy prominence as an artist, a wish which remained nothing but a dream while he went to school and through his long-drawn-out sickness. These day-dreams in the case of young Hitler had an uncanny vigour and importance and determined his entire existence. They reached such a stage that he no longer distinguished between dream and reality, and he, for instance, talked constantly about his tremendous building projects, comprising the change and transfer of entire streets and towns—things which he indeed in later years carried out, which made it appear as if he had been helped by some god. After a performance of Richard Wagner's *Rienzi* in his beloved Linz he led Kubizek to the top of a nearby hill and in a kind of vision spoke about himself as the future saviour of Germany. For a man of his kind, his decline into social non-existence was even more painful than it would have been for the average member of the lower middle class from which he came. With remarkable insight he says of this class in *Mein Kampf* that it was an unstable social element "which only recently had emerged from the level of the manual

---

[1] Unfortunately Dr. Jetzinger has somewhat marred the worth of his many discoveries of documents and facts concerning the youth of Hitler by being over-critical of some witnesses such as Kubizek, especially as far as the latter corroborated facts also mentioned in *Mein Kampf*—which Dr. J. (justifiably) mistrusts. For instance I cannot find that Dr. J. has succeeded in invalidating the story of Hitler's lung illness, or Kubizek's various tales about Hitler's suppressed sex life, which have recently been corroborated by the memoirs of Ernst ("Putzi") Hanfstaengl, a book which seems to have been underrated by many reviewers because of the clownish nature of its author. Hitler's syphilitic affliction, however, which Hanfstaengl makes responsible for this attitude, and which is documented by the Dr. Kersten memoirs, would appear to have influenced him only at a much later stage.

workers" and showed a much greater fear of declining into the ranks of the proletariat than the high bourgeoisie.

To what extent he himself suffered from such feelings is shown by the well-known description of his unsuccessful career as a mason's hand, which he abandoned almost at once for fear of permanent social decline. The young Hitler had become one of the most sensitive and irritable representatives of that section of the German-Austrians which fought against the Habsburg policy for its supposed favouring the rise of the Slavs, Jews and workers in Austria-Hungary. The Austrian of the von Schönerer type had a strong psychological relationship with the "poor white trash" in the South of the United States, whose standard of life is hardly different from that of the negro population which surrounds him, and who lives on an even lower level, but who, for this very reason, clings desperately to the political and social privileges which distinguish the white from the coloured.

In the sexual sphere this colour-consciousness was especially true. The obstinacy with which the "poor white trash" banded together in Fascist-like organizations such as the Ku Klux Klan to protect the white woman from the negro and which even lynched the negroes if they dared to commit the smallest sex offence, is an exact counterpart of the fanaticism with which Hitler later on forbade the hated Jews from having any sexual intercourse with the rest of the population. The greatest service in pursing this aim was rendered to him by the works of Wagner and Houston Stewart Chamberlain, which influenced him in part directly and in part through the medium of or jointly with the local anti-Semitic literature which grew up in a similar atmosphere. Both enabled him to transform the *petit bourgeois* ersatz *élite* which drew his interest into an "Aryan race" that needed protection. On the basis of a thorough analysis of *Mein Kampf*, Rudolph Olden, one of Hitler's earliest biographers, voiced the opinion even in the 1930s that the specifically Hitlerian form of anti-Semitism, with its strong emphasis on the concept of "race pollution", appears to have been caused in part by Hitler's jealousy of individual Jews. He always complained that Vienna was crowded by Jews, and his anti-Semitism might have come from his being ousted by Jews in wooing non-Jewish girls. When writing this Olden did not know that Hitler, according to a certain Greiner who evidently knew him well, tried to rape a pretty Viennese model whom he drew and who was engaged to a half-Jew, and when the girl shortly afterwards got married Hitler was seized by attacks of frenzy and caused a street scandal by shouting public insults at the couple during the ceremony. It seems that the self-imposed suppression of his sex life drove Hitler at times close to complete madness.[1]

The bitterness of the "poor white trash" from the Waldviertel about his experiences in Vienna strongly resembled those of the young Wagner in the Paris of the early 1840s and was hardly less unfounded. Just as Wagner appeared to the Frenchmen as *"un homme hargneux et insociable qui écorchait le français et déblaterait contre tout le monde"* ("a bitter and asocial character whose French was atrocious and who shouted invective at everybody"), Hitler was a socially impossible figure in his Viennese years, of ragged and miserable appearance, who in his worn-out long coat and whiskers looked at times like a Jew from the East, which must have strongly increased his hatred of these elements as well as of the Poles and Czechs who surrounded him in the doss-houses. Just as Wagner came home from Paris, which he was going to hate all his life, to his homeland Germany, Hitler, full of bitter resentment, turned his back on Vienna in the beginning of 1913 and settled in Munich, the capital of Bavaria, whose population was referred to in Vienna as "the transition from the Prussian to the human being". (In Prussia the same slogan was used with reference to Bavaria's relations with the Austrians.)

In leaving Austria Hitler avoided serving in the Austro-Hungarian Army, but since he did not shun military service as such it would seem that his motive was to avoid serving the Dual Monarchy, which he hated, but to enlist under Prussia, which he admired. He worshipped Frederick the Great and the Prussian generals, not least because of their many victories over the hated Habsburg monarchy, and at the start of the first world war he entered the German Army with enthusiasm, where he, unmistakably Austrian, and serving in a Bavarian regiment, surprised everybody with his militarist views and his love of strict Prussian

[1] Dr. Jetzinger, it is true, announces that he is going to publish material which will practically discard everything Greiner wrote on Hitler. But since Dr. J. in his endeavour to explode what he calls the Hitler myth has even gone so far as to deny that Hitler was ever a mason—possibly one of the most significant confessions contained in *Mein Kampf*—one would have to be most careful before yielding to his arguments.

discipline, thus cutting a very strange figure. Germany's military collapse in the autumn of 1918 threatened to deprive Hitler of the new home he had found in the German Army and thus was attributed by him to the activity of the same forces he made responsible for his fiasco in Vienna, and which, he thought, had meanwhile succeeded in building a solid castle for themselves by bringing about the Russian revolution of 1917 : Jews, Slavs and Marxists.

From the First World War to the International Depression

Hitler spoke an awkward German, a grammatically frightening mixture of the semi-Bavarian dialect spoken in his native Waldviertel and the wooden style of the Habsburg-ruled bureaucracy in which he later stated that even before the first world war he had received a "true, granite-like foundation for his personal philosophy", with the result that he "was never able to change his viewpoint in this decisive question afterwards". There is little doubt that Hitler's character had been formed by the end of the first world war, but as with all other dictators events enabled him to seize the dominant position. What made Hitler great was that his formative personal experience, his decline from the lower middle class into the doss-houses, coincided with the experiences of the broad masses in postwar Germany and preceded them in time; Germany capsized while he was at the helm because of the belief that a man who could voice these sentiments convincingly possessed the right prescription for healing that sickness. The tremendous crowd of Hitler's admirers rarely realized that Hitler's political prescriptions originated really in a bygone time, had been composed under conditions which no longer existed, and that their application to the German situation of those years was bound to cause the death of the patient— the German Reich. They remained blind, although they only had to look in *Mein Kampf* to recognize what a grotesque development had taken place in this case. His service in the German Army during the first world war had given the former picture postcard artist something of the feeling of having found a shelter, like that of Richard Wagner while he stayed with King Ludwig II, and there is indeed a common trait in the enthusiasm both men displayed at the start of that particular phase of their lives. But the disaster of 1918 threw Hitler back into the maelstrom of events, and forced him, just as Wagner after his involuntary separation from the King and Munich gradually developed into the Bayreuth Messiah, to start a political career of his own and to play the saviour of the German nation. Just as Wagner's Parsifal during his temptations by the flower maidens of the magician Klingsor, symbol of the Jews and the underworld, suddenly sees the light and decides to "save" King Amfortas and the Knights of the Holy Grail, so Hitler, who at that time was confined to the military hospital at Pasewalk due to temporary blindness from poison gas, became at the news of the outbreak of the German Revolution "knowing by compassion", and took the vow to replace the old *élite*, which had failed, by a new one.

At the same time the German military collapse gave birth to one of the leading groups of the German ersatz *élite* which was to carry Hitler to power: it was the many *Freikorps* (volunteer units) which emerged only a few weeks after the outbreak of the German revolution to protect the German Republic, which then went through a process of political formation against Communist attempts on its life. This not too difficult task was hardly more than a pretext; the real struggle of the *Freikorps* was directed much more against the Republic, which had used them for a short while, than against the Communists. In their endeavour to safeguard secret German weapon deposits and conceal them from the Western Powers, who had limited German armament, the *Freikorps* developed a new ethic: the man who helped to carry out the Peace Treaty of Versailles limiting these armaments, which Germany had signed, and who therefore betrayed the secret caches, became a victim of the so-called *Fehme*—a secret illegal tribunal—and was "disposed of"; the cunning and insidious protector of these caches in turn who knew how to mislead the Entente control commission became a hero; thus black became white. By this "transvaluation of all values" German nationalism inadvertently renewed the Teutonic ethics of the Edda myths; the spirit of the Christian centuries that had elapsed subsequently looked like a varnish which could easily be scraped off; the man who was most unscrupulous was the most successful in this race in republican Germany. The men of the *Freikorps* and related units had something in common with Hagen of Tronje of the *Nibelungen* song, who without any scruple commits murders and does all kinds of damage in the service of his lord and who at the end perishes defiantly in flames, proud of having been faithful to his master.

Like the time of the Merovingians and Langobards and the age of early feudalism, the period after the first world war displayed primitive and barbaric traits; it was an ugly struggle of everyone for himself, the leading elements of the ersatz *élite* struggled against the lower classes as well as against the old upper class, with which, however, it joined in opposing the Republic. Above all it was a struggle for political leadership. To be successful required more political experience and knowledge than the average *Freikorps* leader possessed, especially as the military arm of the new Republic, the *Reichswehr*, headed by General von Seeckt, followed a rather ambiguous line. While in agreement with the *Freikorps* in its general policy regarding German rearmament and the desire to prepare a war of revenge against France, it figured, as an official body whose superbly trained commissioned and non-commissioned officers were earmarked to lead the future German mass army, it would be the most expedient if the rearmaments took place in a legal fashion, by simply enlarging the official army, a method which the *Freikorps* highly disliked since it practically involved their dissolution.

The aim of the *Freikorps* was secret rearmament in opposition to the Republic and, if necessary, even against the Reichswehr. Politically the Reichswehr as an official body was superior to the *Freikorps*, but it felt unable to achieve its aims unless it became popular with the masses. The *Reichswehr's* endeavours to influence the population became the starting-point for Corporal Hitler's political career. As political observer of some units of the Army which helped to put down the short-lived Munich Soviet Republic of the spring of 1919, he discovered the political group, still insignificant, which was to become the German National Socialist Party, and whose leadership he shortly afterwards assumed. The new party very soon cut the tie still connecting it with the budding new *Reichswehr* and became an ally of the *Freikorps*, whose members played a prominent rôle in its half-military "protective" organization, the SA (*Sturmabteilungen*, storm troopers), and also in the party itself. From the beginning the Nazi Party was the party of the lower middle classes, even though the broad masses of this stratum did not join it until after the big depression of 1929.

It is incorrect to blame only the depression for Hitler's success. The unpopularity of the German Republic drove the masses into Hitler's arms, even though the depression was needed to make these feelings general. From the very beginning the new German State was hated by the persons and classes thrown out of power in 1918, the monarchs, the junkers—members of the Prussian nobility—the ranking officers and the big industrialists. That these groups controlled the largest sector of the German Press gave their aversion to the Republic and the entire Western world an importance out of proportion to their numerical strength, and helped to transform the political views of the middle and lower classes in a way highly favourable for Hitler's plans.

The constant attacks of this Press against the French and the German republicans, pictured as the political tools of the French, were accentuated by open anti-Semitism. The Jews had been given full civil rights in the new Germany, known from the place where its constitution was framed as the Weimar Republic, while they had been excluded from all leading positions in the Reich as well as in Prussia in Imperial Germany. This made them look in the eyes of their foes like conspirators and allies of the revolutionaries of 1918, especially of the Socialists. The revolutions in Eastern Europe and the liberal immigration policy of the Weimar Republic caused many Jews from Russia and other Eastern countries to settle in Berlin and other large German cities, to the discomfort of the indigenous Jews, who saw in this unexpected increase in their numbers a handicap in handling their ever-increasing problems in Germany. Not all of their foes preached extreme racial doctrines. Most rightist papers and parties were still influenced by the Christian tradition and felt that a total suppression of Jewry might be an overture to an expropriation of the rest of the property owners, whose interests they tried to protect. This very moderation proved a boon for an impecunious figure such as Hitler, the arch-foe of the Habsburgs and of the Catholic religion, to which he outwardly belonged. For him, the conditions of the Weimar period offered an excellent opportunity for propagating the racial doctrine of the Wagner circle and of Houston Stewart Chamberlain, combined with the more primitive anti-Semitic doctrines he had absorbed while in Austria, all of which appealed to deeply rooted sentiments reflecting dark recollections of the German feudal past.

The defeat of the Reich in 1918, the signing of the Versailles Treaty, and the unsuccessful resistance which the Weimar Republic, disarmed by the Reich's former enemies, tried to put up against their financial demands, gave Hitler's propaganda the welcome opportunity to revive the average German's traditional military and domineering instincts. He presented himself as the Parsifal who attempted to free the Knights of the Holy Grail—defunct monarchist Germany—from being strangled by the tools of the underworld—the French, Bolsheviks, Marxists and Jews. His movement was greatly helped by the ascent to power of Mussolini—whose movement with its flag parades, protective guards (*squadristi*) and its Fascist salute he copied both technically and socially—and three months later, in January 1923, by the invasion of the Ruhr valley by France. To the disappoinment of the German Cabinet of Chancellor Wilhelm Cuno that organized the German resistance in the Ruhr, and which stood further to the right than any former cabinet of the Weimar Republic, Hitler remained defiant and unco-operative, unprepared to support any movement which would take the wind out of his sails. This attitude—incomprehensible to most German patriots—proved, however, to be greatly to his advantage. The collision between the Reich and the French in the Ruhr brought about the complete collapse of the German currency, an event which gave the Nazi doctrines a popular basis that extended far beyond the boundaries of Bavaria, which remained the main bulwark of Nazism until the time of the big depression.

The enthusiasm which Hitler during the months of the Ruhr struggle stirred up among the main victims of the monetary inflation—small capitalists, recipients of fixed incomes and pensions, and small employers who were dispersed over the entire Reich—gave him the rather premature impression of enjoying a kind of mass support which he did not possess at that time, at least from the organizational angle, and which, unlike the gigantic social basis the depression of 1929 with its general unemployment was to create for him, proved to be too thin and fragile socially, since it consisted of the weakest elements, old and worn-out people without much political impetus. The *fata morgana* of his success with this stratum appears to be partly responsible for Hitler's conceiving the plan for his famous *putsch* in the autumn of 1923; the main reason for this decision, however, was his fear that he would be eclipsed in the general race for dictatorship which had then begun in Germany.

This race was unchained by the efforts of the Reichswehr and of its political and military satellites to maintain the mighty position they had reached during the Ruhr conflict in spite of the Reich's final capitulation in the Ruhr. Among the runners was the founder of the Reichswehr, General von Seeckt. Not the type of person to be a dictator, the General tried to foster his plans by establishing a directory. Seeckt's main rival was Gustav von Kahr, whom the local Bavarian Government, to check Hitler, had made "General Commissioner of State" and equipped with dictatorial powers, and who, being a Bavarian monarchist and also a Protestant from the provinces of Franconia, evidently aimed at a solution in which he would call back both the royal family of Wittelsbach, expelled from the throne of Bavaria in 1918, and also—with Seeckt's assistance—the royal house of Hohenzollern, which had ruled Prussia and had worn the German imperial crown. The impression that von Kahr, after a grave initial conflict with von Seeckt, had come very close to the realization of his plans and that the National Socialist Party would be by-passed, prompted Hitler to strike before being confronted with accomplished facts.

Hitler's so-called *putsch* or *coup d'état* of November 9th, 1923 —not by mere coincidence the anniversary of the German revolution of 1918—was a failure, but its plan and execution remained a perfect model of Hitler's political technique. The main targets of his attack were not the much-blamed revolutionaries of 1918 —Socialist left-wingers who had prompted the rest of the population to drive out the monarchs—but the old German society as such, whose South German leaders assembled in commemoration of the November revolution in the Munich Bürgerbräu to hear a speech by Herr von Kahr on the subject of how that event could be eradicated from German history. From the angle of their political philosophy these men belonged in different, although all conservative, camps. Most of them were Bavarian monarchists, but mixed with them were Greater Prussians and pan-Germanists, members of the pre-first world war ersatz *élite* which had been formed in the age of imperialism, absorbing the ideas of Houston Stewart Chamberlain who had not dreamt what use Hitler would make of his thoughts; typically enough he had declined the offer of an industrialist who was ready to spend 10,000 marks to distribute Chamberlain's *The Foundations of the Nineteenth Century* in a cheap edition among the masses. Before the first world war, good society saw no use in influencing the common man. Hitler reveals with astonishing frankness in *Mein Kampf* how his fear of the *petit bourgeois* who was facing social decline shaped his entire mentality. He admired rather than hated good society, a sentiment which in his case was mixed with aversion towards the upper classes of the Dual Monarchy and especially the Jews, whom he considered social invaders. But in those months he had the distinct feeling that his mission of saviour was rejected by the German ruling classes and he thus felt compelled to use force to make them love him.

The *putsch* was unusual because Hitler, the "revolutionary", who had surrounded the Bürgerbräu with his armed guards, did not arrest those inside as might have been expected. Instead, firing a pistol into the ceiling and gesticulating wildly, he rushed to the rostrum and forced them to become his ministers and join in his conspiracy. It was the beginning of that crafty game which after Hitler's dictatorship had started was to lead to assassinations by both sides and to culminate in the futile attempt on Hitler on July 20th, 1944, which led merely to the slaughter of his would-be assassins. Von Kahr and his friends, all monarchists, were about to overthrow the Bavarian and German republics which they served, and hoped for help from von Seeckt, whom they had previously considered their political opponent. They accepted the positions offered them by Hitler "in the name of the monarchy". They thus succeeded in regaining their personal freedom, only to outwit their blackmailer and turn against him at once. Von Kahr paid for this in 1934 by being tortured and finally murdered.

Human memory is short, especially when it wants to forget. Monarchist Germany regained the upper hand in the Republic shortly after the *putsch* by the election of Marshal von Hindenburg as Reichs President, Germany's grand old man of first world war fame. She soon forgot the lesson she had been taught by the fratricidal struggle of 1923 which had ended with

the defeat of Hitler and his men at the steps of the Munich Feld-
herrnhalle, but which had also spoiled the chances of the monarchists for the time being. This assisted Hitler in his second,
more forceful bid for power which was to lead him to his goal.

The story of this second attempt by Hitler confirms the theory
that even the mightiest dictator would remain a nonentity, were
it not for the help of tremendous social and political influences.
Until the beginning of the international depression of 1929
Hitler was a political nonentity, even though the German people
were in the mood for a man of his kind. The "Hitler trial" of
1924, in which he was charged with attempting a *putsch*, had
been used by him for making much public propaganda for his
cause, unconsciously imitating Louis Napoleon. While imprisoned in the fortress of Landsberg he wrote the first volume
of his book *Mein Kampf*. Despite its high price, twelve marks,
it found thousands of buyers—by 1930 the total number of copies
sold reached 23,000, while the figure for the second volume,
which came out in 1927, two years after Volume I, was 13,000.
This success was far exceeded by the sale of a one-volume edition,
which was cheaper. By January 30th, 1933, no less than 287,000
copies were sold. But this preparatory propaganda, however
efficient, did not produce political results before the big depression threw the masses into his arms. The wave of unemployment
which started in 1929 carried him like a cork. The Nazi Party
or N.S.D.A.P. (*Nationalsozialistische Deutsche Arbeiter Partei*)
became a power overnight. In their deadly fear of sinking to the
level of the working class or even lower, crowds of German white-
collar workers embraced the cause of the "Führer" with an
anxiety which recalled Hitler's own early feelings, and it was
indeed these which enabled him to give the sentiments of the
masses the convincing expression that explains his success.

His political movement, permeated with this spirit, was greatly
helped by the formation of a new social stratum of deeply
resentful elements which, coming between the proletariat and
"good society", could be used, as things developed, against either
the upper or lower classes. By its mere existence, it gave unheard-
of dimensions to Hitler's blackmailing tactics, which had already
been so conspicuous in the *putsch* of 1923. Originally this new
stratum consisted merely of workless lower-middle-class elements
and of small artisans and craftsmen who had been ruined, but it

soon increased to such an extent that within the framework of Hitler's own movement new classes began to develop. This evolution gained momentum by the influx of new elements into his camp, such as ruined peasants—especially in Schleswig-Holstein —bankrupt members of the nobility and the high bourgeoisie, and, finally, Communists who were formerly unemployed.

The dormant anti-Semitism of many of these circles, long nourished by the German rightist Press and the numerous local papers, received an explosive character by the experience of the depression and by Hitler's agitation. The depression automatically revived the instincts in those depressed classes to which the scandal sheet *Der Stürmer* of the "Führer of Franconia", Julius Streicher, appealed when describing in detail acts of violation and rape allegedly committed by Jews, thereby transferring the readers' own sentiments into the souls of the Jews. A considerable section of the German people itself had become "poor white trash" as a result of the depression, and by beating the Jews even the poorest among them still felt master.

By an irony of history the theatre of these events coincided geographically with the outer belt of the Communist fortress centred on Moscow. German Communism, like the Nazi Party, was guided by a small group of leaders, not the type of men which headed the Nazi movement such as members of the *Freikorps,* nationalists from the German boundary districts, or declining lower-middle-class elements, but by exactly the opposite human type : proletarians to whom the unions had nothing to offer, such as highly paid specialists or the unemployed, also members of the lower class of Jews who had immigrated from the East.

Just as with France under Robespierre, Russia in the time of Lenin and Stalin felt socially isolated and attempted to secure her political position by mobilizing all her ideological partisans in the neighbouring countries, whom it is true in Stalin's time she used to desert ignominiously whenever her political interests seemed to call for it. The rise of National Socialism took place after the Locarno treaties of 1925, which Moscow regarded as a symptom of German collaboration with the West which had to be answered by increasing Communist activity. Thus two different political offensives collided, both prompted and made socially possible by the economic depression; the declining lower middle class, which was increasingly attracted to Hitler as time went on, clashed head on with the rising Communism, whose ranks were swelled by the unemployment of the industrial workers and which provoked the fury of the Hitlerites, especially because of the type of men who headed it. There was hardly a copy of the *Völkischer Beobachter*, Hitler's main paper, or especially of *Der Stürmer*, which failed to abound in spiteful invectives of the Communist leaders, whose original, Jewish, names were usually quoted in parenthesis after their pen-names, figures such as Litvinov ("Finkelstein"), Radek ("Sobelsohn"), Trotsky ("Braunstein"), Zinoviev ("Apfelbaum"), and many others.

The existence and activity of these men furnished that perverted anti-Jewish rabble-rouser, Julius Streicher, the "ethical" pretext for the shameful obscenities that made him well known : the publication of those pointedly sexual articles and anti-Semitic caricatures which the rising Führer, the White Knight of the German nation, devoured with a rapture that betrayed his true motives. Having the impression that he was a social nonentity, Hitler—as shown in part by the Kubizek memoirs—had suppressed his sexual desires until the time in which he became *Der Führer*, and could thus wreak frightful vengeance on Jews, Marxists, Catholics and Slavs, whom since his Viennese days he made responsible for undermining his existence and hampering his character as a painter and so having forced him to remain abstemious and to miss the pleasures of the normal bourgeois. His impotence, being obviously rooted in this psychopathological motive, was thus related to his subsequent rejection of alcohol and meat : both were caused by his instinctive feeling that his years of starvation in Vienna had affected his physique so strongly that he could no longer exist as a normal human being. Making a virtue of necessity, he interpreted this as the purity of the "pure fool", or, in other words, young Parsifal.

Even his success as a Führer could not change this. His forcibly suppressed sex life remained hampered for the rest of his career, which explains his frightening lack of sentiment; in the company of women he behaved awkwardly and uncertainly; his belated and rather frigid relation with Eva Braun exhausted what still remained of his erotic feelings; he had finally succeeded in conquering one of those "impossible flappers" for whose silent admiration he was ridiculed in party circles. This came much too late to change his terrifying character, whose basic traits were by then fully developed.

So it can be seen that despite the similarities of fate and thought that connected him with the creator and creature of the Wagnerian world, he remained separated from the maestro by the deepest possible gulf, as Wagner was the most fertile and fascinating artist of his age, whose Parsifal regenerates mankind through love, and who neither drowns, strangles, burns nor otherwise murders man, as did Hitler, the sadist without even the hint of a soul. Neither then nor earlier did events correspond with the psychological or social picture Hitler had drawn for his own use when he saw himself enacting the part of a haloed Lohengrin or Parsifal saving Germany from Communism. Germany did not need such a saviour; the rise of Communism before 1933 was not caused by an expansion of the Marxist sphere of influence but merely by rising unemployment, which led to a shrinking of its social-democratic sector, exactly as National Socialism before 1933 did not increase the numerical strength of the anti-Socialist front, but merely gained followers at the expense of the moderate non-Catholic bourgeois parties. Even at the height of the depression, Communism hardly received one-sixth of the available seats in the Reichstag, and met with the determined opposition of the entire remainder of the nation, and especially of the police and Reichswehr. On the other hand, National Socialism was almost three times as strong as Communism in the elections of the summer of 1932, for instance; it controlled the powerful organization of the storm troopers (SA), which rose to 600,000 men under the capable leadership of Captain Röhm; and the Nazis also, different from the Communists, possessed countless friends and helpers even among the non-Hitlerian part of the nation.

From the end of 1931 the Hitler movement began to dominate the German social picture. Both the Nazi political organization (P.O.), led by the bull-headed pharmacist Gregor Strasser, and Captain Röhm's SA became known to practically everybody; the brownshirts of the SA marched through the streets, singing the movement's theme song, the Horst Wessel Lied, or they stood on the corner, rattling their coin-collecting boxes; "motorized shock troops" of the SA *Standarten* (regiments; literally: "standards")

raced through the cities; more and more people appeared
in public with the swastika sign in their buttonholes; SA and
Communists battled openly in the suburbs; even before Hitler's
coming to power the SA controlled entire districts of Berlin;
during the economic depression murder and terrorism spread
over the rural areas, especially in Prussia; the Hitler movement's
monster meetings with their entries of flag-bearers and their wild
military music were always overcrowded; the Führer himself
loved to arrive late, combining his usual lack of self-discipline
with shrewd calculation, since this made the audience wild with
enthusiasm. He finally had twenty cars at his disposal and
dashed from city to city when electioneering, which was then
something new; the monumental "Brown House" or party centre
was built in Munich, taking its name from the movement's
favourite colour, and whose cost was paid for by the big industrialist Fritz Thyssen after having brought the party close to
bankruptcy.

January 30th, 1933

Just as with Mussolini, Hitler's attitude towards heavy industry, as is his entire conduct towards the ruling classes, is among
the most discussed problems of that entire period. Since the last
decade of the nineteenth century, German politics were supposedly determined by an alliance of junkers with heavy industry.
The great revolutionary force of the past, industry, had combined
with its former opponent, the land-owning nobility, especially in
Prussia, to obtain high tariffs profitable to both parties, to fight
the workers, and to embark on imperialism. Certain individual
peculiarities remained; the landowners, as a conservative element, were less desirous of expanding geographically than the
producers, who clamoured for markets and raw materials, but
they could not extinguish the impression that the alliance of both
big groups, in spite of their continuing rivalry, was an important
fact. For Germany, as a modern industrial country but a late-
comer as a nation, and for different reasons also for Italy—likewise a late-comer nation and with a tremendous population problem—imperialist expansion was much more urgent than for
other Powers. The results of the first world war were unsatisfactory for both nations, though Italy belonged to the victorious
group, and they increased this need for additional space. Checked

during the middle of the 1920s by the influx of American invest-ments which, at least outwardly, had a pacifying effect, this ten-dency became overwhelming after the start of the big depression. The end of the influx of capital from the United States showed suddenly that Germany had "rationalized" its industrial machinery too strongly and as a result had done the opposite of what was to be expected of a nation whose expansion had been cut short by the Versailles Treaty, and which, instead of expan-ding, had even lost much territory. The "scissors" between the pressure exercised by the German economy and the political possibilities open to the Germans thus became wider than ever before; Germany had to expand, but could not.

It was under these circumstances that Germany's struggle against the Versailles Treaty and paying reparations reached a climax, thus furnishing excellent grounds for Hitler's propa-ganda. It is true that Germany's old ruling classes, which con-tinued to play first fiddle both socially and economically in spite of the establishment of the Weimar Republic, were not inclined to let Hitler conduct the orchestra. Most junkers, contemptuous of the plebeian ersatz *élite* that suddenly emerged from below, looked upon Hitler with the open disregard shown him by their peer, old Reichs President von Hindenburg. He spoke mockingly of this "Bohemian corporal" and would not give him a better portfolio than that of Mails and Communications, and even the bulk of heavy industry, though convinced that a change was necessary, showed little indication to submit to Hitler. Not only the owners of the big department stores, the export traders and the big stockbrokers, most of them Jews whose commercial interests collided with those of the lower middle classes, but also the bulk of the chemical industry which was strongly interested in export, and the old family enterprises in the Ruhr valley, such as Krupp, Hoesch, Haniel, Klöckner, and Stinnes combines, dis-played a lack of enthusiasm for the Führer. But even the non-Hitlerian firms approved of many parts of the Hitler programme and National Socialism was extremely popular in the ranks of the big banking and the main steel combines, which by receiving public anti-depression assistance had been brought practically into the hands of the Reich, since all of them wished for Hitler's help to regain the independence they had lost. Divided as to the tactics to be followed, all these elements, together with the

Reichswehr, which wanted to expand the Army, were unanimously agreed that the National Socialist wave should be used, and that it would be possible to keep Hitler on the leash.

Hitler himself had no knowledge of economic matters and only little experience in dealing with the nobility, but he knew the value of his movement to both spheres. But he was not inclined to grant his assistance to anyone without exacting a tremendous price. While he admired his forerunner, Karl Lueger, Mayor of Vienna, for his skill in "successfully soliciting the help of the mighty", and while he used exaggerated and oily assurances of personal devotion which recalled the nauseating phrases with which Wagner signed his letters to King Ludwig, he spoiled the hope of the monarchs that they could use this little lackey for regaining thrones lost in 1918. Instead of serving others, he sought power for himself.

Perhaps the spring of 1932, when the upper classes began their efforts to utilize but leash Hitler, was the most difficult of his peacetime career. Leading in these endeavours was General Kurt von Schleicher, the dominating figure of the *Reichswehr* politically if not militarily. In May 1932 the political parties supporting the Weimar Republic re-elected the monarchist-minded von Hindenburg as Reichs President because he was the only candidate who could beat Hitler. A few weeks later von Schleicher succeeded in making von Hindenburg appoint the von Papen Cabinet by cleverly appealing to the President's old monarchist feelings. The new Cabinet sought the support of junkers and heavy industry, and practically put an end to the Republic, but it kept Hitler out of power. Fortunately for Hitler, the men who tried to leash him were split socially. While von Schleicher's *Reichswehr*, being the army of the Republic, tried to keep its political frame intact, as this allowed it a leading rôle in the planned rearmament, and von Schleicher himself was even ready to combine with the trade unions, the powers backing von Papen —heavy industry and the landowners—were not particularly satisfied with this programme.

Von Papen staged several big election campaigns in succession, which almost brought the Nazi Party to ruin. But this split not only saved the Nazi Party from certain destruction, but at the last moment was given an opportunity to rise. In the beginning of January 1933 Hitler secretly met von Papen, who had been succeeded in the Chancellorship some weeks earlier by von Schleicher, and in a lengthy discussion in the home of the Cologne banker von Schröder laid the ground for a political alliance between them, which led to von Papen persuading old von Hindenburg to appoint Hitler Reichs Chancellor. The great moment saw Adolf Hitler, the one-time homeless inmate of Viennese poor-houses, in the rôle of a saviour of society he had dreamed of; as in 1923, it was tainted with blackmail and corruption. While the preparatory talks were going on, the Hitler papers without interruption supported the demands in the Reichstag to investigate the subsidies known as "Osthilfe" which the "suffering" Prussian junkers, including the von Hindenburg family, received during the years of depression. As soon as Hitler came to power these attacks stopped; Hitler gave the von Hindenburg family about five thousand acres of tax-exempt land, and the son of the Reichs President, who had advocated Hitler's appointment, was promoted to major-general. No less beneficial was Hitler's rise for the big banks and the United Steel Works (Vereinigte Stahlwerke), which had backed him and which had practically slipped into the control of the Reich due to the debts they had accumulated during the depression. Both groups got rid of Reich control and were reconditioned economically, and the banks profited greatly from the elimination of their Jewish competitors. Herr Vögler, director-general of United Steel, had joined the banker von Schröder and the ambiguous Hjalmar Schacht, the Reich's "financial wizard", in putting pressure on the other big capitalists in demanding that Hitler be made Chancellor; immediately after Hitler had met von Papen, this group assisted the Hitler party in ridding itself of some of its debts of twelve million marks. Just as with Mussolini, the Cabinet formed by Hitler on January 30th was a coalition Government, but Hitler was not slow in reshaping it in the Nazi sense. By outsmarting his conservative colleagues in the Cabinet Hitler received their consent to new elections, and by a typical act of dictatorial provocation, the burning of the Reichstag building on February 27th, for which he blamed the Communists, he succeeded in depriving them of their seats in the Reichstag, thus securing for himself the majority in Parliament which allowed him to do as he pleased. Whether he, personally, had been informed in advance of the burning of the Reichstag will presumably remain as doubtful as the degree of Mussolini's responsibility for the assassination of Matteotti. It is certain, however, that the head of the propaganda service, the malicious club-footed Dr. Josef Goebbels, planned this action, that the second big man in the party, President of the Reichstag Hermann Göring, supported it (he had been appointed Minister of the Interior on January 30th), and that a detachment of Röhm's storm troopers carried it out by using the underground corridor which connected Göring's official residence with the Reichstag building. The gradual strangling of the political opposition by the tremendous terrorism of those days, and the outrages of the SA, which Göring raised to the rank of auxiliary police, were accentuated by propaganda just as terrifying, which was paid for at Hitler's request by the big industrial combines, which from then onwards supported the Nazi movement.

The Third Reich

The more dictatorial a Government is, the more it reflects the characteristics of its chief personality. It is true that the most despotic tyrant can never free himself entirely from the social conditions that favour his rise to power. If unable to satisfy his followers who carried him to power, or, at least, to checkmate them by creating social counterweights, as well as defeating all foreign nations which attempt to hamper his plans, he is lost. His entire political activity is guided by his own social interests and ideas and by those of his followers. But as long as he is able to stay at the helm he is much less restricted by outside interference in making his political decisions than are other political leaders, which gives his psychological development, his motives and his social limitations an unusual significance. Viewed from this angle, the Third Reich, as Hitler himself referred to his creation, was a tremendously magnified picture of the Hitler of the Viennese years who had been suddenly grafted on to the German tree; under his rule Germany's politics were made to serve purposes very alien to most Germans. Hitler, said a popular joke of those days, was "Austria's revenge for Sadowa", meaning the battle of 1866, also known as Königgrätz, by which Prussia expelled Austria from Germany. In his neurotic impetus to revenge himself on the foes of his Viennese days—Jews, Slavs, Catholics, Marxists—this man resorted to measures no one dared to use, which appealed strongly to the Germans of 1933, who did not know that the enemies this pan-Germanist fought were not automatically those of German pan-Germanism; later, when his prescriptions no longer worked, Germany perished from continuing to use them.

The worst result was that his neurosis infected his followers, as can be heard in recordings of the hysterical shouts of the crowds in the speeches he delivered in the Berlin Sportpalast at that time. A sceptic among his listeners who heard the first of them from a distance—it was the first time that Hitler had his speeches broadcast—made the following entry in his diary: "Voice and conduct of a complete lunatic. It sounded as if he were constantly foaming at the mouth. A funny feeling: I know the captain of the boat I am on [von Hindenburg] to be feeble-minded, and the pilot [Hitler] to be a madman; now, am I a lunatic, or are the others?" A few weeks later, that same witness, having seen Hitler emerge from his Munich flat, beleaguered by a small curious crowd, and drive off in his black Mercedes, had this to say: "The slogan of an electric shock that goes through that crowd is no mere invention. There was for a moment something immeasurable, almost unreal, to be witnessed, and clearly so. Just as if they wanted to fall on their faces in prayer. 'Don't you know that I am Christ, the Son of the Almighty?' "

In the eyes of his followers *Der Führer* had something of the emperors of the German myths who sat in the Kyffhauser of the Untersberg mountains—the latter very close to Hitler's Berchtesgaden retreat—and planned Germany's salvation. His most prominent helpers—though all of middle-class descent—had grown up at a time when the nobility had still been leading socially, suffered from the feeling that they were not noble born, and regarded the Nazi movement as the start of a new feudalism. Heinrich Himmler, for instance, was the son of a high-school teacher known for being ridiculously devout towards the upper stratum, who had succeeded in persuading the Bavarian Prince Heinrich (whose tutor he was) to play godfather to his boy. This inspired the latter with the idea of furnishing a room in the parental apartment with relics of his family and with family trees which he used to worship for hours. The strange desire of this very shortsighted bureaucrat of death, who wore glasses from childhood, to replace the old nobility by one of middle-class descent with Hitler's help, appears to be rooted in part in certain of his experiences while at the high school. Here he was surrounded by newly born royal pages who stood far beneath that ambitious teacher's pet in the intellectual field, but who outranked him greatly in the social scale; the well-tailored dark blue uniforms and the caps they wore are quite clearly the prototype of the uniform of the SS (security guards) he was to organize.

While Himmler, having grown up in this Bavarian atmosphere, had rather similar views to those of Hitler, Hermann Göring, though likewise born in Bavaria, was the son of an official in the Reich colonial service that used to be controlled by the Prussians. This made the young Göring an admirer of the junkers, the Prussian type of nobility whose sons surrounded him in the training school for officer candidates at Grosslichterfelde. Tremendously vigorous and intellectually capable, young Hermann outdistanced these boys even more than Himmler outdid the pages, but socially they outshone him just as much. In addition to these two Nazi leaders, Hitler's party harboured a third prominent would-be aristocrat: Joachim von Ribbentrop, who owed his aristocratic-sounding "von" to his having been adopted, for the promise of a cash payment, by a distant aunt, and who as a native Hanoverian followed the local tradition by playing up to the British aristocracy, and as a youngster went to Canada, where he succeeded in gaining access to its social circles. A fourth would-be aristocrat in Hitler's entourage was the good-looking and outwardly cultured "peasant leader" R. Walter Darré, a German from overseas, whose ideas about the creation of a new nobility from peasant and middle class were close to Himmler's way of thinking. Germans from abroad or from frontier districts, all of them ardent nationalists, were conspicuous among the leaders of the movement, which apparently envisaged a renewal of the German-controlled Holy Roman Empire in modern form; the only one of its leading men who did not join it for reasons of social or national resentment was Josef Goebbels. His icy and spiteful but deadly efficient tirades against the Jews were prompted by his bodily defect, a club foot: the fear of the "darkened and shrunken 'Teuton,' " as a racial publication referred to him in dead earnest—with the club foot to be taken for a Jew or to be regarded as their equal. Consequently he was the only one among the leading Nazis who did not behave at the end like an independent feudal vassal trying to save his neck, but who perished with his Führer.

Taking its cue from that medical optimist, Dr. Coué, Goebbels's propaganda tried to convince the German lower middle classes that under the Führer their situation was getting better and better hourly. To stimulate these feelings, Goebbels interpreted the average German's daily routine work as being an expression of Germanic habits and customs. The success of this treatment was undeniable. The brown shock troops marching like conquerors through the cities, pushing along maltreated Jews hung with crude posters bearing inscriptions insulting their race; the boy-cott of Jewish enterprises which started at once "as a try-out"; the countless arrests and maltreatment of political prisoners in the Berlin "Columbia Haus" and other places later transformed into concentration camps; the termination of the political inde-pendence of the German Länder (individual States); the sup-pression of all non-Nazi parties and newspapers; the *Gleichschal-tung* (synchronization of Nazification) of all professional organiz-ations in every field of human life, were signs of a complete political change which made the German lower middle classes master of the German Reich after they had been serflike from time immemorial. The German *petit bourgeois* were driven almost hysterical by their feeling of unbounded happiness which was fanned by Hitler's gigantic mass festivals, but they failed to see that the splendid chances offered were based on political rather than economic premises and were bound to disappear when the régime vanished. In keeping with its counter-revolu-tionary nature, National Socialism left the economic foundations of society, the industrial combines and big estates, almost un-touched, and restricted itself to securing employment for its followers by "synchronizing" public administration and the nation's entire cultural and private life as well as by suppressing and despoiling the Jews. As well as this it procured new positions steadily increasing its party organizations and public sector of the armament industry, such as the Hermann Göring Works, and by supporting private enterprise.

By much activity to help the lower middle classes, by its winter relief and the huge *Kraft durch Freude* (Strength through Joy)

organization and by the much-publicized "peaceful" undertakings, such as the construction of the Autobahnen (modern
highways which could be used also for military purposes) and the
Volkswagen, the Hitler régime deliberately camouflaged the true
character of its plans—all of which served the preparation for
war. The great increase of social welfare and mass entertainment,
paid for by the taxes that resulted from the rearmament boom,
impressed even the workers. Admittedly the régime had dissolved the unions, opposed any rise in wages, attached the
labourer firmly to his place of work and fought unemployment
by forced labour. But the increase in employment raised the
household budget even of those workers who had not lost their
positions during the depression, and in the ranks of those who
had been unemployed—many of them Communists—Hitler
gained very strong support.

Incomparable, however, were the profits the big industrial
combines made as a result of the régime, even though in many
cases they had to give back part of them to influential party
members, as the merchants in big American cities gave to gangsters who promised them "protection". The lack of enthusiasm
some of those combines had shown during Hitler's rise, the producers' constant struggles against the restrictions of the second
world war, and their anger at the blackmail for which these
regulations were used by Göring and other party leaders must not
obscure the way in which industry as a whole exploited Hitler's
system. The sales of the big combines rose overnight; the profits
were retained, thanks to Hitler's monetary policy, to a much
larger extent by the producers, who used them for enlarging their
plants. The producers also benefited from the wage freezes and
the prohibition of strikes; individual industrialists such as the
redoubtable Friedrich Flick—later sentenced by the Allies for
war crimes, but today once again Germany's leading industrialist
—profited from the enforced sales of Jewish property, which they
cleverly made permanent by blackmail. Hitler's expansionist
policy after 1936 and especially during the second world war
brought numerous foreign-owned works into the hands of their
German competitors; the German appropriation of these plants
in turn was followed when machines and tools became scarce in
Germany a few years later by a systematic spoliation of the
premises. The execution of this spoliation campaign and the

employment of forced labour from concentration camps in Germany and the conquered areas were supervised by Hitler's party agents, whose activity often displeased the producers. But the big companies adapted themselves to the system and profiteered from it since it was the basis of their expansion; Krupp, I.G. Farben (combined dyestuff interests) and other combines established branches at the sites of some Eastern concentration camps where inmates worked before being gassed. The so-called Berta works erected by Krupp, named after Berta Krupp von Bohlen, the grand old lady of that dynasty of industrial giants, used exclusively cheap labour from concentration camps. Among the men who staged the attempt on Hitler's life on July 20th, 1944, were many members of the German nobility, but not one industrialist.

The nobility, the Churches and the old German society which had been leading in the time of Imperial Germany soon found reason to regret the rise to power of their supposed saviour, Adolf Hitler, no less vehemently than did the working class, the Jews and the intellectuals, who had been the primary targets of his attack. Having assumed control, National Socialism at once declared war on Christianity and on all existing society. Even Hitler himself temporarily resented the ferocious fury of the lower-middle-class elements he had unleashed and the violent deeds of Captain Röhm's SA, though he was of course less prompted by love of the old ruling classes than by fear that Röhm and his men, who regarded themselves as chosen military leaders in the coming war, might antagonize the *Reichswehr,* Germany's official army, whose support, training and experience he needed for carrying through his plans. When the future of his pet ideas was at stake, Hitler never hesitated a moment to use the most cruel brutality even against his own followers; on June 30th, 1934, he staged a crafty surprise attack upon the unsuspecting Röhm and his men, and slaughtered all the SA leaders and also some suspect rightists, among them General von Schleicher and his wife. It was the political purchasing price Hitler paid for gaining the backing of the *Reichswehr* for his succession to the old Reichs President von Hindenburg, then on his deathbed. While continuing to be addressed as *Der Führer,* Hitler henceforth combined his old function of Chancellor, or Prime Minister, with that of chief executive. The initiative for the action against Röhm came in part from Göring and

Himmler, the dreaded chief of the Gestapo, or secret state police, whose black uniformed SS then began to replace the SA as first power in the Third Reich. The SS in the ten years that followed reached the goal Röhm had merely dreamed of : to subject the Army to the Party. In Himmler's "SS State" the National Socialist dictatorship was to reach its terrifying climax.

Night over Europe

The rearmament of Germany, which formed the main background for these events, would have been unthinkable had Germany's Western neighbours and their political allies insisted on controlling Germany's armaments, a right granted to them under the Treaty of Versailles, which should have been exercised to safeguard their own populations. Each presentation of the Hitler dictatorship, however brief and sketchy, must therefore attempt to explain the fantastic deception by which the master of black magic at the top of the Third Reich prevented Europe from making use of its privileges. Hitler's personal development was suited to the mood of the time, when not only the German middle classes but those of other countries saw in economic Fascism and rearmament a possible way out of the depression; moreover, Hitler served these purposes even better than anyone else, in an exaggerated and pathological way in which he simply had no equal. The German Führer was still the Hitler of the Viennese days, the foe of Jews and Slavs, who surrounded him in the poor-houses and came mostly from the East. His hatred of France, though ardent, was less genuine.

This explains his successes and failures and much of what his contemporaries could not understand, such as his originally peaceful attitude towards the Western nations, which the German nationalists hated intensely, and his alliance with the despised Poles, whom it was known that he himself looked down on. Those surprised at this failed to see that Josef Pilsudski, the dictator of the Bolívar type who ruled Poland in those years, was susceptible to Hitler's fine flatteries and that there was one element he hated still more than the Poles : "Russo-Jewish Bolshevism". Seen in this light, his alliance with Poland was merely intended to check the Power he saw as his arch-foe : Soviet Russia. It would last until he felt strong enough to dispense with Poland's help. The same was true of his peaceable attitude towards the West, which was intended to camouflage Germany's rearmament long enough for him to have attained the strength needed for forcing Europe by peaceful or military means to join the campaign against the Russians that he had planned.

The Führer's demonic game was to blind his foreign enemies, allaying the suspicion of the rightest parties in his neighbouring states by anti-Bolshevist and Fascist slogans, and those of the leftists in turn by unctuous pacifist phrases. He tore up one international treaty after another without fear of reprisal, openly planned the conquest of Europe, and finally conducted his war, recalling the infernal devices by which Goethe's Doctor Faust, in the second part of the great tragedy, wins his battles with Mephistopheles's help. From the moment when the world of Hitler's imagination began to deviate hopelessly from the reality that surrounded him, during his decline in Vienna, his thoughts had more and more assumed the form of dreams. Now, in the 1930s when his old pet ideas—the construction of tremendous buildings and cities—started to materialize, he still continued to dream, but now of different things. His unleashed imagination, spurred by his thirst for revenge and punishment of the elements he made responsible for the sufferings of his youth, penetrated into human spheres and produced results which no other statesman, let alone general or bureaucrat, could either match or even know of. The development of psychological warfare, the permeating of foreign countries by "fifth columns", the dropping of parachutists and the organization of sabotage in the rear of the enemy and the staging of "provocative actions by the foe"—this entire devilish mixture of lies, deception, cunning and betrayal was to a great extent Hitler's personal work; it was the world of the Nibelungen, of the Tarnhelm and of the magic rings and swords that grant the hero superhuman power, but without stopping his ultimate fall. Like Siegfried who slays the dragon but whose back remains vulnerable, Hitler, anxious to start his crusade against Russia, neglected to seek proper protection for his rear, an attitude which he shared with Mussolini, who made the same mistake when challenging Great Britain.

The Horsemen of the Apocalypse

Until the middle of the 1930s *Il Duce* co-operated with the West rather than with Germany in the international field. The

American billions which had encouraged this attitude had now ceased to flow to Europe. But Mussolini had sleepless nights from fear of Hitler's invasion of Austria—that disobedient Mecca which the National Socialist prophet who had no honour in his own country tried to reconquer with the help of the men from Medina. In 1934, when the Nazis murdered the Austrian Chancellor Dr. Engelbert Dollfuss, who had opposed Hitler's annexation plans, Mussolini almost went to war against the Führer. His concern about Hitler's advance in the north, however, was mixed with secret admiration and with a desire to match the Nazi's efforts. It was rather like professional jealousy and it led his country into the abyss. His urge to found an "Impero" and to surround the Mediterranean with a revived Roman Empire clashed with the interests of Great Britain, then still the paramount Power in most of the area, and this practically drove *Il Duce* into Hitler's hands. His occupation of Abyssinia (1935) and his intervention in the Spanish Civil War obliged him to seek the help of the Führer more and more. The price he had to pay was the loss of his political independence, which in the end vanished completely.

The chief decisions in this competition between the dictators came in 1940, when Mussolini, green with jealousy, jumped on Hitler's war chariot just before the Führer concluded an armistice with France. A few months later he started an aggressive war against Greece to compensate himself for the smallness of the share of the French prey he had received, and thus in turn forced Hitler to change his plan of attack against Russia which was being prepared in deep secrecy in those very months. The final outbreak of the Russo-German war threatened *Il Duce* whose entire plans were aimed at attacking Great Britain in the Mediterranean, just as dangerously in the rear as the Western Powers' armed resistance against Germany menaced Hitler's back while he moved against Russia.

It was still the Viennese Hitler who was only moderately interested in the West and its problems. The list of his conquests, Austria, Czechoslovakia, Memel, Poland—clearly indicated the road to the East he intended to follow, the stages of the extensive and terrible revenge that was to compensate him for his former failure in life and for the execution of which he now marshalled the might and power of Europe's leading military nation. The understandable pride of the little man from Austria to have brought about the famous "Anschluss", the reunion of his home-land with the German Reich, was obscured by the orgies of hatred which followed and which showed the main motives of his action. Refusing to admit to himself that his rise was the result of temporary historical conditions with which he stood or fell, Hitler behaved as if the satisfying of his thirst for revenge were something ordained by Providence and as if each effort to stop his conquering legions were a struggle against the divine world order. The constant political retreat of the Western Powers, shown so clearly in their concluding the Munich agree-ment with him in which they abandoned Czechoslovakia in 1938, made him feel that his planned crusade against the East would not be hampered by anybody; the sudden resistance of England and France after his treacherous occupation of Prague (March 1939), capital of the central part of Czechoslovakia he had promised to leave untouched, appeared to him as a violation of the plans Providence wanted him to carry out. With the flexibility for which he was known he changed fronts with light-ning speed and in August 1939 concluded his famous non-aggres-sion pact with Stalin by which he tried to prevent the West from interfering with his attack against Poland. He later wooed the West when the hour for coming to a reckoning with Russia would strike.

That the Western Powers, despite this pact and the seemingly hopeless situation it created for them, began to make war against him, made Hitler furious. Possessed with the gigantic idea that he was called to establish a new "Aryan" *Ostreich* (Eastern Country) on the debris of the Slav world, he felt that his campaigns in Scandinavia and the West which followed his conquest of Poland involved an unwelcome delay, a fatal postponement of his holy crusade against Moscow. By political trickery he had hoped to prevent the West from intervening in this crusade before it was too late. In the tormenting feeling that he had to solve the chief problems of his career at an age at which Napoleon on St. Helena awaited his end, he regarded the conquest of Western and Northern Europe—perhaps his greatest achievement—merely as a transitory stage in the fulfilment of his chief mission, and thus gave away all the trump cards which a Bismarck in his place would have used to Germany's advantage.

9—DOS

From the angle of international politics the outbreak of the war of 1939 matched the moment in Goethe's *The Sorcerer's Apprentice* when the ghost conjured up by the apprentice changes from a domestic servant into a dangerous monster which threatens to drown everything. Down to that moment the ruling classes of all Europe had refused to listen to the warnings of exiles and their own social equals in Germany. With deadly terror they saw their supposed saviour take off his mask and emerge as a devil who moved the whole gigantic machinery of total war for their suppression.

The unfolding of Germany's military might in the West—a result of Great Britain's stiffening attitude—and the chain of victories that made Hitler master of Europe were, however, not an unmixed blessing for him. The tremendous triumph, the coronation of a decade of almost constant successes, had rather the effect of the prophecy of the witches in Shakespeare's *Macbeth*, and turned his head completely. Instead of recognizing that these successes, like Napoleon's victories, were merely the strategic results of a temporary social advantage and that German superiority in the fields of motorized warfare, tanks and military aviation could soon be matched and even outdone by other nations, he saw his victories mainly as the product of his personal intuition. But the extraordinary energy and demoniacal creative imagination which had carried him to the top started to work against him as soon as the ship he steered began to sail in the wrong direction. From the moment he had conquered all Continental Europe, the political and military reality deviated more and more from the world of his dreams which pressed him to start war against Russia.

In keeping with the "anti-Eastern" ideas he had first conceived in Vienna, he had relied on the protection of his rear by the British throughout his career and even after the start of the war. He had signed a naval agreement with Britain, and had failed to develop his navy sufficiently or to make adequate preparation for a landing, had led a "phoney war" for months in the West, had allowed the British to escape from Dunkirk, and finally, after having endorsed the idea of air attacks against the British Isles, had broken them off without result. Just as Napoleon had once marched away to start a campaign in the East after the failure of his landing attempt, Hitler, while still threatening England, prepared his famous "Barbarossa" plan, with the difference that the attack in the East involved a much larger risk than in Napoleon's time, given the development of the air arm and the political solidarity of the Atlantic nations. A Siegfried, but with his entire back vulnerable, he set out with resolution to fight the dragon of Eastern Bolshevism, though ample warnings foretold him his fate.

The huge campaign in the East increased the natural conflict between the Army and party, which is typical of the entire Fascist system, and which had not been ended for any appreciable period even by Hitler's *coup* against Röhm. As successor to von Hindenburg, Hitler was the supreme commander of the Army. This permitted Heinrich Himmler and his SS—the true victors in the struggle against Röhm—to carry out his underground war against the Army in a much more efficient manner than Röhm had ever been able. A few weeks before Hitler's invasion of Austria, Himmler, by his usual mixture of lies, blackmail and intrigue, had succeeded in bringing down both the War Minister and the Chief of the Army Command, which increased Hitler's personal control of the armed forces. During the tremendous struggle against the U.S.S.R. the conflict between Army and party continued, with the Army coming out second best.

It was the success of Hitler and Himmler in every respect. The Prussian junkers, who still controlled the Army, had been inclined for centuries to regard Russia as an ally against Poles and Frenchmen rather than a foe; at any event not as the terrible monster as she appeared to many South Germans and Austrians. In opposing the leaders of the German ersatz *élite* who were all eager to conquer *lebensraum* in the East, the Army leaders could give very sound strategic arguments showing the risk of the adventure, which later proved correct. Their arguments were the same as those Napoleon before him had neglected, even though a blind man could recognize their validity, taking into account the dangerous nature of a large-scale offensive in a gigantic area with a most inhospitable climate. The region seemed to be made for conducting partisan warfare against the attacker's communications, and invited the defender to lure the attacker into an increasingly difficult position by constant withdrawals. But dictators like Napoleon and Hitler are not only blind, but possessed by manias. Confronted with the example of his great predecessor, whose coffin in the Dôme des Invalides in Paris he had pensively regarded in 1940, he hurried east to meet the same fate. Some wits in enemy countries contended that he had saluted the dead man with his "Heil Hitler" and a voice from the tomb had answered "Heil Moscow".[1]

The tremendous campaign against Russia which began on June 22nd, 1941, revealed the natural limits of his mind, as well as the way in which the social forces that had exploited his régime gradually failed him. This development pushed his most radical followers into the foreground the more the tragedy approached its end. Hitler's efforts to annihilate the Russians by the kind of gigantic motorized pincer movements and tank attacks which had been so effective in the West bogged down in the Russian mud. In his centre the enemy slipped out of his grip three times before he was caught. The southern wing of the German army, which had encountered stiff enemy resistance, was disengaged by strong tank forces Hitler detached from the centre, which had advanced a long way, and this led to the greatest battle of encirclement known in history. But this operation, although successful, hampered the execution of Hitler's overall plan of attack and spoiled the success of his surprise and blitzkrieg strategy, which was the only way he could win that campaign. The freezing of the front lines and the long-drawn-out positional warfare were difficult in themselves because of Russia's vast dimensions, and were bound to bring the vastly superior war potential of the enemy coalition into play, which was certain to cause Hitler's defeat. Insisting like a madman on defending each square foot of his conquests, to save the *Ostreich* he had planned, at the approach of the first winter of this campaign, Hitler flatly rebuffed his generals who suggested a tactical withdrawal. The success of this strategy corroborated his perilous belief in his personal intuition and seduced him the following year, 1942, into ordering a dual attack against the Caucasus and against Stalingrad, during which—unlike the previous year—he met with a strongly reinforced opponent, which made impossible a repetition

---

[1] "Heil Hitler", pronounced with the right hand raised, was the German form of the Fascist salute. "Heil Moscow" was the salute of the German Communists. The city of Moscow was also the spot where Napoleon's luck turned.

of the strategic miracle he had performed. As a result of his decisive defeat before Stalingrad, the blame for which, being a small man, he laid on his foes and his followers his conflicts with his generals reached unheard-of dimensions. Like a scorned prophet of ancient times, he withdrew to the solitude of his bunker, bearing a grudge and cursing his fate. A saviour and prophet is never wrong. His failures are the work of black magic. For the solitary man in the Wolfsschanze, as his secret headquarters in East Prussia were referred to, his chain of defeats seemed to be the work of infernal demons that bring about the Twilight of the Gods; being the prophet of the holy crusade against Russia he still, however, believed in his own magic invulnerability; he loved to think that his uncovered rear—the Atlantic front—was protected by his new miracle weapons, the V1 and V2, which, though products of the highest stage of science, were presented in his propaganda as a sort of Nibelung device.

The Führer's intuition was by far the best ally of his enemies. Instead of using the immense war potential of conquered Europe to defend himself against the Atlantic world he had challenged to a life-and-death struggle, he whittled it down in his campaign in the East and exposed the bulk of his empire without any adequate protection against the attacks of the enemy air fleets and later the onslaught of the invasion army. The increasing outside pressure on the Third Reich encouraged the European nations he had conquered to raise their heads once more; it thus stimulated organized sabotage and political and military resistance, and opened the eyes of many a German who hitherto had believed in the Führer's star. The social picture of Europe and especially Germany under this dictatorship assumed a grotesque aspect. The old Continent had become practically an immense slave state. While Hitler's total mobilization made the last German man—the oldest as well as the youngest—carry arms and sent him to the front, millions of foreigners under forced labour, deported by the régime from their homelands, worked under rigid SS supervision in the offices and factories. They were joined there by the wives of the German soldiers. Females deported from foreign countries looked after the German *Hausfrau's* household. On the lowest step of this new society stood the gipsies and the Jews, whom the demon from harmless little Braunau ground to death in his concentration camps.

The longer the war lasted and the more mischief it did, the more did the German producers, like the generals, lose their freedom of action. As armament production was of overwhelming importance for their big combines and individual plants, the products were much more subservient to the régime than the old nobility, whose claim for leadership in State and Army was threatened by an uncanny plebeian. Their authority, formerly unchallenged, and their freedom to act were increasingly restricted. From the spring of 1942, when the Führer created a special armament ministry under Albert Speer, total war became a reality in the economic field as well. Through the so-called *Reichsvereinigung* (Reich production rings) Speer controlled the allocation of materials and labour, the wages and prices for practically all enterprises. The labour force needed was raised by slave hunts all over Europe. At the same time, these slave hunts served Hitler's favourite aim : the depopulation of the East and freeing it from all non-German elements. Despite the imminent loss of the war, the Führer and his henchman Heinrich Himmler stuck to this plan with pathological tenacity. The German Reich was to form a national nucleus which was to extend far into Russia in the East, and was to be surrounded by tributary people. It was to be based on slave work. When the war ended the SS was actually rising to the rank of an *élite* within the Nazi ersatz *élite*; it had replaced or subjected the old *élites*—nobility, big industrialists, intellectuals, Church leaders, and bureaucrats—and with the help of its partisans in conquered Europe was bringing the old Continent under the rule of a new warrior aristocracy.

Twilight of the Gods

The increasing outside pressure on Germany had the strange effect of bringing these terrifying and grotesque schemes nearer to their realization the closer Hitler's Germany moved towards its inevitable end. Hitler's defeat at Stalingrad and subsequent retreat from Russia, the destruction of his Mediterranean position which led to the downfall of Mussolini in the summer of 1943, the round-the-clock appearance of Allied bomber squadrons all over the Reich, and, finally, the successful Allied invasion of France, kindled the low-burning flames of the German resistance movement which culminated in the attempt of July 20th,

1944, against Hitler's life. Its failure permitted Himmler and his SS to tyrannize the Reich without any further restraint. The attempt was not mainly the work of the junker opposition to the Nazis, as observers assumed at the time, but rather the result of a resistance movement springing from common emergency action of pre-Hitler Germany which fought the Nazis' satanic neo-paganism. Junkers, officers, high officials, Catholic and Protestant priests, ministers and intellectuals, Socialist politicians and labour leaders co-operated in this work. Big business was practically un-represented. It still flourished, though Germany perished. Given their ethical views and mental fortitude, the men who perished in Plötzensee and other places of vengeance as a result of the failure of the attempt belonged to the finest flower of German manhood. Their death brought Germany into the hands of the most neuro-tic of the leaders of the German ersatz *élite*, who were abysmally inferior to their victims in knowledge of human and religious problems. They could now yield to their inferiority instincts towards real nobility without any inhibition. Their efforts to stay afloat under those conditions where the tide had turned against them, their increased terrorism against the old *élites* which reflected their rising anxiety for their own fate, were interpreted in their political propaganda as the moral independence of born supermen not hampered by the law of Christian ethics.

After July 20th Himmler became the true master of the nation and went even farther in this field than the Führer, who in the solitude of his mountains or his bunker brooded over his fate. Having been well informed about the movement against the Führer from the outset, he seems to have been ready to make himself supreme leader had the attempt succeeded. We now have evidence that this most trusted of Hitler's trusted ones had extended his hand to the enemy countries for months to offer them peace conditions about which the Führer remained unin-formed, and that his closest advisers tried to persuade him to murder Hitler by means of his favourite astrologist. For the greatest mass murderer in history such matters had lost their frightening aspect. "Whether ten thousand Russian females fall down in exhaustion while digging an anti-tank ditch", he had told his SS in a Poznan speech in 1943, "interests me only in so far as the anti-tank ditch is finished for Germany." The medical reports of the so-called experts working in his concentration camps informed him about the mass sterilizations performed there, the extermination of thousands of people by inoculating them with various diseases, freezing them to death in ice-filled containers, the laceration of their blood-vessels in pressure chambers that simulated the change of atmospheric conditions during the fall of a body from the stratosphere, and other vile forms of torturing and killing human beings.

The SS which he commanded and made the leading power in the Reich, formed the upper crust of Hitler's ersatz *élite*. It stood far above the majority of party members socially. German sociologists call it a *Geschworenenschaft*, a community formed by a solemn fidelity oath, which they say consisted of young men who had become outcasts from the nobility and bourgeoisie in the troubles of the late 1920s and early 1930s. In addition to these men who controlled the many SS offices such as the *Reichssicherheitshauptamt* (Reich main security office), and the *Wirtschafts- und Verwaltungshauptamt* (main economic and administrative office), the SS comprised the huge personnel in charge of the concentration camps, who stood on a somewhat lower level. It was recruited from bankrupt barbers, dismissed policemen and prison guards and from the many old party members who had been expelled from non-German countries because of their political agitation in the years before Hitler's conquest of Europe and had sought shelter in the Reich. By maltreating political prisoners most of these men compensated themselves for the loss of the dubious pleasures connected with their work which they had missed for some time. The camps often had an enormous number of inmates—Auschwitz alone had a floating population of 180,000 to 200,000 people who lived in 620 barracks and of whom up to 10,000 were killed each day—and served at the same time to enrich the SS. They rented their slave labour to private producers to a large extent, where they worked under the most rigid supervision, but they also founded factories of their own, for leather and textile production, for construction work, or for the manufacture of concrete, and they further expanded into the fields of agriculture and forestry. The monetary value of the average concentration-camp slave which was realized from the exploitation of his work and utilization of his belongings, his body and his teeth, was reckoned by the SS to be 1,600 Reichsmarks (about £145 10s.). Certain factories acquired the bodies on the spot and made superphosphate from them. The gold from the teeth was sent to the Reichsbank, which paid the SS 60 million marks for sixty-seven shiploads. The special service troops of the SS which followed Hitler's armies on their march east like revolting hungry vultures and slaughtered Jews by the thousands served at the same time economic purposes; the loot they took from their victims was sent to the SS *Wirtschafts- und Verwaltungshauptamt.* In the last year of the war, because of overcrowding of their gas-extermination facilities in Auschwitz, the SS began to burn their victims, most of them children, on grills in open fields. The shouting and moaning became so insufferable to the inhabitants of the nearby towns that the camp formed large orchestras to drown it by playing music.

To present a complete picture of the systematic mass killings which took place all over Europe under Hitler and Himmler, but especially in the East, is quite impossible, especially in a short work giving a general picture of the period. It is certain that the basic plan was devised by one single man, a demon haunted by the furies of his past : it was the Hitler of the Viennese period who in this way took the most awful revenge for the failures of his early life. This thirst for revenge collectively infected an entire social stratum which followed him as the saviour from the depression and resembled him in its desire to compensate itself for the psychological damage that crisis had done it, and had sworn to follow him to the very end.

The last act of the Hitler drama saw the Führer, beaten on all fronts in the military sphere, emerge as conqueror from the attempt on his life of July 20th, 1944. In the mind of a man of that type all forces which dared to oppose him were radiations of some devilish magic which threatened to destroy his life's work. His feeling of resentment against his personal opponents who dared to attack his position as Führer and head of the ersatz *élite* overshadowed all other sentiments. While the Reich faced military destruction, he watched with glee the film of the death of his would-be murderers of July 20th and enjoyed his victims' agonies, which he had sharpened artificially in some instances by ordering the hangman to use thin piano wire. To the last moment he saw in himself the Messiah who had to protect Europe against the danger from the East. His desire to perish in this convincing pose caused him to abandon his long-considered idea, to wage his last battle at his Berchtesgaden retreat. Instead, the final scene took place in the Berlin Reichs Chancellery, under fire from Russian guns. Immediately before his death he heard the news that Mussolini, whom he liberated from the grip of his internal foes in 1943 and who like himself had since been planning his revenge, had met his fate near Como while trying to flee from his country, and was hanging with his mistress head downwards in a Milan street. Not unlike Napoleon, Hitler felt deserted by all he once trusted when the end came. While Russian shells exploded outside, the bunker beneath the Reichs Chancellery reverberated with the curses he launched against Göring and Himmler. Even then he refused to admit that he had made mistakes. A Messiah is always right. If things turn out badly, it is the guilt of others. Eva Braun, the little shopgirl whom he took along with him to eternity, gave proper expression to this Hitlerian idea. "No good Germans left", she jotted down in her last hour, "but those in the bunker." Flames devoured their bodies in the very same moment that the Prussian junkers, whom Hitler had approached as their saviour, collapsed like the gods in the last part of Wagner's *Der Ring des Nibelungen*, deprived by the Russians of their seats, their might and their lands. In his last days Hitler wrote the text of two documents, one of a more private nature, the second aimed at eternity. Each symbolized one of the two souls he in fact had: the Austrian *petit bourgeois* and the Führer. In the first of them, his last will, speaks the "Hitler from Leonding" (near Linz), as he was known in his youth. He bequeathed whatsoever valuable pictures he possessed to a museum to be erected at Linz—one of his oldest day-dreams. The other document, entitled testament, contains his legacy to mankind. It gives a lengthy argument which tries to show that he was always right in politics, and also makes some recommendations for a successor—a meaningless gesture under the circumstances. But Hitler could not leave this world without a catch-phrase. A monomaniac more than a maniac, he left this planet with the following words that form the end of his testament:

"Above all, I enjoin the government of the nation and the people to uphold the racial laws to the limit, and mercilessly to resist the poisoner of all nations, international Jewry."

Part V

DICTATORSHIP IN OUR TIME

Chapter Thirteen

THEIR FORM AND THEIR PLACE IN HISTORY

WHEN Sir Isaac Newton saw an apple fall from a tree in his orchard, he had the sudden inspiration that what he had observed might be subject to the same law which governs the mutual attraction of the stars in heaven. Similarly insignificant historical phenomena are frequently controlled by the same fundamental laws as important ones. The rules of the small city tyrannies of Greece, Sicily and the Renaissance and of the countless military dictators of the Hispanic world were determined by the same basic law that explains the appearance of stars of the first magnitude such as Caesar, Cromwell or Napoleon: all these men were born leaders carried into power by a revolutionary wave which they used to establish an aristocracy. The tremendous dynamic drive of these figures came from their being neurotic characters, i.e. they were men who developed complexes in their youth caused by emotional conflicts between their self-esteem and their social surroundings, which predetermined them for their subsequent rôles. Psychopathological cases of this kind are very numerous, but only very rarely do such men gain political or historical significance. In a way, they resembled bacteria whose effect depends on whether they find an adequate seat. Just as there are different bacteria that become virulent under different circumstances, so the types suitable to become dictators are unable to climb to the top unless favoured by the time and social conditions. Quiet times do not encourage dictatorship; even in more stormy years when the tendency is towards dictatorship not all types of candidates have the same chances. Had Hitler lived in Robespierre's France he would have been socially misplaced, just as Robespierre would have had little chance of success in the Germany of 1933. To imagine that Lenin could ever have enacted the part of Bonaparte on 18

Brumaire would be absurd, just as Bonaparte could never have staged the October Revolution of 1917.

The chances of a man becoming a dictator depends on social circumstances. From this angle it would appear that up to the nineteenth century and in some parts of the world for even longer the leader of a bourgeois revolution who might be called a fallen aristocrat had the best chances. We might call him the "classical" dictator.[1] The rise of capitalism in ancient Greece, Sicily and Rome, of commercial capitalism and incipient manufacture in the Renaissance and in seventeenth-century England, and, finally, the growth of the industrial bourgeoisie in France and in the Atlantic world created the climate in which these men rose. Being military leaders, most of those men were supported by the younger sons of the peasantry who recruited their armies or by the native primitive tribes, quite often coloured. Very few of them were originally wealthy; in addition, they lacked the support of a wealthy bourgeoisie, especially in areas such as ancient Sicily or the Spanish-American world, where dictatorship consequently became a standing institution. But their struggle against the landowning nobility and their function as protectors of "peace and order" made them indispensable to the bourgeois stratum, and where it was lacking led, as a rule, to their being supported by foreign capitalists, desirous of opening up their countries. Their whole careers, their *coups d'état*, the way in which they handled finances, legislation, administration, religion, culture and international affairs, made them champions of the middle classes socially though not politically.

The opposite numbers of these "classical" dictators were the representatives of counter-revolutionary dictatorship, the defenders of nobility, landed property and altars, who often acted as lieutenants of the monarchs driven out in a preceding revolution but who used to put stones in the way of those monarchs in case they tried to return. While much less frequent numerically than the "classical" dictatorship, this form is also very old.

Younger than these two older types of dictatorship is that of

[1] The types of dictatorships briefly presented here were described in more detail in the author's book *Why Dictators?* (New York, Macmillan, 1954) which in contrast to the present history of dictatorship, tries to formulate the general empirical laws governing the rise of dictators, and discusses the characteristics of each form of dictatorship.

the lowest classes—we might even call it ultra-revolutionary dictatorship. It first emerged in the time of the Renaissance and the Reformation and in a more developed form in Revolutionary France, finally to culminate in Lenin's Russia.

The most recent form of dictatorship is the tyranny of Fascism and National Socialism, which in view of its strangely deceptive character has been called the "pseudo-revolutionary type" by us.[1]

The age after the second world war is marked by the almost complete disappearance of the "pseudo-revolutionary" type which perished in the ashes of the international conflagration and merely left some stragglers, all in the Hispanic world. One of them—the Argentine dictator Juan Perón—disappeared from the scene in 1955. While in some countries—especially in Italy —small Fascist parties continued to exist, it was not before the spring of 1958, when France went through a bad internal crisis for fear of losing Algiers that the possibility of large-scale Fascism loomed again. The second world war led to a tremendous rise of the ultra-revolutionary form of dictatorship, which profoundly changed its original character. It now developed from a battering-ram of the lowest classes against the ruling society into the pyramid building of a modern Pharaoh, though one dedicated to promoting material progress. After his disappearance from the scene the fate both of his overseers and of his scores of labourers and peasants in turn became dependent on the outcome of a struggle for power between his henchmen.

Along with these more recent types, their older brothers, the classical and counter-revolutionary dictators continued to live on. In keeping with the general development which led to a division of the world into two spheres, not entirely dissimilar, of capitalist and Socialist monster combines, classical dictatorship changed its geographical location. Being the political midwife of bourgeois society it no longer had its place in the Atlantic world, where it was now eclipsed by the counter- and pseudo-revolutionary forms. It continued to exist instead in the non-Sovietized countries of the colonial areas, which are at present still in a stage reached by Europe hundreds of years ago, from which they try to jump straight into the year 2000.

It cannot be denied that dictatorships on the whole are slightly

[1] This nomenclature is taken from the author's book *Why Dictators?*

receding, as compared with the period of the second world war. Looking backward from the year 2000, the dictatorships of the Stalin and Hitler period may appear as the crest of the social wave which can be compared to other waves of dictators in history and which began at the end of the first world war. Most of these waves produced entire series of dictatorships, and the historian must be selective in presenting them, especially in a short manual written for general orientation. Just as our analysis of the tyrannies in Greece, Sicily, the Rennaissance and the Hispanic world had to concentrate on describing some examples, the presentation of the totalitarian dictatorships of our age has had to be very sketchy. It was impossible, for instance, to mention Hitler's lieutenants all over Europe, even by name. Similar considerations must limit the scope of our remarks which follow on the dictatorships which came after Hitler.

Chapter Fourteen

NON-COMMUNIST DICTATORSHIPS
AFTER THE SECOND WORLD WAR

Dawn of Freedom in Latin America

UNTIL the middle of the 1950s Latin America on the whole continued to be ruled by military dictators, even though some of the major states in which the economic progress of the century had given the civilian element the upper hand did not fall under the yoke of military dictators except in times of depression and political crises. The main exception to this general rule was the evolution in Mexico, where the endless iron tyranny of General Porfírio Diáz, that trusted champion of foreign investors, stirred up at a very early stage those anti-colonial and anti-capitalist instincts which led to the elimination of dictatorship in this country, and made it a forerunner of things to come.

The plight of most of these dictators in the big depression of 1929 and the following years, the drop in the exports from their countries and thus in their public revenues, and the stopping of their payments to foreign creditors whch resulted from it, led to difficulties of all kinds with United States investors, making the dictators listen eagerly to the Nazi and Fascist propaganda, to which were added alluring trade offers. But Hitler was concerned with building up Germany's armaments, and did not live up to the promises he had made in the course of his barter policy, which somewhat dampened these pro-Nazi sympathies. To this was added the fear that Hitler, using the huge network of agents he had established there, would intervene in the affairs of individual Latin American countries—which in fact he did in Bolivia, Brazil and Argentine. Thus when prosperity returned to the United States, finally culminating in a war boom, which revived the economic relations between North and South America, most Latin American dictators, including those who had temporarily favoured Hitler, hastened to grab the outstretched hands of their big northern neighbour and to make the public forget the past.

The connection with the Latin American dictators had both advantages and disadvantages for United States policy. It helped the United States—and thus the Western Allies—win the war and enabled Latin America to participate, mainly through her dictators, in the United States war boom and postwar prosperity. It thus restricted Fascist, Nazi and Communist infiltration to some few vulnerable areas especially open to it, and even in the end led to financial agreements between the United States investors and all those countries providing for a resumption of the interest and loan payments that had been stopped during the depression. But it discredited the United States in the eyes of the foes of the dictators, who became constantly more powerful and vociferous, due to the social repercussions of those economic boom years. Thus, when those republics, like ancient Greece or nineteenth century France, finally got rid of the dictators in the 1950s the United States, while ideologically a foster-father of Latin American freedom, looked like its enemy to many. Given the impossibility, under international law, of interfering in the affairs of other nations, the reproaches made against the United States diplomacy for maintaining friendly relations with the dictators were in many cases substantially unfair. But the recollections of the dollar diplomacy of the past, which preceded Franklin D. Roosevelt's good-neighbour policy, the extent of American investments, and the dubious nature of the dictators tended to create that needlessly dark picture of United States Latin American policy which led to a bad political fiasco in 1958 during a trip of United States Vice-President Nixon through former dictator-controlled countries.

Just as the period of Latin America's liberation from the Spanish yoke, that of the final overthrow of military dictatorship in those areas offered an extremely diverse picture. The one trait common in all these cases was the rise of a new society, stimulated by the boom of the 1940s and 1950s, which owed its growth in part to the dictators' own modernization and industrialization policy. This led to long and bloody mass upheavals —something unheard of in Latin American history—and made the dictators look like midwives who, having done their work, were expected to leave. But the political stand taken by them in these last big struggles and by the various classes that overthrew them was different in each instance. The first of these new-type revolutions was in Bolivia in the spring of 1952. Headed by Dr. Paz Estenssoro, as the leader of the Bolivian masses, especially of the poor tin miners, it was directed against the dictator General Ballivian, a tool in the hands of the absentee tin-mine owners, who paid the miners less than a dollar a day for working eight hours underground, while the leading mine-owner, Simon J. Patino, originally a poor *cholo* from Cochabamba, built palaces for himself in Nice and Paris and was said to be worth a billion dollars. Though originally a close friend of the Argentine dictator, Juan Perón, a Fascist-type ruler who had supported the uprising, Dr. Paz Estenssoro became the first president in the history of strife-torn Bolivia to start thorough social reforms in favour of the poor peasants and miners, thus transforming the worst-ruled State in the world into something resembling a social republic.

That a man of this calibre should have been close to Perón can astonish nobody familiar with the form Fascism assumed in Argentina. An Army officer of foreign extraction, Juan Perón received his decisive ideas while on missions to Berlin and Rome in the days of Hitler and Mussolini and lacked the sort of supporters that backed the European dictators. Instead of leading an infuriated *petit bourgeois* against the working man and his trade unions, Perón and the blonde Eva Duarte, the variety artist from the slums, whom he married and who became his political partner, were compelled to woo the elements that Hitler had despised. While Fascist in its forms, its regulating of the economy, and the building up of huge organizations for women, youth and social purposes as well as a dreaded State police, the Perón dictatorship was mainly supported by the *descamisados*. These were the shirtless masses of Italian immigrants, and thus the dictatorship from the outset stood in stronger opposition to the old classes—plutocracy, creole landowners, and clergy—than Hitler and Mussolini had done, with the possible exception of their last two years. The blackest spot of this rule was a degree of corruption unusual even among Fascist dictators. The Peróns behaved as if they owned the State. A former radio announcer and night-club beauty, Eva Perón played Cinderella turned Lady Bountiful. Wrapped in the most precious furs in the world, displaying jewellery from the largest collection on the American continent, and famous for her Paris wardrobe, by her fanatical speeches and primitive form of social policy, in which the distribution of gifts from stolen welfare funds played a major rôle, she gained support among the *descamisados*, who acclaimed her with delirious fanaticism.

Neither Juan, a tall, good-looking man, but from very small Italian immigrant stock, nor Eva—Evita, as the masses affectionately called her—who came from a still lower station, could ever forgive the upper classes for the condescending way in which they were treated. Their secret police matched all its predecessors regarding the refined methods it used, its speciality being the torture of its victims with electrically charged pins. Evita's almost unconcealed neurosis affected her followers; after her early death there was an outbreak of mass hysteria which outdid even that after Caesar's assassination; aerial photographs of Buenos Aires at the time show an endless compact stream of people, reaching to the walls on both sides of the main avenue above which in gigantic letters the words "*Perón cumple*" and "*Evita dignifica*" (Perón fulfils; Evita dignifies) are visible. Evita's death greatly weakened this dictatorship.

The régime's economic troubles, caused by over-hasty industrialization, were accentuated by Perón's struggle against the Catholic Church. It abandoned its passive attitudes as ally of the big landowners and started to woo the city poor who had become orphans through Evita's death. Encircled from all sides, Perón assumed the traits of late Roman Caesars to an increasing extent. The ageing dictator used to surround himself with a crowd of young girls in shorts, with whom he practised motor-cycle racing. After his downfall, very large buildings were found, filled with the odours of heavy oriental perfumes, where he had harboured this harem. The tremendous street fighting of the autumn of 1955 forced him to follow the example of Rosas, who almost one hundred years earlier had fled from furious crowds on to a foreign gunboat in the harbour, which ended his dictatorship. After a period of transition, in which the country was ruled by a military caretaker régime, the republican system was resumed. While the social weight of the *descamisados*, who had backed Perón, continued to be felt, they adapted themselves to the new situation by supporting the election of a presidential candidate without apparent dictatorial ambitions, Señor Frondizi.

It is significant that the revolution against Perón was backed by the Catholic clergy and given its decisive turn by the rising of the middle classes and military units near Córdoba, the university city, which was an old bulwark of the clergy. Made over-confident by the lack of political opposition to the Army, Latin American dictators underrated the disintegrating effect on the old military circles caused by the growth of modern capitalism and industrialism, as well as its disturbing results among the old ruling classes, both landowners and clergy, whose submissiveness they had taken for granted. This was especially true of Colombia, which after several years of grave political disturbances had fallen under the rule of a conservative-minded dictator, Rojas Pinilla, under whom industrial development reached a peak. Antioquia, for instance, began to vie in industrial importance with such centres of modern progress as Caracas and São Paulo, while the city of Medellin, which previously had resembled a sleepy European *"Kleinstadt"* (small town), became a modern metropolis of fabulous wealth. Confronted with these modern trends, Rojas felt he needed mass support for his tyranny, and began to make overtures to the women and the workers. But, like Perón, he encountered the resistance of the clergy, especially in the industrial city of Cali in the west, which during the 1950s had doubled its inhabitants, reaching 300,000. Influenced by this opposition, the workers failed to respond. When Rojas staged one of those fake elections in the spring of 1957, which used to be commonplace to secure the continuation of his rule, he met with the solid resistance of both upper bourgeoisie and the masses. His efforts to break a bank strike, called to cripple the finances of his régime, failed completely and led to a bloody mass upheaval. Like that against Perón, this revolt abounded in heroic actions, but led to Rojas being driven from the country as a result of a defection of the generals. Gradually the country returned to republican government.

The experience of Rojas, that it was dangerous to "rig" presidential elections and to challenge the Catholic clergy by vying for the support of Indios and other Labour elements, was shared by the dictator of Venezuela, Marcos Pérez Jiménez, who had been able to stage such an election in 1952 and be unscathed. With its oil wells and iron ore deposits, controlled by the dictator's foreign bankers, Venezuela lacked an independent middle class

such as the one that had brought down Rojas. But the industrialization of the country had led to a strengthening of the
working class, which was ready to become the chief foe of the
tyrant. There were plenty of men to stir up the workers' feelings.
Catholic dignitaries, led by Archbishop Raphael Arias Blanco,
competed with middle-class intellectuals and Communists in
condemning the régime for investing the country's huge income
from its natural resources in tremendous building projects, for
the benefit of Caracas only, and even more because only a few
big promoters benefited. Units of the Army and Air Force met
the dictator's faked re-election by an uprising, but were suppressed. But the well-planned assistance the revolutionaries received from a secret committee of intellectuals and workers threw
the country into such turmoil overnight that even those generals
who had supported the dictator abandoned his cause. At the end
of January 1958, after a series of fantastic street battles, the
triumph of the revolution was complete, and the dictator fled
from the country, taking with him an amount of roughly two
hundred million dollars.

With Venezuela returning to constitutional life under the
auspices of a military caretaker régime, military dictatorship
reached its lowest ebb in the history of Latin America and was
restricted to four countries: Paraguay, Nicaragua, Cuba and the
Dominican Republic. Of these countries Paraguay, then ruled
by General Felix Stroessner, had not yet recovered from the
depopulation it had suffered in the wars of the younger Lopez,
and was thus one of the most backward areas of the whole
continent. In Nicaragua the system of dictatorship was somewhat
weakened in 1956 by the assassination of General Anastasio
("Tacho") Somoza, one of its most conspicuous representatives,
also famous for the way he enriched himself. He was succeeded
by his son, Luis Somoza. In Cuba, the tyrant Fulgencio Batista,
a former sergeant and a somewhat primitive specimen of the
classical dictator type, who had ruled the country for decades,
was waging a shifting civil war with a rebel leader, Fidel Castro,
whose mountain retreat in the Sierra Madre he proved unable
to take. This brought the leadership among the Latin American
dictators of this time into the hands of the mouse-faced, but wily,
Rafael Trujillo, head of the Dominican Republic, which he ruled
in the way of a benevolent but crafty and cruel despot. The

undeniable progress his country made under him in the fields of
hygiene, technical development, city planning and public construction was cancelled out by his gigantic self-enrichment and
that of his family, which finally owned almost the whole State,
by his mass butcheries of negroes in the neighbouring republic
of Haiti, whom the Dominicans despised for being a few shades
darker, and finally by the cold-blooded torture and murder of
his republican foes. This was the man that his newspapers called
"his *excelentísimo, generalísimo*," Rafael Trujillo, the "*salvador
de la Patria*" and "*benefactor de la Republica*"! By the kidnap-
ping of his critic, the exiled Professor de Galindez, who was
abducted from a New York subway, and by his assassination of a
United States citizen and a Dominican who had staged this plot,
Trujillo created an international scandal in 1956.

Dictatorship on the Iberian Peninsula

While dictatorship in Latin America was shaken by the social
evolution, its development on the Iberian peninsula, although
following the ebb after the second world war, was more affected
by the fact that its dictators were reaching retirement age. The
dictatorship in Portugal, headed by Antonio de Oliveira Salazar,
had been founded during the Fascist wave of the 1920s and
1930s and was thus one of the longest of this century. Its leader
was a professor of economics who had originally been trained
for the priesthood, and this made him strongly resemble all other
great clerical dictators in history, especially García Moreno of
Ecuador. An admirer of Mussolini, whose constitution and
handling of State affairs he copied, Salazar was much more
successful. Like his neighbour, General Franco, he understood
how to keep his country out of the second world war. Although
he resembled other Fascist dictators in not raising the low wages
in his country, from his collaboration with the Church and protecting property, he enjoyed such prestige that his rule was never
seriously threatened since it started in 1932. At the end of the
1950s everyone agreed that the Portuguese National Union,
which he led and on which he based his rule, would have to make
concessions to the parliamentary system on his disappearance,
since he had no political heir apparent.

The succession problem plagued Francisco Franco, the most
important Spanish dictator in the twentieth century, to an even

greater extent. Franco's rule was a product of the stormy period in Spanish history that started with the downfall of the dictator Primo de Rivera in 1930, which led to the end of the monarchy the following year. The crisis reached its climax in 1936 through the formation of a Popular Front Government supported by the leftists. The political development of Spain in those years was determined by the refusal of the bourgeoisie to join the people in carrying out the long-overdue agrarian reform. The effort of the Popular Front Government to make up for this omission and to break up the big estates led to a kind of unofficial civil war in which republicans or monarchists, foes or defenders, respectively, of the big *latifundia* of the nobles and the Church, fought each other with bitterness. On the right of the monarchists stood the so-called Falange (from the Greek word *phalanx*, battle line), the political organization of the Spanish Fascists, who, it is true, were never to play such a conspicuous rôle as Fascism did in Germany, with her millions of bankrupt bourgeois and *petit bourgeois*, or in Italy, with her tremendous surplus population which could no longer emigrate. The increasing Fascist terrorism which was to block the threatening land reform caused the leftists to counteract with a terrorism of their own, to burn churches and monasteries, and to answer killings by murder.

This was the background for the long-prepared uprising of Spanish and Moorish colonial troops stationed in Spanish Morocco. It was a rightist rebellion which was led by General Franco after the death of its original leader Sanjurjo in an air crash. In spite of all the denials that were broadcast, from the very start this revolt was supported by Mussolini and Hitler. Without this Fascist assistance, and the help he obtained from the Western democracies (very strange considering he was the arch-foe of democracy), his final victory would have been totally impossible. The Popular Front Government was backed in the main by workers, peasants and progressive middle-class elements —at the start there was almost no Communism. Unfortunately for it, Franco's assault took place when the so-called appeasement policy of Western Europe towards Hitler and Mussolini reached its climax. It was the time when the broad masses in the West were too pacifist, lackadaisical and shortsighted to prepare for a struggle against Fascism, while the rightists in their enthusiasm about the helping of the economy by rearmament found nothing but praise for the Führer and the Duce. This led to the ill-fated policy of "non-intervention", which involved a blockade of Spain against the import of armaments, supposedly in order to secure peace. In reality this system harmed only the republic, which the big Powers, in defiance of international law, thus deprived of all means of self-defence, while the anti-republican rebels who controlled Spain's western boundary received all the material they wanted by having it shipped through Portugal.

Franco's destruction of the valiant Spanish republic, helped by his Moorish colonels and by Fascist accomplices, is one of the most depressing spectacles in history, especially as the republic was deserted by all its friends. The reports of the best-informed contemporaries, for example the United States ambassador in Madrid, Claude C. Bowers, prove that Franco's foes in the first year of the war did not include any Communists, despite statements to the contrary broadcast all over the world. In fact the "Ultra-Revolution" was emerging, a system which, as shown by the history of France after 1789, generally does not appear before the upper class of the revolutionaries have brought their country to the verge of disaster. The turning-point was in March 1937, when Franco's columns were marching on Madrid. Just as in Paris in 1793, a radical Government formed by determined defenders took over. It was only in this belated or "Jacobin" stage that the control partly slipped into Communist hands. Just as in revolutionary France, the lowest classes of the city— supported by an international brigade—succeeded in stopping the enemy, and by exploiting the advantages Clausewitz says that defenders possess, brought their foes into a dangerous position. The fight for life of the Spanish Republic can be compared with the defence of Jacobin France or Lenin's Russia in the Civil War, but the epic courage of its defenders could not in the long run arrest the course of Fate, the less so since the hostile international situation was accentuated by geographical and social difficulties. The defence was centred in three separate areas, around Madrid and Barcelona and in the Basque territory. The defenders were further divided by grave conflicts between Communists and syndicalists.

Strangely enough, the long duration of the Civil War, which ended only five months before the outbreak of the second world war, proved to be, in a certain sense, an asset for Spain, since it prevented her from entering the European conflict. At the decisive moment Spain had been ravaged by her own internal conflict to such an extent that the victor, General Franco, did not dare join Hitler and Mussolini in attacking the Western world. He was no born demagogue like the totalitarian tyrants, and he largely owed his position to the plane crash that killed Sanjurjo, the original leader. He therefore was not blinded by dictator complexes from the outset, nor was he over-eager to expand. His cruelty which became manifest through his slaughter of countless political foes during and after the Civil War, was more the result of the natural character of the Spaniard than that of a dictator. His ostentation in turn reflected the tradition of feudal grandees rather than the ambition of a *parvenu*. A dictator of the counter-revolutionary brand rather than a Fascist, he saw in the Falange he was forced to lead after its chief had been killed more a means of power than a purpose in itself. Remaining a monarchist, like most dictators of this century, he played with the idea of re-establishing the rule of the dynasty, of course under conditions that would suit him. In the interest of his followers he saw to it that the Falange kept its privileged position in State and society while following this course of action.

The moderate course Franco followed in international affairs made his contemporaries quickly forget the blood-spattered hatchet-man of democracy he had been, and will remain in history. His negative attitude towards Hitler, who tried to enlist his help against Great Britain, paid extremely well politically. The political influence of the Catholics in the United States, who had been instrumental in making Spain follow this line, helped him conquer the political crisis that threatened him in 1945 through the downfall of his former allies, Hitler and Mussolini. Assisted by the growing tension between East and West, this Catholic pressure led to his political recognition by the United States and to his being accepted as a member of the so-called Free World. Although the Catholics were for centuries the friends of Spanish governments opposed to freemasonry, before long even they began to criticize Franco's rule. It became increasingly evident that the General by his counter-revolutionary programme and his defence of the big estates against the entire country had turned the clock of history back in a way obnoxious to the interests of the Church. Well aware that Franco's antiquated social policy drove scores of believers away from the church, both the clergy in Spain and even more the masses of Western Catholics interested in social welfare increasingly attacked the Franco régime. Nor did the United States' assistance in building military power and constructing fortified bases compensate for the industrial, social and political backwardness of the Franco system. Given for non-productive purposes and constructed by firms selected by the Falange, this programme strengthened Spanish Fascism and the creeping monetary inflation which made the masses increasingly bitter. Since the winter of 1955–56, for the first time since the end of the Civil War, the régime faced major trouble in domestic politics and proved unable to suppress strike movements. In 1958 the Cortes—the Spanish Parliament then filled with Franco's yes-men—was forced to permit collective bargaining, though strikes continued to be prohibited. The most promising tendency in modern Spain, if looked at from the democratic angle, was the constant tension between the Falange and reactionary monarchism, which Franco tried to mitigate in vain by obliging a young Bourbon prince, who was being trained to succeed him, to acknowledge the Falange. The frictions between Fascism and monarchism, which had brought about Mussolini's downfall and which had been so conspicuous in Hitler's last years, threatened to become fatal for this dictatorship also.

Dictatorship in the Islamic world

Just as Latin America freed itself under the "liberators" from Spanish domination in the beginning of the nineteenth century, the twentieth century has seen numerous new nations, led by energetic individuals, break the yoke of the super-national empires. The collapse of Tsarist Russia, the German imperial Reich and the Habsburg Dual Monarchy in the last years of the first world war led automatically to the liberation of a series of nationalities in Eastern Europe, and after the second world war, when most of these nations had slipped back under foreign yoke, although under different circumstances, this evolution continued in Asia and Africa.

As leaders of popular national movements against monarchies and colonial empires the heads of these new States belonged to the liberator species of the classical dictator type. The prestige they acquired during the struggles for liberation gave even those among them who did not become dictators proper, distinctive authoritarian traits. Men such as Thomas Masaryk, the President of the bourgeois Czechoslovak Republic after 1918, his successor Eduard Benes, Prime Minister Nehru of India, or President Soekarno of Indonesia, some of them leaders of unity parties, had an influence which lifted them above the level of their fellow citizens. In all cases where the liberation did not take place automatically by the military collapse of belligerent empires or by political concessions made by the colonial Powers, as in India, the leader of the liberation was usually a politically inclined soldier who became dictator. Modern Turkey, being the nucleus of the old Ottoman Empire which disintegrated in 1918, was created by an officer, Mustafa Kemal, who staged an armed uprising against the last Sultan and the Allied Powers of the first world war who backed him. In a victorious campaign, Kemal forced the Sultan to abdicate and the Allies to grant his country better peace terms. Since his days Turkey has been ruled by a kind of "classical" dictatorship, even though in a somewhat concealed fashion. The newly liberated nations in Northern Africa, Arabia and along the southern coast of Asia were socially backward. Where they had passed the stage of a primitive monarchy, this backwardness usually stimulated the establishment of military dictatorships of the kind Latin America possessed until quite recently. The reason was that in all countries which do not possess a modern social structure, the Army was the only element that could check the old feudal powers.

One of the best examples of this evolution was the development of Egypt, where the old dynasty which had ruled the country since the last period of the Ottoman Empire was expelled in 1952. Considered a tool of Great Britain, this dynasty was hated for its corruption and lack of even the most elementary ethics. The leader in the struggle for liberation, and the first President of Egypt, Mohammed Naguib, turned out to be a figurehead for a clique of young officers, and a conservative but rather weak creature, picked chiefly in order to soothe the feelings of the class of corrupt notables and parliamentarians that had been supporting the defunct régime. Unable to solve the social problems in the way the younger officers expected, Naguib was replaced by the main ringleader, Gamal Abdul Nasser, in a tumultuous fashion in the spring of 1954. Nasser would have been content had Naguib carried on as he was expected. He was of giant build, but basically shy, and for his very shyness was defied by the common man, who interpreted it as democratic modesty. Carried along by a popularity which threatened to impair his sound judgment, Nasser, however, displayed a certain slyness—not uncommon among men of his silent type—which made him use his prestige as a club, but without actually imperilling his régime. The people saw in him the chief conqueror of the last king, the fat and pleasure-loving Farouk, as well as the man who had made England leave the Suez Canal, the liberator of the Sudan, and especially the champion of the struggle against Israel. They liked his simple life, his devotion to the Mohammedan religion, and his work for the poor *fellahin,* among whom he divided the big estates. By the middle of 1956 about 635,000 acres had been distributed, and this was only the beginning. The tricky and vicious methods he displayed in his struggle against Israel and his Nazi advisers strengthened rather than weakened his popularity. No enemy of the business world, but a political autocrat, no Communist, but a reformer, and above all a military man, he represented a modern edition of the classical dictator of the liberator species, and might one day be succeeded by other military dictators until the people have developed far enough to replace dictatorship by democracy, as has been done in Latin America. His sharp conflict with Israel and his alliances with other Arab States gave the Soviet Union the opportunity of wooing him both politically and economically.

Nasser's conviction that he had Soviet backing caused him to meet an American challenge—the sudden refusal of financial aid for rebuilding the Aswan Dam—by nationalizing the Suez Canal in 1956. This in turn led Great Britain and France to join Israel in a war of aggression against him which was stopped by the other big Powers and the United Nations in November 1956. This immensely increased his prestige. His increasing popularity in the Arab and Mohammedan world soon broadened the social and political rift that separated his Egypt from the more backward Arab areas where the rule of despotic monarchs continued. It made Nasser the chief figure in the Arab world and their main champion in Algeria and the entire Middle East.

Thus the foundations were laid for the unification of all Arab
States; this began early in 1958 when Egypt and Syria joined to
form the United Arab Republic. Given both the rivalry among
the Arabs and that among the big Powers involved, there was a
fair chance that this development would lead to a new general
world conflagration.

Chapter Fifteen

THE SOVIET UNION UNDER STALIN
AND HIS SUCCESSORS

Marxism à la tartare

THE development of the Soviet Union after Lenin's disappearance from the scene showed a growth of State-controlled economy which would have greatly astonished Marx and Engels, but under conditions which were almost the opposite from what they had expected from the economic as well as from the psychological angle. Instead of the conquest of highly developed industry by workers made unemployed by capitalist production, industry was developed from nothing by State workers and State employees driven by the whip under a tyrant who was more like Genghis Khan or Tamburlaine than the leader of a modern workers' party. The Bolshevist Revolution of 1917 and the establishment of the Soviet Union were preceded by a destruction of the existing economic machinery on a scale almost unparalleled in the history of modern capitalism, and not by abundance and over-supply. Under these circumstances the usefulness of the leading Communists sank rapidly once their revolution had succeeded; what was needed from then onwards was not the ideologist or political fighter, but the slave-driver, technician and henchman, who forced the people by all possible and impossible means to transform the wrecked remains of the machine production of the Tsarist age, then still in its infancy, into modern industrial giants. It was the tragedy of the leading party members that they failed to recognize this situation in time; many of them, beaten bloody and unconscious by Stalin's henchmen, racked their brains to the very end to find out why they, of all people, the celebrated martyrs of Tsarism who had dreamed for years of the proletarian victory in Tsarist prisons, were to have such a terrible fate.

The man who brought all this about was almost unknown up

to the time of Lenin's death in January 1924, although he was then in his forty-fifth year. He had already played an important if secret rôle, which most actors on the political stage—especially Leon Trotsky—had failed to recognize, to their undoing. Perhaps Stalin was the most successful statesman of the twentieth century—not only his outward circumstances but also his appearance and psychology fooled the observer; the medium-sized, insignificant-looking figure with a moustache, the lengthy nose, the wry, somewhat Asiatic smile, and the inevitable pipe made no particular impression, and his outward calm camouflaged the outbursts of deep and uncontrolled hatred of which this son of the Caucasian mountains was capable.

Just as Napoleon spoke French with a harsh Corsican accent all his life, Joseph Dzugashvili did not know Russian originally, but merely one of the Georgian dialects spoken in his homeland. Stalin (man of steel) was his pseudonym in revolutionary papers. The harsh discipline of the theological seminary in Tiflis where the son of a poor cobbler grew up had by its slight military colour something in common with the war school of Brienne in which the great Corsican spent the decisive years of his youth; most probably his character, like that of the young Bonaparte, was formed to a large extent by envy and hatred of better-situated and socially higher-placed schoolmates. But while Napoleon, the scion of an aristocratic family, tried to revive his faded claim for social recognition, Joseph Dzugashvili, the cobbler's son, became a revolutionary in this atmosphere. What we know about his earliest years shows that he tried to outdo his classmates' hatred of Russian Tsarism, which was caused by their being Georgians. Like young Hitler and young Napoleon, he was a ravenous and insatiable reader. The study of prohibited literature served the satisfaction of his complexes of hatred and vengeance; the complaints of his supervisors about this increased constantly, until the seminary finally showed him the door. In doing so the good monks did not know that their ward had already become a Marxist. Young Soso (nickname for Joseph) knew how to conceal his feelings well and learned to practise this to such an extent that all his life he showed some of the traits he had developed as a student in the seminary. He was the kind of person who would be thoroughly convinced of the truth of the Marxist slogan that religion is the opium of the people, but who for this very reason would be inclined to tolerate religion; at the height of his career he resembled less a Socialist revolutionary than an irate Circassian tribal chief.

Penniless and unemployed, the young student expelled from the seminary could hardly help following the Lenin line, though subconsciously he might have dreamed of using this policy from the outset for becoming an oriental despot one day, and for forcing the other revolutionaries to acknowledge his mental and political leadership. His tremendous class hatred, that was not only directed against the old society of big landowners and businessmen but also against the upper crust of the revolutionary camp; his feeling of inferiority towards the revolutionary intelligentsia which came from the bourgeois stratum was to permeate the entire history of his dictatorship. Those sentiments were to gain him the sympathies of the broad masses and after he had finally destroyed the revolutionary upper crust induced him to play dictator not only in politics but at the same time to make his incompetent efforts and views in the field of the entire mental and cultural life the supreme yardstick of Soviet culture.

The main secret of his methods and thought was his hidden resentment at being doomed as a champion of Leninism in Russia to be the scapegoat of the movement, whose main wire-pullers in those years—before and during the first world war—sat unmolested in Western countries. While he granted Lenin this privilege unbegrudged as the leader and indefatigable protagonist of the movement, he regarded the others more or less as drones; that most of them were Jewish made him no friend of the Jews, though no anti-Semite. His own agitated life compared unfavourably with those of the exiles, which indeed were not any too comfortable either. Until the spring of 1917, when the revolution finally materialized, Stalin's life offered the typical picture of the chased and persecuted party agent and agitator. The centre of his activities were the oilfields on the Black and Caspian Seas with their masses of Russian, Tartar, Armenian and Turkish workers, which helped him whenever he slipped back from prison or his periods of exile in Siberia to the main theatre of his political propaganda—like a kind of acrobat breaking his chains. The details remain in an historical mist. The constant deportations inspired him with deep hatred; his many escapes sharpened his cunning; his working among the labourers made him a leader,

10—DOS

though a kind of leader unable to resist Lenin and his brilliant right-hand men in fascinating the masses; he therefore disappeared into the background when the revolution of 1917 finally brought these men back to Russia. He was thoroughly disappointed at being obscured by the men from outside, and he resisted his rivals wherever he could.

The Civil War after 1918 offered him a good opportunity to do this. During the struggle in the southern theatre of war which centred round Tsaritsyn—later renamed Stalingrad in his honour —a series of clashes took place between a group of front-line fighters, led by himself and a few former sergeants, and the then omnipotent War Minister Trotsky which marked the start of the historic duel between the two. Trotsky and the other leading Bolsheviks underrated the powerful position the insignificant-looking man with the pipe had created for himself since the earliest phase of the new order. Not much more than two years after the end of the Civil War the Soviet Union was practically ruled by Stalin, which was not recognized while Lenin, who was gravely ill, lived on.

In the first days of the October Revolution Stalin had become commissioner for nationality questions. A man from Georgia, he seemed just the person needed to carry through Lenin's ideas on this subject, which involved careful preservation of the many non-Russian nationalities suppressed by Tsarism, especially of the people along the southern and south-eastern boundaries which connected the Tsarist empire with the Orient. This expectation was quite unjustified. Just as the Corsican Bonaparte quickly lost interest in the liberation of his homeland as soon as he found the chance to rise in the hitherto hated oppressor country, Stalin not only abandoned the cause of his native Georgia but also the idea of protecting the dozens of other nationalities originally entrusted to his care. The "freedom" they were granted remained as much a dead letter under his rule as the freedom of the average Soviet citizen; the natives who rose in the local Government became more and more instruments of Greater Russian nationalism. Greater Russian policy became one of the main characteristics of Stalinism and did not vanish after his death.

Stalin's increasing control of the nationality issue was matched by his rise in inner Russian affairs. The birth of his dictatorship was on April 3rd, 1922, the day he was named Secretary-General of the Communist Party—an event that passed unnoticed at the time. Before long the Secretary-General had succeeded in building up his office in such a way that its supervisory agency, the Politbureau of the party, was gradually filled with its leading figures, and floated helplessly in space while its Central Committee—its parliament—was not convoked unless he wanted it, and from his control of the executive was gradually filled with his pawns. The dying Lenin was greatly perturbed by this development which he himself had conjured up, and especially by the reappearance of Greater Russian tendencies. "The political responsibility for this entire truly Greater Russian business," he wrote when informed about the way in which his agents treated Georgia, "lies fully on the shoulders of Stalin and Dzershinski."

Joseph the Terrible

The combination of the names of the new dictator and the dreaded founder of the State police is significant; Stalin in fact controlled almost the entire State machinery when Lenin passed away. In his last clear moments Lenin had sharply admonished the party not to pass on his authority to Stalin, but he had taken no measures to stop the approaching mischief. In the post-revolutionary years a great part of the old Tsarist bureaucracy had put itself at the disposal of the new régime; this new class of officials and the State police gave the Secretary-General the necessary backing for holding in check the Politbureau and the party's Central Committee. The bureaucracy in turn was controlled by Stalin's mastery of both police and party, enabling him to control the promotion and thus the fate of the officials, especially as his system of differentiating salaries gave promotion special importance. The enormous differences in pay stood in the sharpest possible contrast to the basic tenets of Communism, but they fitted this type of dictatorship perfectly.

The old Bolshevist élite, exiled abroad until 1917, were thus in a difficult position. Trained in staging mass unheavals, they saw in the Russian Revolution the prelude for an international revolution and believed that it would otherwise be lost. They had no hope of remaining in power unless they worked their hardest both for world revolution and the maximum industrialization of Russia. Trotsky, the leading ideologist of the opposition, insisted tenaciously on both, but Stalin, in control of the State power, refused to co-operate and in addition—since power corrupts—knew how to induce two members of the old Bolshevist guard, Zinoviev and Leon Kamenev, to join him.

In the first years of his rule, when the old Bolsheviks were still in key positions, Stalin still ruled in a constitutional manner, solving his main problems without shedding blood. In 1926 he forced Trotsky to resign his position as War Minister and shortly afterwards alienated Zinoviev and Kamenev. But instead of butchering the three, as he was to do in later years, for the time being he merely opposed them by forming a new so-called "rightist" Bolshevist group consisting of Bukharin, Tomsky, and Rykov in the Politbureau, with whose help he succeeded in spoiling Trotsky's idea of a speedy industrialization. But hardly had he succeeded in banishing Trotsky to a distant province and then driving him into exile proper than he took off his mask. The year 1929, in which Trotsky crossed the frontier as a political fugitive, while the Black Friday at the New York Stock Exchange began the international depression and the period of Franklin D. Roosevelt and Adolf Hitler, also saw the beginning of Stalin's unrestricted tyranny and of the terrible but stupefying development it produced.

Having made sure that the long-discussed total industrialization and the restlessness of the masses it was supposed to produce could not be used by professional demagogues like Trotsky for their personal aims, Stalin began to carry out Trotsky's programme with fantastic speed and tremendous energy. It was an incredible undertaking in form, dimension and scope. It transformed Russia into one of the world's largest industrial Powers, covered the entire inhospitable and gigantic area with a dense network of electric power stations and factories within a quarter of a century, tore one hundred million small peasants, five-eighths of Russia's population, from their primitive surroundings and drove them into collective State farms, pushed many thousands of tractors into areas which had hardly seen a steam engine, and put many illiterates from uncivilized areas into classrooms, with the result that shortly after Stalin's death this country, formerly the most backward of the world's Powers, far outranked the United States in producing engineers and highly qualified technical specialists. But in the exploitation of men and material, it was probably the most wasteful enterprise in history, and dwarfed everything seen in this field since the erection of the Pyramids.

Strangely enough, the gigantic experiment of the first Five-Year Plan in no way followed an established programme. It was made politically possible by the expulsion of Trotsky and put into operation to relieve a famine. The plan began with a State-sponsored revolt of the small peasantry against the medium and big peasants (*kulaks*), staged to secure the food supply of the cities. This situation was unforeseen in its scope and forced the dictator to exercise the strongest possible pressure on industrial production so as to procure the necessary machines for carrying through the agrarian revolution. The result was confusion of fantastic proportions, accompanied by an increase of famine which the régime tried to conceal from the outside world, and by the destruction of millions of *kulaks*. The *kulaks* that were not mown down by the machine guns of the State police were arrested with their families and shipped to Siberia in unheated cattle trucks in the middle of the Russian winter. Left there without shelter or proper means of subsistence they met a pitiful fate.

There was, however, method in this madness. Stirred up by the so-called Stakhanov system—a modern edition of the ill-famed "Taylor" or "sweat-shop" system known from early American capitalism—the industrial labourers worked increasingly rapidly; this led to "Socialist competition", the race of millions of work-horses to obtain Stalin's decoration, gifts or public acknowledgments which at the same time was to bring the pipe-smoking foreman at the head of the vast State close to the heart of the masses.

Like the Goebbels propaganda, the incredible Stalin propaganda gave the word "Communist" a thoroughly wrong meaning and transformed the mind of the masses in such a way that, forgetting both their misery and the increasing rift that separated them from the industrial managers and from the Stalin State party, they thought that they lived in a kind of paradise. Having psychopathological natures themselves, tyrants such as Stalin and Hitler are usually much better authorities on mass psychology than the representatives of other forms of government who never even consider finding out what miserable treatment the masses are ready to accept if duly dealt with both by big sticks and carrots. In most other things Stalin and Hitler had little in common. Stalin was not a nervous "Saviour of Society" like the *petit bourgeois* Hitler, whose tyrant complex came from his fear of social decline, but was a scion of former serfs turned small peasants. Even though Stalin's past and his hatred of the Bolshevist Old Guard developed a hatred complex in him also, he acted with more prudence, slyness, cunning and realism than the Führer, and above all he was not a gambler who put all his money on one card.

Stalin's task in the social field was very different from that of Hitler. Hitler's problem was to adapt his rule to the requirements of an overdeveloped capitalist industry whose unsolved marketing problems, enforcing the dismissal of millions of employees, called for mass rearmament and military conquests. By contrast, Stalin commanded an industrial machinery part of which existed merely on the drawing-boards of his engineers and whose establishment involved both a desperate search for trained and untrained labour and a peaceful attitude in international affairs to secure the Soviet Union against sudden surprise attacks during that very critical period. The rapid deterioration of Europe's international situation resulting from Hitler's appearance on the scene forced the Russian dictator to accelerate his work on an enormous scale, and to this end he steadily built up his enforcement apparatus. Not only the labourers but also the technical managers and bureaucrats of this police State felt driven day and night. They were terrified and knew that each move they made was watched and checked. He who failed to reach the fantastic production targets the régime expected of him, who felt frustrated by the lack of raw materials, and who did not master the illegal methods used by the individual managers in pirating trained labour, accumulating stocks and influencing the State machine, were hourly in danger of being arrested by the State police and of being accused of sabotage.

In the régime's struggle against sabotage, the fear of a slackening of the required speed combined with the fear that the discontent of the masses might be used by the old Bolshevist opposition, Stalin proceeded against his old foes with all the means at his disposal. In 1929, when he started his stormy first Five-Year Plan overnight, occurred the first of those never-ending sabotage trials which have become so typical as a result of the self-accusations of the defendants. From Khruschev's revelations during the Twentieth Communist Party Congress in Moscow in

1956, we can now state with perfect certainty that those so-called confessions, which in the course of years became more and more fantastic, were brought about by inhuman torture of the defendants ordered by Stalin himself.

The Communist Party organization, which had been transformed in the 1920s from a kind of guard mainly of old Bolshevist fighters into a mass organization consisting largely of workers, became as much a target of the fury of its omnipotent Secretary-General as did the old intelligentsia. Convinced that most of these working-class officials lacked the qualities required for supervising the gigantic industrialization, Stalin began to direct the "purges" he carried through with the help of his rapidly growing State police even against these trusted agents. The struggle against his own followers is one of the routine features in each dictatorship. The more powerful a tyrant and the more complete his victory over his opponents, the greater the danger that the tyrant's followers—the only remaining power in the State—might attack and destroy him. Nowhere did this danger reach more colossal dimensions than in the Soviet Union under Stalin, who commanded the biggest bureaucratic machinery of dictators in history, the more voluminous and sensitive since Stalin was the first dictator in history not only to direct the political life but to control the entire economic life of a rapidly advancing modern State.

The size of the potential sabotage determined the scope of Stalin's counter-action and the violence of the methods he used. After December 1st, 1934—the day when his trusted agent Sergei Kirov was assassinated by young members of the Communist opposition in Leningrad—an uninterrupted chain of purges began which turned the entire State topsy-turvy. Two of the first victims were Stalin's former assistants against Trotsky, Kamenev and Zinoviev, who were tried twice in 1935–36, and having "confessed" to having mentally encouraged Kirov's murderers were finally executed. While the "confessions" of these seasoned old Bolsheviks were still rather carefully phrased—their final wording being the result of months of negotiations between the Kremlin and the prisoners—things went more smoothly after 1936, when Stalin replaced the chief of the secret police, Herschel H. Yagoda, by the dwarfish and poisonous Nikolai I. Yezhov— he later killed both of them. This appointment saw the start of what became known as the "Yezhovchina", a modern St. Bartholomew on the broadest scale and with no time limit. Victims of this mass slaughter were both the Bolshevist Old Guard and a tremendous number of unknown proletarian party functionaries and other supposed foes of the régime. Spread over the entire gigantic territory of the Soviet State, the action lasted until just before the second world war, when Stalin suddenly stopped it.

In his famous speech of 1956 Khruschev revealed the secret history of these events, of which the outside world had guessed from the outset. He produced document after document originating in the basement cells where the secret police used to torture their victims. These documents literally "cry to Heaven". "Unable to stand the torture any longer", one of them declares, "to which I am exposed by Ushakov and Nikolaiev [two secret police agents], especially by the first one, who uses his knowledge that my broken ribs have not healed properly and hurt me badly, I have been forced to accuse others." "I am crying for help", writes another victim, an old Bolshevik and close friend of Lenin, in addressing a member of the Central Committee of the Stalinized Communist Party, "from a dark prison cell. Hear my cry of despair. . . . I suffer without being guilty, believe me. Time will show it. I am no counter-revolutionary stool-pigeon, nor member of an anti-Soviet group, as I am said to be on the basis of a denunciation. . . . For almost forty years I have fought in the party for the welfare of the State. Today, at sixty-two, I am threatened by the judges with increasingly hard, cruel and dishonouring bodily punishment. . . . I cannot defend myself against the sudden, repeated and heavy body blows . . . my torture has reached its climax. My health is gone. . . . To die in a Soviet prison, branded as a traitor—could anything be more terrible for an honest man? . . ." It was all to no avail. In many thousands of such cases the party member finally did his duty. The infamous show trials against leading Bolsheviks, the procedures against Piatakov, Radek and others in January 1937, against Bukharin, Rykov and Yagoda in March 1938, and the secret court action against the leading mind of the Soviet Army, Marshal Tukhachevsky, and seven other generals who were shot by Stalin in June 1937, were but an insignificant fragment of the real events; in 1937–38 the dictator approved in advance a gigantic series of such verdicts which the State police submitted to him on 383 lists, without putting a single one of the accused on trial.

The strange fact remains that this bloodshed did not make the tyrant unpopular. Absolute monarchy had already learned how to make its servants responsible for its sins. The larger their number and political weight, the greater was the success of this method. The harshness of the Stalin régime, its increasing Greater Russian despotism, its lack of consideration for the workers, who were tied to their jobs, lived in sub-standard conditions and were forced to build up industry, were compensated for by Stalin's rough treatment of the hated slave-drivers; Stalin thus appeared as the god whom the masses had to thank for these acts of grace. This must be almost taken literally. Even a newspaper of the importance of *Pravda* published rhymes praising Stalin as the creator of daylight, fertilizer of the earth, rejuvenator of the century, bringer of Spring, and producer of the human race!

Stalin regarded this deification of himself and his ideas with malicious delight. It was a substitute for the almost open lack of recognition shown him by the intellectuals, the high bureaucrats and the leading military men. Like many tyrants from a humble station in life, he was eager to excel in cultural matters. Despite his terribly dull and painfully trivial style and his basically pedestrian appreciation of the arts which he shared with Hitler, Stalin wished to be recognized as a writer, a leading philologist, scholar and even art expert and be presented as such by historians. In the proof sheets of a little Stalin biography published in the Soviet Union in 1948, which describes his personality with the most tasteless flatteries, there are numerous edifying passages inserted in the text in his own handwriting. "Comrade Stalin's genius", so one example goes, "enabled him to see through the enemy's plans and thus frustrate them. The battles in which Comrade Stalin commanded the Soviet armies are brilliant examples of leadership talent in conducting military operations." Self-knowledge was not one of his strong points. "Though he fulfilled his task as party leader with supreme skill . . .", he scribbled at another place into the text, "Stalin never permitted his work to be marred by the smallest trace of vanity, conceit or self-glorification."

Strangely enough, this ridiculous-looking despot was at the

same time easily the most successful tyrant in world history, his gigantic achievements placing him high above Ivan the Terrible and Peter the Great, whom he was eager to copy. This demon who "stamped armies out of the earth and made cornfields grow on his outstretched hand"[1] forced the Russian *mujik* to help him create the most powerful industrial empire on the Eurasian land mass. In the ten years preceding the second world war the consumption of electric current in the Soviet Union, for example, rose from 6 million to 40 million kilowatts, the production of coal from 30 million to 133 million tons, that of oil from 11 million to 32 million tons; the production of iron from 4 million to not less than 18 million tons and the annual output of machine tools and instruments from 3 million to no less than 33 million tons. If it is also taken into account that the number of industrial workers rose at the same time from about 11 millions to 28 millions and that in 1938 more than 31 million people attended schools and colleges, compared with 8 millions in 1914, it can be understood why the working masses as such, in spite of the terrible deeds of the régime, had no reason for revolting against their master and overlord, who in any case was better guarded than any other despot in world history.

War and Peace

The most vulnerable aspect of the régime during the big economic change Stalin had inaugurated was its lack of protection in the international field. Each rising nation when it arms itself passes through a danger period when its neighbours can attack it with ease. This was true of the Soviet Union. From the days of Lenin one of the main motives of Soviet international policy was to create the impression of living in a beleaguered fortress, typical of all ultra-revolutionary dictatorships. This did not of course exclude the possibility that at some time in the future the tables might be turned, and when Russia had developed from an agrarian country into an industrial giant its besiegers might become the besieged. For the time being, however, Stalin had to proceed with the utmost caution and adapt himself to the conditions of the outside world, of which he knew hardly anything. His outwardly strongest weapon in dealing with foreign politics, the Third International, often proved unusable.

[1] A quotation from Schiller's *Die Jungfrau von Orleans*.

His political method, to combine with his big neighbour States, Germany and China, against the hated Western nations and against Japan, pleased the radical wing of the Labour movements in the countries he opposed, but at the expense of his followers in the nations he befriended. Thus it created centres of opposition in his own Communist camp.

In fighting this opposition, the master of the Kremlin, even though he could not always use the revolver as he did at home, displayed the same hatred, arrogance and heavy-handed methods used in his own country. From 1923, when he made a close understanding with the German Reichswehr, which was then fighting the Ruhr invasion, he drove the German Communists from crisis to crisis. Very similar was his procedure in China, where for years he collaborated with the rising military dictatorship of Chiang Kai-Shek, and with the wealthy Chinese middle class, especially in Shanghai, thus rousing bitter resentment in the ranks of the Chinese Communists. It was only after Chiang Kai-Shek had caused him a long series of political disappointments, and had finally staged a real blood-bath among the Chinese Communists, that very much against his inclination Stalin gradually revised his policy and re-established his connections with his partisans in the south of the gigantic country who were led by Mao Tse-Tung.

The unfortunate experiences he had had in both political theatres, Chiang's lack of Communist sympathies, and especially the rise of Hitler, finally forced him reluctantly to approach the Western democracies, though not without interruptions and not permanently. The changes of the party line he decided used to take place quite suddenly and caused the Communist Party leaders and the functionaries in the countries involved to fall over like ninepins; for each possible major change the dictator usually kept entire teams of candidates in readiness for party positions which suddenly emerged from behind the screen. During the Seventh Congress of the Communist International, which took place in Moscow in August 1935, the Bulgarian George Dimitrov announced such a change of policy. (Dimitrov was the hero of the Leipzig trial in which the Nazis had tried to "prove" the Communist responsibility for the burning of the Reichstag. Being innocent, he had dared to point at his accuser, Hermann Göring, which made the fat Nazi leader scream in outbursts of uncontrolled

rage). Dimitrov's Stalin-inspired speech of 1935, calling for
a common front of all anti-Hitlerian labourers, parties and
nations, involved a complete breach with the traditional Communist party line, which demanded a struggle against all enemies
of the working class, without compromise. In deepest secrecy,
however, and in contradiction to this new, so-called People's Front
policy, Stalin continued to extend his hand to German militarists,
the more eagerly as the Western democracies' policy of appeas-
ing Fascism made him mistrust their intentions. The international situation of spring, 1939, when the Western Powers,
formerly so lame and inactive, began to oppose Hitler's annexation policy, thus driving him into Russia's arms, brought Stalin a
triumph and the fulfilment of his most ardent wish; he hardly
ever appeared as radiant and happy as during the signing of the
Stalin-Hitler pact by his Foreign Minister Molotov and Hitler's
von Ribbentrop.

Nothing is more dangerous for a dictator than when things
develop as he wishes. The tremendous political and material
profit the pact with Hitler brought Stalin, the bloodless conquest
of the Baltic States and half Poland and his diversion of the
dangerous Hitler towards the West made Stalin hope that this
paradisical situation would last for ever. He heard the news of
the defeats of the Western Powers with glee; in the depth of his
heart he had always wanted it to happen so. This started a
tragi-comic play of grandiose dimensions. The anti-Western
complex of the Russian dictator, and the urgent desire of the
German dictator to erect a big empire in the East, were incompatible. The way in which the two dealt with each other, deceived
each other, and made great mistakes in calculating has hardly
its equal even in a history as rich in grotesque happenings as in
that of dictatorship. As we now know, Hitler had foreseen for a
long time that he might have to seek a reconciliation with Russia
at the decisive moment, but he hoped that it would be as short
an interlude as possible; for Stalin, however, this combination
meant practically the fulfilment of his fondest day-dream, which
made him reject the thought that it could ever end. Stalin's
incredulity when faced with the steadily increasing reports on the
preparation of Hitler's "Barbarossa" plan—the code word for
the attack on Russia—was the exact counterpart of Hitler's
refusal during his Eastern campaign to give due credit to the

intelligence on Stalin's creation of a gigantic war industry in Central Asia. That the Soviet Union, despite the incredible mistakes of the dictator and the terrible weakening of the Russian armies by the purges—especially the Tukhachevsky trial—was able to stand up to Hitler was largely due to Hitler's making worse mistakes than his foe. Compared with the military and political megalomania of Hitler, who tried to outdo the old Prussian nobility in its own field—warfare and Eastern colonization—Stalin, the arch-enemy of Tsarism and the upper classes, was after all a peasant, with a carefully calculating mind; there his psychology matched the situation of his country, which fought for its soil and existence, and which only at a later stage, when the aggressor had been bled white, could hope to overcome Fascism.

The fearfully dangerous situation of the gigantic Stalinist empire which had been attacked overnight by a mighty invader called for uncanny harshness towards the dictator's own troops as well as enormous energy and brutality in the technical organization of defence; in both, Stalin was master. Just as he defended his front lines with tanks, guns and heavy weapons of all kinds, he permeated everything with State police agents and units. Communist "Politruks" and even common soldiers were ordered to fire upon everybody appearing to retreat. Russian prisoners of war, liberated by Stalin's troops from German prison camps, self-mutilators, or Russian partisans who happened to say something favourable about the conditions behind the German front, were shot without ceremony. The Kremlin informed its troops about the shooting of generals accused of cowardice or of having issued orders to retreat. The methodical transplanting of 1,300 factories from just behind the front line to Central Asia was something only a dictator like Stalin could perform. This is also true of the uninterrupted march of live cattle over distances of 1,800 to 3,000 miles from collective farms in Kazakhstan or Siberia to the fighting front. Only a State as abysmally tyrannical as Stalin's possessed the machinery and organizing capability to organize a series of monster offensives and at the same time to mobilize sufficient labour to increase gun and aircraft production five-fold, tank production fifteen-fold, and ammunition production four-fold during four years of war —and in spite of a yearly loss of about four million dead and seriously wounded. Stalin's best ally was Hitler himself, both from the Führer's senseless over-expansion of the German potential in men and material and of his treatment of the population in the gigantic area he had occupied. The broad masses of Western Russia and of the Ukraine, which, sick of the Stalin tyranny, had received Hitler with friendliness and even with enthusiasm in the beginning, soon realized that they had jumped out of the frying-pan into the fire, and at the end welcomed the hammer and sickle as signs of their liberations from the swastika.

Atoms Stop a Giant

Stalin's victory in the second world war made the bloodiest and most malicious tyrant of all times—next to Hitler—not only the mightiest man of the postwar world but it also allowed him to yield almost without limit to his anti-Western inclinations, which he had had to repress so often previously. The agreements concluded with the big Western Powers, his allies in fighting Hitler, were misinterpreted by him with complete perfidy, even though they were most generous towards him and granted him the lion's share of the prey. Eastern Europe, the Balkans, and the parts of Germany occupied by him were transformed into Soviet satellites in violence of these agreements. Even during the war there had been no lack of sinister deeds which showed the West that the mask of self-control and wisdom the dictator wore when with his allies in person concealed an abyss of hatred and cunning. Just after the invasion the ill-famed slaughter of thousands of Polish officers in the section of Poland occupied by Stalin in 1939 had taken place, for which Stalin later blamed the Gestapo. During his victorious advance upon Warsaw in 1944 he had encouraged a Polish uprising against Hitler which he failed to support and thus caused to collapse, apparently in the expectation that the ensuing slaughter would rid him of opponents of his Stalinization programme. After Hitler's disappearance he no longer knew any limits.

Eastern and Southern Europe were almost completely Stalinized within a few years and were forced to join the former enemy countries in working for Russia's reconstruction. This undertaking—important and in itself justified—was carried out in a way that suited the tyrant's political interests. Bracing himself to fight for supremacy in Europe, Stalin performed the incredible feat of reaching or even exceeding the figures of Russia's industrial prewar production within four or five years of the war's end, in spite of the tremendous destruction. An inveterate enemy of the West, he exploited the natural political frictions with his allies that were bound to emerge after the collapse of the common enemy to burden them with the responsibility for the continuation of the drudgery and slavery to which the population had been subject during the war. In the years after 1945 this international propaganda reached its climax and steadily increased in intensity, since it hit a target which had troubled the dictator all his life. The tension in the international field and the rapid growth of the Soviet bureaucracy it involved simultaneously deepened the rift between the man at the top and the machine, and thus stimulated the activity of the State police; under its new chief, Lavrenti P. Beria, the purges became worse than ever.

About this time the State police had exceeded the scope and size of Himmler's SS and fulfilled all its functions. Known as the O.G.P.U., later as the N.K.V.D., and finally as the M.V.D., which meant that like all other so-called "People's Commissariats" it had gained the rank of a regular State ministry, it had command of about 800,000 special guards and controlled the entire military intelligence, not to mention the regular police, numbering 400,000 men. Like all totalitarian police forces it watched each single member of the population; its control of the forced labour camps, of road and railway construction, the planning and building of new canals and the tremendous electrification projects made it by far the most important State authority. *Kulaks* and other members of suspect national groups—which Stalin and Hitler transplanted, as had been done in ancient Sicily—met the remnants of the old ruling classes, common criminals and Trotskyists in the forced-labour camps, and joined them in slaving on the "Big Soviet Construction Projects" such as the Stalin Canal between the Baltic and the White Sea (where thousands of these men died), the Moscow-Volga Canal, the railway from Lake Baikal to the Amur, or the second track of the Trans-Siberian Railway. The most notorious camps were located in North-east Siberia in the Kolyma area, near the gold mines from which prisoners rarely returned alive.

In spite of the terror for the individual human being and

the fearful pressure the régime exercised on the entire population, millions and millions regarded the Soviet Union as their
saviour. For the poor labourer in the rice-fields of South China,
for the despised rickshaw man in Shanghai, the downtrodden
coolie in Singapore, the longshoreman on strike in San Francisco,
the struggling porter at the Gare Saint-Lazare in Paris, the dis-
franchised coloured intellectual from South Africa, or the miserably paid workers in Sicily, the Soviet star lighted a hopelessly
black night. Communism was the dream of gigantic masses of
underdogs all round the world to whom no French Revolution
had offered a piece of land, some political control, or even a faint
inkling of a better world. It can be said without exaggeration that
the international policy of the Soviet Union was heir to the
French Revolution and filled all spaces not touched by its predecessor. In all areas unaffected by the older movement, the land
problem had remained unsolved and thus offered the most fertile
soil it could find to the spread of Communism. The boundary of
the area with unsolved land problems roughly indicates the limit
of efficient Soviet propaganda. The most successful way to breed
Communism is to hamper the solution of land problems, or to
create a new one artificially, such as has been done in the Union
of South Africa. In Rumania, Hungary, Poland and also East
Prussia, Stalin's Russia profited immensely from the obsolete and
often harsh rule of generations of feudal landlords. In China and
other Asiatic territories, the hunger for land was likewise decisive, even though the land ownership in those areas was not
always based on feudalism. Even the invasion of South Korea by
the North Koreans in 1950 was partly provoked by the existence
of an unsolved land problem which appeared to make South
Korea a natural area in which to spread Soviet influence.

In carrying out his agrarian revolution in Asia and Eastern
Europe Stalin did everything in his power to damage or embar-
rass the West, especially by influencing international opinion. A
tremendous peace propaganda campaign tried to preserve the
inequality of power relations which had been created until the day
when the man in the Kremlin would launch a decisive push in
the West after the rapid reconstruction of his country. This propaganda carefully neglected to mention that the Western countries had disarmed after Hitler's downfall, while Russia had not.
"Fifth column" activity in all parts of the world, the establish-

ment of Communist power centres, that could also serve military purposes, the influencing of the foreign Press, foreign Parliaments, educational institutions and art, and many other tricks that the totalitarian dictators had learned from each other forecast that one day the enormous military supremacy of the Soviet Union would shake the Eurasian land-mass. In 1949 the man in the Kremlin successfully staged his main *coup*: the gigantic Chinese republic was brought into the Communist camp by Mao Tse-Tung's revolution.

In this procession of victories which it appeared no one could halt, the giant was finally stopped by the smallest-known unit on earth—the atom. Without the West's monopoly in the manufacture of atom bombs—short-lived it is true—and its continued superiority in the manufacture of atomic weapons after the end of this monopoly, there is little doubt that he would have reached his goal. When the Soviet Union had finally caught up with the West and a balance had been created, Stalin was dead. The temporary Western superiority in this field and the increasing international resistance to his régime brought him a series of political disappointments and failures in the last few years of his life with which the ageing dictator could hardly cope mentally. His effort to blockade Berlin and thus to achieve supremacy in Germany was frustrated by the Western Powers' provisioning the city by means of the famous air-lift. The political rebellion of his erstwhile partisan in the Balkans—Marshal Tito of Yugoslavia—was victorious, even though Stalin uttered with furious contempt that he needed merely to shake his little finger to make Tito fall. Finally Stalin also failed in his attempt to eject the West from East Asia by making the North Koreans invade South Korea.

The Imprudence of Killing One's Doctors

The more Stalin was infuriated by these defeats, the more violently he raved against all whom his revenge could reach. His last years offer extraordinary material for a psychological study on the delusions of an ageing tyrant. As early as the struggles of the North Koreans and Mao Tse-Tung's China against the United Nations, the world discovered that Stalin's technique of "brain-washing" his victims and his dissemination of falsehoods had also infected his allies. His accusation that the United Nations had started bacteriological warfare, and the shallow "proofs" he submitted in substantiation, perfectly matched his general methods of falsification and propaganda, as Khruschev described to the world in his speech in 1956. Stalin's suspicion became morbid. It could mean death if anyone talking to him showed fear and allowed his eyes to shift. Like the tyrants of the Renaissance, he saw traitors and spies everywhere. His right-hand man from 1938 onwards was Beria, his Georgian compatriot. Beria had risen to power in an administrative district (*krai*) by doing away with a predecessor in 1931, and in the course of his activity as director of the State police had killed tens of thousands of party functionaries and Soviet officials on the basis of fabricated accusations, mostly without any trial at all. When Stalin and Beria felt, for instance, that their Greater Russian centralism caused dissatisfaction in their native Georgia, they staged a blood-bath there in 1952. Everyone who was not 100 per cent Russian and 120 per cent Stalinist had reason to tremble before the two. In the autumn of that year the dictatorship began to emphasize its anti-Semitic side, which it always denied officially, and hanged, for instance, twelve leading party members—mostly Jews—in Prague because of supposed sabotage. Under the influence of the highly coloured reports submitted to him by Beria, the aged Stalin lost contact with reality. In the last months before his death, which took place in March 1953, he seriously suspected that his old friend Voroshilov—the highest dignitary of the Soviet Union next to himself—was an English agent; at the same time his old confidants Molotov, the Foreign Minister, and Mikoyan, Minister of Commerce, fell into disgrace; informed circles feared justifiably that the unusual enlargement of the Politburo, thenceforth called Praesidium, enforced by Stalin on the Nineteenth Communist Party Congress in the autumn of 1952, showed that he intended to kill all old members of this leading party agency. On top of all this, the public learned with astonishment that the man in the Kremlin had suddenly arrested the leading physicians of the Soviet Union entrusted with the care of himself and the other high officials, and accused them of having plotted the assassination of their patients. The sole "proof" Stalin submitted against these doctors was, as is now known, a letter of denunciation from a woman doctor who served the State police as an occasional stool-pigeon. Stalin ranted. He ordered one of the accused to be chained and another to be beaten up. The official of the State police charged with investigating this affair, Ignatiev, was told by the dictator that he would lose his head unless he submitted the confessions of the prisoners. Then Stalin ordered the investigating judge to appear before him and explained to him the method he was supposed to follow; to beat, beat, and beat again.

In February 1953 the situation had become practically untenable. No one at the top in the Soviet Union was sure of his life any more. Stalin distributed the utterly fantastic confessions of the accused doctors, produced under torture, to the members of the Politburo and accused the bureau of political blindness. Furious invectives in *Pravda* against a series of high officials foreshadowed the coming of a new purge. Then the world learned the unexpected news that the dreaded tyrant had suffered a stroke. A few days later, on March 5th, he lay on his bier. Had he been murdered, as many say? That cannot be proved. That he was closely guarded by the omnipotent Beria, who used the furious old despot for his own purposes, makes this unlikely. It is certain, however, that at that moment plenty of men had excellent reason to desire this result. Had Stalin lived longer, some of the mightiest members of the Politburo would have lost their heads. His sudden disappearance from the scene brought these men, instead of death, political control.

Rise of Khruschev

Even though Stalin's death may be natural, the situation when he died strongly resembled that of the last days of Robespierre, whose disappearance was also in the interest of leading members of his own party, the Jacobins, who conspired against him as they feared a purge. The "dictatorship by committee" which started after Stalin's death was a dictatorship of leading party members and some high-ranking military men and closely resembled the rule of the Thermidorians and the Directory that followed it during the French Revolution. Stalin's successor as Prime Minister, his confidential secretary, Georgei Malenkov, obtained neither of the two key positions which had formed the basis of the power of the dead dictator: the position of Secretary-General of the Communist Party and that of Supreme Commander of the State police. The position of Secretary-General, which Malenkov seized in the first few minutes, was taken away

from him after a few days by his colleagues in the Cabinet and
was later given to Khruschev, and the command of the State
police, which was in the hands of his former friend Beria, by that
time a rival, did not pass to him at all; it was his struggle with
Beria which made him acceptable for the time being to the remaining members of the Praesidium—the heads of the technical
bureaucracy and the Army—and caused them to support him as
Prime Minister. Beria himself, fully aware that the life-and-
death struggle for place meant winning over the masses, which
began to breathe more freely after the death of the old tyrant,
started at once with utmost determination to outdo his colleagues in this field. To the surprise of the outside world, Stalin's
death led to immediate competition between the men in power to
influence the common men of the Union, and especially the
suppressed areas, which threatened to wreck Stalin's harsh
centralism and his almost antisocial economic policy. It was a
struggle with weapons reversed, like the one between Laërtes and
Hamlet, and it led Beria into a position which made him appear
to be the strongest opponent of the harsh centralist trend he had
represented previously. His concessions to the non-Russian
nationalities, regarded as treason by the military and their
friends, accelerated his downfall four months after Stalin's death.
His downfall was also speeded by his raising of false hopes which
had led to events such as the revolt in Eastern Germany which
threatened the rule of the Soviet Union.

The military in the Government saw to it that after Beria had
been arrested and executed, his State police were brought under
the control of a committee presided over by a colonel-general.
The old rivalry between Army and State police was thus decided
in favour of the Army. The weight of the high technical bureaucrats and military men in the Government after Stalin's death
was so strong that Malenkov himself could not resist it for very
long. In his effort to copy Beria's post-Stalin policy by inaugurat-
ing popular measures such as concessions to consumers, he met
with the jealousies of his colleagues in the Cabinet and was
brought down, even though he was not killed as had been the
hated master of the secret police.

The political figure who won the greatest advantage in the
downfall of both Beria and Malenkov was the rising new tyrant
of the Soviet Union, Nikita Khruschev. One of the leading

members of the party secretariat, he had helped to foil the attempt of Malenkov to seize the position of Secretary-General of the party in March 1953, and a few months later had succeeded in securing this position for himself. He used this as a jumping-off point for his race to power, as Joseph Stalin had once done. This does not mean, however, that the Secretary-General was automatically the strongest person in the Soviet Union. It would be more correct to say that the position served as a good springboard to power and was sought mainly by ambitious men. Even Khruschev, rotund, robust, earthy, and 100 per cent more Russian that the scheming, mean and lean Stalin, would seem to have been less free from dictator complexes than outwardly appeared. Born in 1894, Nikita Khruschev was the son of small peasants from a village near Kursk and when he was a boy received a merciless beating from a gamekeeper and a policeman when caught fishing in the pond of the wealthy Prince Koslovski. One writer thinks that perhaps this incident had a significance in the life of Khruschev similar to that produced upon the young Lenin by the hanging of his brother Alexander Ulianov. Be this as it may, it is certain that young Nikita soon became acquainted with terrorist and Marxist literature, and as a metal worker employed in the factory of one Helferich in Kharkov, stirred up the workers in the Donetz Basin against their employers before the 1917 Revolution. Having risen in the party in Kiev, he was called to Moscow in 1934, and was made Secretary-General of the Party in the Ukraine in 1938, replacing one Kosior, who was felled by the purges, and in the following year obtained a seat in the Politburo. The prestige he acquired as Stalin's right-hand man in the Ukraine both before and after the German occupation helped him to climb to the top of the party in Moscow, whence he reached for the supreme leadership.

His rise, like that of Stalin, makes it necessary to modify the old slogan that dictators usually find no successors. Since the days of Lenin, the Soviet State machine had reached such dimensions that it was imperative that some solution of the successor problem be found, however crude. While Khruschev lacked the control of the secret police and the armed forces, at least to the extent that Stalin had possessed it, and before March 1958 was not even Prime Minister, he matched his mighty predecessor in the art of overpowering his opponents, though he lacked the power of killing them outright. Like Stalin, he was a master at proceeding in a pseudo-democratic fashion by forming "majorities" in what was now the Praesidium against the unhappy targets of his attacks, and by reinforcing these "majorities" if necessary with trusted lieutenants co-opted on to the Praesidium. Thus having first combined with the old Stalinists such as Molotov and Kaganovitch and the military, led by Marshal Zhukov, against Beria and then against Malenkov, he played Zhukov against Molotov, Kaganovitch, and the latter's ally Shepilov, only to turn on his former ally, Zhukov, when these three had fallen. He brought Zhukov down by combining with another military faction, lead by Marshal Malinovsky. In March 1958, he succeeded in turn in ousting Marshal Bulganin, the paternal figure with the goatee who had accompanied him on his many visits to foreign capitals, and to replace him as Prime Minister; the reason being, apparently, that Bulganin had failed him in the Zhukov matter.

Like Beria and Malenkov, but with more success, Khruschev succeeded in making political hay of the fact that after a tyranny as harsh as Stalin's even the smallest concessions make a Government popular. By restricting the State police, reform and dissolution of the labour camps, liberalization of the court procedure, a switch to the production of consumer goods, easing the labour laws, a slight relaxation of the censorship, the freeing of the arts from many of the ridiculous chains to which the deceased would-be art expert had subjected them, and similar methods, the "dictatorship by committee" had succeeded in creating a better atmosphere both inside and outside the Soviet Union. These features were not merely "tactics", as fanatic enemies contended, who saw in everything that happened in Moscow the outcome of an infernal secret world plan—a kind of "Plot of the Elders of Zion" in which pseudo-educated men like Hitler had believed. They rather reflected the ideas and political concepts of the new class of officials, functionaries, high military men and leading intellectuals from whom Stalin had formed a kind of neo-bourgeoisie by his system of paying widely varying salaries, which he could hold in check only by constant bloodshed. Khruschev decided to use these ideas, but without granting the neo-bourgeoisie the degree of freedom it had enjoyed since Stalin's death. In the field of foreign politics, once he had become unrestricted ruler, he withdrew some of the concessions made to the outside world in the period of "dictatorship by committee". He no longer maintained friendly relations with Marshal Tito, Stalin's inveterate foe, with whom he had tried to come to terms in the intermediate period. By a state visit to Budapest in April 1958, he supported the Hungarian satellite régime which had put down an anti-Communist uprising in October 1956 with the military help of the Soviet Union. Encouraged by Khruschev's attitude, Soviet Hungary killed the chief figures in that uprising, Maleter and Imre Nagy, whom it had kept in prison until then. In internal politics the Khruschev trend was marked by a stupendous technical advance, symbolized by the appearance of the various Sputniks high above the earth, and by a tremendous agrarian reform which involved handing over the State-run machine and tractor stations to the agrarian collective farms. The aim of this measure was both to relieve the Soviet Union of a considerable financial burden and to gain support for Khruschev in the collective farms, which he could use to build up his power in the face of the high bureaucracy. Very soon after the start of his unrestricted rule, it was clear that a Khruschevist party was being formed to fight the big men in the party and thus to replace Stalinism, which Khruschev had debunked. Appearing on certain occasions in Army uniform, the dictator was evidently copying his great predecessor whose might to a great extent had been based on his position of Generalissimo. At the same time Russian textbooks began to emphasize Khruschev's merits in winning the Russian victory at Stalingrad in the second world war!—a version historians found rather novel. Apparently a new Russian "personality cult" was in the making, not very different from the one Khruschev had condemned in the case of Stalin. While very much of the merry living man himself, Khruschev was evidently unwilling to share his power with anyone else, or to tolerate defections from the Soviet orbit by figures such as Marshal Tito.

Marshal Tito

Tito, whose proper name was Josip Broz, was originally a day labourer who came from Catholic Croatia, which was ruled by the Habsburg Monarchy until 1918. While serving in the Habsburg Army in the first world war, Josip Broz became a Russian

prisoner. An ardent opponent of the Habsburg State, he participated in the Bolshevist Revolution of 1917 and was later used by
Moscow as one of its agents in the Balkans. His main task was
the political disruption of the new Kingdom of Yugoslavia,
which had swallowed his native Croatia after the collapse of
the Habsburg Monarchy. As a Croatian he seemed to be especially fitted to agitate against the Serbs who backed the Yugoslav
monarchy and counteracted Moscow. Even when Yugoslavia,
occupied by Hitler, started to fight the German invader, these
divisions remained; Tito's entire political career was determined
by this dual struggle against the Führer and against the Serbs,
which fitted Stalin's programme perfectly. That the ruler of the
Soviet Union subsequently broke with this trusted vassal was due
both to Stalin's vanity, which tolerated no criticism, and to
material reasons: the importance of the Serb element—mostly
small peasants—in Yugoslavia was such that Tito, after he had
liberated Yugoslavia, or subjected her to his rule, which was
synonymous, would have dug his own grave had he followed
Stalin's programme of total collectivization of his agriculture; in
addition, he refused to buy Russian products at exaggerated
prices, which Stalin expected of all his satellite States.

The zeal with which Russia tried to appease Tito in the transition period between Stalin's death and the establishment of
Khruschev's unrestricted rule was rooted in the political and
economic programme of the "dictatorship by committee".
Instead of making the adjacent States tributary slaves of what
was then called Stalin imperialism—rather a copy of the predatory expansionism of the French Revolution than imperialism
in the usual sense—they tried to win them over by peaceful
means and thus make them useful tools in their rivalry with the
United States of America. The efforts to come to terms with Tito
failed under Khruschev, as Tito refused to abandon his independent position between East and West. That this did not make
him a Western humanitarian is shown by the fate of his friend
and biographer Vladimir Dedijer, silenced and jailed for assail-
ing the régime of the ruling technical bureaucracy. Shrewd, but
pomp-loving, fond of pleasure, somewhat overbearing and fat,
Tito preferred to sacrifice a friend to offending the important
men in the party. But he was not disposed to develop his State

along the line followed by the industrial giants of the Soviet system, the Soviet Union itself and its faithful copyist, the People's Republic of China, and he developed his propaganda accordingly. This earned him the bitter hatred of the rulers of both big States and led to an odd war of words between little Tito and his big brother-in-politics in Asia.

Chapter Sixteen

DICTATORSHIPS IN THE FAR EAST

Chiang Kai-Shek

THE Asiatic Continent, although a cradle of big empires, was as little a genuine area of dictatorship as was Africa. The big Oriental empires were classical centres of despotism, a thing closely related to dictatorship, but until recently they lacked the bases of revolutionary unrest, the big cities, which were a hotbed of tyranny in the West. In the Orient, dictatorship proper was imported, an outcome of the appearance of the white man, of Western imperialism and Western capitalism, under whose auspices the Eastern world produced phenomena which the West in part no longer knew. As in some underdeveloped areas transport is furnished today both by camels and mules as well as by aircraft, modern China, for instance, saw a sequence and even coexistence of several forms of dictatorship; she thus had her Napoleon and her Lenin at the same time, the dictator of the bourgeois and that of the peasants' and workers' revolutions, whose gigantic planning of his country's economy made him China's Stalin at the same time.

As everywhere where the Soviet system advanced, its progress in China was due to an unsolved land problem. In spite of this, however, the Communist Revolution had to wait here, as elsewhere, until a series of wars and the resulting mixing up of social strata had prepared the ground for it. The chain of events started with the attack by Japan on Imperial China in 1894, and the ensuing advance of all the big world Powers, who regarded the vast helpless empire as a welcome prey for imperialist expansion. The atrocities of the entire Western world in this area, especially before the first world war, are still remembered in China and helped her leaders in her struggle against the West.

China's development in the decisive decades was strongly determined by the evolution of her southern and south-eastern provinces, where, under the influx of Western capital a national bourgeoisie emerged. Since the expulsion of the Manchu dynasty in 1911, the prestige of this new bourgeoisie and of its political mouthpiece, the Kuomintang Party, rose steadily. While a great part of the country, especially in the north, fell under the rule of a series of generals who fought each other after the disappearance of the imperial house, the new middle class and the intelligentsia, led by Dr. Sun Yat-Sen, a moderate reformer, aimed at the establishment of a unified democratic republic. After Sun's death in 1925 the leadership in this struggle and in the party fell into the hands of Sun's brother-in-law, Chiang Kai-Shek, then director of the Whampoa military academy.

A capable and disciplined officer, almost Prussian, irate, irascible and haughty, Chiang was very soon called the Chinese Bonaparte. His career as dictator, his achievements in the military unification of the country, and later in his struggle against Japan as well as his collaboration with the Chinese plutocracy would seem to substantiate this comparison, even though Chiang was never as popular with the peasants as was Napoleon. There were good reasons for this. Different from the French bourgeoisie at the time of Napoleon, which practically co-operated with the peasants against the feudal landowners, the wealthy financiers behind Chiang regarded the peasant merely as a target for exploitation. Wealthy merchants, bureaucrats and large clans who lived on the terrible usury which robbed the worn-out humans in the rice paddies of their wages. The centres of South Chinese rice culture, especially in the provinces of Hunan and Kiangsi, were the breeding ground of Communism.

Mao Tse-Tung

These surroundings formed the natural basis for the activity of Chiang's irreconcilable enemy and eventual conqueror: Mao Tse-Tung. Like Stalin, the scion of generations of poor serfs, Mao Tse-Tung came from the lowest strata, and like so many other dictators—Robespierre, Napoleon, Mussolini, Kemal Pasha and others—he was much more impecunious than his fellow students. Such an experience often forms the character of a man. If the boy comes from the sphere above—as did Napoleon, the son of a nobleman—it makes him ambitious; if he comes from below, he is likely to turn revolutionary. That is not

310 DEVILS OR SAVIOURS

to say, however, that Mao Tse-Tung would have copied Stalin
in fanatically turning against the West. The students at Peking
(now called Peiping), where he attended the university, were
friendly towards the Western world, despite their hatred of
imperialism; what finally alienated Mao from the West was the
feeling of solidarity of this earthy and robust peasants' son with
the peasant stratum which the Chinese middle class and the
foreign Powers treated equally badly, and which was neglected
even by Stalin, until Chiang Kai-Shek's antisocial attitude forced
him to change his policy.

Chiang's mass slaughter of the Communists in the cities made
the peasants behind Mao Stalin's only true supporters and
Chiang's main domestic enemies; thus began the epic struggle
between Chiang and Mao which began in 1926 and was to last
more than thirty years. It was inaugurated by a seven-year
peasant war in the provinces of Hunan and Kiangsi. When
Chiang's numerical and technical superiority in this area finally
became too strong, Mao and his cohorts set out on their famous
"long march" across the Tibetan mountains all the way to
Yenan in the extreme north-west of the country, which became
one of the legends of history. When Chiang followed him there
and ultimately fell into a trap of a pro-Communist Chinese war
lord, he was finally released upon a hint from Stalin, who
attempted to play both Chiang and Mao against the constantly
advancing Japanese, who tried to swallow up the entire country.
This Russian policy, which was continued in the second world
war, and endorsed by the nations allied to Stalin, especially the
United States and Great Britain, was rooted in Stalin's old desire
to combine with Chiang against all maritime invaders. Stalin
desired to follow this policy even after 1945, when Japan, which
had over-expanded, collapsed under the impact of Hitler's downfall and the explosion of the first atomic bombs, while the
Western Powers, who had been Stalin's allies, took over Japan's
function of chief opponent of Russian expansion in the Far East.

Just as in the 1920s, Stalin was quite willing to subordinate
his connections with Mao to the alliance with Chiang, and even
made an agreement with the latter, but this was spoiled by the
rising tensions between the political camps involved. With the
past history of Chiang and Mao and the classes they represented,
it was only to be expected that the political armistice both during

and after the war would be called off as soon as their common opponent was beaten. The extensive negotiations between them, mostly at the behest of Americans, will look to historians more like stages in their struggle for power. Mao's popularity among the land-hungry peasants, especially in Manchuria, forbade a real reconciliation. Chiang's attack on Mao, the corruption in his administration, his incapacity to solve the land problem, his fatalistic toleration of the monetary inflation which was exploited by big speculators and threatened the country with financial disaster, and his co-operation with the conservative foreign Powers of that time recall in many respects the policy of the bourgeois Gironde Party whose sins provoked the Ultra-Revolution of its day and the Robespierre dictatorship. In the first months of 1949 Mao Tse-Tung, the Robespierre, Lenin or Stalin of the new China, was master of the situation, and his foe Chiang withdrew full of spite to Formosa, whence, protected by the Americans, he never tired of telling the world that he would one day reconquer his country.

"New Democracy"

Like most Soviet satellite States in the West, China stood socially and economically in the 1950s at the stage reached by Russia in the time of Lenin's New Economic Policy. Well aware of the peculiar form of the Chinese situation, Mao Tse-Tung, in his famous book *New Democracy*, had, just like Lenin, subdivided the economy of his country into three sectors: nationalized production; agriculture, which at first slowly but painfully was being transformed into a collective economy; and the small and medium industrial production, which he promised to protect for the time being. He knew, just like Lenin, that during the transformation of agriculture, his main task, because of the rural structure of his country of 600 million people, he would not be able to do without the activity of the small and medium industrial producers, who still operated on a profit basis. This did not mean that he let them have just what they wanted during this period; by State propaganda campaigns for wage rises, against sabotage, corruption, tax fraud and similar misdeeds—praiseworthy goals in themselves, but like the word "democracy" were not meant here in the usual sense—the producer class was purposely divested of its power. Pilloried as "bourgeois" in the

official propaganda, in the eyes of the masses the producers were
regarded as allies of Chiang Kai-Shek, whose supposed or real
agents were produced from time to time before local peoples'
assemblies and summarily sentenced and were executed in public
squares a few days later in the presence of the peering city population, convoked for this special purpose.

In the collectivization of agriculture, the main concern of his
régime, Mao used force and authoritarian methods too; he
methodically stirred up the small and medium peasants against
the wealthy ones, he threatened with the same fate Stalin had
prepared for the *kulaks*. The results of the Chinese collectivization were astonishing even in terms of the progress made soon
after the start. Assisted by the co-operation of many intellectuals
who had come over to him from the Kuomintang to serve as
propagandists, Mao increased the number of farmers' families
working in the agrarian co-operatives—the preparatory stage of
complete collectivization and technization—from 14 per cent in
the summer of 1955 to 60 per cent in January of the following
year and 90 per cent in March; in one-half of these cases even
full collectivization was reached.

The imminent boom of the colossal area and the relative backwardness of its industry urged the European Powers to break
through the economic blockade with which the United States
had surrounded the country for strategic reasons since its intervention in the Korean War. The increase in China's international relations and the rise of the country, especially in the fields
of education and teacher training, gave Mao's régime a leading
rôle in preparing for a co-existence of the Soviet and capitalist
systems that started after Stalin's death. The "dictatorship by
committee" suited the Chinese Communist system and even
Chinese history much better than Stalin's rigorous centralism
had done; Chinese historians emphasized that the staging of
agrarian reforms by a benevolent bureaucracy was a standing
feature in old China, as shown by the history of the Han and
Ming dynasties, whose founders were themselves farmers.
China's Foreign Minister Chou En-Lai played a leading part in
the "Titoization" of the Soviet bloc in the autumn of 1956, but
he approved of the rough handling of Hungary, who, in Soviet
eyes, had overstepped the permissible line. It also appeared that
the liberalization of the Soviet bloc which followed Stalin's

death was more than a temporary stage and was not a purpose in itself. For the Mao State, which was aiming at surpassing the Soviet Union, this was most acceptable and useful as long as China went through her period corresponding to the New Economic Policy. That explains the acrimonious discussions between the Mao and Tito propagandists which accompanied Moscow's new collision with Tito in the spring of 1958.

Postscript

DOWN THE BLOOD-PATH?

Two main dangers threaten our generation; modern super-weapons with powerful nuclear warheads, and neurotic statesmen. The two must not be allowed to meet. Had Hitler possessed the hydrogen bomb, he would have transformed the Twilight of the German Gods of 1945 into a general world disaster.

From their early days, most dictators live in a state of unusual tension with their fellow men, which usually leads to grave neurosis. The professional worries of the dictator tend to accentuate this neurotic condition. In most of these cases terrible explosions and tragedies ensue. None of these figures would ever have come to power had not the social conditions of the time carried them to the top. He who wants to prevent the rise of dictators would therefore do well to study the circumstances which usually favour their rise, even though the individual opponent of dictatorship is hardly in the position to change these conditions. Neither is a single individual in the position to prevent a psychopathological person from taking up what he calls his political mission. It is possible, however, to enlighten the world about the nature of these men. Under healthy democratic conditions they do not achieve very much as a rule, since the egotism of their rivals in the political field forms a kind of protective cover against them. Where a nation is steeped in democratic ideals, the danger of dictatorship is small. The United States Senator Joseph R. McCarthy, who conducted a political propaganda campaign of almost Hitlerian dimensions and in almost Hitlerian fashion in the United States only a short time ago, aiming at presenting himself as Saviour of Society, was soon forgotten—a victim of the mechanism of democracy. At the time of his death at the early age of forty-eight in May 1957, his glory had faded to such an extent that it was reminiscent of Talley-

314

rand's remark when he heard that Napoleon had died in St. Helena, after six years of exile : "It is no event, just a piece of news."

The defence of the Western democracies against their totalitarian rivals and the prophylactic treatment of dictatorship is much more difficult in countries where the democratic system is weak or still in its infancy. This is especially true under the present conditions where the cold war between the West and the Soviet Union forces both parties to woo statesmen whom they would otherwise prefer to ignore. The Soviet Union recently invited potentates from the darkest corner of Arabia for a "visit of friendship" to the Kremlin—a policy the United States immediately copied—and the list of the members of the so-called Free World include such trusted friends of democracy as President Batista of Cuba, Rafael Trujillo of the Dominican Republic, Rojas Pinilla of Colombia and Marcos Pérez Jímenez of Venezuela—the last two now politically defunct—Salazar of Portugal, Francisco Franco of Spain, Chiang Kai-Shek of Formosa and formerly China, and others. The more the democracies woo these men, the worse for their cause. This must not lead to undue generalizations—since politics make strange bedfellows, and since in some instances the industrialization provoked by financial aid helped to undermine the social structure of such régimes. But the systematic encouragement of such reactionaries by the Western world for the sole purpose of fighting the Soviets has a demoralizing effect on its best friends.

Looking at the total picture the two parties in the present world struggle are not only mixed politically but even the moral aspect is blurred. Not everything in the dictatorships is black, nor white in the democracies. In the case of most "classical" dictatorships—the midwives of the Western world—the positive points often exceed the negative ones. An examination of the merits and demerits of individual dictatorships would need a painstaking investigation of the way they handled economics, social problems, education, religion, the Press and the arts, which in a small volume like the present cannot be given, even on a very small scale. The results of such an examination would presumably cause much surprise. In spite of our horror at the unspeakable atrocities of Stalin, and our aversion to the heavy-handedness and cynicism of his methods, the Soviet Union would probably

11—DOS

come close to the top in such a test. In many fields connected with education and social hygiene the citizen of the Soviet Union —even under Stalin when the freedom of the individual did not exist—was ahead of the citizens of the so-called Free World, including those of the United States. Among these fields were the care for the individual's use of his recreation time, the methodical, stimulating education, the results of which became visible at the time of the Sputniks, the lack of cheap and worthless literature including detective, criminal, murder, sex and "Western" stories, and their appearance on the films, radio and television, the cutting down of sports news to a reasonable amount, and the lack of the society news and gossip columns. It must also be admitted that the Western Press, although outwardly enjoying complete freedom, is to a large extent in the hands of wealthy financiers and so does not reflect all shades of public opinion. By the same token, the Western labourer and employee, while unrestricted in his freedom to change his position and seek work, on the whole enjoys less security against unemployment than does the Soviet worker, who, with some modifications, has to accept the positions assigned to him, but need not fear to be put out on the street.

The most destructive side of all dictatorships is undoubtedly their lack of freedom of expression, which can hardly be fully described in a book—especially a small one. The censoring of all news, combined with the dictator's one-sided propaganda, gives the masses in the cities and country a coloured and totally unrealistic picture of the situation in the world which determines their lives and actions. Inmate of a gigantic prison, the individual hears only what the prison director wants him to hear, and in the end he starts to believe it. Thus the struggle against this kind of mental tutelage and against all efforts to restrict freedom of expression must form the main basis of the defence against the methods we have pictured. Of equal importance will be the struggle for world disarmament. Militarization and arms races have so often formed the hot-house in which the tyrants rose. The most important task, however, is to learn a lesson from history and see to it that the dictatorships which have hurt humanity so strongly in the last few decades will not reappear. Whether we are approaching this goal is uncertain. As long as the question of German unity remains unsolved and a unified

Germany has not entered the United Nations, the return of another Hitler is not beyond the bounds of probability. A modern German Hitler would not necessarily need SA and SS guards, nor would he have control of a Nazi Party. He could very well be a kind of "iron chancellor" of the Bonn Republic, supported by the *Bundeswehr*, atom-worshippers and German remilitarized industry, and he might well start on his road to power by a repetition of the Hitler-Stalin Pact. Be this as it may, the fact remains that Germany since 1945 has entered the ranks of those "armed republics" which are the very breeding ground for dictatorship, as shown among others by the history of France from 1789 to 1958.

Should it be impossible to solve the German question, the ensuing complications might also lead to a super-militarization of the Russian dictatorship. We have compared the post-Stalin governments in the Soviet Union to the French governments after Robespierre's downfall. One should not forget, however, that when those French rulers started facing trouble—especially in the field of international affairs—a new dictator appeared in France: Napoleon Bonaparte. It will have to be the aim of the Western Powers to prevent a repetition of this development. A collision between West and East, unchained for instance by the German unity question, could easily lead to the rise of a Russian Bonaparte. The problem is of cosmic importance. *Videant consules ne quid detrimenti capiat mundus.* May our statesmen prevent the world from perishing in flames.

EPILOGUE

Fidel Castro beats dictator Fulgencio Batista

NEW Year's Day, 1959, was one of the proudest days in the history of the fight against dictatorship. The sound of the fire-crackers announcing the turn of the year could still be heard, when the wily and hated Fulgencio Batista, who for decades had intermittently been the strong man of Cuba, secretly boarded a plane carrying him into exile. His flight marked the end of an epic struggle which had entered its main stage two years and one month earlier, when the final victor, Fidel Castro, at the head of a handful of men, landed on swampy ground at Oriente Province, to wrest his native country from the hands of the dreaded tyrant.

Through Castro's victory the system of military dictatorship in Latin America reached its nadir, though it seemed to revive in old war-torn Europe. Eclipsed by the gradual rise of new classes, the prestige of the military man in Latin America was on the wane, while in the Old World it was raised by the struggle against the USSR and the international social crisis which followed World War II. This situation was accentuated by advances in military techniques. Due to the development of atomic warfare, standing armies, a threat to all republics, had become obsolete in all cases where they were not supported by adequate atomic power. Consequently, many Latin Americans tended to believe that the military aid given by the United States to backward states such as Cuba had no longer any military value, but served mainly to suppress the common man with the help of local dictators eager to protect the economic needs of the "Colossus in the North". For Fidel Castro, this widespread belief became certainty when one of his secret helpers, who was actually in the Cuban Embassy at Washington, sent him

transcripts of messages from U.S. generals who, naïvely identify-
ing the interests of hemispheric defence with those of Batista's
régime, expressed their sympathy with the dictator.

It was Batista's undoing that the type of régime he represented
had outlived its social usefulness. Originally a mere army sergeant who, in common with the older Dionysus, held some sort
of clerical position with the army staff, he participated in August
1933 in the overthrow of his forerunner, the terrible Machado.
The bloody inner fights which followed gave him and the other
non-commissioned officers of the Cuban army the chance of
playing saviours to the badly shaken Cuban society, and of
setting up a dictatorship under his command. As a dictator,
Batista followed in the footsteps of so many Latin American
strong men of his time. Having become the protector of "law
and order" he defended the property of the rich sugar planters,
the foreign investors and the budding middle classes against the
poor rural workers, on condition that he and the thugs surrounding him be allowed to dip liberally into the public funds, and
that his dreaded police be free to manhandle anyone who
refused to play the game. American businessmen supported him
as eagerly as they had backed the terrible Machado, and so did
the U.S. diplomats and generals. Due to Havana's leading rôle
in gambling, prostitution and the narcotics trade the ranks of
the U.S. investors who backed the dictator were joined by
numerous gangsters, which gave the foreign interests of this
country a particularly nasty flavour, especially since the dictatorship was known to be "in" with all these elements.

Batista knew quite well that a régime as hostile to the freedom
of the press, freedom of thought, the proper functioning of the
courts and individual liberty as his would antagonize above all
the middle class intelligentsia, and he therefore tried, not without
success, to find followers among the workers. In wooing a certain
labour element he copied the two Peróns. But he failed to gain
the mass of the poor workers, and he could never hope to
impress the main mass of the bourgeoisie which in the mid-
1950s, received much encouragement through the revolutions in
most other big Latin American states, where dictator after dictator toppled. As an area which still lacked a large industry,
Cuba, it is true, could hardly hope to overthrow her strong man

by a sudden shock, as did Argentina, Colombia, or Venezuela. In a country controlled by tobacco growers and sugar planters and firmly ruled by organized graft, a regular military campaign was needed to root out the evil from the area. The man to lead this campaign, Fidel Castro, was the son of a poor immigrant from Spain, who had become wealthy through hard work as a labourer on American-owned plantations and later as a sugar planter. In helping his father, Fidel Castro himself became accustomed to hard work, but he also set out to study law. This double background determined his future. A giant, who never shunned any physical challenge, Fidel—as Cuba affectionately called him—displayed at the same time a rare resourcefulness as a military and political leader. Unselfish, and totally unimpressed by "good society" he was in every respect the opposite of Batista, the stocky former sergeant who had long forgotten his own revolutionary past, and, chief of a cohort of thugs, made a tremendous fortune by serving the mighty. A basically small and spiteful man, Batista cold-bloodedly tortured and killed all the enemies he could lay his hands on, while Castro left prisoners unscathed and sent them home.

As might be expected, Batista tried to convince the world that his foes were Communists. It is indeed true that the men surrounding Castro, Argentine-born Ernesto ("Ché") Guevaras and Castro's brother Raoul, had some slight Communist tinge. It is further correct that Fidel himself, at the age of twenty-two, participated in the tremendous street fights of 1948 in the capital of Colombia, Bogotá, which followed the assassination of Leftist leader, Gaitán and which disturbed the Bogotá conference of the American states. Bogotá authorities later ascribed the presence of Fidel and other intellectuals from foreign countries to the desire of the Communists to break up the Bogotá conference, though the Communists could not, of course, foresee the murder of Gaitán and the dimensions of the outbreaks that were to follow. But Fidel's rôle in this matter must be seen in proper perspective. Some degree of connection with Communism has become commonplace with numerous statesmen of awakening nations, a fact which did not prevent them from shaking off these ties whenever it served their interests. The considerable influence exercised upon Fidel by his teacher, Father Armando

Llorente, would seem to exclude the view that he is under Moscow's influence. The numerous speeches we have of his sound convincingly democratic.

A sworn enemy of the system of dictatorship, on July 26th, 1953, Fidel led a band of armed youngsters in an attack on the Moncada barracks in Santiago, capital of Oriente Province, but failed and was captured. Condemned to prison, he was finally freed by an amnesty, and then lived in exile in the United States and in Mexico. There, he and his followers were trained in the art of guerrilla warfare by a former colonel in the Spanish Civil War who owned a ranch.

On December 2nd, 1956, he started his historic invasion of his native island, landing there with eighty-one men, most of whom were dispersed at once, leaving him with hardly more than a dozen. The way in which this handful of fighters established a stronghold in the Sierra Maestra, and in the course of hardly more than two years defeated Batista's police forces plus his army of 15,000 officers and men, which he finally almost doubled, is an epic of human endurance, resourcefulness, courage and bravery. Known as the "Bearded Ones" (los barbudos), since they had no time for shaving, the men of the 26th of July movement, as they called themselves in commemoration of the attack on the Moncada barracks, would, of course, never have reached their goal, had they not been assisted by the mounting admiration of the entire population for their intrepid leader, that bearded and bespectacled giant with the unfailing telescopic rifle, in whom the students and workers saw their Robin Hood. Kept informed by his sympathizers about every move Batista's forces made against him in a pathless area where the dictator's planes and tanks helped him little, Castro again and again managed to slip through the fingers of his attackers. Besides, the sympathies he evoked enabled him to harass his enemies' rear and to organize a large-scale technical terrorism and sabotage which the attackers tried to combat by tremendous physical terrorism. But this proved to be their undoing, since it alienated even many people who would have supported their cause. Exploiting the general indignation about the torturing of his followers, in Spring 1958 Castro declared total war on the government, to be topped by a general strike. The strike movement did not come off as planned, but the strict orders to officers and public servants to cease to obey the dictator, issued by Castro on this occasion, were of importance in the future. So was his warning that all Civil War criminals would be court martialled and shot.

The end of the Batista tyranny came through virtually the same element which had decided the victory of the armies of Robespierre, Lenin and Mao Tse-Tung over their opponents. His hopes raised by the collapse of the general strike, Batista launched a general offensive against Castro's mountain fortress, thus giving his opponent the chance of starting a counter-offensive, the mightiest move that can be thought of in classical strategy. Steadily gaining momentum, Castro's move finally prompted the army to desert Batista's cause.

Castro's victory was so decisive that he was able to dispense with the usual military caretaker régime, as a preparation for complete democracy, but appointed a president of his own choosing, who in turn made him Prime Minister. His assumption to this office contradicted his oft-repeated assurances that he would avoid taking over any official duty. The reason for his changing his mind was the necessity for seeing through the execution of his programme, which called for a thorough cleansing of the administration, agrarian reform favouring the poor peasant, industrialization, and the punishment of what were called Civil War criminals, in accordance with his proclamations of 1958. To meet the indignation of the outside world, especially of the U.S. public, which protested passionately against the summary and often theatrical proceedings which led to the shooting, by April 1959, of about five hundred Batista followers, Castro pointed out that this type of justice seemed to him fairer than the famous War Crimes trials in 1945–46, inasmuch as he had laid down the law beforehand. His defenders also said that in a country where the machinery for the enforcement of law had been wrecked so thoroughly as in Cuba under Batista, summary proceedings offered the only means of freeing the country from the thugs, thieves and torturers who had formed the basis of the Batista régime. While Batista, who had fled to the Dominican Republic, taking with him tremendous funds, started a powerful press campaign in which Castro was called a dictator, the defenders of the new Cuban régime emphasized, with some justification, that a political leader so strongly supported by the vast masses of his country as was their chief, did not need to betray the people with the help of armed power, in the style of old caudillos. The resistance of the old social powers against Castro's efforts to purify state and society remained so strong, however, that he could hardly have dispensed with the help of his armed followers, even though he might have wanted to.

Since this sketch was written, early in 1959, Castro has developed still further into a kind of Cuban Nasser—a benevolent dictator with a broad mass basis, but still a dictator.

BIBLIOGRAPHICAL NOTES

PART I   The Dictatorships of Antiquity

The literature on the tyrants of antiquity suffers to a certain extent from the customary insulation of the research in this specialist field. The disinclination to make use of comparisons and world historical empirical laws is here particularly unsatisfactory, since, due to the fragmentary nature of our knowledge of antiquity, analogies (obtained with due regard to historical likelihood) often furnish the only possibility of gaining further knowledge. Books which contribute most fully to the understanding of Greek history and its tyrants are "Griechische Geschichte", by *K. J. Beloch* (Strassburg, 1912–27) which is in four volumes; "Griechische Geschichte von den Anfaengen bis in die Gegenwart", by *H. Bengtson* (Munich, 1950); "The Origins of Tyranny", by *P. N. Ure* (Cambridge, 1922) ("useful but too heavily modernized"—Bengtson), and "Class Struggles in Ancient Greece", by *Margret O. Wason* (London, 1946). The author's own attitude comes very close to that of the Swedish scholar *M. B. Nilsson*. For the specialist literature on the tyrants in Sicily, see the classic four-volume "History of Sicily" by *E. A. Freeman* (of which the English edition had already appeared in 1891–94); for the general social background of Roman dictatorship, the book by *G. Salvioli* which first appeared in French translation and has never received due recognition, "Le Capitalisme dans le monde antique" (Paris, 1906; ital. Rome, 1929). For the Gracchi and Sulla see the works of the Frenchman *J. Carcopino* (who, however, rather over-emphasizes the unwillingness of Sulla to abdicate). For the history of the greatest Roman dictator, the biography of Caesar by *G. Ferrero* should be consulted, which, however, goes rather too far in its emphasis on the element of chance in the career of a dictator, and underestimates his striving towards despotism; *M. Gelzer*'s book "Caesar, der Politiker und Staatsmann" (Munich, 1942) is perfectly reliable but rather uninspired; a comprehensive and dramatic biography based on the most exacting study is offered by the Frenchman *Gérard Walter*, who specializes in the investigation of dictator types by means of modern methods. Other books to note in connection with this subject are *Kathleen Freeman*'s "Greek City States" (London, 1950); *A. Andrewes*'s "The Greek Tyrants" (edited by H. T. Wade-Gery; London, 1956) and *R. J. Hopper*'s "The Basis of Athenian Democracy" (Oxford, 1957).

PART II   The Dictatorships of Early Capitalism

Concerning despots of the Renaissance, the most famous work on this period, *Jakob Burckhardt*'s "Kultur der Renaissance in Italien" contributes very little to our subject. As son of the patrician class of a Swiss city-state, Burckhardt sought in politics and art the aristocratic characteristics with which he was identified; the character of the urban masses, their interests and needs, and the development of the urban economy, which gave them their daily bread, interested him very little; with the leaders of the masses whose Machiavellian character he admired, he deals only sporadically and in so far as they took over political leadership of their districts. On all these points the other famous historians of this period, the Englishman *John A. Symonds*, has thoroughly outdone him; Symonds's work on the Renaissance in Italy is, in contrast to that of Burckhardt, which is essentially a portrayal of art, spirit and way of life, a comprehensive full-blooded general history of the time and its despots, and even today—seventy years after its first edition—remains supreme. For information as to more recent research into the economic and social picture of the time which provided a background to the despots of the Renaissance, see *Alfred Doren*'s brilliant "Italienische Wirtschaftsgeschichte" (Jena, 1943). For the history of the numerous individual despots it is mostly necessary to consult specialist literature dealing with single parts of Italy and above all, with individual towns. The book by *Ernst Kantorowicz* on Frederick II, though written in the mannered style of the Stefan George school, is nevertheless considered the classic work on this subject; for the history of the Bentivoglio family in Bologna, see the monograph of *Cecilia M. Ady* (London, 1937); for those of Florence see (should time permit) the thorough nine-volume work by *Robert Davidson*, and for Lorenzo Medici—in particular the older work by *A. v. Reumont*; the Gonzagas in Mantua have been dealt with by *Selwyn Brinton* (London, 1927), and Vincenzo in particular in "A Prince of Mantua" (London, 1956) by *Maria Belloni*; the Scaligers of *A. M. Allen* in his "History of Verona" (New York, 1910); of the numerous works on the Borgias, and on Cesare Borgia in particular, those to note are *William H. Woodward*, "Cesare Borgia" (London, 1913), *Guiseppe Portigliotti*, "The Borgias" (English edition; New York, 1928), *Baron Corvo* (pseudonym of *Frederick W. Rolfe*), the author of a history of the Borgias (New York, 1931), and *Rafael Sabatini*, who emphasizes Cesare's French nationality in "Cesare Borgia" (Boston, Mass., 1930).

The material on Oliver Cromwell is all collected in the 540 pages of the "Bibliography of Oliver Cromwell", edited by *Wilbur C. Abbot* (Harvard Univ., 1929). Amongst the best-known biographies of Cromwell, the works of *Samuel R. Gardiner* (London, 1901), a short précis of the picture of Cromwell offered in *Gardiner*'s works on this period, and *Charles H. Firth* (New York, 1933) suffer due to the failure of the average Victorian and post-Victorian to understand the psychology of revolutionary periods and leaders of the people. A good concise picture of the social background of the period and its struggles is given in the work of which several editions were brought out by the Dietz (Stuttgart) press before Hitler came to power, by the leader of the Socialist "Revisionists", *Eduard Bernstein*, entitled "Sozialismus und Demokratie in der grossen englischen Revolution". The best character study of Cromwell known to the author is offered by the British lawyer *George R. St. Taylor* (obviously inclined towards Roman Catholicism or the High Church) in his brief study of the Dictator (Boston, 1928).

PART III Dictatorships during the Rise of Industrial Capitalism

The literature on the French Revolution and the dictatorships arising out of it is limitless. The most important work on the period and in particular on Robespierre is the work in several volumes on the history of the French Revolution, by the pioneer French scholar *Albert Mathiez*, which freed the picture of Robespierre from the misconceptions arising out of the clash between the parties; most of the more recent biographies of the dictator are based on Mathiez, one such work being the

American *Ralph H. Korngold*'s "Robespierre and the Fourth Estate" (New York, 1941). A very apt portrayal of the Committee of Public Safety and its policy is that of *Robert Palmer*, "Twelve who Ruled" (Princeton, 1941). The comprehensive and dramatic biography of Robespierre by *Gerard Walter* (Paris, 1946) is a worthy companion to the biography of Caesar by the same author.

The material on General Bonaparte, later the Emperor Napoleon I, is so vast *in toto* that the Napoleon biographer, *Friedrick M. Kircheisen*, who, starting shortly after the beginning of the nineteenth century, drew up a comprehensive Bibliography on Napoleon, had already listed 80,000 works, and the number has grown considerably since then. To gain an objective picture without wasting time it is best to discard at the outset the books by such uncritical gushers as *Gustave Aubry*, the monomaniacs like *Kircheisen*, and on the other side the more or less witty professional grumblers like, for instance, *Werner Hegemann*, "Napoleon oder de Kniefall vor dem Heros". Works disappointing due to the lack of necessary understanding of the neurotic features of the picture are once again productions of British biographers such as the famous Napoleon biography by *J. Holland Rose*, or the still weaker one of *I. M. Thomson*. The same is to be said of many French biographers, such as the late Academy Member *Louis Madelin*, whose vision was impaired by the brillance of the Napoleonic era. The older work, in three volumes, by *August Fournier* (Vienna, 1904–06) is a useful and carefully considered piece of work, as are the comprehensive biography by *William J. Sloane* (7th edition; New York, 1939) and the no less excellent work on Napoleon by Louis Villat (Paris, 1942). A very good biography, though rather deficient on the psychological side, is that of the Russian historian, *Eugen Tarlé*, who had already made his name before the Bolshevik period, and was counted amongst the greatest scholars in the U.S.S.R. *Emil Ludwig*'s book on Napoleon, the best of his sensational and popular life-stories, is also worth reading. Furthermore here, as in the case of almost all these men, analyses made by psychologists and psychiatrists, such as the paper by *Leon Pierre Clark*, "Napoleon Self-Destroyed", are of very great importance.

In spite of the extensive literature on Napoleon III, a good

comprehensive work, portraying the rise and social background of this dictatorship, is still lacking. The biography
of *Albert Leon Guérard* (Cambridge, Mass., 1943), although a
product of Harvard University, takes Napoleon far too seriously,
portrays him very strongly and is too indiscriminate in its facts;
the small book on Napoleon by *Pierre de la Gorce*—condensed
from his fat volume on the history of the Second Empire—is out
of date. But several individual studies such as *Emil A. Rein-
hardt*'s "Napoleon and Eugenie" and *S. A. Maurois*'s "Miss
Howard and the Emperor" (Collins, 1957) are useful.

Concerning the literature on dictatorships in the Spanish
cultural traditions, the extraordinary fragmentation of this world
renders impossible a single all-embracing treatment. The best
and most discerning work on the development of dictatorship in
Spain itself is the book by *Antonio Ramos-Oliviera*, "Politics,
Economics and Men of Modern Spain" (London, 1946). General
treatments of Latin-American history (paying due attention to
dictatorships) are given by *Carlos O. Bunge*, in his "Nuestra
America" (Buenos Aires, 1918) (excellent) and *John Crow* in
"The Epic of Latin America" (New York, 1946) (recommended).
Another comprehensive study is that of *H. Herring*, "A History
of Latin America from the Beginnings to the Present" (London,
1956), and "Government of Latin America" (New York and
London, 1957), by *W. W. Pierson* and *F. G. Gil*, is also to be
recommended. For individual works on the best-known dictator-
ships, see *Th. Rourke* (pseudonym of *Daniel Clinton*), "Gomez,
Tyrant of the Andes" (New York, 1936); *George Wise*,
"Caudillo, a Portrait of Guzman Blanco" (New York, 1951) (dis-
tinguished study by a student of M. Weber); *Ralph Roeder*,
"Juarez and his Mexico" (2 vols., New York, 1947); *William E.
Barrett*, "A Woman on Horseback, the Biography of Francisco
Solano Lopez and Eliza Lynch" (New York, 1938); *Wilfred H.
Colcott*, "Santa Anna" (Norman, Oklahoma, 1936); Carlton
Bearls, "Porfirio Diaz" (Philadelphia, 1932), etc.

PART IV Dictatorship in the Era of Working-Class Movements

The literature on the meaning, spirit and form of totalitarian
dictatorship is extremely diffuse. The only things given here are
a few bibliographical pointers for studying the development of its
history.

For the history and antecedents of the Lenin dictatorship see the works on the Paris Commune by *Edward S. Mason* (New York, 1930) and by *Frank Jellinek* (New York, 1937), and in particular the work in several volumes of the former English diplomat and expert on Russian affairs, *Edward Hallet Carr*, on the Bolshevik Revolution, a serious attempt at objectivity which began to come out in 1951 (Macmillan, New York) but was attacked by both anti-Communists and Stalinists. A general work on the period leading up to the Revolution is *Avram Yarmolinski*'s "Road to the Revolution. A Century of Russian Radicalism" (London, 1957), and on the period in general *Zevedi Barbu*'s "Democracy and Dictatorship" (London, 1956). Indispensable for the understanding of Lenin is the study of his collected works which have appeared in all the European languages and in many others. Amongst the biographies of Lenin to be recommended are those of *Nina Baker (Brown)* (New York, 1945), *Ralph W. Fox* (London, 1933, pro-Communist), *Christopher Hill* (New York, 1950), *Christopher Hollis* (Milwaukee, 1938) *Platon M. Kerzhentsev* (New York, 1938) and particularly the book of *David Shub* (Doubleday, New York, 1948), the best work in this field to date.

It is difficult to gain an impression of the enormous amount of literature on the Communist (Third) International; amongst the best and most objective works on this subject is that of *Hugh Seton Watson*, "From Lenin to Malenkov, the History of World Communism" (New York, 1953). For further works of this kind, see the Bibliography for Part V.

For the history of the period prior to Fascism and National Socialism the amplifications of Richard Wagner's political thought in the biography in several volumes by *Ernest Newman* is to be recommended together with the four-volume correspondence between Wagner and King Ludwig II, and the correspondence, published in 1934 in Leipzig, between Wagner's widow *Cosima* and *Houston Stewart Chamberlain*, Wagner's son-in-law.

On Annunzio there are biographies by *Gerald Griffin* (London, 1935) and *Frederico Nardello* (New York, 1931); a comprehensive study is offered by *Filippo Masci* (Rome, 1950), but the most intimate work is the description of his life and work by his secretary *T. Antongini* (Boston, 1938).

For the rise of Mussolini see the comprehensive background study (Italian revised edition, 1950) by *Angelo Rossi* (pseud. of *Angelo Tasca*), on the birth of Fascism (also published in French in Paris, 1938) and the Italian work on Italy in the thirty years preceding 1945 (Rome, 1945-47) by *Giacomo Peticone*. The personal career of Il Duce is dealt with in the classic work by *Gaudens Megaro*, "Mussolini in the Making" (Boston, 1938), and in that of *Paolo Monelli* (Milan, 1950), (American edition published New York, 1954) which shows much more clearly his natural limitations. Both works, however, suffer from underestimation of the testimony important for his earlier years contained in *Angelica Balabanoff*'s "My Life as a Rebel" (translation of her memoirs already published in serial form in "Die Weltbuehne" and elsewhere; New York, 1938). A more modern work on the subject is *R. Dombrowski*'s "Mussolini : Twilight and Fall" (London, 1956; translated from the original Polish). For an overall history of Fascism see *Giovanni Mira* and *Luigi Salvarorelli*: "Geschichte des Faschismus" (Rome, 1953; in Italian). The book on Mussolini by *Richard Wichterich* (Stuttgart, 1952) portrays Mussolini too much as a powerful, self-assured *condottiere*.

The situation for a general picture of National Socialism is just as unsatisfactory as that for Fascism. For rapid orientation the reading of works on Hitler and his "paladins" is advisable. The most important of the biographies of Hitler up to the end of the second world war were those of *Konrad Heiden*, which for the early history of the movement are still indispensable. The general expectation that Heiden, making use of his great factual knowledge and the enormous number of documents and reports available after 1945, would at last produce *the* book on Hitler, has unfortunately not been fulfilled; today the leading book on the subject is that of the English historian *Allan Bullock*, which appeared in 1952 in London, and proves that there are amongst the younger generation of English intellectuals, and especially the intellectual participants of the second world war, men with a deeper understanding of the psychological problems of the Continent than was formerly the case. The well-written biography of Hitler by *Walter Goerlitz* and *Herbert Quint* contains a great deal of material, but does not give a sufficiently wide picture of the social background and, in particular, of the horrors of the dictatorship, such as the effects of concentration camps. Personal reminiscences of closer acquaintances of Hitler are given in *H. Hoffmann*'s book "Hitler was my Friend" (London, 1955), and in *A. Kuebizeck*'s "Young Hitler. Story of a Friendship" (London, 1954). The authentic picture of Hitler at the height of his power is contained in his "Table Talk, 1941–44" (English edition, London, 1953), and at the end of it in "The Last Days of Hitler", by *H. R. Trevor-Roper* (London, 1956). Amongst the biographies of leading National Socialists those to note are *Willy Frischauer*'s books on Goering and Himmler, the book on Goering by *Ewan Butler* and *Gordon Young* (London, 1951) and the "Biography of Goebbels" by *Curt Reiss*. In an attractive study on the Austrian Fascist journalist Georg Lanz "von Siebenberg", a former monk and would-be nobleman who founded a fantastic order of Templars, the Viennese scholar *Wilfried Daim*, a student of Freud, presents Lanz as the main father of Hitler's ideas. That Hitler was strongly influenced by Lanz appears certain, but Daim fails to analyse the influence of political Wagnerism on Lanz, and undertakes that on Hitler ("Der Mann, der Hitler die Ideen gab" (Munich 1958)).

For the background history of the period and the study of individual problems it is advisable to use the comprehensive current bibliography which is published in the *Vierteljahresheften fuer Zeitgeschichte*. It is also a good thing to consult the literature published in other countries during the time when Hitler was in power, which were mostly directed against Hitler but made use of a great deal of contemporary material. A few of these works, such as the book *S. H. Roberts,* "The House that Hitler Built" (London, 1937) and *Franz Neumann*'s "Behemot; the Structure and Practice of National Socialism" (London, 1944), are still worth reading today. The banned material in publications like *Otto Nathan*'s "The Nazi Economic System" (Duke University, 1944) or *Guenther Reimann*'s "The Vampire Economy" (New York, 1939) is still useful as a contrast to the euphemistic literature which seeks to conceal facts, represented by such works as that of *Louis P. Lochners*'s "Die Maechtigen und der Tyrann", refuted also in content by the author's own publication "Hitler, Reichswehr und Industrie" (1950), which appeared shortly before it. In the period immediately after the war a flood of memoranda of Hitler's colleagues, opponents and victims and of leading military men was added to this literature. To these belong the publications of *Von Papen, Hans Frank, Schwerin-Krosigk, Meissner, Diels, Gisevius, Hassel, Schlabrendorff, Halder, Heusinger, Guderian, Speidel,* etc. Today the tide has ebbed and given place to a period of scientific individual studies.

PART V   Dictatorships in Our Time

Concerning the general character of dictatorship, to judge the different kinds of human "bacteria", which as time goes on have become "virulent" and turned into dictators, it is best to consult the writings of professional psychologists and psychiatrists, who have occupied themselves with these problems. In this category belong among others, the books of *David Abrahamson,* "Men, Mind and Power" (New York, 1945); *Gustav Bychovski,* "Dictators and their Disciples" (New York, 1948); *G. M. Gilbert,* "The Psychology of Dictatorship" (New York, 1950), and *Wilhelm Reich,* "Mass Psychology of Fascism" (New York, 1946, translation of a practically unobtainable German book published in Scandinavia). Individual studies of average types in the Fascist period are offered in works like *Th. W. Adorno*'s "The Authoritarian Personality" (New York, 1950).

The literature on the non-Communist dictatorships of the present day is abundant, but naturally fragmented. The best survey of the modern dictatorships of Latin America is given in *German Arciniegas*'s "The State of Latin America" (New York, 1952). For the Peróns see *Robert J. Alexander*: "The Perón Era" (London, 1952), *A. P. Whitaker*: "Argentine Upheaval" (Pennsylvania University, 1956), and *Fleur Cowles*: "Bloody Precedent" (New York, 1952). For Spain under Franco see the aforementioned book by *Ramos-Oliviera*; a no less critical attitude towards this dictator is that of the book, written from a Catholic point of view, "This is Spain", by *Richard Pattee* (Milwaukee, 1948).

A good general book on the most recent happenings in the Near East is *W. Z. Laqueur*'s "Communism and Nationalism in the Middle East" (New York, 1956).

For the study of Soviet dictatorships since Lenin it is most expedient to take first of all works on Stalin. At the head of the biographies is the well-known book of *Isaac Deutscher,* but due to the disclosures about the Twentieth Party Congress a few other works have come to light again, which place more stress on the coarser side of Stalin; to these belong the biographies of *Boris Souvarine (Suwarin)* (Paris, 1939); *Yves Delbars*'s work in English (London, 1939); *Suzanne Labin* (Paris, 1938) and not least Leon Trotsky. The best way of gaining information on the general development of the U.S.S.R. is through the bibliography of the *Vierteljahreshefte fuer Zeitgeschichte*; of the extremely abundant literature which tries to light up every corner of this enormous field, those recommended are the works of *F. Beck* and *W. Godin*: "Russian Purge and Extraction of Confession", (New York, 1951); *David Dallin*: "The Real Soviet Russia" (New Haven, 1947) and "The New Soviet Empire" (New Haven, 1951); *Ygael Gluckstein*: "Stalin's Satellites in Europe" (Boston, 1951); *Ruth Fischer*: "Stalin and German Communism" (an extremely important Harvard study by the former German Communist; 1948); *Alexander Inkeles*: "Public Opinion in the Soviet Union" (another Harvard Study; 1950); *Boris Meissner*: "Russland im Umbruch" (a good sociological examination; Frankfurt, 1951), and "The Communist Party of the Soviet Union" (1957); *Salomon Schwarz*: "The Jews in the Soviet Union" (New York, 1952) and "Labor in the Soviet Union" (New York, 1952); *Alexander Baykov*: "The Development of the Soviet Economic System" (indispensable; New York, 1953) and *T. Cliff*: "Russia from Stalin to Kruschev" (1956).

Biographies of Marshal Tito have been written by, amongst others, *Leigh White* (New York, 1951), *Koni Zilliakus* (London, 1952), and Tito's friend (since deported), *V. Dedijer* (New York, 1953). "Tito and Goliath", by *H. F. Armstrong*, is one of the latest books to have been published on the subject.

Books helpful for the study of dictatorships in the Far East are, amongst others, *Edward Hunter*: "Brainwashing in Red China" (New York, 1951); the book on Mao Tse-Tung by *Pierre S. R. Payne* (New York, 1951); the valuable Harvard Study "Chinese Communism and the Rise of Mao" (1951), by *B. J. Schwartz*, and a more recent work by *Peter S. H. Tang*: "Communist China Today" (New York, 1957). Mao's own opinion is to be found in his paper "On the Correct Handling of Contradictions among the People" (1957). Other useful works in this field are those of *C. J. Friedrich* and *Z. K. Brzezinski* : "Totalitarian Dictatorship and Autocracy"; *M. D. Kennedy*: "A Short History of Communism in Asia" (London, 1957); *R. L. Walker* : "China and Communism : the First Five Years" (London, 1956); and *K. A. Wittfogel*: "Oriental Despotism : A Comparative Study of Total Power" (London, 1957).

INDEX